D1282188

# NEGOTIATED CARE

*The Experience of*
*Family Day Care Providers*

In the series

*Women in the Political Economy,*

edited by

Ronnie J. Steinberg

# NEGOTIATED CARE

## *The Experience of Family Day Care Providers*

Margaret K. Nelson

Temple University Press
Philadelphia

Temple University Press, Philadelphia 19122

Published 1990
Printed in the United States of America



The paper used in this publication meets the minimum requirements of American National Standard for Information Sciences—Permanence of Paper for Printed Library Materials, ANSI Z39.48-1984 ♾

Library of Congress Cataloging-in-Publication Data
Nelson, Margaret K., 1944–
Negotiated care : the experience of family day care providers / Margaret K. Nelson.
p. cm. — (Women in the political economy)
Includes bibliographical references (p. ).
ISBN 0-87722-728-4
1. Family day care—United States. 2. Family day care—United States—Management. I. Title. II. Series.
HV854.N45 1990
362'.0425—dc20 90-10860
CIP

*For Bill, Sam, and Jeff*

# CONTENTS

# ACKNOWLEDGMENTS

I wish to thank the Middlebury College Professional Development Fund for supporting this research at various stages and Vermont EPSCoR for supporting the collection of data from unregistered providers.

I have been lucky to have available a wide range of support services at Middlebury College. These include the willing and able assistance provided by Terry Plum in the Library, John Thompson-Rohrlich, Chip Winner, and Linda Knutson in the Computer Center, and Wayne Fazestskie, Beth Dow, and Ann Wheeler as departmental secretaries. I am grateful for the work done by my research assistants, Lissie Bates, Susan Dutton, Katie Edwards, Sarah Furber, Jennifer Nelson, and Gwynne Williams.

The child care community in Vermont has consistently given support for this project. I have appreciated the time and energy offered by Joyce Shortt and the staff of the Burlington Childcare Resource and Referral Center, Cheryl Mitchell and the staff of the Addison County Parent-Child Center, Coley Baker, Helen Keith, and Helen McGough.

My thinking about the issues surrounding family day care has been challenged by my discussions with, and the critical readings of drafts by, family members, friends, and colleagues. I want to thank Emily K. Abel, Eve Adler, Lynne Baker, Myra Marx Ferree, Joanne Jacobson, Kathy McDermott, Ruth Milkman, Bill Nelson, Burke Rochford, Kate Sonderegger, and Joan Smith.

As the manuscript was nearing completion, Carol Offen's careful editing and Sandy Vivian's persistence in locating elusive references were much appreciated.

Finally, I am especially grateful to the many women and men who gave freely of their time and who trusted me to convey the rich complexity of their daily lives. I hope this trust was not misplaced.

# NEGOTIATED CARE

## *The Experience of Family Day Care Providers*

# INTRODUCTION

Child care has recently evolved from a personal issue to a public problem. Popular and academic presses abound with overviews, policy statements, surveys of current arrangements, evaluations of different kinds of care, and advice to parents.[1] In the last presidential election, candidates from both parties addressed this new political issue; in the last session of Congress politicians debated a wide range of child-care proposals. The word "crisis" is bandied about.[2]

This book is about one specific aspect of this public problem. It focuses on a particular kind of child care—family day care, defined as "non-residential child care provided in a private home other than the child's own"[3]—from a perspective that has been generally ignored: *that of the caregiver.*

The literature specifically addressing family day care is scanty. The largest study of the issue, and the one most commonly cited, is the *National Day Care Home Study* (NDCHS). It has three limitations. First, the data are now ten years old. Second, it was conducted only in urban areas. Third, the goals of the study—to provide a description and evaluation of family day care—precluded attention to the kind of issues under consideration in this work; it did not offer a detailed analysis of the meaning of family day care as an occupation for the providers.[4] Many of the other analyses of family day care rely on small samples and many place first the concerns of children.[5]

To a great extent, popular stereotypes (for the most part negative) substitute for knowledge. A Doonesbury cartoon shows Joanie, arriving late with Jeff at the day-care provider's door. She apologizes and the provider says, "No skin off my nose. Of course the other kids have started." Joanie asks, "Started what?" "Watching the tube. You got this week's check?" The implication is clear. The stories that reach the newspapers are even more dismaying in their import. Reports abound of child abuse in unlicensed homes; in 1986 three children in New York City died in a fire while in the care of an unlicensed provider; in 1988 a ten-month-old child died in the home of a "sitter" with a child-abuse record; even little Jessica McClure had a lesson beyond her courage and the generosity of her rescuers: she was being attended to by an unregulated family day care provider (her aunt) when she took her spill down the well.[6] These largely negative stereotypes are balanced—in a kind of cultural schizophrenia—by articles expressing concern that this source of child care might be drying up and by portraits of women who, weary of their struggles in the "working world," have returned to the home and taken up family day care as a way to enrich their lives.[7]

But by slighting or treating impressionistically family day care, the literature has ignored an important phenomenon. Family day care represents the site of much of today's child care, accounting for the primary daily location of approximately 40 percent of children under the age of one, 38 percent of children aged one or two and 15 percent of (the full-time care for) children between the ages of three and five. Many children are in more than a single kind of care; family day care often completes the picture for older children who spend time there before and after preschool or elementary school programs. All together as many as 5.1 million children may be cared for in this setting.[8]

Family day care is also the site in which a large number of child-care workers are located.[9] In 1981 the NDCHS suggested there were as many as 1.8 million different family day care providers in this country. (A piece of proposed federal legislation uses the term "family child care provider," which it defines as "1 individual who provides child care services for fewer than 24 hours per day as the sole caregiver, and in a private residence."[10] This terminology, like that used by the NDCHS, makes no distinction between women who care for unrelated children and women who care for related children. As the data in this study [like that collected by the NDCHS] show, many women who offer child care in a private residence care for both relatives and nonrelatives.[11])

This book goes beyond stereotypes to offer a close analysis of the family day care provider's daily existence. It argues that the experiences of family day care providers and, in particular, the kinds of dilemmas they face in their relationships with clients, children, family members, and representatives of the state's regulatory system, emerge from the broad social context of a massive demand for child care (to meet the needs of women working in wage labor) combined with a faltering social policy. It also argues that the experiences of family day care providers are shaped by ideologies about women's role (and the centrality of caregiving to that role) and by the concrete reality of women's lives. Women who transform caregiving into a paid activity located in the domestic domain both challenge and reconfirm traditional definitions of womanhood; the limited material resources with which they do so circumscribe the possibilities for resolving persistent dilemmas. Ironically, a group of women who resist some contemporary social dislocations—by remaining (or returning) home rather than working in the public sphere—both facilitate and bear some of the burdens of the very process they have tried to sidestep.

## *Child-Care Needs and the Social-Policy Response*

The increased need for any kind of child care is created by the recent transformation of the wage labor force. In both absolute and relative terms, more women than ever before are entering the labor force and they are staying longer. Since 1975 two out of every three new labor-market entrants have been women, and forecasters predict the trend will continue through 1995. In 1950 the labor-participation rate of all women was 33.9 percent; by 1987 it had risen to 55.6 percent. Women now constitute almost half (45 percent) of the civilian labor force.[12]

These numbers conceal the dramatic change in the kinds of women who work. Formerly married women and women with children were underrepresented in the labor force. This is no longer the case. The participation rate of married women rose from 23.8 to 54.7 percent between the years 1950 and 1986; the rate for women (married or not) with children under eighteen years of age grew from 45.9 percent to 54.7 percent in the same time period. Equally striking is the change in the rates of labor-force participation of women with children under three years of age (the group most likely to use family day care), which has increased from 34.1 to 50.8 percent over this same span.[13]

Looking at these statistics from a different perspective, about 25 million children—more than half in married-couple families—are in families where the mother is absent from the home for part of the workday on a regular basis. In March of 1987, 10.5 million children under six years of age—more than half of all children these ages—had a mother in the labor force and needed day care on a part- or full-time basis.[14]

The fact that so much of this need is met by family day care reflects our societal ambivalence about the consequences of women's engagement in wage labor, in particular as it requires the transfer of the care of dependents from the private to the public domain. It also reflects a set of economic and political priorities. The women's movement proposed a variety of solutions to the problem of daily child care:

more male participation, employer-sponsored on-site child care and other benefits for working parents, and a vast network of state and federally funded child-care centers.[15] The vision did not materialize. Few men were willing to sacrifice the power derived from full participation in the public sphere by assuming the responsibility for daily care of their own children; because child care remained low status (and low-paid) work, few chose child care as a full-time occupation.[16] As for corporate and governmental sponsorship, until very recently, the absence of money and a clear policy, and the tendency to privatize child care, resulted in an overall situation in which family day care thrives and remains the only option for many parents. The United States has the least well developed child-care policy of any industrialized country.[17]

In spite of numerous studies demonstrating extensive advantages from an investment in child care (e.g., easier recruitment, decreased turnover and absenteeism, increased morale), and in spite of Reagan-administration support of such actions, corporate employers have only reluctantly begun to take on this responsibility. Corporations are used to assuming that the costs of the reproduction of the labor force are covered by wages and leaving the responsibility of locating and paying for child care to the initiative of individuals; they can justify this decision as one that maintains a distinction between private and public spheres.[18] Nor have corporations been more responsive to other kinds of benefits such as parental leave or flex time.[19]

The inadequacies of our welfare programs also help to push caregiving into this informal realm. Child-care policy in the Reagan administration was marked by three trends: decentralization, deregulation, and privatization. The government cut back funding of all kinds: in 1985 twenty-four states were serving fewer children with federal funds than they had in 1981. The government also ceased its overview of how funds from the Social Services Block Grant (formerly Title XX of the Social Security Act) were to be spent by the states. By bypassing the Federal Interagency Day Care Requirements the government left child care subject to state standards only.[20]

There was also a concomitant emphasis on the private provision of child care. From the mixed economy of privately funded and operating programs coexisting with totally public programs, the United States moved to a more extensive reliance on private care. This was accomplished through a policy of subsidizing demand rather than supply, an encouragement of private-sector providers to produce and deliver services through contracts with the state, and stress on the value of informal rather than formal care.[21]

The renewed attention on child care in Congress suggests a major shift in social policy. The child care bills under consideration have ranged widely, from the tax credit proposals favored by the Bush administration, to the proposals (passed by the House in 1990 and the Senate in 1989) that combine tax credits with support to Head Start and school districts for before- and after-school care and grants to the states for child care subsidies.[22] Even if these latter proposals are not enacted, at the very least the burden of paying for child care among low-income families will be eased. But the more extensive proposals, whose potential impact should not be minimized, also remain in significant ways congruent with earlier policies.

Three issues dominate discussions of child-care policy: availability, affordability, and quality. Most observers agree that locating child care is a central problem for working parents. Articles report on the extensive child-care needs of parents from all income groups and the paucity of available slots.[23] Paying for care poses additional problems: Family day care in urban areas can cost as much as $160 a week; day care centers can be even more expensive; and in-home care can cost twice as much. Many studies suggest that the absence of acceptable child care is a major constraint on women's employment as well as on the economic self-sufficiency of poor populations. Women for whom staying home is not an option are often forced to choose between affordability and quality in their selection of day care. And although many parents say they are satisfied with their child-care arrangements, the frequency with which they change them suggests otherwise.[24]

Both the Senate's Act for Better Child Care Services and similar portions of the House's Early Childhood Education and Development Act would address all three child care issues. They would place the greatest emphasis on the problem of affordability, and they would continue to do so through demand subsidies supplemented by contracts with appropriate agencies that provide services. In both proposals the bulk of the allotments to the states is designated for the provision of "child care services . . . to eligible children in the State on a sliding fee scale basis . . . with priority being given for services to children of families with very low incomes." The market sets the rates for reimbursement to providers:[25]

> An eligible child care provider shall have a right to payment *at the same rate charged by providers in the State or substate area for comparable services* to children of comparable ages and special needs whose parents are not eligible for certificates under this title or for child care assistance under any other Federal or State program. (emphasis added)

The remaining monies are to be spent to address issues of availability and quality. In one of the many compromises made to promote passage of this form of child care legislation, federal standards were dropped in favor of state regulations. Under the proposed legislation states are directed to evaluate their policies and to improve quality by supporting resource and referral programs; improving the monitoring and enforcement of licensing and regulation requirements; providing training, technical assistance, and scholarship assistance to caregivers; ensuring that adequate salaries are paid to child-care staff; and making grants to libraries and providers for purchases of books and toys. States are also directed to use a variety of mechanisms to increase the availability of child care, for instance by making grants or low-interest loans to child-care providers and by establishing a loan fund to make capital improvements.[26]

Thus even the legislation with the greatest potential for altering the delivery of child care upholds the priorities of parental choice, state rather than federal control over standards, indirect government responsibility for the creation of new child-care facilities, and reliance on the market for setting rates. It would *not* establish a federal child-care system, and it would leave ample room for the continuation of family day care (including care by relatives) as a major component of the child-care system.

Of course, the location of care in residential settings is also fostered by personal preferences. Although ideology certainly plays a role in shaping these preferences, many people have concerns, legitimate or not, about whether institutions can render the personal care that women in families used to provide. Even when cost is not an issue parents often express a desire to find in-home care or care in home-like settings, especially for children under the age of two. For some groups, relatives are considered the only appropriate caregivers.[27]

The persistence of family day care is thus no surprise. Accurately or not, family day care is perceived as desirable because it is most like mother care and because it is least expensive. It thus "suits the priorities of those who would like developments to be as localized, community-based and informal as possible."[28] Because family day care requires neither extensive ongoing funding nor initial capital investment, it does not require any long-term public commitment; it continues to privatize this responsibility. If women are doing the work of child care, and if they do it cheaply at home, capital does not have to pay the full costs of the reproduction of its labor force. And as a society we can overlook altogether the fundamental challenge current trends pose to the notion of the separation between private and public spheres even as the responsibility for the care of children is moved outside the nuclear family (and sometimes into a different domestic domain). We can also overlook the challenge these trends pose to traditional ideas about women's role when child care is defined as a "woman's problem" and is shifted from one woman to another.

But family day care providers must manage and make sense of their work within these fictions and contradictions. In analyzing how they do so, we seek answers to a series of questions. What pressures do they experience as they strive to meet the needs of workers in wage labor? How do the underlying assumptions that they will at the same time remain informal, cheap and flexible *and* willingly subject themselves to public scrutiny affect them? How are these assumptions reflected in the expectations of parents? What kind of relationship with providers are parents seeking for themselves? What kind of relationship with providers are they seeking for their children? Do parents recognize that in transferring care to another they have to be willing to accept a more socialized vision of child rearing, or do they continue to see child care in completely private terms?

## *The Activity of Family Day Care and the Theoretical Response*

Family day care providers care for young children as paid work in their own homes. A variety of theoretical analyses offer useful insights into both the role of caregiving in women's lives and the phenomenon of home-based work. At the same time, some of these analyses have overlooked issues that can help us understand the family day care provider's distinctive situation.

### CAREGIVING IN THE MARGINS OF PUBLIC AND PRIVATE LIFE

In spite of the shifts in its location, caregiving, to young children in particular, remains women's work. Feminist analyses of the meaning of this activity fall within two general groupings.[29]

Some feminists have described caring as work, as the specific kind of labor women perform in our society. Writers from this perspective highlight a series of related issues. First, many suggest that caregiving is intrinsically disagreeable. They note that the tasks associated with caregiving include the "dirty work" that many occupations strive to shed or pass onto others, and that caregiving is boring and repetitive. Not surprisingly, then, many also argue that women's continued involvement in this activity is evidence of (and in turn contributes to) their subordination both in the private family and in the society as a whole. Socialist feminists in particular argue that although through such activities women make a significant contribution to the capitalist economy, they receive neither social honor nor economic rewards for doing so. In fact, much of this work remains invisible and devalued.[30]

This approach advances the analysis in this study by drawing attention to the coercive elements that shape a family day care provider's entrance into the occupation, the benefits employers reap from the low cost of family day care, the tasks that compose her daily activities, and the limited rewards available for fulfilling this role. But the approach has limits. As Hilary Graham has noted,[31]

> Such a perspective can quickly lose sight of the personal significance of caring. Stripped of the emotional bonds which encompass it, caring becomes redefined as 'tending,' 'the actual work of looking after those who temporarily or permanently, cannot do so for themselves.' But caring is more than this: a kind of domestic labour performed on people. It can't be 'cleaned up' into such categories without draining the relationship between carer and cared-for of the dimensions we most need to confront.

Acknowledging these emotional bonds, another group of feminist scholars, starting from a psychological perspective, offers a more salutary vision of caregiving.[32] They stress the personal meaning women derive from, and the intrinsic rewards to be gained by, attachments to care recipients and relationships grounded in reciprocity rather than coercion or a market exchange. They also locate caregiving not just as the work that women happen to do in our society, but as "the constitutive activity through which women achieve their femininity and against which masculinity takes shape."[33]

This approach brings into focus the deep affection that emerges between family day care providers and the children who come to them on a daily basis, as well as the complex and often supportive relationships between family day care providers and the parents of these children. But this perspective has its own problems. As Emily K. Abel and I have argued elsewhere,[34] "the emphasis on the personal fulfillment women derive from caregiving shades easily into a celebration of differences which serve as the rationale for women's inferior position [and] runs the risk of enshrining activities which are entwined with women's subordinate status." Furthermore, to the extent that these analyses are drawn primarily from the experiences of mothers, the question remains whether the same satisfactions can be reaped when the care recipients are not related by kin. And no more than the alternative view does this approach tell us how the experience of caregiving is shaped by the particular context in which it occurs.[35]

The distinctive setting in which family day care providers work creates unique problems and unique possibilities for experiencing caregiving as "work" and as "identity." On the one hand, family day care providers remain in the private domain; on the other hand, they are offering a public service that, although it has an ambiguous occupational identity (baby-sitter? child care worker?), is increasingly subject to state scrutiny. As scholars have noted, the dichotomy between public and private, though flawed as a description of reality, does have the function of isolating sets of appropriate norms.[36]

People expect their private and public lives to make different claims. These differences may be highlighted with respect to the issue of care. The private world demands unstinting care without regard to remuneration. Ideally relationships there are "nurturing, enduring, . . . noncontingent [and] governed by feelings of morality." In the private domain care of others is presumed to follow automatically from caring about them; the latter kind of caring is a normative requirement of family life. Public life places a cash value on the former kind of caring. Relationships there may remain "impersonal, competitive, contractual, and temporary."[37]

These norms are also gendered. As the feminist scholarship on caregiving argues, if care is the work a woman is compelled to do, it is also an essential component of her identity. Since the nineteenth century when men and "work" moved into the public world, women were left in and given complete responsibility for the activities of the domestic domain; they were also identified with those tasks that, because they were now defined as "not work," were assumed to flow from innate nurturance. Women were thus assumed to have no independent rights or interests, but to subordinate their needs willingly to those dependent on them. Even when women followed the domestic tasks into the public world (as nurses, teachers, social workers), they were caught in a dilemma: "forced to act as if altruism (assumed to be the basis for caring) and autonomy (assumed to be the basis for rights) are separate ways of being, even human characteristics distributed along gender lines."[38] Their activities there are judged by standards—warmth, intimacy, friendliness—that were formerly applied only to services in the private domain.[39] In contrast, men were free to pursue (and, indeed, compelled to seek) a life in the public sphere that assumed they were acting as autonomous individuals, as individuals with rights. Autonomy is the linchpin of a (male) professional model of caregiving in the public domain; professional caregivers adopt a norm of detachment that systematically precludes an identification with clients, and, arguably, the possibility of intense caring about them.

We want to ask, then, how family day care providers negotiate between these two sets of norms—those that dominate the family and those that dominate the world of paid employment—in their relationships with parents and children. How do they distinguish between the manner in which they respond to their own children and those of clients who come to them on a daily basis? To what extent are they motivated by love and affection in their participation in this occupation? To what extent are they interested in maintaining a businesslike stance and emotional distance? Do they define family day care as a distinct occupation? Are they constrained by the expectation of altruism? Does their own gender socialization and the expectations of others inhibit their assertion of rights?

## HOME-BASED WORK

If analyses of caregiving ignore context, some analyses of home-based work ignore caregiving. The resurgence of home-based work in the United States has stirred a series of debates about its significance, for those who do this work and for the broader society. Some scholars and policy analysts see in such activities both the vanguard of a promising new life-style and the solution to the set of problems created by women's employment outside the home. Others view these activities in a far less positive light, and still others note mixed effects. The dispute is complicated by the suggestion that home-based work has a different meaning for women than for men because of women's role in the home. The many different kinds of work addressed in this debate intensifies the confusion.[40]

Whether child care is included in these discussions or not often depends on the stance of the analyst. Those who are intent on demonstrating how either technological change or capital's search for cheap labor has spurred the current reliance on home-work dismiss offhandedly child care (as well as a variety of other occupations).[41] This is not surprising. Family day care providers are not employees whose work has been moved from the factory or office into the home; compared to industrial home-based work or telecommuting, for example, family day care is less easily seen as part of the recent transformation of work. Since many of these analysts are highly critical of the effects of homework, they are anxious to exclude those occupations that might blunt the thrust of the critique. Alternatively, those who use broad census categories such as "self-employed workers" often have a more benign attitude toward home-based work and include child care among a range of occupations that can substantiate the claim that this setting confers benefits.[42]

Two further sets of discussions cut across these debates. A number of economists and sociologists have become interested in the persistence of nonwage labor activities alongside of and, some would argue, vitally intertwined with, wage labor in the formal economy. Here, too, the place of child care is open to dispute as scholars attempt to define activities that "belong" in the informal sector. Some scholars reserve the term "informal economy" for those activities that take place "off the books" and thus are not registered by the economic measurement techniques of the society; by this terminology, family day care providers are divided down the middle on the basis of whether or not they report their income.[43] Others define the informal economy differently. Joan Smith, for example, includes, "nonwage labor . . . that actually produce[s] goods and services *relatively* independent of the formal sector and those that are associated with the circulation of these goods and services outside a formal market system."[44] If state regulation is one dimension of "relative independence," family day care providers now straddle the fence in the process of shifting from one side to another.

Historians have also "discovered" home-based work; for them it is evidence that women have always worked at home, that for women the dichotomy between home and work is always a fiction.[45] From this last perspective, the distinction between activities that stretch the family income (e.g., household provisioning, reciprocal exchanges of goods and services between kin, household, and neighbors) and activities that provide access to an additional income (e.g., illegal work and informal work unrecorded by the employer or self-employed individual) is emphasized less than the fact that by all such activities women make a significant contribution to household survival.[46]

Because family day care is uneasily located within these (sometimes strictly arbitrary) categories and because the categories themselves shift depending on the political goal of the investigator, it is easy to lose sight of the issues that stand at the heart of this study. Yet each of the perspectives outlined above can help identify relevant questions.

Clearly family day care providers differ in significant ways from industrial wage workers or telecommuters. As Sheila Allen writes,[47]

> Homeworking must be examined as waged labour incorporated into capitalist relations of production. This means challenging the many ways in which homework is disguised by its superficial similarity to other forms of work done at home . . . The relations between homeworker and supplier differentiate homework from all these other forms of work. Homeworking is a form of casualised employment but is nevertheless *waged* employment.

Nevertheless, we can ask some of the same questions about family day care as we might about home-work even if we reserve that term for those home-based activities that are waged. Why do family day care providers "choose" to do this work rather than work outside the home? How do they compare with workers who work outside the home with respect to personal characteristics and working conditions? What conflicts do they experience in merging paid and unpaid work in a single setting? And what are the personal, social, and economic effects of working in the home? We also want to ask how child care as a home-based occupation *differs* from industrial home-work: What particular complications derive from the fact that the paid work of a family day care provider is much the same as the unpaid work she does in the home?[48] How do the problems of negotiating with several parents about payment differ from those of negotiating with a single employer about wages?

Family day care providers also differ from many professionals and entrepreneurs who view the private domain as a location for carrying out their work without the impediments of bureaucracy. At the same time, some family day care providers do define themselves in precisely these terms. Thus we might ask, what are the obstacles to successful entrepreneurial or professional activity in a home setting? Conversely, what benefits does this setting offer to workers with entrepreneurial or professional goals? Are the obstacles and benefits the same for women and men?

If it is difficult to locate child care precisely within different definitions of the informal economy, this very fact suggests questions. One set of questions has to do with the importance of the informal economy in the abstract. As Joan Smith argues, "the informal sector maintains low subsistence costs to capital by directly augmenting the wage. Informal economic activities actually generate income, and, to the extent that they are sufficiently widespread, any form of income is worth more because it can be spent in an informal market where prices are low."[49] Hence we might ask, for example, whether increasing state control over the business of family day care means that it is coming to play a different role in the process of capital accumulation. A different set of questions emerges when we look at the providers themselves: Is income reporting relevant to the decisions a family day care provider makes about regulation? Do women at different stages of incorporation into the formal economy (e.g., regulated versus unregulated providers) experience their work in different ways?

Finally, the work of historians suggests continuities in women's engagement in a range of home-based activities, and some persistent questions: Is the distinction between domestic labor and home-based work a meaningful one? Does an involvement in these latter activities contribute to women's gender subordination in the family? What role do these activities play in the development of community? We might also focus on some possible changes over time. As more women work outside the home, how do women justify their continued involvement in informal activities? How does the experience of home-based work change as it is increasingly subject to public scrutiny?

As we answer these questions there are others that are left unaddressed. This book can not serve as a manual to parents interested in knowing more about whether family day care will suit their needs. Nor does it evaluate the impact of this kind of care on young children. The information here may, however, have relevance to both sets of concerns. And although it is not a broad policy statement per se, an examination of the daily experiences of family day care providers can teach us something about why they resist regulation, how they use available training programs, why they fail to assume a professional occupational identity, why turnover rates are high, and, in general, why the occupation appears not to live up to the expectations society imposes on it.

But this book has other issues as its priorities. Much of the contemporary debate about *the family* represents a concern about what might happen to the care of dependents—children, the frail elderly, handicapped persons—and, more broadly, to our sense of community, as women seek the privileges of autonomy and, whether motivated by this search or not, leave the domestic domain for wage labor. This concern is addressed here from the perspective of the women who now assume (at least some of) these responsibilities.

## *Methods*

This study uses two complementary approaches to explore the experiences of family day care providers. (For a more detailed description of methods, see Appendix A.) In some places, and for some purposes, I am content to describe the family day care providers as an outsider, relying on statistical information to portray, for example, the age distribution of the women doing this kind of work and the money they earn over the course of a week. The data employed in these sections are drawn primarily from my own mailed survey of 345 family day care providers currently engaged in the occupation in Vermont.[50] The questionnaires used in this survey covered a range of issues including the number of years the women had been providing child care, reasons for opening a day-care home, attitudes toward child care, future plans, problems, and background information. I also draw on a telephone survey of 75 women who had ceased doing this work within the past two years.

Most of the research, however, is designed to explore the subjective experiences of the family day care provider, to get inside the provider's head, as it were. For these purposes I rely on intensive, semistructured, taped interviews conducted with 70 current family day care providers and 16 women no longer in family day care. Questions in the interviews cover a wide range of issues, including relations with children and parents, the impact of the work on members of the provider's family, and sources of stress and satisfaction. Each interview lasted at least one hour; many ran for several hours. All of these interviews were conducted in the provider's home, and although I made an effort to conduct interviews during a time when the children would be napping, I found myself becoming a participant observer in the operation of family day care homes. I watched providers settle disputes with children, attend to their ongoing needs, and find distractions for them so the interview could continue. I was also called into service myself: I changed diapers, comforted children frightened by the momentary absence of the day care provider to answer the doorbell or telephone, and (at the end of many interviews) taught children how to record their voices and listen to themselves on a tape.

Since the provider's experience is embedded in relationships with a variety of significant others, I also interviewed nineteen employing mothers, seven providers' husbands, and a variety of other individuals in the provider's world: outreach workers, state licensers, and providers of center-based child care.

The core of this study, then, is a microanalysis of the experiences of family day care providers. One by one, each facet of their lives becomes the focus of detailed attention as I draw on the providers' words, as well as their gestures and emphases, to understand and convey the acutely personal—yet common or shared—meaning of their work.

## *Outline of the Book*

Chapter 1 offers information that provides the background for the analysis of family day care as a distinctive form both of caregiving and of home-based work. This chapter has four parts. The first section presents seven case studies, three from the most typical kinds of family day care providers and two each from two variants of the general type. The next section, drawing on information obtained in the questionnaires, describes the population of family day care providers in Vermont. In considering family day care as a career, I explore the dual motivations for entrance to this occupation: Providers want to make money *and* they want to remain at home and be full-time mothers to their own children. Finally, I describe family day care as an occupation, giving the number of children providers care for, the hours they work, and the income they earn. I also look at the number of years women remain in the occupation and their feelings about the work.

Each of the next three chapters is organized around a relationship between the provider and a "significant other." Chapter 2 focuses on relationships between family day care providers and the parents who bring children to them. The major dilemmas for both parties in this relationship are deciding which set of norms prevails and establishing boundaries between them. I suggest that while each party has reasons for wanting to adhere to the norms of a market exchange, each also has reason to find the impersonality of the market unsatisfactory and to view the relationship as embedded in the norms of a social exchange. I explore the roots of these two sets of norms and the complications stemming from alternation between the two. I also show how overlapping responsibilities aggravate the tensions of shared mothering.

Chapter 3 examines how family day care providers resolve the dilemma of distinguishing between how they feel about their own children and those who come to them on a daily basis. To a certain extent, family day care providers are expected (by parents) to respond to children according to the norms that govern family life; at the same time, parents want to maintain control over this relationship and they reserve the right to define it as temporary. Providers also have reasons for approaching child care for nonkin as they do care of their own children and they draw heavily on the model of "mothering." But because they lack the privileges of motherhood they must learn to differentiate between the care they give to others and that which they give to their own. I discuss the providers' stance of "detached attachment" and the manner in which they exercise the right to choose the children for whom they will offer care.

The two chapters just described, then, focus on dilemmas of establishing relationships with "outsiders" and the manner in which family day care providers mediate between the contradictory norms of the family and the market. In Chapter 4, I discuss the relationship between family day care providers and family members. Here the issue of home-based work becomes prominent. The major dilemma for providers lies in transforming the home into the site of paid work. The chapter explores the provider's relationships with her own children, her husband, and other family members and friends, and analyzes the conflicts that arise. In particular, I explore the irony of choosing to do this activity because of what it can do *for the family* and then finding the family transformed as a result of this work.

The public critique of family day care centers on three issues: the lack of public control because of the vast number of underground providers, the lack of professionalism on the part of providers (including their limited training), and the high rates of turnover. The last three substantive chapters address these issues.

Chapter 5 looks at regulation, examining relationships between family day care providers and representatives of the regulatory system. But because this is the only relationship that is in some way "optional," a major portion of the chapter is devoted to understanding the provider's decision about whether to exercise the option of regulation. This decision occurs in the context of her *other* relationships (i.e., with parents, children, and family members).

Chapter 6 examines the experiences of a group of women who defined themselves as offering a "preschool program" as well as family day care. These women are of interest because they shed light on the question of what might happen if family day care were to be transformed not just into a more businesslike endeavor (as might be the case with increased regulation), but into a more distinctly professional one as well.

In Chapter 7, in analyzing the reasons for turnover among family day care providers, I focus again on the context in which family day care providers work. By demonstrating the links between context and the kinds of problems and dilemmas highlighted throughout the book, the chapter serves both as a summary and an identification of issues that should be addressed in any policy designed to improve the working conditions of family day care providers. The Conclusion outlines a series of policy recommendations.

# Chapter 1

# FAMILY DAY CARE PROVIDERS AND THEIR WORK

Two goals compete in this chapter: on the one hand, an attempt to describe the "typical" family day care provider; on the other hand an intent to indicate the individuality of women who do this work and the idiosyncratic features of their experiences. The case studies below consequently convey simultaneously a woman's uniqueness *and* what her story reveals about a shared experience. And it could not be otherwise. A recurrent argument in this book as a whole is that the individual characteristics that differentiate among these women are insufficient to overcome the essential dynamics of this kind of work. In each set of relationships (with parents, with children, with their own family members, and with the state) family day care providers face certain dilemmas; the particular attributes of the providers may enable them to "fiddle" around the edges of these relationships—but rarely can they alter them altogether.

## Case Studies

I have selected seven women to describe in some detail. Three of the women care for their own preschool children as well as those of others: Gerry Porter and Rena Milks each have only one child; Shelley Tompkins has three. These women represent the typical day-care provider. The next four women were selected to represent the most common variations. Both Nancy Bingham and Cara Brown have preteen children who are now in school all day; Patsy Lincoln's two children are both in high school, and Joan Bolton's four children are all adults with children of their own.

### WOMEN WITH PRESCHOOL CHILDREN

*Gerry Porter* started taking care of children in her home a little less than a year before I interviewed her. She had found that she could no longer bear to be separated from her own daughter who was one year old at that time. She had no qualms about the care her child was receiving, but she was distressed and became increasingly certain that she wanted to remain home. She was not sure, however, that she could afford to give up her job as a secretary in a lawyer's office. Her husband also was hesitant—his own work as a car salesman entails seasonal changes in income. He agreed at last and, as Gerry says, "the financial end has been acceptable."

Gerry was caring for three children on a full-time basis and a couple of others part-time but she was not looking for more clients. She knew from taking her daughter to another home that she wanted to keep the group small—"If that was comfortable with me I would offer that to the other mothers." She also wanted to be able to offer the children in her care "a lot of attention." Her own family "was broken up a lot," and she was raised by her grandparents. She feels that her past experiences are relevant to her now-intense desire to devote attention to her daughter: "I just want her to have everything."

As we talked, she held Peter, a little boy of eighteen months, because his cough was keeping him awake during what would normally have been a nap time. Gerry was concerned: She wondered whether the child was really well enough to be with her that day. She was also angry at Peter's mother for not calling a doctor and for not leaving any medication. Aside from this kind of ongoing problem, so far Gerry had not had much trouble with parents. She did lose one child following a disagreement about how much structure there should be in the daily routine. When the mother took the child to a preschool, Gerry said she didn't mind: "He wasn't a good kid, to be honest."

Thinking back, Gerry said she was surprised to realize that she had "more experience than [she] had thought": Although she had never had any formal training in child care, she used to tutor younger children in reading and she taught music lessons for a time. Nevertheless, Gerry felt she had had a lot left to learn about children and that she had grown during the past year:

> It's strange to take care of other people's kids—it's almost like having babies—but you just sort of learn like you did with your own. . . . It's been a long year, learning the different things and about different age groups. I didn't know what to do with a four- or five-year-old. It's been sort of different. I didn't know what to expect. It sounded easy but it's like life. It isn't easy. You just have to experience it.

Gerry plans to have only the one child and to offer family day care until her daughter enters school full-time. At that point she would like to get a job with the same hours as her child. She wishes she had the training to be a teacher. But she thinks she might use her secretarial skills to find employment in a school system.

---

*Shelley Tompkins* met me at the door with her sleepy infant in her arms; her middle child peeked out to see who had arrived and was hustled back to take her nap; her seven-year-old son was still in school. Two other children were napping in the "master" bedroom; a third, who was dropped off for the afternoon while we were talking, knew the routine well. As soon as she had kissed her mother goodbye, she marched in to join the other sleeping children.

Like Gerry, Shelley had worked after the births of her own children. But she faced a different set of problems when, after a six-week maternity leave, she returned to her job as an unskilled worker in a local factory:

> I had one baby-sitter who was pregnant and decided that she couldn't handle [both children] so I had to find a new one. We had moved and I found another baby-sitter who took both of them. But that got expensive, with hiring a taxi to transport my son to kindergarten in the middle of the day. So I found another baby-sitter closer to the school. I wasn't happy with her. Two weeks into it I said, I don't like this. The baby-sitter had a lot of children and she didn't seem to spend much time with them. . . . And I just started saying I should stay home and take care of my own kids and I like children and then I can be home.

As was the case with many of the women I interviewed, Shelley's initial caution gave way to openness as she warmed to her subject and became interested in conveying her interests accurately. Her first rendition of how she began family day care slurred over critical aspects of her life. As she tried to explain more fully what the work meant to her, and how important it was for her to stay home, she added information about a divorce after her first child was born and a period as a single mother. She also revealed the deep roots of her current commitment to home-based child care:

> When I was a kid I was going to grow up and be a mom and have ten kids. . . . I don't know. I always wanted to have kids. I remember when I was growing up writing to this orphanage and asking what it required to work there. . . . And then in high school I was just your run-of-the-mill

> teenager who didn't get along with her mother and father. But I always wanted kids and I've always liked kids. . . . And I really wanted to be with my kids and I never thought that I wasn't going to be allowed to take care of them. With [my son], his father and I got divorced when he was seven months old and I had to work, I had to have a job because I was on my own. And I never thought that would happen. . . . I always thought that's why you had kids—to be with them. . . . So then, really, I did [day care] selfishly, to be with my own kids. But now when the [other children] come I like them. I enjoy them. . . . I still think of [the day-care children] when they're not here. When we went on vacation last year I sent all of them postcards. . . . I guess there isn't any real thing that made me want to do it, just that I always liked kids.

Having a day care in the home has not been easy for her. First, the transition was financially difficult: "The worst part was losing insurance and then not having too many children in the beginning. And then I had to take a month off to have my third child." And because her husband, like Gerry's, does work with seasonal variations—he has his own contracting business—there were some very lean times. Second, Shelley's children have not always appreciated having extra children around: Her son resents not having his mother's attention when he comes home from school; her daughter dislikes one of the little girls who comes three days a week. And there's also the wear and tear on the house: "This house looks like it's got a lot of kids in it. And it does." Even so, Shelley thinks she will keep up this work until the baby is in school. And since she thinks she would "really miss having kids around," she fantasizes about an alternative: "The ideal would be to work in another day care so I could come home to my own home."

---

Unlike Gerry and Shelley, *Rena Milks* never worked outside the home

---

once her own (and only) child was born four years ago. She knew when she got pregnant "that it would be one or the other . . . because it doesn't make any sense for me to have one and then leave it with somebody." When she started doing family day care she watched a four-year-old in addition to her own child; later she cared for two nephews who sometimes stayed with her for several weeks at a time. When we spoke together, she had just agreed to keep an infant for forty hours a week; this was the only child she was caring for beside her daughter.

Rena came from a big family herself, and when she was nine her oldest sister had a child and Rena spent a lot of time with that family, so she has had a lot of experience with children. At the same time, she knows that she provides different care from that which was offered by her own parents who showed little physical affection. Rena enjoys "hugging and kissing the children and making them feel really loved."

Although she has always cared for small groups of children, she is sometimes in conflict with her husband about her work. He is appreciative of the money, but he feels that this additional income does not make up for the extra stress. Since they are not strapped financially (her husband is co-owner of a sporting goods store; they just built a new house in a "nice" part of town), Rena feels little pressure to expand the group. But Rena likes having a little money to call her own. At $1.75 per hour for a child who comes full-time (and $2.00 an hour for a child who comes part-time), Rena's fees are at the high end of the scale. She says her feelings about these rates vary from day to day: "Sometimes you feel almost guilty taking the money; other days it's like this isn't worth it. I guess it balances out. . . . Sometimes I feel it's a lot of money that you're getting when you're home anyway and fixing meals for your own; but then there's days—you're stuck at home all day long with cranky children—when $5 an hour wouldn't be enough."

At the time of the interview Rena thought she would continue to do child care for two more years—until her daughter was in school full-time—and then would search for something else. Like Gerry, she sees work in the school system as being ideal since, "I still want to be there when Katrina comes home." Less than a year later another provider told me that Rena had stopped doing child care. "She never really liked it all that much," Robin said. "Don't get me wrong," she added, "Rena was good to the children. But she just wasn't cut out to be tied down like that."

## WOMEN WITH OLDER CHILDREN

I first heard about *Nancy Bingham* from a friend who had taken her son to her: "Nancy's wonderful," she said. "She really loves the children. You have to talk with her." This contact proved lucky. When I called Nancy for an interview, she was very hesitant. "I'm very private," she said. "I'm not good at expressing myself." When I mentioned Helen's name, she warmed a little. When I promised to bring pictures of Helen's son—they had moved to California in the interval—she agreed to meet with me: "It would be nice to see what Daniel looks like now."

Nancy lives in a small town where "everyone knows everyone else." She started doing child care eight years ago when her second child was born because she needed extra money, and she did not want to go out to leave her children: "I would have felt so horrible leaving them and sending them to a baby-sitter." She also sees herself as being very domestic in her orientation: "I like to be home—I like to bake and things like that. I'm real domestic." A strong religious faith underscores her conviction that she made the right decision: "I feel it was meant to be . . . I live close to the school and I have a sandpile and playhouse. So I really feel that this is what I am supposed to do right now, and it's neat how it always works out. I always have enough children. And any time I've lost one I have gained another."

Nancy is careful about the number of children she will accept—"I know my limits"—and she tries to maintain a consistent group of regulars. She does not otherwise protect herself. Like Gerry, Nancy held a sick child for much of the time we were talking, a little girl flushed with fever. But Nancy did not mind: "I give them good care when they're sick. The mothers trust me to know what to do." She also becomes deeply attached to the children in her care. During the interview she wept, speaking about how much she had missed Daniel after he left.

Nancy's commitment to children—both her own and other people's—shapes her plans to continue for about four more years. At that time her son will be in seventh grade, "and he will be old enough to stay alone." "Also," she adds, "with one exception [a baby 'on the way' who will come to her at six weeks old] all the other children I care for will be in school, and I will have seen all those children through."

Nancy does not know what she will do at that time: She did not receive any education after graduation from high school. She likes to cut hair and she thinks that hairdressing is a possibility; she also considers going back to school. For now, however, she is willing to wait: "I'll see when the time comes."

---

*Cara Brown* first got involved in paid child care as a teenager when she ran a play group for several neighborhood children. Following college she pursued an entirely different career as an office manager for the telephone company. When her own children were born, she returned to child care, first taking an extra one from time to time and then, when all three were finally in school all day, doing it in earnest. At the time I interviewed her she had been doing child care for two and a half years as a registered provider; she thought she would continue for several more years and then return to her earlier job.

Cara's days are fairly loose, structured largely around her own domestic responsibilities and the children's needs. She thinks her success lies in the fact that she likes "to be crazy and silly" with the children, to read to them, and to listen to music. Occasionally she supplements these casual interactions with more structured activities: "I go in spurts. Sometimes we do arts and crafts and sometimes we take nature walks. But I'm not like a teacher who sits down and plans." And, in order to keep her options open, she cares only for children from the age of two up: "I don't take care of babies anymore. With so many kids I don't want to have infants. I can't do the things I want to do then."

Most of Cara's clients are found by word of mouth. She likes it best when she can check out a new family with someone else: "I sort of know what I am getting into then." She always has clients come on a trial basis, and she has turned away those who don't seem to have the same values. To her this is one of the advantages of a home-based occupation: "I have a lot of control over the way I run my business." And she does take the business end seriously: She takes full advantage of the available tax breaks, she has separate fees for part-timers and full-timers, and she relies on written contracts. Nevertheless, from time to time, she finds herself in the same kinds of conflicts as other providers: with parents who arrive late to pick up their children, with parents who don't give enough notice when a child is not coming, and with parents who forget to pay. She also resents the attitude of some people toward her work: For everyone who says "more power to you," there's another person out there who says "you must be crazy to do this." She wonders, "Who is supposed to take care of these kids anyway?"

---

*Patsy Lincoln* and her husband Mark live in the same town where they

---

grew up. In fact their home is built on a piece of land they share with Mark's parents. The setting—high on a hill with views of the surrounding countryside—is lovely, and the house itself is immaculate: Even though there were four children there when Patsy and I spoke, you could have, as the expression goes, eaten off the kitchen floor.

Patsy started to care for children other than her own six years ago when her younger child was in fourth grade: "I started when my kids didn't need me anymore because I need little ones." She now cares for six children from three different families: Three of them are from one family and have been with her since they were born (the oldest is in school now) and, because their mother is a nurse, they are often with Patsy for twelve days at a stretch.

Basically Patsy uses as a model for the children's care the way she treated her own: "You did what you thought was right." She also feels there are some ways in which she has changed: "I can tolerate their naughtiness a lot more than I used to and I pay more attention to nutrition now." Patsy's husband Mark has also changed since they had little ones of their own: "He worked harder back then and he had no patience. With these kids now, he spends a lot of time. If he is home they want to be with him and he'll take them sugaring and things like that. He didn't do that with our own."

Patsy's teenage children also help out. Sometimes they resent the extra demands. On the whole, however, Patsy thinks they too enjoy having the children there: "We're one big family here really."

And Patsy is satisfied with the way things are although she has had disagreements with parents—especially over pickup times and fees. But she rationalizes away the latter: "I'm not in it to make a killing either." And she feels amply rewarded by the children: "I love holding them and cuddling them. It's a good feeling to know you are needed. I love seeing them take a first step, the funny things they come out with, the little things they say. And then they come up and hug me and say, 'I love you.'" Even so, Patsy has taken her last infant. "I will leave it the way it is. I get so attached, if I keep on taking little ones I will do it until I'm sixty-five. I want to stop with this baby." She is not sure what will come next, although she knows it will not be full-time work outside the home. But she is not worried: "There's so many things to do that I don't get to do now."

---

At age sixty-one *Ruth Bolton* is among the oldest of the women interviewed for this study. But her story is not atypical of the women who do family day care as a lifetime career.

Ruth grew up in a family of fifteen children and, as she says, she has "always taken care of children." While she was raising four of her own she often took in a couple of additional children "to make a little extra." She also engaged in a wide variety of other activities to supplement or augment the family income: "I would take in wash or rent rooms during carnival and stuff like that. I love doing these things though. I've always been very happy and content to stay in my own home . . . I could do almost anything so I didn't have to go out—caning, rugs, patch clothes, canning." Her own education stopped at high school, and she has never had any training for work with children. She relies on her own experience, and she believes that any woman who loves children and has raised her own can do this work.

There are few limits around Ruth's work life. She will often care for a child through the evening if the parents have some special plans, and since she sees no need to wake a sleeping child, she lets him/her stay over. And she is very involved in her relationships with parents whom she sees as an extension of her family: "The mothers need me as much as the kids and I am like a mother to some of those girls." At the same time, however, she notices that the parents do abuse her. Like other providers, she minds when parents don't call to say they will be late, when they haggle over how much they owe that week, and when they bring sick children. The parents view the situation in somewhat different terms: "Ruth never tells you what *she* wants. It's always, 'Whatever you want to do, whatever you want to give me.' "

Ruth's child-care style is among the most "traditional" of the women I interviewed. She stresses discipline: "If they're with me they have to mind." And she prefers to start with babies: "That way they get a good start and I don't have to go around screaming and yelling." Ruth is also set in her ways. Her living room is full of knickknacks and evidence of her handicrafts. She does not move these objects: "The children know not to touch them." Her morning routine includes a trip to the food co-op where she pours each child a cup of milk laced with a little coffee; she does this even though one mother repeatedly asked her not to: "The children enjoy acting like grown-ups."

Occasional conflicts notwithstanding, Ruth is proud of her status in the community, the fact that she has been doing this for years, and "everybody knows me." She relies on her reputation for new clients: "Most people have come to me by word of mouth—people say, get Ruth Bolton if you can. . . . [The pediatrician] recommended me to someone. A lot of them have told me, 'You're the number one baby-sitter in [town].' "

## *Demographic Characteristics of Family Day Care Providers*

We now turn our attention to family day care providers as a group, looking at such demographic variables as marital status, number (and ages) of children, age, and indicators of social class.[1] I also include here a couple of case studies of atypical providers.

### FAMILY STRUCTURE

Family day care providers are almost uniformly married women with at least one child of their own. These characteristics are a product of different aspects of the experience of working in family day care. First, family day care rarely can pay enough to support a woman living on her own; the occupation thus relies heavily on the population of women who, because they are married or living with someone, have access to a second means of support. Only 14 percent of the providers are not currently married. Three percent of the providers are living with someone, 2 percent have never been married; 8 percent are currently divorced or separated and 1 percent are widowed.[2]

---

*Sarah Stern* was in her third baby-sitting job following her graduation

---

from college when she married a man "who had me really fooled" and got pregnant. Although she knew right away that she "had made a big mistake," she stayed in the marriage until her son was six months old. She then moved back to her native state and started doing child care in her home. Making ends meet without child support ("I'm supposed to get it but it never comes") is not easy. Sarah's parents paid for the down payment on the house in which she lives with her child, who is now two and a half. Even so, Sarah had to rely on food stamps and food assistance for a while ("I never thought I would see the day when I would need welfare"). But she would not consider expanding her group beyond four children, and she will not leave her son until he goes to school: "I would never do that. I would never put Josh in a home. I couldn't imagine leaving him. Trusting someone else to form part of your child's personality—it's so important!" Financial difficulties are not Sarah's only problem. As a single woman she feels isolated and lonely much of the time. She knows she is going to have to find alternative work when her son goes off to school: "I don't know how people do this for years and years. I don't want to do that. I really enjoy being with people, and you don't get that in this job."

It is not only the low income of this kind of work that ensures its reliance on married women, but the fact that this is also predominantly an occupation that women begin when they have young children.[3] Only 4 percent of the women interviewed had never had any children of their own—like Judy Dalton.

---

*Judy Dalton* is a single, childless woman whose interest in caring for

---

children was sparked by her work in a local high school's child-care center. Following graduation she enrolled in a nearby junior college where she majored in early-childhood education; for several summers she was employed by a woman in her community who was a family day care provider. If this training encouraged her to believe that she could offer appropriate care without having been a mother herself, she was also motivated by her own past: "My own childhood was not the total best—I wanted to give kids what I didn't have." At the time I interviewed her she had just purchased her house with a loan from FHA and was managing to meet the monthly payments with the fees from keeping (relatively) close to the limits set by state regulations.

Among the more typical group of family day care providers, number of children ranges from one to nine; the most common is two.[4] More than half of the women (56 percent) have at least one child of preschool age; 25 percent have no children under the age of six but do have at least one child who is in elementary school (i.e., between the ages of six and twelve); ten percent have children between the ages of thirteen and eighteen; and the remaining 9 percent have children who are over eighteen. The age of the day-care provider's youngest child is an important variable, affecting the nature of her work. Those with preschool children care for their own as well as others throughout the day. (Very few providers send their own children to nursery school.) Those whose youngest child is in elementary school are likely to find that the family-related burdens on them change during the course of the day. At three o'clock, when many people are at their weariest, they have to respond to the needs of their own returning children. Those whose youngest child is a teenager, like those whose children have left home, are unlikely to have to respond to their own children in more than a perfunctory manner; in fact many of these women, like Patsy Lincoln, rely on their older children to offer occasional relief.[5]

The providers in this study range in age from 21 to 71 with a mean of 34.5. Not surprisingly, there is a relationship between age and presence of one's own children: The younger women are more likely to have their own children at home full-time during the day. A. C. Emlen has suggested that providers are generally older than their clients.[6] This age discrepancy may underlie the finding that although parents occasionally report that they rely on providers for advice about child-rearing, the reverse is seldom the case.[7]

## SOCIAL-CLASS INDICATORS

Social class is assessed separately by the variables of education, income, and former occupations.[8]

The vast majority (94 percent) of family day care providers have completed a high school education, and half of the women have some education beyond high school; 24 percent have completed college or received a graduate degree. Vermont's providers are somewhat better educated than Vermont women as a whole: In almost every age group higher proportions of providers have completed high school and four years of college than have women in the broader population.[9] This suggests that family day care is not selected by women only because they lack marketability.[10]

Median family income for providers falls between $20,000 and $24,999. The income distribution for Vermont households consisting of a married couple with a wife in the labor force and a child under the age of six in 1980 was slightly lower (with a median of $21,137) than the distribution among similarly situated (i.e., married, child under the age of six) family day care providers (with a median between $25,000 and $30,000).[11]

Most of the family day care providers (87 percent) had worked outside the home at an earlier point in their lives. Their previous occupations were distributed among the major occupational groups much like Vermont's female labor force as a whole.[12] Forty-four percent of the women had previously been employed in the broad category of "technical, sales, and administrative support occupations." Twenty-eight percent had previously worked in some kind of service occupation. Eighteen percent had worked in "managerial and professional specialty occupations," mostly as teachers, nurses, and social and recreation workers.[13] Ten percent had worked as "operators, fabricators, or laborers."

Four features of the former occupations of family day care providers are worth noting. First, most of the women have been employed in highly sex-stereotyped occupations; they have not chosen to challenge traditional gender expectations—nor was their employment likely to present them with opportunities to do so. Second, few women were in skilled occupations or in occupations allowing much room for self-direction or advancement. This has two implications: Some of the women may be able to return to their prior occupations relatively easily; for many of these women, family day care might represent an increased degree of autonomy and challenge (82 percent of the respondents agree with the statement, "I like [family day care as a] job because it allows me to be my own boss"; 79 percent agree with the statement, "I like my job because it allows me to be creative"). Third, these occupations do not pay well in Vermont (or elsewhere). For women at the lower end of occupational earnings, keeping family day care may represent an economic improvement.[14] Finally, most of these occupations lack the flexibility that is part of the class privilege of professional work; the women employed in these jobs probably could not negotiate easily around their own domestic responsibilities. It is not surprising, therefore, that some of them, like Shelley Tompkins, find that once they have a child of their own they no longer can afford to continue in, or manage the complications of, wage labor.

## *Entering the Occupation*

The similarity of family day care providers to the female work force as a whole raises the question of why these women choose this occupation rather than remaining in or reentering wage work following the birth of a child. Given the recent concern that an insufficient number of women will be available shortly to do this kind of work, this question achieves a certain pressing significance.

### MOTIVATIONS

The motivation for offering family day care can be linked to a variety of factors: a personal or ideological commitment to remaining at home, enjoyment from working with children, the need to earn an income, and perceptions of the problems entailed in earning an income as wage employees.

Let us begin with the financial motivations. If changing economic circumstances serve as an underlying cause of the demand for family day care providers, so do they serve as an underlying cause of the supply of this kind of care: 75 percent of the questionnaire respondents said the need to earn an income was one of the reasons for starting to offer family day care. No more than other families can those of day care providers afford to live on one wage.[15]

The money earned from family day care constituted, on average, slightly more than one-third (37 percent) of the total household income among family day care providers.[16] The percentage contribution toward the family income varies with total family income: 45 percent of those providers with family incomes below $15,000 are contributing at least half of that income; only 10 percent of those with family incomes over $35,000 are contributing that much.[17] Eighty-two percent of the respondents indicated that this additional income was either "very important; I could not get by without it" or "important; I need the money for both necessities and extras." These findings should dispel the notion that family day care providers are working for "pin money" or that their earnings are marginal to their families; family day care is a job that provides a second income for a family without alternative resources.[18]

A woman's decision to open a day-care home rather than go out to work may be connected to the structure of wage labor in other ways as well. Whether or not they work outside the home women continue to have responsibility for child care, and because a woman's work is often justified within a family *only* if it can cover that expense, the difficulties of finding and paying for adequate child care become significant issues. Many women reported they felt these pressures acutely. Some of the women interviewed, like Shelley, had worked outside their homes and found the struggle to find acceptable child care arrangements too great. Seventeen percent of those responding to the questionnaire said this was another motivation for opening a family day care home:

> When I did work full-time [outside the home] during the day, that was probably the most difficult because we had two different day-care situations that my kids were involved in. One was good but I wasn't that crazy about [the other one]. . . . It was terrible, getting up in the morning, getting them ready to leave, and I just decided that I wasn't the type of mother that could deal with that.

Twenty-seven percent indicated that the available care was too expensive given the wages they could earn:[19]

> I really have thought of [finding a different job] but it doesn't work out. It just doesn't work out. We can't afford it. If I went to work, you're going to make $100 a week, if that, and you end up paying a baby-sitter at least $50 or $60 a week.

> I figured it out the other day—I wanted to go back to work—and sat down again and realized that I could not afford it. I can't come out ahead.

Some women face a different set of constraints. For women relying on AFDC (Aid to Families with Dependent Children), family day care may be an ideal way to earn a little extra money; some women choose to do so "off the books."

---

*Hillary Brush,* for example, has three children of her own. When she was married and had access to a second income, she was able to work part-time. Now that she is divorced she would have to work full-time—assuming that, without a high school education, she could find a job that would enable her to support her children. She does not want to leave her youngest daughter for that many hours a day. But since AFDC does not provide enough for some of the "extras" she wants, she makes up the difference with occasional child care. This leaves her enormously vulnerable. She has to limit the number of clients so that she will not be visible, and she has to trust the parents to maintain confidentiality. She accepts only cash payments.

Thus one motivation for entering family day care as an occupation is linked to the dynamics of wage labor and the difficulty of finding and purchasing child care on women's wages (or on AFDC payments). We can not, however, ignore ideology. The rapid entry of women into wage labor suggests that a traditional ideology about woman's place is eroding. Among some women, however, this ideology remains compelling. Family day care, like other forms of home-based work, appeals to women who wish to find a way to earn money while staying at home.[20]

In most cases the desire to remain at home is experienced as a commitment to caring for one's own children. Eighty-five percent of the questionnaire respondents said they started offering family day care because they wanted to stay home with their own children; 68 percent of the women said this was their most important reason. "My top priority was to be with my children. That to me was more important than anything else. . . . That's why I had the children—so I could raise them myself."

This commitment is not always anticipated in advance. Some of the women stated they "always knew" they would not work when their own children were born. But some attempted to do so and found, like Gerry, that, in addition to the difficulties mentioned above, the pain of daily separation from their child was greater than anticipated. Some women, like Patsy Lincoln, find that once their own children have left the house they miss the presence of babies and toddlers.

As we will see in Chapter 2, this ideological commitment to staying at home constitutes the basis for a mutual misunderstanding between family day care providers and the women who come to them as clients. The providers frequently use words like "traditional," "old-fashioned," and "behind the times" to describe their life-style. They *know* that by contemporary standards they are deviant. They are sometimes defensive about their choices; this defensiveness can be transformed into a critique of those who choose otherwise.

Although most of the women indicated that their desire to stay home was self-initiated, some make it clear that this ideology about a woman's role is filtered through a spouse. While no woman interviewed for this study said her husband had *forced* her to work at home, many implied that their interest in maintaining a traditional household conveniently converged with their husbands' wishes.[21] Cara Brown, for example, said of her husband and his influence on her decision: "He's real traditional anyway. I think he likes it this way. I'm pretty traditional too. So it works this way. . . . I'm not comfortable with being in a full-time job where I'd have to find a baby-sitter during the summer for my kids. And my husband isn't comfortable with that either."

Women give other reasons as well for opting to stay home and take in other children. Some can not find another job they enjoy; others are bound to the home because of their own or others' disabilities or because they lack access to transportation.[22]

Enjoyment in working with children is numerically among the most common responses, offered by 84 percent of respondents as a motivation for family day care. Curiously, however, it rarely emerged in interview discussions as a *primary* factor in the origins of family day care in these women's lives. Although the women see their current engagement in family day care linked to previous kinds of involvement with children, they rarely said they chose any of these activities because they enjoyed working with children. In caring for younger siblings or babysitting they were simply responding to customary expectations. The absence of an affirmative commitment to working with children in these more complete stories leads me to conclude that, although the women find now (and perhaps found in the past) enormous satisfaction in these activities, this pleasure is less a causal factor than it is a facilitating one; it is a reason why a woman who wants or needs to stay home may find family day care an acceptable option.

This discussion of motivations should not be misinterpreted. Most of the women checked more than a single motivation (the mean number was three); more significantly, the manner in which women who were interviewed discussed occupational entry suggested a web of interconnected causes. We will return to this issue later in the chapter.

## PRIOR EXPERIENCE AND TRAINING

Prior experience with children and direct training for this kind of work might also facilitate entry into the occupation. Almost all of the family day care providers had worked with children before entering the occupation. Eighty-five percent baby-sat as teenagers, and for 35 percent of these women prior experience is limited to this activity. Some worked in day care centers as paid employees or as volunteers; some worked with children as teachers, as nurses, and as classroom aides. Among those who listed another form of experience, teaching Sunday School or leading a scout group predominated.

---

*Brenda Jackson* engaged in a range of these activities. She was trained as

---

a pediatric nurse, and after she had her own baby she decided that she wanted to do day care at home. After three years she also chose to be a foster parent. At that time, as she said, "It all went together—day care, my own family and foster children." Over time she found the stress of family day care so great—particularly the problems she was having with payment—that she decided to work in a child-care center. Although she enjoyed this new setting she resented having to pay for the day care for her own children. She also found the constant observations by a group of highly-educated parents unnerving: it made her wonder whether she "did the right thing or said the right thing." One year later she decided to reopen her family day care home, hoping that it would be less stressful this time around.

Slightly more than half (53 percent) of the providers had received some kind of training for work with children. Two-thirds of those who said they had some training mentioned attendance at conferences (this is particularly true of registered day-care providers who have access to an increasing range of support activities); almost half said that they had training in high school or college courses; and approximately one-third said they were trained on the job (usually as preparation for becoming a teacher or a nurse).

## RECURRENT THEMES IN DISCUSSIONS

Two themes stand out in providers' discussions of occupational entry. First, few providers can separate consciously their current activities from the manner in which they have always fulfilled a traditional gender role. Some women can not answer the question of why they opened a family day care home without going way back. They had always baby-sat; they came from large families; there were always extra children around the house. (For some women the continuity is less with informal care of children than with formal care of children in an occupational role such as nurse or teacher.)

Second, some women can not point with precision to the moment at which they began to offer family day care as such in their homes.[23] Many women started very casually. One's first clients were often friends and family members who asked a "favor." (Eight women said on the questionnaire that this was the reason they began offering family day care.) Some women began because they were simply searching for a playmate for their own child. Only gradually did they take on "outsiders"; often this did not happen until their own children were grown.

---

*Millie King*, for example, started baby-sitting in someone else's home

---

right out of high school. After she married at age twenty she cared for a nephew in her home—sometimes for several weeks at a stretch—through the period when her two children were born. She then started caring for another sister's children, who stayed with her until they started school. Her brother's three boys were then included in her care. Millie did not "start with the public" until twelve years ago when her own two children were in school full-time.

As this example suggests, to view entrance into the occupation as a discrete choice occurring at a specific moment in time is to ignore significant continuities that reveal the way women's lives are constructed, both in their own families and in the broader community. Many family day care providers learned early that they were supposed to be nurturant and altruistic, and to share their love (and their homes) with others. These are the lessons that are relied on when parents choose a family day care provider who is a mother or one who has grown up in a large family; it is also assumed by a public policy structured around the willingness of women to provide this kind of informal care. (Ironically, this policy assumes that these lessons have taken root *and* simultaneously attempts to regulate providers—just in case.)

Thus, although I use the word "choice" to describe how women find themselves in family day care, it is important to stress as well the material limitations (the structure of wage labor, the requirement that they earn some income) and the prior socialization (the commitment to the ideology of domesticity, the acceptance of woman's traditional role) that constrain these choices. Family day care as a career represents the dynamic outcome of a range of factors.[24]

## Family Day Care as Work

We now turn to a description of family day care as a job and to a brief review of providers' attitudes toward this work.[25]

Three sets of factors shape the working conditions of most family day care providers. First, the average provider is offering a service to individuals involved in wage labor. This affects the timing of her work as well as the kind of fees she can earn. Although a second factor is less obvious, it is important to note that family day care providers also have to negotiate around the rigidity of other formal institutions; at times they have to provide flexible care to make up for the intransigence of the public world. For example, as is the case for a woman who cares only for her own children, the rhythm of the provider's day is shaped by school schedules. She may simultaneously have to send one group of children off for afternoon kindergarten while preparing to greet and feed children returning from morning programs; at three o'clock the return of school-age children can alter the structure and dynamics of her group; when schools are closed (for vacations, snow days), her work load can increase dramatically.[26] These links also result in a reduced autonomy for family day care providers, a reduction that makes a mockery of the notion that women's work in the home—whether paid or unpaid—can ever be fully dissociated from the broader social structure in which it is located. Third, the family day care provider must respond to the demands of the domestic domain *at the same time and in the same place* as she responds to the demands of her paid work. This fact is a critical determinant of her relationships with parents, children, and family members, as we will see in the next three chapters. Here it is sufficient to note that although the demands of the domestic domain vary widely, all women face some such constraints. And while care of their own children may more easily be integrated into their paid work lives than is the case for some other home-based workers, this integration often comes at the expense of their own definition of "good mothering." Moreover, the fact that she is offering care rather than creating a product may intensify some conflicts.

Eighteen percent of the respondents to the questionnaire said they held another job as well as family day care: 43 percent of these women work at the other jobs less than ten hours a week; 35 percent work between ten and nineteen hours a week; only 22 percent work twenty hours or more. For this group of women a fourth constraint operates.[27] The jobs that demand a smaller number of hours include clerical work and housecleaning. Marie Plout, for example, takes care of four preschool children as well as her two teenage daughters. She takes the younger children with her when she goes to clean a neighbor's house. Ann Strayer cleans a beauty shop one day a week; on those days the day-care children are at another family day care home. Some of the women have even more demanding second careers. Two of the women interviewed were registered with the state as foster parents. They have an unpredictable child-care group: An emergency placement can mean an extra child for several weeks. Because these children often have special problems, fulfilling their needs while responding to the needs of one's own children *and* the day-care children can be very difficult. Two years after our initial interview, Brenda Jackson told me that her return to family day care, combined with foster care, had not worked out: "It was just one glass of water too much." Several women care for the elderly in their homes. The three women I interviewed who did this work found that the two occupations complemented each other, that the children benefited from exposure to elderly persons and that, in return, the elderly were cheered by the presence of young children in the house. Nevertheless, the burdens on these women, like those who did foster care, were tremendous.

*Marjorie Black* started taking care of children in her home eight years ago, when the oldest of her four children was born, because she needed the extra money. She was well prepared for this work: She had cared for two children (in their home) for a short period before her first daughter was born; she was one of fourteen children herself. After her third child was born Marjorie began taking care of elderly women in her home as well. Marjorie finds this a good way to earn money (about $1.25 an hour "around the clock") and fulfill a social need: "It's nice to be able to give someone a home and love and affection they won't get in a nursing home."

Some of Marjorie's paid child care has been stressful. Timothy, who came to her for six years (and who still comes after school), is mentally handicapped, and his care has required coordination with a team of specialists. Polly had yet other needs: "Her parents loved her but they just put themselves before their children always. . . . I often offered to keep her for weekends and overnight and stuff just because I knew she would be better physically cared for here than she was at home."

Not surprisingly, Marjorie's days are very long. She describes her mornings this way:

> I get up at 5:30. My husband is a construction worker and I fix his lunch. Sometimes I have a little time for myself. Then I help the two oldest children get off to school. I get the ninety-five-year-old up and bathe her and give her breakfast. I dress the other two children and then the baby-sitting children are dropped off at 8:30. I do housework and laundry—four loads a day. At 11:30 two more children are dropped off.

But Marjorie makes this appear effortless. As we talked, four children (two of Marjorie's, two nephews) played a fantasy game in the stairwell and peeked at the bees that were going to be added to the hives outside; one of the elderly women swept around the kitchen table at which we sat talking over a cup of tea. And, perhaps because it is all working well now, Marjorie thinks she will carry on: "I don't forsee any close end to this—but I don't want to either."

## SCHEDULING THE WORK

That family day care providers offer a service to individuals employed in wage labor has consequences for scheduling their work. While some forms of home-based work do allow a modicum of flexibility, child care can not be tucked into "convenient" times or put off until the evening; it has to be offered when it is needed.[28] A provider who offers her services to even a single full-time wage earner must make herself available for forty hours, plus the time required for travel to and from the workplace. Unless she is exceptionally lucky, a provider is likely to find that her clients' work hours are staggered such that her own work extends well beyond the eight-hour day. Sixty percent of the providers worked fifty or more hours a week or more than ten hours a day.[29] Providers rarely get a break in this time. Only 29 percent of the family day care providers say they *ever* have a time when someone else comes to cover for them. Nap times constitute the only possibility of a break for those who have no backup. Negotiations with parents about this time are, not surprisingly, extremely tense.

When domestic chores are added, the demands on a woman can become overwhelming. Her time is entirely structured by the combined demands of paid and unpaid work. A typical day-care provider described her day this way:

> I get up at 5:00 and clean the house and put the laundry in and just get everything ready for the day. My husband will come down and the kids will come down and have breakfast. And the first child arrives at quarter of seven. The one that came at quarter of seven would end up eating with us. Seven-thirty the [older] kids would get out for the bus—luckily the bus stops right out here—and by then the rest of the kids would come. Then we would have a day planned. . . . [At 1:00] they would nap. I didn't always get a break when they napped; sometimes there would be a child who needed some special time when the others weren't around. I had a friend who was unemployed who would come down during that time. I should have taken that time off. . . . Because then the kids have recharged their batteries. Parents get home between 4:00 and 5:30—hopefully 5:00. And then I had no relief because my children came home from school and my husband came home at 5:30 and I was preparing dinner.

Providers work long weeks as well as long hours. Thirty-nine percent of the providers said they took no days off for illness or personal needs during the previous year; only 29 percent said that they took off more than two days. A quarter of the providers had no vacation during the preceding year; half of those who did have a vacation took one week or less. (Not surprisingly, the children of schoolteachers are given priority by some providers who may even advertise that this group of children is preferred because the provider can be assured that the children will be picked up relatively early in the day and that she can get some relief during vacations.)

Although the family day care provider is bound to provide a steady, but flexible, service to multiple clients, she may be unable to hold the clients to an equally steady commitment. Many providers have to handle client requests for extra work. Fifty-eight percent said that during the previous year they had offered overnight care at least once; 55 percent said they had offered weekend care at least once. Parents also often arrive late to pick up a child: only 7 percent said this was rarely a problem; 25 percent reported that it happened regularly.

## NUMBERS AND CHARACTERISTICS OF CHILDREN IN CARE

All caregivers by definition are expected to be attentive to the needs of others. The work is unpredictable and highly contingent, demanding flexibility rather than adherence to set schedules. While the provider may not always be fully engrossed in the activities of the children, she does need to be attentive at all times: "My entire day, five days a week, that entire day I have to be on the alert for somebody all the time. It's bothersome."

On average, the family day care providers in this study deal with 6.7 children over the course of a week; 24 percent care for more than 10. Although these children may rarely all be present at any one time, the provider has to become familiar with each child's idiosyncratic needs: This one needs to be held after a nap; this one cries when her mother leaves; this one is allergic to chocolate.

Group size fluctuates over the course of a day. By 7:00 A.M. the typical provider already has two nonresident children present as well as her own; by noon her group size has increased to four nonresident children; at five she may still have three nonresident children present.[30] Fifty-nine percent of the providers have at least one time during the day when they have six or more children present.[31]

A range of ages can further complicate the provider's job. Some providers limit their groups to children of a specific age; and some refuse to take babies because of the especially trying demands of this age group.[32] But most providers (87 percent) care for children of at least two different age groups, and many (47 percent) care for children spanning three or four age groups.

The children may also range in backgrounds. Some providers feel acutely the demands placed on them by, for example, middle-class parents who want their children to attend a preschool for part of the day, thereby complicating the provider's schedule. A third also said they had at least one child for whom the state provided support. These children can pose special dilemmas. If the state is paying for the child care as part of its protective services, the children may have (and often are perceived as having) serious emotional and behavioral problems. But even if the state is simply supplementing a family's income by paying part of the child-care costs, providers are often reluctant to include such children in their groups. At the time of this study, because the state reimbursement was lower than the customary rates for child care, providers had to decide whether they would accept this reduced rate alone or ask the parents (illegally) to make up the difference.[33] Providers also said they did not like receiving payment only once a month and that they resented the paperwork involved. Among some providers, a reluctance to be involved with the state at all and a prejudice against low-income parents solidifies resistance to caring for this group of children.

Some providers (16 percent) also include in their groups children with physical and emotional disabilities, although many say that they are reluctant to do so because they do not feel qualified—or because they do not have the time—to respond to this particular set of demands. Marjorie Black, however, was proud of having participated in Timothy's rehabilitation and she enjoyed being part of a team.[34]

## FEES AND EARNINGS

That family day care providers offer a service to individuals employed in wage labor also has consequences for the money they can earn. Low wages for women in the labor force have traditionally been justified by the assumption that women are secondary workers making inessential contributions to family income. This assumption affects day-care providers who set their rates in relation to what the *women* who are their clients earn. The providers become aware of the customary charges for child care: "When I started I asked around about what was the going rate. Now I would like to raise my rates but I know I can't in this area." They are also conscious of the difficulties faced by working women. One woman said, "I think it is hard for mothers to pay much for sitters because they aren't making much." Another woman who had herself purchased child care for a year and a half before opening her family day care home, said, "I charge $1.25 an hour and I have learned that that is low. But I was on the other end of it. I know that when someone makes minimum wage it is not possible to pay more."

The rate that can be charged for any child's care is thus closely linked to the public wage structure for women.[35] Family day care providers charge, on average, $1.37 an hour. Almost a third of the women charge $1.00 or less; only 18 percent charge $1.50 or more. An increase in fees has to be negotiated with each client separately; raises in provider's fees will not likely coincide with raises in their clients' wages. Providers and clients sometimes negotiate bitterly about these issues. Two-thirds of family day care providers offer a reduced weekly rate for women who bring their children on a full-time basis. (The median weekly fee was $50 a week.) Although providers may lose money by giving a discount of this sort, they gain in predictability and in not having to keep track of their time.

Providers give two other kinds of discounts even though their work is not lessened proportionally. First, three-quarters offer a reduced rate (on average fifty percent of that charged for a first child) for the second child in the family; this rate is explained on the grounds that families bringing two children constitute an exceptionally stable clientele. (This practice, however, makes providers reluctant to accept families with three or more children.) Thirty-five percent of providers care for a child of a relative; about a fifth of these women give reduced rates in these circumstances.

The mean weekly income for the providers responding to the questionnaire was $171. For the median fifty hours worked per week this comes to hourly earnings of $3.42. The median annual income of $7,500 from child-care earnings is well below the (1980) median income ($9,089) for full-time female workers in Vermont.[36]

In addition to the significance of these incomes for the maintenance of the family day care provider's household, other issues should be noted. First, these incomes come without any benefits. Day-care providers have to pay their own Social Security (if they report their incomes; if they don't, they lose this future resource), they are not covered by unemployment insurance or disability insurance, and they have no paid health coverage.

Second, although a family day care provider may save money by not going outside to work, there are extensive costs associated with keeping a day-care home. The incomes have to cover the expense of food (whether or not they are on the federal food program), toys and supplies, insurance and household depreciation. At an average of $17 a week, these costs reduce the provider's weekly earnings to $154 and her hourly earnings to $3.08.

Finally, the income earned from child care is erratic. Day-care providers' earnings are unpredictably and adversely affected by the withdrawal of children for illness, mothers' maternity leaves, family vacations, and job transfers. Only a third of the providers say they charge whether or not a child comes; only 27 percent of family day care providers say their earnings are "very predictable." Late payment is a constant problem. Only 21 percent said they were never paid late by parents; 15 percent said that this happens regularly.

## EXPERIENCING THE WORK

The providers in this study had been engaged in family day care for a median length of three years; 38 percent had been offering care for two years or less; 31 percent had been offering care for three to five years; and 31 percent for six or more years. The typical family day care provider views her work as "temporary." On average, the women anticipate they will spend 3.6 more years in the occupation.[37]

For the time being, however, most women appear satisfied with their jobs as family day care providers: 52 percent indicate they are "very satisfied," and an additional 37 percent say they are "somewhat satisfied"; only 4 percent say that they are "very dissatisfied" or even "somewhat dissatisfied." At the same time, many women (64 percent) find the work to be "very" or "somewhat" stressful. Sources of stress are revealed by the frequency with which providers report certain kinds of problems. In addition to late pick-ups by parents and late payments, another difficulty cited is the frequency with which parents bring children who are sick: 58 percent say this happens often or sometimes. Providers also mention as another source of stress the frequency with which they have to deal with difficult or abused children (47 percent and 7 percent, respectively, say this happens often or sometimes). In addition, some women find the isolation of the work to be a source of stress, especially during Vermont's long, cold winters. They also mention the loss of family privacy, their own children's reactions, and the low status of child care.

The ways in which these various problems intersect were often indicated by respondents at the end of the questionnaire; I include here three typical examples:

> I really love my work and often have less trouble with the children than I do parents. They think little of being late for pick-ups of their children with minimal compensation financially (if any), forgetting additional clothing or change-of-weather clothing, often dressing a child for early A.M. temperatures. It is a constant job keeping after these moms.

> In three years of providing child care I've had experience with a child that was sexually abused, two families going through divorce, the tragic death of one father, head lice, and chicken pox! At the end of last summer four families—

> equaling six full-time children moved out of town. . . . Providing day care is rewarding, frustrating, and always a challenge.

> The bad is the long hours. Fifty is tiring but I have to be available this much because of the working hours of different people. I am too soft when it comes to charging for certain situations. First is vacations and I lose money when children are away for several weeks a year. I am thinking of limiting more strongly vacations, late pick-ups, etc. I don't like the way I have handled these things. I am shortchanging myself a lot.

In short, the work lives of providers are the result of a careful, if constrained, weaving of various demands. They are also shaped by their own commitment to providing a certain kind of care. It should be obvious that in many cases these demands and "desires" contradict one another and that these conflicts produce stress: For example, a woman who wants to limit her clientele because she has a commitment to providing intimate care (to her own and other children) finds that she has to enlarge her group if the family is going to pay this month's bills; a woman who wants to attend to her family's dinner at five o'clock finds that she is inhibited by the presence of three children whose mothers are late yet again. Yet providers frequently explain their working conditions as the result of a kind of free choice—to respond to the request of an individual client for additional time, to give a discount to a family bringing a second child, to care for groups as large as twelve children; as the examples cited above illustrate, they also frequently blame themselves for the problems they face.

## *Conclusion*

The family day care providers in this study do not differ dramatically from the broader population of women from which they are drawn: They have similar levels of education, occupational status, and family income. This suggests that family day care providers are not compelled to offer this service only because they lack the means to find other employment. For many of these women, family day care is a particular, transitional stage of life. What does delineate them, however, is their greater commitment (experienced indirectly in some cases) to "domesticity."

But domesticity is not the only motivation; the women also have financial needs. The current tasks of most family day care providers emerge from, and are shaped by, a dual motivation of business and family—or what I later refer to as a market and social perspective. The difficulties in satisfying both sets of interests is a theme that resounds throughout this book. Moreover, the providers locate themselves within a very traditional conception of women's roles. Not only have they "chosen" to remain at home at this point in their lives, but they have *always* been involved in caring for others; in fact they often begin this activity out of responsiveness to friends, neighbors, and the broader community. As one woman said when asked why she started a family day care home, "the need was there." This self-definition prepares them inadequately for transforming child care into a rigidly confined paid employment and frequently underscores resistance to regulation; these difficulties are compounded by attachments to children (and parents) that emerge in the process of the work.

Constraints on the family day care provider's activities and her high degree of vulnerability are significant features of the provider's work life. Some of her actions can best be understood as an attempt to pursue and protect a limited form of autonomy. Family day care providers might seem autonomous to a casual observer, as they sometimes seem to themselves. Indeed, some providers can exercise individual control over the selection of clients served; they may also drop clients with whom relationships have soured. The setting is free from bureaucratic requirements controlling both the hours and pace of work, and the provider is unlikely to have to handle such tasks as record-keeping, which compete with care. No superior evaluates her performance, and she may thus be free to develop an individual style of care based upon personal experience and knowledge.

But the broader context within which she works generally limits these freedoms. If the demand for her services is low, she can not pick and choose a clientele. Although she stands outside the formal economy, her hours are determined by the needs of clients who work as wage laborers and her pace by the necessity of taking on large numbers of clients. Moreover, her work is not free of conflicting demands, including the demands of her own family and those of the broader community in which she is located; sometimes too her clients request particular types of care. Her wages are subject to negotiation; they are low and frequently unpredictable. And there are other areas of vulnerability. Without the protection of an institution that sets rules for *both* clients and providers, she has little recourse when clients abuse the relationship. She may also be more directly vulnerable to the state. Those who operate at the margins of legality live under the threat of license revocation or prosecution. Even those who run legal businesses fear spot checks and selective application of rules.

Of course, as the case studies illustrate, any attempt to generalize about providers obscures differences among them. If some providers, like Rena, live comfortably on the incomes they and their husbands earn, others, like Shelley, struggle constantly to make ends meet. If Cara sees family day care as a transitional stage of life from which she will easily return to another occupation, Nancy wonders what will happen to her in the future. And if Marjorie is content in spite of the enormous demands on her, Brenda is in the process of burning out. Nevertheless, all of the women are working at home, with young children; all are engaged in the same daily round of activities; all of them have to mediate among the demands of parents, children, and their private lives. While their backgrounds might provide them with different tools with which to negotiate the choppy waters of family day care, they all experience the same kinds of dilemmas.

# *Chapter 2*

# RELATIONSHIPS BETWEEN MOTHERS AND PROVIDERS

As more women enter the wage labor force, and more household tasks are transferred to the market economy, women purchase services that they previously supplied without pay ("out of love") in the home. The new service providers are often women as well and thus the relationships that develop between women who provide services and women who use them have emerged as a subject of inquiry.[1] For example, in a perceptive analysis of Italian day care, Chiara Saraceno notes that the increasing reliance on purchased services entails both "the redefinition of boundaries between private and public spheres and the reallocation of responsibilities between them," and she goes on to dissect the "relationships and conflicts between women differently located in these two areas."[2]

In this chapter I extend Saraceno's analysis by looking at relationships between family day care providers and the mothers who use their services. Because these relationships are based on an exchange of services for money, they may differ from those between family members and friends who informally exchange goods and services.[3] Yet because this kind of child care remains in a private domain, these relationships have a different context than those between institutional employees and their clients. Family day care providers are not constrained by bureaucratic norms of impersonality, efficiency, and rationality; nor are they protected by rules that outline appropriate behavior for both parties. Most have no access to the distancing techniques available to professionals.

These relationships can also be differentiated from those that occur in the more privatized employment of domestic workers because it occurs in the *provider's* home. Research on domestic workers suggests that conflict between such workers and their employers may revolve around how to view the exchange. Employers often want the domestic worker to think of herself as being governed by a social ideology based on the values and practices associated with family life. As Bonnie Thornton Dill notes, however, the employer may be more mystified by this ideology than the worker who knows she is entitled to a fair wage for a day's work.[4]

The location of family day care in the provider's household creates a different uncertainty about what kind of transaction is occurring. Both parents and providers have reason to prefer the norms of a *market exchange*, with clearly specified obligations, stated rules, and social distance. And to a certain extent this style of interaction prevails. Providers and parents agree to hourly or weekly fees for the care of young children; they may agree to other conditions as well (e.g., providers will supply snacks and not meals; a fee will be charged for time scheduled if parents do not give twenty-four-hour notice; parents must bring diapers and a change of clothing). They thus mimic the form of a contractual service. But, the full definition of obligations between mothers and providers is rarely so simple. Both parents and providers also have reason to find the impersonality of the market unsatisfactory and to view the relationship as embedded in the norms of a *social exchange* with diffuse obligations, negotiated decision making based on trust, and intimacy. These two alternate sets of norms governing the parent-provider relationship generate enormous ambiguity and occasional conflict. The problem is compounded by the fact that parents and providers do not have the same motivations for shifting from one set of norms to the other. And their definitions of their mutual obligations are often asymmetrical, exacerbating the tensions inherent in this form of shared parenting.

A considerable body of literature has addressed the issue of relationships between caregivers in different domains. Much of this literature argues that each party to the relationship should have a clearly defined and a clearly distinguished role.[5] But parents and family day care providers necessarily have similar and overlapping responsibilities. The activities of each party cross arbitrary lines such as those separating instrumental and emotional tasks; the boundary between the two caregivers is permeable. Parent-provider negotiation about such issues as control and intimacy are plagued by uncertainty and confusion.

## *Overview of Mother-Provider Relationships*

Two features of the relationships between family day care providers and mothers who use their services are relevant as a backdrop: Although the relationships are generally characterized by social-class congruity, they are also marked by mutual misunderstanding.

The extent to which child-care providers and child-care users are divided by barriers of class is currently disputed. Sheila Kamerman, for example, expresses concern that society may "recreate a stigmatized, low-paid role for working women in which women now do for low pay and for other women's children what they previously did for no pay but for their own children."[6] But others argue that, although enormous disparities exist in the in-home employment of child-care workers, this is not the case in institutional care, even though salaries for child-care workers are extremely low.[7]

In family day care as well, there is evidence of broad, though imperfect, class congruity. In Chapter 1 we saw that family day care providers appear similar to the population of working women from which they are drawn in terms of occupation, education, and family income. Data from national consumer surveys suggest that women of all social backgrounds use family day care (see Table 1). These surveys also demonstrate that the precise form in which women use this kind of care varies with their social characteristics: If women with more education or higher occupational status rely on this kind of child care in almost the same proportions as do women with less education or lower occupational status, they are considerably less likely to draw from relatives as their care providers.[8]

If those using relatives are more often assured of class congruity, the manner in which other parents locate providers tends to the same result. First, parents frequently seek a provider conveniently located near home: The majority of day-care providers were found within one mile of the child's home in Portland, within two miles in California, and within three city blocks in New York City.[9] Given the high degree of residential segregation in this country, proximity increases the chances of finding a provider with similar social characteristics. Second, each party relies on informal networks to hear about the other. A provider often begins her "business" with the child of a friend or neighbor; ultimately her clientele may include family members, close friends, "friends of friends," and former coworkers. Similarly, parents start their search for a family day care provider by consulting others in their social and familial networks.[10] Furthermore, several of the women interviewed had previously been users of this kind of child care, and at least one of the mothers was considering entering this occupation.

In addition, each side searches for indicators of potential compatibility. Social class is often implicitly a factor in the *provider's* selection of clients. In a small town they rely on the fact that they "pretty much know everyone." Although some providers have no choice but to take any and all who seek their services, many screen potential clients. One woman, for example, said that she "sort of filters out

*TABLE 1*
PROPORTION OF U.S. EMPLOYED WOMEN
(BY SELECTED CHARACTERISTICS)
WHO USE FAMILY DAY CARE

| | % of U.S. Employed Women Using Care in Another Home by | | | |
|---|---|---|---|---|
| Characteristics | Grand-parent | Other Relative | Non-relative | Total |
| *Occupation Categories* | | | | |
| Managerial and professional specialty occupations | 6.2 | 3.4 | 28.1 | 37.7 |
| Technical, sales and administrative support occupations | 10.9 | 3.9 | 22.8 | 37.6 |
| Service occupations | 7.7 | 4.7 | 14.5 | 26.9 |
| Operators, fabricators, laborers | — | — | — | — |
| Precision production, craft and repair occupations | 19.3 | 8.7 | 22.1 | 50.1 |
| Farming, forestry, and fishing | — | — | — | — |
| *Educational Attainment* | | | | |
| Not a high school graduate | 10.5 | 8.4 | 14.8 | 33.7 |
| High school graduate | 13.9 | 4.4 | 22.3 | 40.6 |
| College: 1–3 years | 8.3 | 4.0 | 22.6 | 34.9 |
| College: 4 or more years | 4.2 | 2.3 | 27.4 | 33.9 |

SOURCE: U.S. Bureau of the Census, *Who's Minding the Kids? Child Care Arrangements: Winter 1984–85* (Washington, D.C.: Government Printing Office, 1987): 17.

people on the phone—assessing the way they are, the questions they ask, and the things that are important to them." Those who are simply seeking the cheapest care possible might be eliminated in this manner: "One lady [called and] her first question was, 'How much do you charge?'" Many providers also ask that parents interested in using their services come for an interview: If they don't like what they see (either in terms of the mother or the child), they sometimes use the subterfuge of high rates. Sarah Stern, for example, said:

> I hear that in [some towns] it's hard to find the right kind [of parent]. It sounds snobby but I'm not happy working with people that I just can't talk to. I did have this one girl come with her daughter and I knew when she came in the door

> that I did not want to watch this girl's daughter. . . . The daughter was off the wall. The mother kept saying, "Don't do that" [and] the kid would not listen. And I'm thinking to myself how am I going to get out of this. . . . Plus her father worked in a cow barn and I didn't want my house to smell, so right as she is getting ready to leave . . . I told her I charged $4 an hour which was a lie. . . . I did not want her to even consider me. . . . I didn't know how [else] to get out of it.

(Another provider unsuccessfully attempted to use the same subterfuge to sever her ties with a more middle class woman who made her nervous and whose child-care style she found offensive:

> This one particular mother, it really hurt me when I started sitting for her. She is a career woman. . . . I used to die every morning when she would kiss [her daughter] good-bye, it was so false. I didn't really like the woman. . . . When I found out that she was pregnant I was kind of iffy if I wanted a new one. I decided to charge her $3 an hour and figured that she surely would find someone else. But she said, "No problem.")

The other side also screens for compatibility. In an analysis of the manner in which the contemporary market provision of services continues to rely on the family to ensure that a caregiver has the proper orientation toward her work, Berenice Fisher and Joan Tronto argue that a person employing a caregiver may seek information about her background.[11] The parents I interviewed certainly did so: "I knew she comes from a large family and therefore I had the feeling that a lot of kids together would not frazzle her nerves." The emphasis they place on having similar values ("I liked knowing that she shopped at the [natural foods] co-op") may often be a coding for similar class location. Parents also rely heavily on what they learn from others: "I had heard good things about Anne from my sister-in-law and friends that had heard that she had left work to babysit. . . . I wouldn't go to a complete stranger and leave my children with them"; "My husband knows her children from school and he thinks they are okay"; "I thought of the mothers I had known from teaching. I called a woman whose daughter I had had at school and who I knew has two younger ones at home. I didn't know the woman had done baby-sitting in the past, I just thought she would be good."

Regulatory status is not an important consideration. Only one of the mothers interviewed said that she relied on state licensing at all.

The others dismissed the issue completely (if they even knew about it): "Registration is not a concern because I know her personally"; "I never used a registered sitter. I was never concerned about licensing by the state. I went by knowing who the people were or what other people said about them."

The provider's motivation and commitment to child care, however, is an important variable.[12] No mother wants a provider she thinks is "in it for the money": "She always told me she was not in it for the money. She wanted to be home as long as she could be there. That's what she was there for."

The relationships under examination are thus often ones between women of equal social status. Of course, this is not invariably the case and each side has a different attitude toward status differentials.[13] Middle-class mothers tend to prefer relationships with women of a somewhat lower social-class position. In such cases they feel freer to "dehumanize" the caregiver and ignore her personal needs. Some parents, however, feel that in such cross-class relationships they have to be particularly sensitive to the provider's possible feelings of inferiority: "I also think I am in a situation where because I'm a teacher I sense that this lady was always on her guard thinking that I was judging her." Moreover, these cross-class relationships can create conflicts. Moral values, cleanliness and language are areas of concern raised by middle-class women who consider taking their children to a provider of a lower social status: "There was another person who baby-sits where I wouldn't leave my daughter because her grammar is so bad—the constant exposure is something that I didn't want my kids to deal with. I would have to undo things."

Providers too generally seem more comfortable with same-class relationships. They resent the *noblesse oblige* attitudes of those they call "business women"; they feel greater hostility when they perceive a large gap between the available resources and the money received. They do not like being given instructions by women they feel are both overly concerned about a child's intellectual development and insufficiently concerned about discipline. When they deal with women of a lower social status they complain about bounced checks, children who are inadequately fed and clothed, and maternal indifference toward the content of care.[14]

Although social-class congruity and careful selection might ease interactions between mothers and providers, there remain significant ideological differences between the two groups that retard mutual understanding. As we have seen, most family day care providers hold conservative notions about a woman's proper place and the importance of motherhood; on the other hand, the mothers employed outside the home have made some accommodation to a changing world.[15]

Both mothers and providers make sacrifices to maintain the "choices" they have made. Justification of these sacrifices can take the form of an almost willful misunderstanding of the "other."

Mothers employed outside the home give up daily interaction and good times with young children: "I get jealous that the babysitters have them during their good hours. You just don't get to see [your children] then. I'm extremely jealous that [my daughter] does cute projects and crafts at the new sitter's and I wish that I could be doing that with her." Although the mothers who are employed are often uncomfortable about leaving their children (particularly infants), they talk about the financial necessity underlying their decision, the search for excellent substitute care, and the benefits and pleasures of their paid work. They resent it when providers imply that, because they leave their children, they might not be good mothers: "I have felt that both Anne and Kate look down on me because I do not stay home with my child. Kate has said about other mothers, 'If they only stayed home.' It makes you feel, 'Oh shit.' "

Some women assert, however, they might not be "good mothers" if they did as the provider suggested: "I'm not sure that I believe it is the best thing for a mother to be at home with her child all the time and I know for a fact that for me it's not what's best. Having been home fifteen months I was a crazy woman. I am not meant to be at home all day. . . . I know that I am a better mother when I am out of the house." They say they can't understand how "these [other] women can care for all those children all day." "I couldn't do it," they say. "It's a mystery to me how anyone can."

From the other end, day-care providers repeatedly say they can not understand how mothers can bear to leave their children. Although the providers who had formerly worked outside the home offered a variety of reasons for leaving wage labor, they placed *first* that they could not bear the thought of having someone else rear their children. Gerry Porter said,

> I took three months off after I had [my daughter]. I never really thought that I would ever not work. . . . It was just about a year to the date after I went back to work that I decided, well, I really don't want to work any more, because I felt that I really needed to stay home—because of Alice. I wanted her to have a nice family life and I wanted her to have a mom and dad that knew her. . . . [I had] a real good person taking care of her . . . so I never had a second thought about leaving her as far as the sitter was concerned. But when I left her I felt kind of empty almost and I couldn't wait to get done with work.

Some of them are so embedded in their current choices they "forget" they ever led a different life: One woman told me her son had not done well in child care during the year she was employed outside the home, and then later in the interview insisted she had never had anyone else care for her child. Because many of the providers feel it is wrong for mothers to leave their children, they are in the curious position of offering a service in which they have no faith:[16] "The bottom line is I feel every mother at every expense should stay home with their child. . . . I always felt in the back of my mind, why don't they stay home with their children. . . . I can't understand why it was more important for them to shuffle papers. . . . And I still haven't figured it out." Thus neither side fully respects or comprehends the other.

This misunderstanding may be exacerbated by the information and advice available to each party in the relationship. Women's magazines today are full of suggestions about how to locate, evaluate, and interact with child-care providers.[17] Much of this information echoes social stereotypes. Parents are cautioned that although family day care can offer the best care, it may also offer the worst; that abuse can be a problem and that "too many women are in it just for the money" and take too many children; that family day care providers are untrained and unsupervised; and that parents taking a child to family day care might lose control over "child-care philosophy or routines." Parents are also advised to be thorough in the selection process, using the resources of references as well as both scheduled and unscheduled spot checks: "Try to visit in the morning when the children are fresh and at the end of the day to watch the leave-taking process. You should be able to visit any time unannounced." They are urged to remain "suspicious."[18]

Less advice is available to providers. Over a two-year period, a newsletter sent to all registered providers in one county in Vermont carried no articles about how to negotiate with parents.[19] The registration guidelines focus almost exclusively on the rights of parents in the relationship.[20] The public critique of family day care fuels the provider's feelings that she stands alone and unprotected in a relationship that begins with mistrust and suspicion.[21]

## *Defining Obligations*

### THE PROVIDERS' PERSPECTIVE

When I began interviewing family day care providers, I assumed that although some questions would be difficult to answer, the simple factual questions—such as how much they charged—would elicit simple factual responses. This proved to be a naive assumption. With the majority of the providers, questions about fees and what they expected from parents generally revealed their ambivalence about whether market exchange or social exchange norms should prevail.

It is easy to understand why providers have at least a partial commitment to a straightforward market perspective. At one level the provision of family day care is a job. Providers have to charge enough to make a living. And they want to be able to predict their incomes; thus they set rates and try to hold clients to a fixed fee. Providers also want to regulate their clients to make their own lives as easy as possible. They want to offer care for limited and inflexible hours, to have advance notice of exceptions to the schedule, and to avoid caring for children who are sick.

When they focus on these needs, providers often speak very bitterly about parents. They complain about parents who don't let them know a child is not coming, about parents who arrive late to pick up a child, those who don't bring the necessary supplies, and those who bring sick children. These are all common occurrences. They also complain about parents who forget to pay on time, who haggle over every nickel and dime, who make a fuss about a slight increase in rates, and who assume that "overtime" is free. They say they especially resent the assumption that they will be happy to give care at odd hours because they are "at home anyway": One woman reported angrily that when she chided a mother for not picking up her child on time, the mother responded, "I didn't realize you had anything else to do." Through such complaints they express a sense of exploitation and an acute awareness that their interests collide with those of parents. As one provider speaking about these matters concluded, "It's an issue of bread and butter on my table or bread and butter on yours."

With many providers, a market perspective grows as a result of repeated abuses at the hands of parents. While initially they might accommodate almost all parents' requests, they often become less flexible as time passes. Some handle overtime by charging time and a half; others say they are reluctant to do so because that "solution" simply legitimizes parental negligence. Slowly they acquire the skills necessary to enforce their rules:

> I'm firmer now 'cause they walk all over you. It's a business. After being in it four years you have to look at it as a business.

> In the beginning I was really easy. I didn't say too much to anybody. And then I said, no, I'm not doing it anymore.

> Because they will take advantage of you . . . if you don't put your foot down and say something. . . . Now I lay down the rules when they first start. I just tell them what I expect from the time of the first meeting we have.

At the same time that providers may want to handle their business in a cut-and-dried manner, they express a totally different set of attitudes as well, attitudes that reflect their awareness that the terms of the market exchange not only conceal, but even distort the full nature of what they are offering and what they want from parents in return. They indicate a commitment to giving care without anticipating a cash return—or sometimes even any return at all. Providers preface their remarks about wages with comments suggesting they are "not in it for the money," that they are doing their work out of love. They speak about the enormous amount of unpaid care they offer, and they indicate they would like to do so more often: "I wish I were in the situation where I didn't have to take money . . . just so that you could do it for the parents, because it's nice to have someone give you a break." This more social perspective has both situational and ideological roots.

Note that these different views do not come from two different groups of providers but represent a contradictory set of perspectives offered by the same providers. Regulatory status is relevant to the emphasis with which providers adhere to one or the other perspective: Those who are regulated can be characterized as having a stronger market orientation. Even so, as we will see in Chapter 5, they too express adherence to the norms of a social exchange. Thus although some providers express more commitment to the market form and some express more commitment to the social form, most providers, at some level, express *both* attitudes. Moreover, the commitment to one or the other viewpoint is not clearly based on the level of family income. The women I interviewed range in social-class position from the wife of a bank president to single women living on AFDC or SSI (Social Security Insurance) grants. Clearly these women have different needs. But these differences do not appear to be relevant to the manner in which they make decisions. Each woman came to her own, ongoing, assessment of the income she wished to derive from child care. When she felt she could manage without payment she might give free care; when she felt she could not afford to do so, she resented parent lapses. Some were explicit about this. The same woman who spoke bitterly about money being an issue of "bread and butter on my table or bread and butter on yours" later commented, "When I have enough money to put food on my table, I let things slide. I feel good about that. When I am doing fine and they can't afford it, I let them not pay. But when things are tight here, I feel it more." Marjorie Black, who had previously relied on her child-care income exclusively and now also cares for the elderly in her own home, commented on how her perceptions shifted: "I'm not doing this for the money [now] and probably if I was I'd be more careful about it. I let them keep track of the hours. I'm not very professional about this at all, that's for sure. I do remember that [before] when people didn't pay you on the night they were supposed to—I needed that money and I expected to be paid."

The social perspective emerges from four sets of factors: the location of family day care; the dynamics of entry into and engagement in the occupation; social attitudes toward pricing care; and the constraints incumbent on offering a service to wage workers.

*The Location of Family Day Care.* To begin with, family day care providers are situated in the domestic domain where caregiving follows the norm of reciprocity.[22] Paid and unpaid care is merged in a single setting. There is no separation between private and public work spaces: Children color at the kitchen table and nap in all the available bedrooms. There may even be no temporal separation: A woman might put in her laundry or prepare dinner while keeping an eye on nonresident children. Providers offer family day care because they want to remain home and care for their own children, and they often merge care of their own with the care of others of increasing distance: stepchildren, foster children, and the children of relatives, neighbors, friends, and finally, clients. If they are trying to treat all children the same way, to be fair, they can not easily distinguish between what they do out of love and neighborliness, and what they do because they are paid: "There are times in the middle of the afternoon there are thirteen, fourteen kids in the backyard and my daughter comes in and gets snacks for everyone."

Since "clients" often include friends and relatives, providers sometimes feel compelled to—and sometimes freely choose to—adopt a purely social exchange. For instance, women might watch the children of friends, neighbors, and relatives without charging because "they would do the same for me."[23] One woman was explicit about reciprocity: "I don't get paid for taking care of [my nephew] but his mother is with my mother today. On the day that I go [to take care of my mother] she takes [one of my daughters] home with her." Others modify rates for these groups: "Somebody told me I should charge more for a baby. But I'm not going to do that—because I feel comfortable [the way it is]. I told her I'd charge her $2.25 an hour for the three children. She's my friend too, so I can't charge more"; "I charge less for my niece because I couldn't [charge the full price] to my brother."

At the same time, some providers, recognizing the complications entailed in these close relationships, prefer to keep a distance from their clients: "It was harder when I was friends with my clients. I think that's the hardest thing. Because you are in a business and they don't take it business-wise as far as paying you on time. You know, I'll see you Monday, I forgot the check today."

For similar reasons some absolutely refuse to care for the children of relatives:

> I had my cousins here for a while. And after a while it started being pretty sticky. They expect a little more. And I'm almost doing it for ten hours a day and sooner or later she's getting a little later and later. . . . I gave them a cheaper rate because they were relatives and she was having a hard time, which didn't bother me at all—my ends met. But I think she was just taking too much advantage of me.

> My brother and I had quite a falling out. He was becoming a chronic offender of fifteen minutes late, twenty minutes late, at 5:30, [he's] not here. . . . His older daughter went to school and he wanted to bring her after school. And some days he would bring her and some days he wouldn't. And I asked him to please call me and let me know if he was bringing her or not. And apparently because he was my brother—well for one thing he felt that he had done me a favor by having me take care of his kids in the first place to get me started baby-sitting—so anyway one day he came and I was about at my wits' end. I had asked him several times really nicely, and I just said to him, "You know I really don't want to get in a fight with you, but I think I should say this to you now so we can clear the air." I said, "I really need you to be on time and I really need you to call me and let me know if Melissa is coming." . . . So I thought that would be fine and that he would understand. And he said, "We're giving our two-week notice and we're going to be taking Melissa somewhere else." . . . And this was a really awful scene and I felt just rotten. For one thing I felt rotten that he would do that without even thinking about his daughter first, how she would feel about going to someone new. . . . I haven't seen Melissa much since. I was pretty close to her. I still am. I love her, obviously. I felt real bad. She made a space here for the kids and for me. But I had known about

> his feelings about having done me a favor for quite some time—he had expressed it to some other brothers and sisters—and I was uncomfortable with that. I mean, like he did pay me fifty dollars a week. But I *earned* it.

Many of the providers I interviewed still live in the small, rural communities in which they themselves were raised (60 percent were native Vermonters). They are tied to networks that assume collective responsibility for others, and they adhere to the ideology that sustains this assumption. As one woman said, "You help someone but you don't expect to get paid for it. That's the way I was brought up." Other women confirmed they also worked with a social-exchange model, although they suggested they might limit this kind of caring to specific situations or specific times:

> I guess if one of my day-care friends wanted me to take care of their kids so they could go shopping, I would say, okay, you can pay me for that. But if there's a sick relative or they themselves are sick and in the hospital—if they're not making any money—it's hard for me to charge them. . . . I had some friends—well their mother was a dear friend of mine and she was dying of cancer—and I watched their children for probably three or four months, I don't know, maybe twenty or thirty hours a week, for nothing. I may need somebody some day, too, you know.

Some women begin working with this model; when clients fail to reciprocate they diminish their offerings:

> I'll sew their clothes . . . different things like that. . . . I'll bring their child to them if it's more convenient and I can do it . . . or I'll help out with [taking the child to] the dentist. There are some families I'm right there to offer it and there are some families I wouldn't offer it at all. So it's sad that people don't see that. At first I'll do it for all families but when it's not reciprocated, after a while, you just stop.

But, the *preferred* style of interaction remains informal reciprocity:

> Baby-sitting for this certain family is a give and take situation. It's not all give and it's not all take. We work together on it. We rent [from the parents] so I usually take the baby-sitting out of the rent. There's nothing that they wouldn't

> do for us as a family that we didn't ask. . . . He gives us beef and doesn't charge for it. . . . I enjoy situations like that, where you don't have to feel under pressure that they're paying you so much and they expect so much. . . . We're just working together.

*Dynamics of Family Day Care.* Because family day care providers work alone, enter the occupation with limited formal training, and are, in fact, "at home anyway," they have trouble maintaining a strict market stance. Institutional workers can "retreat" behind a bureaucracy or a professional identity to create distance from clients and implement regular rules. No such retreat is possible for family day care providers.

With certain clients, however, the providers do more closely adopt the model of the market. Relationships with parents not previously known to them often begin this way; when the relationships are abbreviated in time they remain formal. But if providers are going to fulfill their own ideal of good care, they have to know what is happening in the children's lives. They come to know when other women are themselves short of cash and when they need some extra assistance: "I gave her child care for free for a couple of months because she wasn't getting her child support checks." Daily interaction with mothers can be the basis for warm friendship.[24] As intimacy grows providers begin to speak about obligations to individual women and sometimes to entire families:

> To this day there is a bond there with the whole family. We've seen the mother come a long way. . . . When she graduated from Alcoholics Anonymous [my husband] bought her a watch and I was so touched. That's how you get involved in some of these things. You're not just getting involved in the baby-sitting. . . . You take on the whole family sometimes.

Even if they have not formed such attachments to parents, providers almost always feel strongly about the children. Over months and years of giving care, genuine affection grows. (This issue is discussed in detail in Chapter 3.) A strong sense of commitment can make a provider hesitant about demanding higher wages: "I rarely get the full amount. I wish I had said there would be a minimum. I am reluctant to do it now because I like the child and the mother"; "I would like to require [pay for sickdays]—some sitters do. But I don't know how it would go over with the parents and I don't want to lose any of these kids." It can also lead the provider to give a service for free or for more hours than they wish:

> I had one parent that owed me money when she left. . . . It was as much my fault as it was hers because I just let it go on and on for six months. But she was in the process of a divorce. It was really affecting the child that I had. I just could not put that child through one more trauma of having to go to a new sitter on top of everything else he was going through. He was three years old and I could just see what this divorce was doing to this little boy. . . . It was really my fault. I should have given him up. I just couldn't because I wouldn't put him through not knowing where he was going to go.

> The latest leaves close to 6:00. It's too long for me. But what happened with one of them is—I had her before when her mother worked [in town] and she was getting picked up at 4, 4:30. And then her mother changed jobs and was working [farther away]. And because I had already had her and there was so much going on anyway with the family. . . . I decided to keep her. She'd been through enough changes and I didn't want her to go through another change.

*Social Attitudes Toward Pricing Care.* The question of a "fair price" or an adequate return is inherently difficult to determine. The diffuse nature of the caregiving activity confounds attempts to quantify it.[25] The affection that develops is not easily transformed into a dollar figure:

> It's so hard because you're dealing with their *child.* I mean you're supposed to have unconditional love with their child. Yet that's the hard part, you're getting money for that kind of love. How can you put a price on that?

> You do get attached to them all. I mean every year I do Christmas shopping for all the kids. . . . You watch them when they're sick—they've got fevers . . . they come down with a bug here. You feel like you do so much for them. You try to teach them everything they're supposed to know about the course of a day.

To a certain extent the activity is its own reward: "It's the same rewards a mother gets, the hugs and the little things like that." And haggling over fees cheapens the service:[26] "I had one [mother] . . . [who] would keep track of how much, you know, and pay me just so much, and that hurt me because I thought, here I am giving so much. How can she be so cheap with me."

Moreover, there exists a cultural taboo against even attempting to redefine care as a commodity. As Arlie Russell Hochschild has noted, "jobs which involve processing people demand emotional labor [and] [s]eeming 'to love the job' becomes part of the job."[27] Family day care providers are conscious of this requirement (and the fact that motivation is important to mothers) in their presentation of self. They do not want to be seen as being in it just for the money. In explaining why they offer care, a "but" suggests the constraints derived from social expectations: "Some parents don't like to pay and that makes it hard because I don't want people to feel I'm only in it for the money, because I really . . . enjoy being with the kids. But it is a job for me."

This taboo is particularly strong for women. Nurturance is attributed to a woman as part of her basic identity. Having to demand payment (or other rights surrounding the work of child care) is difficult. And, because socialization for "womanhood" traditionally has stressed acquiescence, many providers find themselves at a disadvantage in situations requiring self-assertion. Some women state frankly that they lack necessary skills; some feel that these skills come more easily to their husbands: "My husband is a lot more forthright and if it was him, he would say this is the way it is and he would know exactly what to say to present it to them and that kind of thing. I'm not comfortable with this." Asserting limits thus requires a complex shift in self-perception and a reliance on inadequately developed skills. The complex motivations that underlie entry into the occupation, as well as the provider's self-identification as a mother, make this shift particularly difficult.

*Additional Constraints.* Even if women could make this shift, they would find themselves blocked by two realities that stem from providing a service to women engaged in wage labor. First, because they have to meet the needs of several families, each having its own schedule, they can not hold their clients to fixed hours. Second, the rewards available for caregiving in our society are limited. Although many providers find themselves in a "seller's market," they are powerless to raise their rates above the local norm. The low value placed on this kind of work and the absence of provider training also preclude the possibility of charging high fees.[28] One provider discussed how two parents—for different reasons—resisted her attempt to raise her wages. Particularly noteworthy is the attitude of one mother (a teacher) who wanted to ensure that the provider's earnings did not threaten her *own* status:

> Last year I was going to raise it to $1.50—the moms got very upset with me that I was going to charge $2 for two children

> and I nearly gave up baby-sitting. I was very upset with them and they were very upset with me. One girl felt that for her income it was too much [and] another mom felt that because she had received a college education—I think she was looking at it not as what she paid me but what I received as a whole—she felt that I was getting more per hour than she was.

Providers thus have to look beyond the terms of a market exchange to make any sense of what they are doing and to feel adequately reimbursed for their work.[29]

Not surprisingly, then, they want something beyond the fees they so hesitantly impose, something reflecting the social nature of the exchange. Ruth Bolton, who early in the interview insisted that she was content receiving enough to put "a little food on my table," later indicated that she viewed a mother's obligations to her in terms that extended far beyond simple payment. She wanted the mothers to have a sense of responsibility to her and to the entire group of children in her care. She mentioned a mother who withdrew her daughter (Susan) from her. She suggested that in doing so the mother reneged on her responsibility not only to Ruth, but to a mildly retarded child (Mary) who was also receiving care:

> [The mother] had taken Susan out to some other woman she claimed was a school—which was really no different from me. . . . The reason she took Susan from here [was that] Mary didn't challenge her. . . . I felt real bad to think that she couldn't wait until the end of the year. . . . Why couldn't she let Susan stay . . . instead of taking her away. I didn't like that too well. I didn't think it was fair. I'd brought the kid up, got her to where she's big enough and smart enough and able to be not too much work for me. And she was good for Mary. . . . I'd given her more than three years and couldn't she have waited until the [summer]?

Other providers indicated similarly that a good client was one who took the time to know the other children in the group and was willing to show them affection.

Many providers (and their husbands) also spoke about wanting expressions of appreciation *as well as* payment. Providers have no supervisors or ongoing evaluaters; they rely heavily on the simple fact that parents trust them. And they "cling" to even casual comments about their work and how well they are doing. Gifts from mothers were also mentioned frequently. One husband said, "The mothers should show more appreciation of her. They do in spells. . . . One mother brings flowers and things and that makes a big difference. At least you feel appreciated then." One provider put it this way: "[Jennifer's] mom is so good to me. . . . On the year anniversary of her being here I got this beautiful bouquet of flowers . . . and it had a real nice card, 'Thank you for all the love and care you've given me. To my second mom.' . . . That's one thing with parents . . . when I feel they appreciate me, that makes a big difference." Sometimes, however, these same gestures are regarded with contempt: "For Christmas I got a bar of soap. I was insulted"; "They might do something—put it this way—give you a big present and then later slough off about what time they come. . . . And then you go, I can be bought but listen, this is going overboard."

And providers can dismiss the market aspect of the transaction altogether or redefine it so that it falls within the norm of a social exchange: "Look at all this I'm giving these kids. And actually, the pay is like saying thank you, you've done a fantastic job." They can also up the ante to keep the mothers indebted in these terms. One provider who gave an anniversary present of overnight care to each couple, explained her decision in the following manner: "The girls are always bringing me something. They're good to me. I take care of their kid but they pay me for that and I thought why can't I do a little something for them."

The muddle of interrelated needs and interests is illustrated in one provider's discussion of the significance of both material and nonmaterial reinforcement:

> I wouldn't have the children in my home if I wasn't charging something because we need the extra money and I would otherwise have to work out. Some Fridays when the ladies forget to pay me—which upsets me greatly—I say to whoever is here, "Do they think I'm doing this just for the fun of it?" The mothers realize I'm doing it for the money. And they are good to me. They remember my birthday [and] they give me a bonus at Christmas. And one mother said to me she was having trouble getting a maternity leave and . . . one of her biggest fears is losing me as a babysitter and they say things like that and it makes me feel good.

A brief description of a "good" and a "bad" relationship *from the perspective of a provider* might illustrate how the ambivalence about making claims affects interactions with mothers. Judy Stone has been taking care of children in her home for six years. She started "as a favor" to a friend with two small children. The friend now has four children. But Judy has barely raised her rates: six years ago she charged $1.00 an hour "and it went up 50 cents and then again and that's the way it has been." Judy is attached to Marie's children but her relationship with their mother has deteriorated. She knows she is not making enough money: "There are times I think, 'two dollars for all I do.'" And she resents bitterly the days when her "friend" arrives late to pick up the children without calling first, or when she says, "I don't have enough, can I pay you next time?" Judy also blames herself for the way things are: "It's my fault. I don't speak up more about it." Two years ago Judy agreed to take the children in another family as well. She charges Kathy at the same rate per child out of a sense of rough market justice: "I couldn't accept [one dollar for each child] from Kathy because I didn't get it from Marie." But her relationship with Kathy is flourishing. Kathy lives up to her narrow obligations—she calls if she is going to be late, she brings a change of clothing, and she supplies snacks. But more importantly, Kathy gives rides to Judy's daughter and "always adds something extra" to the paycheck. Judy's satisfaction thus relies on a deception: Kathy is paying more than Judy feels comfortable charging; the bonus appears to be a "gift," an expression of gratitude and appreciation.

## THE MOTHERS' PERSPECTIVE

We will see why this deception often fails to materialize, as we turn now to the perspective of the mothers—who view the relationship quite differently from providers. Not only do they have less reason to become enmeshed in an intense relationship, they have more reason to avoid actively this kind of entanglement.

First, parents have different needs. Not surprisingly, a mother wants child care that is suitable for all her children so that pick-up and delivery times are easier and because, as one mother said, "they would be together if I were home with them." A provider who doesn't take babies or won't take more than two children from the same family can create enormous complications. A mother wants the child care to cover her entire working day and extend sufficiently on either side to allow her to travel to and from her workplace. Flexibility is also desirable: Some jobs demand occasional overtime; some days it is convenient to pick up the milk before the children; sometimes working mothers need space in which to relax. As an employed woman with small children she has little room to maneuver. Not only are the requirements of her job rigid, but she is unlikely to have a husband who assumes responsibility for an equal share of the housework or child care. Some women simply do not feel they have the time to be concerned about anyone else; they find the requirement of showing gratitude or friendship a heavy burden they do not want to assume.[30]

A mother also wants and needs inexpensive care. At a weekly cost of forty to sixty dollars, family day care takes a healthy bite out of salaries.[31] No mother wants to be locked into paying for care she doesn't use. If she herself is paid on an hourly basis she can ill afford to cover the cost of sick days and vacations: "I had always been comfortable with Carolyn's rates but I was angry when she wanted to get paid for holidays. It upset me some because I don't get paid for holidays." She has reason to believe the provider's stated fees and to hope that having paid those fees she has discharged her obligations.

A mother's needs are thus at odds with those of a family day care provider. She also has a different "interest" in the relationship. The provider must have access to intimate details about the child's family life, but the mother has no corresponding reason to become involved in the provider's life. She may spend a considerable amount of time "checking out" the provider before she makes the decision to leave her child there; but once the mother has established that the provider can give adequate care, she does not need to learn more about her and her family *unless* it directly impinges on the provider's capacity to serve the mother's needs.

Mothers may have other motivations as well for maintaining the relationship on a more formal footing. Just as some providers want to avoid dealing with close friends and relatives, a mother may feel that distance allows *her* to keep options open. If she is not too close to the provider she can expect more honest feedback, and she can communicate her own dissatisfactions. One mother, who had initially said that she was uncomfortable with a provider she felt was "in it for the money," later in the interview spoke about wanting to avoid intimacy:

> I don't think [being friends] would be good. I think it's harder to deal with friends on a business level. . . . [The sitter] wouldn't say things that needed to be said. I think it would be harder [for the sitter] to say she wasn't pleased. . . . A friend would really feel a loyalty to me. As just a business relationship you don't have to worry about that. . . . I wouldn't want my daughter with a friend who was sitting. I wouldn't be apt to say things that need to be said. . . . I couldn't say that I was not pleased with what is going on.

The mothers say they do not want to be trapped in situations where they have to think about another person when they want to put themselves or the child first. One woman stated openly, "I increasingly resented having to care about the provider, especially in having to get home by 4:00." Another woman described what happened one day when she went to pick up her child at the time she and the provider (Ruth Bolton) had agreed on and found Ruth out for a walk with the children. When she went back an hour later, in order to make it clear that she was not annoyed, she said, "It's good for Stephen to get out for some air." Ruth apparently responded huffily, "It's good for *me* too, you know." This incident, the mother said, made her "realize the ways in which I am obliged to care about Ruth and to think of her as a member of the family as well as to think about Stephen and the care he is getting. . . . I have to weigh what a change for Stephen means in comparison with what it means for Ruth."

But most mothers are unwilling to become so involved, so while providers find themselves engaged in diffuse relationships, and ambivalent about what they expect in return for what they give, mothers try to limit their obligations: to pay well, to come on time, and to keep the provider informed of changes in the household.[32]

The provider's failure to define the relationship in neat and tidy terms can be enormously frustrating:

> Part of the problem in dealing with a sitter in her house is that it is not professional and there are no fixed roles. She wants it that way on the one hand, but on the other hand she doesn't want it that way. And I have mixed feelings about it as well. She does not want to feel like she is a business and she wants to feel that she is helping people out. . . . She refuses to say how much she wants to charge—"Anything you give me"—but on the other side she does have needs she only acknowledges in coded ways or by talking about the other women and therefore letting me know what she needs.

In pushing toward a more "businesslike" perspective the parents deny the richness of the relationship. They even discount a provider's attachment to the children: One mother who was thinking about withdrawing her children from a provider with whom they had been for some time said, "They see a lot of kids come and go and they know that they can not keep these babies forever. They're not theirs to keep." Another said that she feels little incentive to maintain the relationship between her child and the woman who cared for him for the first five years of his life: "I feel bad but not bad enough to do anything about it." Class differences can accelerate the process of disengagement; one woman commented that it would be "fake or condescending" to continue her ties with her daughter's care provider.

Not infrequently mothers rewrite the script to justify their own limited obligations. Some mothers describe their children as being extraordinarily lovable and good. A number of women told me that *her* child was the provider's favorite. Such characterizations implicitly suggest that the provider must thoroughly enjoy the child's daily presence. When the mother leaves her child she is bestowing a favor, not incurring a debt. Alternatively, but to the same effect, mothers speak about the "special" characteristics of the day-care provider: "Karen is just a special person with little kids—it's a mothering, nurturing thing that doesn't stop with her own"; "Sally is kind of childlike"; "Mary likes being at home—she's very domestic." Giving love and daily care is "naturalized" and trivialized as a part of the individual's personality rather than considered a service requiring financial reimbursement.[33] There is an ironic analogy here to the way men define women and thereby dismiss reciprocal caring.

One of the mothers, Elizabeth Walker, spoke about relationships with two family day care providers she had used. The first one, with Adele, was not satisfactory. Elizabeth left her children with Adele for fourteen months. Although she had consistent evidence that the children liked the provider and that affection ran on a "two-way street," Elizabeth remained uncomfortable because Adele met her with "scowls and curtness." She tried to balance out her perception that the woman was "being professional and I respect her for that" with "this doesn't feel good." Ultimately, the latter feeling prevailed. When Adele raised her rates Elizabeth used this action as an excuse to place her children with a different caregiver. The relationship with Nancy is better: "It's more than a job for Nancy and she gives quality care; it's a warmth kind of thing. She greets me cheerfully. And she is understanding that I have meetings out of school and may be late." Elizabeth also feels that she is meeting her own obligations which she defines as, "[being] respectful of her time off—I don't ask her to sit evenings or weekends—and [paying] her well." Whereas the first relationship foundered on the provider's adherence to the terms of a strict market exchange for *both* parties, the current one flourishes because Nancy does not limit her caregiving to narrow hours, is deferential, and allows Elizabeth both to remain autonomous and to feel generous.

## *Shared Mothering*

The relationships between mothers and providers revolve around a shared concern for meeting the needs of children. Ambiguity about what norms should prevail, however, complicates negotiations pertaining to the two key areas of control and intimacy. Additional complications arise from the fact that the roles of the two parties are not clearly distinguished.

## CONTROL

One of the reasons mothers choose family day care is because they think that they will be able to maintain control over the style and content of child care.[34] Ironically, they might actually have less control than they would in an institutional setting that had stated rules, an open-door policy, and clear professional norms.

Efforts to maintain control emerge in the planning stage, as mothers begin the process of selecting a family day care provider. Parents start with a list of what they want for their children during their hours away from home: Issues such as nutritional food, a clean environment, small group size, and a range of activities constitute the most frequently mentioned "tangibles." These vary with the age of the child: Women searching for infant care are more likely to stress cleanliness, small numbers, and a close relationship between the provider and her child; women with older children are more likely to stress the possibility of interaction with peers and a more "stimulating" range of daily activities. The concerns also vary with the particular, class-bound, interests of the parents. Surprisingly, the middle-class parents I interviewed were, if anything, *less* concerned about educational activities than were the working-class parents.[35] There are two explanations. First, the middle-class parents were confident they could provide this stimulation at home: "I figured that the life we led in the family was education enough"; "I'm not looking for an academic setting. I'm not concerned about numbers and letters—I'm there for that." Second, many of the middle-class parents could afford, and actually chose, to take their children to a preschool as well; the working-class parents were unable to spend the time and money to ensure this kind of arrangement. (Additionally, many working-class parents consider preschools an unnecessary "frill." This attitude is shared by many of the providers.) Although, as noted above, some of the middle-class parents *were* concerned about issues such as language from the working-class providers, they also seemed to find the "difference" between their house and that of the providers "stimulating" in and of itself:[36] "There are all kinds of people and kids have a lot to learn from difference; I see a benefit to having differences."

Armed with their lists and their "intuition," they start the search for a provider who can meet their needs and interests. They also seek one who will allow them to remain in charge.[37] They soon learn that they have to negotiate and make compromises.

The first shock is the paucity of alternatives. Good—or for that matter any—child care is hard to find:[38] "I got a list of twenty-seven people from various sources—I called all of them before I got to Meg. Some I ruled out right away because they had way too many kids—like Carla Brock. Almost all of them had too many kids and couldn't take another child or would only take one of the kids. Finally it was a toss-up between Meg and another woman but Meg was closer to work."

Some women have tried a variety of different situations before they find one that even approximates their needs: "The first one I found and used for three weeks made me unhappy. It was a house in which there was smoke and the woman talked on the phone and had friends over. There was TV—soap operas. I knew I had to change."

Most mothers include some issue on which they are unwilling to bend. Health is central to many of them, and they eliminate providers who smoke or who "don't know the difference between apple juice and Kool-Aid." Discipline is also a bottom-line issue for many—they would withdraw their children if they had evidence of spanking. But by the time they find someone, almost all mothers are willing to settle for something less than an ideal situation. The woman just quoted as being anxious to remove her child from a home with constant television and smoke found that the next sitter met some, but not all, of her needs: "I went to Sharon's without [my daughter]. I thought it was chaotic. But there was no TV and there was a sign saying, 'No Smoking.' I think she has the kids' health in mind."

The mothers also soon realize that it is unreasonable to demand exceptions for a single child, that the provider may have her own ways of doing things in her home, and that, therefore, they must give in on some items:

> The things I was expecting at first and realized I couldn't expect from anybody else was that the baby-sitters would do things the way I wanted them done. I had this big thing with not too much candy and healthful foods. But I had to realize that if I had made the decision to go to work and let somebody else take care of my child, they might have chocolate milk sometimes. It did concern me but I thought, if I'm going to be too concerned with these things that were not monumental, then I should just stay home. I could not expect other people to change their ways of doing things because my child was there. And after thinking about it I decided it was less serious.

> I don't want Emily watching a lot of television as she gets older. I might say something to Karen about it—I'll see how

> it goes. I think I'll ask her if it's on a lot. I don't know. That's a concern—I sort of feel, like oh God, I don't have the right to tell her I don't want you to have your television on. It would feel more right in my own house. I give up some because I take her to someone else.

As these examples suggest, the fact of purchasing a service located in another person's home is one basis for distinguishing relationships that develop between family day care providers and mothers from those found between women and domestic workers. Domestic workers are disempowered in part because they work in another woman's private domain.[39] Both providers and mothers note that the former gain some power because they offer the service in *their* homes. In comparing the degree of control she had when she hired a woman to come into her home with that available to her when she took her children to a family day care provider, one mother noted bluntly, "Whoever's home it is has the upper hand."

Just as providers find their socialization to be *one* of the factors inhibiting them from directly claiming their rights as workers, mothers also indicate that their own (similar) socialization can prevent them from directly expressing their needs and interests. Moreover, they are dealing with something of the utmost importance, and they often feel guilty about not living up to social expectations of good mothering. Their emotional involvement leaves them vulnerable.

Sometimes mothers engage in elaborate rituals to prevent a confrontation. If they doubt a provider's capability to give medicine they rearrange the schedule so that the child does not need to be there at that time; if they are uncomfortable with the back-up person they make sure that the child is not left on those days ("I try to work around Ruth's habits"). Each side sends coded messages. Providers complain to mothers about *other* women, and mothers recognize these complaints as thinly veiled hints:

> She complained to me about other parents. I tried not to be a source of complaints. She would complain about things like people not saying when they would be back and not being paid by some of them.

> She complains about the amount of money she is getting from other people. Mostly she complains about the other *women*. She does not think men are in charge. But she never lets me know directly. . . . It has occurred to me that I might be the source of complaints but I think it would be my attitude toward my children rather than my taking advantage of her.

Because these relationships are extremely important, accurate decoding is crucial. Psychologists with an academic concern about the potential weakening of the parent-child bond suggest that parents and caregivers must form a close enough link that a true partnership will develop.[40] Mothers have a more concrete interest in maintaining this relationship. They are afraid that any irritation they elicit will be taken out on the child:

> On one level I know that if I'm not in a good relationship with her she won't be nice enough to my children. . . . I haven't really worried about it too much—but I noticed that when she was having a hard time with another woman she wasn't really as fond of her children. She was always complaining about the two kids . . . and she talks about the mothers in front of the children and pretends that they don't understand when, of course they do. That really horrified me.

As this example suggests, their fears are not always groundless. Some providers acknowledge openly, "If you like the parents you can work well with the kids." The opposite may remain unstated, but it is perceived as a threat. Because mothers, at least implicitly, ask the provider to act as if she were engaged in a social relationship, they become aware that imposing too many demands violates the trust underlying this expectation.

Of course parents do have some "negative" power: They can report a provider to state officials; they can also withdraw their child. But, knowing how hard it is to find a replacement, they may be reluctant to do so. They wonder whether they have enough information to make a final judgment.[41] They want to maintain stability in their child's life.[42] Thus although they recognize that they have the right to hire and fire, they rarely see themselves as having a great deal of power. I asked one woman if she felt as if she were her child-care provider's employer. She answered:

> It's much more dependent than that because unless I have the peace of mind around my child care there's no way I can do my work. . . . I never thought about it as . . . an employer-employee relationship, it's much more dependent than that. . . . She had the power. She knew I needed someone to take care of my children and she had encouraged us to look around before selecting her. And we did and we couldn't find anything better or anyone with an

> opening so it felt like we were at her mercy. . . . So that's how she got her power.

In response to the same question, another woman said, "I feel like her employer but I feel like she's got control of the string. Because I'm the one paying her but she's got control—the right for her to say I don't want to take Deborah anymore or my rates are going up or whatever. The power is with her because she could say the relationship is ending."

Providers know they are offering a scarce resource of great importance. But their power remains limited: It takes a long time to break in a new child to day-care routines; they may not be able to find another child who fits into the time slot; and they are often emotionally involved with the children. Providers do say they want to be accommodating: "Parents ask for different things which is fine, I can bend a little." They also make it clear they do not want to, and will not, do everything parents want. If parents are attempting to find someone who will allow them to stay in control, providers are attempting to weed out these same individuals:

> One woman came and said not to discipline the kid and I said no way I'm going to not discipline a child.

> When they first come they tell me what they want and what to do. Like Delia, she came [and] I went along. She questioned me and suggested [this and that] . . . and I did just as I was a mind to. We laugh about it now. But I thought I can't take care of her kids . . . to suit her.

Providers want to maintain control over their work conditions. Using the location in their own homes as a basis for asserting this right, they refuse to bend on such issues as television, smoking, and the presence of pets:

> One mother didn't like TV's and at first she didn't want to leave the baby with me because we have a television. She got snotty a couple of times because she found the TV on [even though] I wouldn't let her kid in the living room where the TV was. I finally said to her, "Listen if I smoked and you didn't want your kids around someone who is smoking, you don't tell me to quit, you find someone else."

For practical reasons as well, providers can not meet the demands of parents for individualized attention or special consideration.

An attempt to treat all children fairly is often translated into treating all children the same way: This includes the same food, activities, and rest periods. The latter is one of the most touchy areas. While a provider may recognize that parents do not want to have a child up late at night, she also wants to preserve her daily break. The manner in which providers discuss this issue sometimes conceals the true agenda:

> I had a real problem with parents and napping. That really was to me a bothersome thing. That parents would say to a day-care provider, they don't want [their children] to take a nap because they want [their children] to go to bed at 7 at night. Now if you're told that if you work all day it's quality time, how are you going to get quality time out of a little kid that is wound out at 5 P.M. That bugs me so much. That child might have gotten quality time from the day-care provider but if they want quality time with them, let them take an hour nap—or a two-hour nap—and stay up until 10 and enjoy them.

The provider's self-esteem is also at stake. They are vulnerable because they lack formal training and have no external sources of support. They are insulted when mothers give too many instructions and suggest they are less well qualified than they feel themselves to be:

> One lady intimidated me. She'd do things like, if I had a lull I would take her son and somebody else with me. And she would say, "Don't forget to strap them into a seat belt and do this and do that." And I thought, wait a minute, I don't like somebody saying and do this and this and this. . . . I thought, does she think I'm stupid, that I wouldn't strap him in? I might say that to a teenager baby-sitting.

Providers are also extremely sensitive to class insults: "[One father] is very opinionated. It's his way or no way. He's younger than I am but he's condescending, always looking down at you. . . . [Both he and his wife] are from very rich families. I often feel like I'm their black nanny taking care of their kids."

Resistance to parental injunctions draws strength from the provider's sense that she is "better" than the real mother, based on the basic premise that a woman who works outside the home is at least marginally negligent with respect to her child's well-being.[43] Observations of interactions between mothers and children and of the children's behavior, dress, and health can confirm this sentiment. Providers sometimes feel they have the right to take over in minor ways:

> Some of the parents I feel that their jobs are more important than their children. . . . Some people I feel don't deserve to have children by the way they're taken care of. I sputter to myself but I never say anything. There's a lot of kids I give baths every day. . . . There's no reason in the world why a kid should be dirty. Soap does not cost that much and it doesn't take that long to give a child a bath. . . . and they should stay home long enough to give the children a bath rather than being here and there and leaving the kid with another baby-sitter at night.

(Mothers recognize that providers make these decisions and they feel ambivalent about them: "She doesn't like the way I raise children. . . . She saw us as so nuts about Stephen and she disapproved and she felt that he was soft and she was going to toughen him up.")

Inevitably issues arise for which parents have left no clear instructions. How should the provider handle a low-grade fever, the first temper tantrum, lying, or a four-year-old's questions about sex? There are also issues about which they receive mixed messages. Sometimes a mother appears to want to shift some of the burden for child rearing onto the provider, especially in those areas the mother feels she handles poorly. A mother who knows that she gives in to her child too often "because I see her so rarely" might want the provider to be firmer in discipline. A mother of an only child on whom she lavishes attention might want the caregiver to treat him less partially.

Daily uncertainty about who is in charge peaks at departure time. This is a tense moment. Many children begin to act up as soon as the mother walks in the door; it is the one time of day when both mothers and providers are present for more than a brief interval. Some mothers say they want the provider to continue to assume responsibility. They defend this choice on several grounds. They feel uneasy about taking over in someone else's house; they want the child to learn to respond to the caretaker in that domain; and they can learn about the provider's caregiving style by watching what happens: "I like to let the sitter handle it. Because it's her house and Katie has to know that she has to respond to that person"; "I leave it up to them because it's their territory, it's their house. You can also find out how they discipline people and handle kids." Moreover, mothers do not want to anger a child at the moment of reunion by being too firm. Conversely, providers say they want the parents to assume responsibility: They want the parents to show that they have respect for and will reinforce the rules they have spelled out for their homes; they think to themselves, after all, "she really is the mother"; and they also do not want to alienate the child whose good will constitutes a major reward.

## INTIMACY

In addition to the specifics that mothers can assess through a preliminary interview and ongoing visits, they want something else that they find more difficult both to evaluate and to articulate. They want to be reassured that the child is receiving loving care. This is often first on their lists: "I wanted her to get a lot of attention, to be held a lot, to have a lot of physical closeness." And many mothers suggest that this kind of warmth and genuine concern can make up for other deficits. The woman who spoke about compromising on chocolate milk explained further why she was willing to do so: "I liked the way she looked at them and touched them and held them. There would be times when she would wake them and would be very gentle. I knew these were things that went on all the time. It made me feel good that this was the care they were getting."

But many mothers feel ambivalent about this intimacy.[44] A mother may want the provider to love her child, but not to claim that child; she wants the provider to be like a mother, but she does not want her to make independent decisions; she wants the provider to become close, but not to threaten the parent-child bond.

Parents think anxiously about the fact that their children may spend almost as much time with someone else as they do with themselves: "I figured out how much time he was at the sitters and how much time he was with us and it was an hour and a half more he spent with us waking time than with the sitter." They wonder whether, "his personality development will be a reflection of [my husband's] and mine or a reflection of [the provider's]." And they evaluate their own relationships with their children for reassurance: "I think he's very attached to my husband and me and I feel real secure about that. I feel that there is real bonding that took place."

In this context evidence of a good relationship between a provider and her child is reassuring to a mother. However, it can also make a mother acutely jealous:

> I remember Halloween night, [the sitter] and her husband and two kids came over . . . and [the sitter] walked over to [my daughter] and picked her up. I was jealous. It's something like a man and his wife and his mistress all being in

> the same room together. . . . I guess I wanted [my daughter] to reject her maybe. But that would be terrible. But I don't want her to forget who I am.

Another mother remembers how she responded to evidence of attachment between her child and the sitter: "I was very picky about what [the sitter] was and wasn't doing. Diddly things like what she prepared for lunch, if he missed a nap. I wanted to pick on things. It was a way for me to preserve the fact that no one could replace me. So I was going to pick her apart."

For providers as well the most complicated boundary issue in "normal" situations is how close to get to the child and how much attachment to feel (this is discussed extensively in the next chapter). They exercise caution in presenting their relationship with a child to his/her parents. Providers are often well aware of what the parents are missing, and they recognize the possibility of jealousy.[45] One provider who worked outside the home until her daughter was two, speaks knowledgeably on this subject: "I think if you get really involved there tends to be friction with parents, kind of like it's your business but it's not your business. You're in a position where they want you to really like their kids but they don't want their kids to like you too much. . . . Parents don't want kids to call you 'mommy.' " Other providers speak about protecting parents: "It's like watching these children grow up and taking their first steps and saying their first words and cutting their first teeth. I try not to say anything. I would like the parents to think they are seeing it for the first time at home." (One provider who is not so cautious said that each time she told a mother about a "first," the mother would deny that her daughter was old enough to have performed that feat. Several days later the mother would come back and report, full of pride, that the child had achieved that same new stage of development at home—in front of her own parents.)

Most of the providers have enormous respect for the parent-child bond, and they do not want to threaten it:

> That's a fine line too. Because some of these kids you could get them to love you more than their parents. It would be very easy to do. I mean, it would be *very* easy to do. Because you spend more time with them. . . . But it would be wrong.

> You want to give the child what he needs without giving too much that you are interfering with the way he or she feels about his own parents.

They do not want to elicit expectations they can not fulfill. They also want to keep a distance to protect themselves. Quite simply, providers do not want to be overwhelmed by love for a child who is not their own.

## *Conclusion*

Both parents and providers believe it is important to maintain good relationships with each other. However, many factors impede a simple resolution of obligations. Although parents and providers may have similar social-class backgrounds, and therefore some similar values, they have to negotiate an emotionally charged territory without established guidelines, and they have reason to mistrust and misunderstand each other. The advice each party receives may exacerbate this mistrust. Parents and providers enter the relationship with different interests. Providers want to limit the time spent caring for other people's children, and they want to be paid well for that time. But providers find it hard to maintain these limits: Both the ideology of care and the nature of the work itself encourage intense attachments—to children *and* to parents; the actual payment available for caregiving makes a mockery of a narrow market perspective. Providers find themselves involved in diffuse, and poorly defined, relationships. Parents frequently need to push at the limits providers set, and they want to pay as little as possible. They want the providers to act out of friendship. But they want *their own* obligations defined narrowly. This imbalance is one of the central ironies.

The fact that these relationships revolve around children complicates the boundary issues. The parental desire to maintain control over child rearing clashes with the provider's interest in shaping her work environment; a mother's assertion of control violates the social nature of the bond. A mother's ambivalence about how close a connection she wants to see between the provider and her child is echoed in the provider's attempt to find the proper balance between attachment to, and distance from, each child in her care.

In their discussions of these complex relationships, each woman speaks as if she were the powerless one. Providers say they feel dependent on the willingness of parents to follow their rules. They note that because of the low prestige accorded child care they have few mechanisms to ensure compliance. They know that they are vulnerable to complaints lodged with state officials. They feel trapped, by their inability to assert themselves and by their awareness of the lack of alternatives, into continuing to offer care for children when they receive little financial reimbursement. And they feel captive in their own homes. Mothers speak of their extreme dependence on the provider they have found after an enervating search. They know that some providers disapprove of them, and they bristle at the suggestion that they are not being good mothers. They resent having to comply with rules that do not meet their needs. They feel vulnerable because they have so much at stake. And they question whether they have enough information to evaluate the situation.

In fact, neither side has much power. Child care *is* hard to find; the resources are limited; and the boundaries between private and public issues are shifting. And mothers are tied directly to the requirements of wage labor and the double burden. Providers are tied less directly, but no less firmly, to the formal economy and, perhaps even more securely, to the demands of the domestic domain. The abuses within the relationship are necessarily the result of each person's attempt to make the best for herself out of an unmanageable situation in the context of a social policy that fails to acknowledge the needs of either of them.

# *Chapter 3*

# MOTHERING OTHERS' CHILDREN

In seeking "homelike" care for their children, parents are attempting, among other things, to purchase for limited periods of time the relations that (ideally) characterize the home. Family day care providers participate willingly in this notion that homelike nurturance can be bought and sold. They too expect that they will be "like mothers" to the children in their care. And, as they go about their daily activities of caring for children, they learn to love them and to treat them like their own. The setting in which they work engenders this attitude. Yet they also find this attitude difficult to sustain because they lack the privileges of motherhood. They have limited authority, and loss is an ongoing reality; they also have to delimit and contain these relationships so that they can demand financial reimbursement. In their relationships with *mothers* providers have to find a middle ground between the norms of social exchange and the norms of the market. In their relationship with *children,* providers also have to find a stance that resolves competing, and even contradictory, pressures.

The first part of this chapter describes what the providers want to be offering to the children who come to them for daily care; we will see that providers align themselves with "mothering" as a model for the care they give. The second section describes the roots of this model: the structural context in which they work, the absence of occupational socialization, the manner in which providers draw on prior experience and training, and the provider's own ideology. The providers experience their caregiving activities in ways that are similar to those in which mothers experience theirs, finding comparable rewards and facing comparable problems. However, because the relationship between a provider and the children in her care is "interrupted" by the intrusions of parents, the state, and a broader public, and because it is bounded by inevitable loss and financial constraints, providers have to find a way to dissociate from the model of mothering. They do this through a stance of detached attachment. The chapter concludes with a discussion of the manner in which providers exercise the right to make choices about which children they will nurture.

First, however, a few qualifications are in order. As we know, the care family day care providers offer to young children is often villified. Family day care providers are aware of this public contempt. They are quick to draw distinctions between themselves and "other" providers. *They* are motivated by love and enjoyment as well as money; *they* do not take so many children that they can not offer adequate care to each. *Other* women are in it only for the money; *other* women take too many children. In describing their relationships with children and the meaning of their work, they may be engaged in an act of self-justification which, some readers might argue, I have swallowed whole. I don't think so. I am aware that I was exposed to the "best" that family day care providers have to offer: No provider was going to state baldly that she hated children or her job (though some spoke quite honestly about feeling burned out); no provider was going to abuse a child in the presence of an outsider. But I am not attempting to judge quality. Rather, I am attempting to analyze how the context within which this particular group of caregivers functions shapes the dynamics of their relationship with care recipients. And while my analysis depends on the statements of providers (and my observations of their interactions with children), it also depends on my own understanding of the manner in which the activity of giving care to children can engender attitudes of affection.

This is not meant to imply that there were no qualitative differences among the providers. The women I interviewed varied widely in terms of training as well as other background characteristics, and they described their days very differently: If some providers built in time to read to the children plus opportunities for drawing and crafts, in other homes the television set loomed large as an activity. However, none of these differences seem directly relevant to the issues under discussion here. While a woman like Ruth Bolton who leaves her knick-knacks on the shelf might have a stronger sense that children have to learn limits early, and whereas one like Cara Brown who takes long "nature walks" with the children might have a stronger sense that a child's growth needs adult direction, all the women engage in a similar core of hands-on caregiving activities. They feed the children, clothe them, put them down for naps, comfort them when their mothers leave, and settle disputes. And it is what happens when they do these things with children who are not their own, within a particular context, that I am most interested in analyzing.[1]

I do acknowledge one set of differences, however. One group of providers takes what I call a "professional" stance toward child care, while most of the providers see their role as being "like a mother" to the children in their care. (Those providers who adamantly deny this self-description in favor of being "like a teacher" are analyzed in Chapter 6.)

## *Provider's Vision of Good Care*

What do family day care providers want to be offering the children who come to them on a daily basis? The most common answer to this question makes reference to the family day care setting being "like a home": 81 percent of the questionnaire respondents feel it is "very important" to provide "a homelike atmosphere." Interviews confirmed this approach: "I try to make the child comfortable here"; "I try to give them the experiences I gave to my own children"; "I want this to be a nurturing place"; "They should be at home here"; "I like this being just like a home." The answer also makes reference to the family day care provider being "like a mother": 75 percent of the respondents agree strongly with the statement "A family day care provider should be like a mother to the children in her care." In discussing their feelings about the children the women use familial analogies: "They are my part-time kids"; "I'm trying to give the children a sense of family"; "I'm like a second mom"; "I think of them as extended members of my family"; "These guys are like my own kids"; "I'm offering closeness and security—my motherhood."

The manner in which providers use these terms assumes that their meanings are obvious, that everyone knows what a home is and what kind of care a mother offers. As providers talk more they reveal the ideal with which they work. This ideal includes protecting the children, allowing them to play and learn, disciplining and loving them.[2]

High on the list of priorities is to keep the children safe and to attend to their everyday needs while they are in the provider's care. They stress good nutrition: 86 percent say this is "very important." They also speak about the burden of responsibility involved in ensuring that the children are cared for competently. Some providers indicate that this burden is a major negative feature of their work lives.

The majority of family day care providers is also convinced that a home is a place where children should play, learn through playing, and where they can be left alone for periods of time to amuse themselves:

> The kids play and do a few things; they read and draw. We have lunch early and when everyone is quiet I enjoy a break. Then my kids come home at two and we try and go outside if it's nice. We have a snack.

> The kids come for a couple of hours and we have free play. I read stories. We have outside play, lunch, rest, and play. They start to get picked up by 3:30 and the last goes by 5:15.

> In the morning the kids go outside. I let them go without me—I check on them. If my younger son is there I don't worry about them. The kids have not gone near the pool. Otherwise they color or play inside with toys. We have lunch around noon . . . and then a nap for most of them.

Most providers do not stress explicit educational activities: While they may read to the children or bring out toys and equipment, the majority of providers does not feel that instruction should be the core of a child's day; only 39 percent of the respondents indicated that they thought it was "very important" to include any "educational activities" in the daily round of events.[3] In fact, a substantial number of the providers feel that too much emphasis on "abc's" is inappropriate and unnecessary for young children: "I'm not one who feels [preschool education] is important." (Some more traditional providers even view it as potentially ruinous: "Nursery schools—as soon as children start there they go crazy. They don't seem to have discipline. They act like little brats. [Nursery schools] let them do anything.") Providers do, however, stress other kinds of learning, particularly the development of social skills: 53 percent said they thought this was "very important." As one provider said, "you teach them everything they have to know about life." And another provider contrasted this kind of teaching with the emphasis on education and drew a boundary between her responsibility and that of parents: "I don't spend a lot of time trying to teach the kids. I tell [the parents] that is their job. I teach them what life is about."

Most of the family day care providers, when asked to describe their style of child care or what they are trying to accomplish with the children, mention discipline (in the broad sense):[4] "With the twins I stress table manners"; "They're taught to behave, to be nice to anybody, not to be mouthy, not to hit, and to show manners whether it comes to playing or eating or sharing or whatever"; "I expect the child to respect me as a person and I, in return, respect them as an individidual, their privacy. If they want to be left alone, fine. I try to encourage manners, politeness, sharing with other children, as well as playing together in a group. Just generally learning to respect other people's property. And if they want something they ask for it."

Homelike care refers not only to the kind of activities that prevail, but also to the pacing of these activities and the attentiveness and affection that make this pacing responsive to children's needs. When asked about the differences between the care they give and that offered to children in a day care center or preschool, family day care providers are quite articulate and insistent. They view these establishments as rigorously scheduled, as places in which individual children get lost in a crowd. In contrast, they view a home as a place where children's needs are met as they arise, where the caregiver can respond spontaneously both to the individual child and to the will of the group; only 24 percent of providers felt it was "very important" to offer children "a structured or planned day." They also feel that day care centers do not encourage the "warmth, love and intimacy" that can be found in a family setting; centers do not offer the "one-on-one" care of a home.

Although family day care providers do not speak forcefully as professionals might about what they are trying to accomplish with the children in their care, it becomes clear that the providers see this kind of "homelike" care as the setting that can best ensure the protection, learning, discipline, and affection that a young child needs.[5]

## *Roots of the Provider's Style*

This alignment with mothering and homelike care clearly has its roots in several structural factors; it also stems from the provider's own experience and her own ideological stance about proper care for young children.

### STRUCTURAL FACTORS

By definition, family day care providers remain at home. As a consequence paid and unpaid care is merged in a single setting. This makes it difficult for the provider to distinguish between what she is doing for her *own* children and what she is doing for the children who come to her on a daily basis.

The structure in which they work also creates certain limitations. There is a material underpinning to the emphasis on homelike care. A preschool pedagogy is expensive.[6] Although the providers spend weekends scouring garage sales for toys and equipment, they can not afford to spend too much on these items. As one woman said, "I'm a *home* day care. I can only do so much with what I can afford. I can't buy luxurious things."

There is also a pragmatic underpinning to this kind of care. Many day care centers divide children into single age groups in order to lessen the variations in the kinds of demands to which they are called to respond. They are then equipped to follow a schedule and plan activities appropriate for a narrow range of children. Family day care providers don't have this luxury. Although many of them try not to take on babies, only 13 percent deal with only a single age group. Given a range of ages, quite simply, they can not plan events or schedule activities: "It's hard with the little ones [around] to sit down and work on our alphabet. . . . I leave that up to the mother to do at home." Moreover, their inability to tie parents to the same (or even similar) schedules impedes such planning. Providers work in isolation. There is no one to help with outings ("We go to the playground—but that is hard unless you have someone with you") and no one to offer them breaks ("In a center workers have a break and therefore children have a person with more gusto. I can't keep up that level"). Many of the family day care providers prepare more than one meal for the children who come to them. This activity takes time that might otherwise be devoted to interaction with the children: "A lot of time I find the kids don't need my attention. But it always seems that when I would like them to be on their own they need me—like lunch time." They have almost sole responsibility for maintaining the environment: "I don't schedule the day. They do their thing and I do mine around whatever they are doing. . . . If the ironing's got to be done, the ironing gets done. If the laundry's got to be done—I don't do all of these things after they leave at night. I don't do a thing any different than I did when I was home with my own two. What's got to be done gets done." Although most women do not find time to attend to much housework, some can, and they see their actions as beneficial to the children: "They see you doing these things and it's just like mom did."[7]

## EXPERIENCE AND SKILLS

If structure provides one underpinning to this style, it also has roots in the absence of any alternative identity or occupational socialization. Professional and semiprofessional workers often consciously seek to evade attachment.[8] Training in occupations like medicine, law, teaching, and nursing emphasizes the necessity to avoid becoming overly attached to, or identified with, clients. Drawing on Parsonian terminology, Sara Lawrence Lightfoot, for example, distinguishes between the appropriate attitudes of parents and teachers:[9]

> Parents have emotionally charged relationships with their children that rarely reflect interpersonal status or functional considerations. Children in the family are treated as special persons, but pupils in schools are necessarily treated as members of categories. From these different perspectives develop the particularistic expectations that parents have for their children, and the universalistic expectations of teachers.

Similarly, Sandra Scarr suggests that professional caregivers should maintain an emotional distance from their charges:[10] "A teacher is not fulfilling her role of impartial instructor about the world outside of the parent-child bond if she spends her time on affection and comfort for individual children." While some observers proclaim the functional necessity for this distinction between the roles of teachers and parents, others suggest that drawing these lines may serve the interests of caregivers who are claiming professional status. As Chiara Saraceno notes, the creation of a distinctive stance may be a critical element in this process:[11] "In order to maintain a professional image and to avoid the 'feminine vocation trap' evoked by working with young children and promulgated by employment policies, [some workers] stress their expertise and professional handling of children, focusing on the more formally educational aspects of their work." Workers in these areas struggle for rights involving working conditions and the exercise of autonomy. But they are not supposed to—and they may choose not to—make emotional claims with respect to the children in their daily care.

By contrast, most family day care providers enter the occupation casually and without either prior experience in formal child care or extensive formal training. They perform their work in isolation from others; they have limited access to a work culture that sets norms for interaction with care recipients.[12] Not surprisingly, then, only the model of mothering is available to them. (Some of the providers are, in fact, defensive about their lack of training: "I am not a school. I'm not qualified to be a teacher.")

If providers lack the occupational socialization that might create a commitment to a professional model, they do draw on a distinctive set of experiences through which they feel they have acquired the skills necessary to perform competently the role they have defined. Good mothering—for their own and for the children of others—comes from experience. Some observers note that with smaller families and less contact with extended families, more women today start parenting in the absence of prior experience.[13] This is not the case for the women in this study. Most of them have a variety of experience to draw on to implement their model of good care.

Many providers, when asked how they learned to care for children, begin with a discussion of their own mothers' care of them. For some, this experience provides a clear model of effective and appropriate caregiving. One provider, for example, when asked what experience she had, said, "Let's go way back because I think it is all important. I'm the oldest of five children. My mother is a saint and just taught me all the basics." Similarly, another woman said, "[My knowledge] probably comes from my mom. . . . She always had fun with us when we were little. . . . She always let us be kids."

Some women are more ambivalent about the care they received. One suggested that although overall she felt she could use her mother as a model, she was making some modifications: "When I was growing up my parents didn't show us a lot of affection and I always missed that. All my kids are very kissy and huggy." Rena Milks said she had learned from her husband's family how to be more affectionate than had been the norm in her own.

And some women believe that they have to overcome completely the model that was presented to them as children.[14] For example, when asked for the source of her child-care style, one woman who had had a rough adolescence (including drug use and giving birth to a baby she put up for adoption) responded:

> Well my child-care style is very different than when I grew up. I wasn't getting . . . the things that I'm giving these kids I baby-sit for. . . . My mother was not loving, she wouldn't cuddle or hold me or much communication at all. . . . I guess I just realized if I can help the next kid not to get into [the kind of] situations I did, more power to me. I want to show some of these kids there's somebody out there who cares because there wasn't anybody for me and I don't want that to happen to other kids.

Another woman said similarly, "My knowledge comes from my experience of growing up. I didn't have a good childhood. But I think about how I felt as a child and I want to make it better for my kids."

Many of the women grew up in large families. If they were among the oldest, they cared for those who came later. In answer to the question, "What kind of training have you had?" one woman said: "Training? I was the oldest of eleven children—does that count? I have brothers and sisters at home right now that are like my own. I potty-trained them, I broke them of their bottle, I nurtured them, I gave them all the things that they needed. . . . I felt I was ready. I come from a big family—there was lots of us around." Another woman, asked whether she had ever cared for children before, answered, "Just my whole life. My mother was sick when my younger sister was born and I baby-sat . . . from the time I was eight." If they were among the youngest, they found themselves thrust into caring for nieces and nephews: "I have been taking care of other people's children ever since I was old enough to take care of myself. I took care of a niece when I was nine." Almost all the women did baby-sitting as teenagers. And, for those whose children are now older, the way they are turning out gives them confidence that they can care for other people's children. Nancy Bingham said, "I've been told—and I feel—that [my own children] are great kids. . . . The way I raised them is what I do with the kids I baby-sit for . . . and [my children] are doing fine so far."

The women who have been doing this work for some time also draw on the experiences of years past. Providers talk about specific knowledge they have acquired. They learn to deal with fights and injuries; they learn about developmental stages; they learn how to manage the complexities of relating to a wide range of age groups; and they learn how to evaluate children's needs. Some women say that they have become more flexible over time as they learn to assess children's moods: "I used to go with a routine and stick to that. Now I am looser than I used to be because I have learned how to be and to get the same thing accomplished while being looser." Similarly, "I have learned that each child is an individual and might be different that day. I evaluate in the morning what kinds of things can be done that day."

Some mention specific skills that ease the burden of their work: "I have gotten better at putting them to bed [for a nap]—I know that sounds funny but it could be difficult. I am also better at learning how long their attention span is." Many providers speak about having become more patient. And although they may think of patience as a natural attribute, their own definitions belie this ready dismissal:

> Patience is understanding the individuality of all of these children. . . . I could have another 181 [children] and each one of them would be different again. There's no two that need the same amount of loving or need the same amount of reprimanding. Each one needs a little extra something of some sort which is fun finding with that individual. I think [that is part of the challenge.]

Two themes predominate in the providers' discussions of the relevance and utility of these experiences. On the one hand, the women firmly believe this kind of experience is the crucial training for child care. For example, one woman in answer to a question about what knowledge she drew on, said, "Being a mother. The strongest child care providers are those who have raised children. They have had the experience of what works and what doesn't. They know how important a nap is." Another woman also said she relied on experience: "I think that anyone that has taken care of kids for as long as I have, sisters and brothers and all the kids I've taken care of, can do this work."

Given this conviction, they mock the idea that anything else is necessary; they are particularly scornful of the notion that book learning or formal training is preferable to experiential learning:[15]

> A woman came the other day and she was asking, "What special training do you have in dealing with children?" And I said, "I'm the mother of six children, that's all the special training that I feel like I need." As far as taking a book that tells me how to deal with children . . . I don't want that. I don't believe in book raising children. . . . So that question kind of disturbed me.

> Some of the new mothers, so many of them go by the book. And I just threw the book out. . . . I threw the book away. You don't need to go by the book. Just let your child grow and out of common sense you should know what to do.

> Well, if they're going to have training I don't think they're a very good baby-sitter. I wouldn't want to put my kids [with] someone that needs book training and stuff like that. No way. I would say if they don't have the ability without being trained I wouldn't want them to baby-sit.

The flip side of this glorification of experiential learning is a denigration of their own knowledge. For many women locating the source of skills in experience is tantamount to a denial of expertise.[16] There are several reasons for this attitude. First, it is hard to isolate the skill learning out of the experience. The skills are acquired without direct tuition: no one taught them to cook or to change a diaper; they simply did these things. When asked what she was good at, one woman said, "What an interesting question." She then answered in a manner suggesting only a hint of awareness that she was acquiring knowledge through the activities of family day care: "I enjoy kids a lot. I like learning and watching stages."

Second, providers share with parents the sense that these abilities come naturally to women: "I don't have any skills. Anyone who has been a mother can do this," one woman who was particularly depressed lamented. Another said, "It's built into you." Although they may acknowledge that child care does not come easily to all women ("I don't think that everyone is cut out to do this"), they do not alter their conviction that the abilities are *natural.* (And some women are concerned that, in spite of their own learning and experience, they are deficient because they are *not* "naturals": "I'm not a natural. I'm learning how to do these things.")

Finally, providers buy into the cultural denigration that comes from the fact that these tasks are passed from one woman to another.[17] And although some recognize that they have acquired expertise, others refuse to acknowledge that what they have is anything of value: "Teaching takes skills. But this? I don't know. Instinct is more what you need and a lot of patience."

Given this self-denigration they have difficulty thinking that they should be richly rewarded: "If I was paying $1.75 for child care I would want one hell of a good job. My kid had better come out almost an Einstein and clean and well mannered. So maybe that is why I don't charge that much because I don't feel that I am giving that much to a child to produce an Einstein."

## IDEOLOGICAL FACTORS

Family day care providers are not just defending a style based on their own inadequacies or the impossibility of providing something else. For the majority of family day care providers, the immediate impulse to care for other people's children is rooted in a desire to stay home and continue caring for their own children while earning a living. Thus the majority of these women define themselves as mothers who are committed to mothering as a primary role.[18] And they see the style of child care they are offering, including the emphasis on discipline and affection, as central to the performance of this role.

Their decision to stay home with their own children generally precedes their experience as day-care providers. But the women who do this work believe they see confirmation of the importance of a *mother's* love and discipline. One of their major criticisms of women who leave their children with them daily is that these women—partly in attempts to make up for the time they do not spend with their children and partly to make the time they do spend with them easier—are inconsistent and inadequate disciplinarians: "You can tell those parents just give in because they really don't want to deal with [their children]." And although the particular emphasis on a specific kind of discipline may have its roots in the class location of some family day care providers, discipline is an aspect of all child rearing. When family day care providers say, as one woman did, "My top priority was to be with the children. That to me was more important than anything else. . . . That's why I had them—so I could raise them myself," they are expressing a desire to shape children who will assume an appropriate place in the social community.[19] The need for discipline may also underlie their deep mistrust of substitute caregivers. And it is a reason for remaining at home even when their children are teenagers: "For me it was more important to stay home and be there when my kids came home [from school] and *to know where they were.*"

Family day care providers also believe that the children who are with them miss out on the sense of attachment to their parents and the daily experience of receiving love. This also is a reason for staying home with their own and the other pole around which good mothering revolves. "What is good care?" I asked one woman. "Most of the time it is just making sure that they are taken care of and showing the love they should be getting at home," she answered.

Finally, the providers think that by including the children in their daily household activities, they are providing an important opportunity to help them acquire the skills necessary to be parents themselves. Familiarity with cooking and cleaning, for example, is valued for itself; in this way these women differ from institutional child-care providers who are more likely to use these activities as the basis for the acquisition of more abstract skills. Even when direct tuition is not involved, the women believe they are important role models. One woman who cares for the elderly as well as a couple of young children, reflecting her own self-pride made this explicit: "As far as sitting down with the kids and doing anything constructive, really I don't. I don't feel that I'm their teacher. . . . I feel that I am an example that they can follow—a productive human being." (Some providers consider these models necessary because otherwise the children would not know "what a mom does.")

Family day care providers clearly believe that the kind of care they are offering is what young children (their own included) need. It is flexible enough to respond to the individual child's needs and demands, and it does not pressure the child into becoming adult before his/her time. And many believe that in providing affection, discipline, and the opportunity to play, they are making up for what the child does not get at home. (Ironically, they are attempting to offer something they do not think it possible for anybody except a "real" mother to offer—something they do not trust anybody but themselves to give to their own children.)

Their descriptions of their days demonstrate this complex admixture of self-justification and positive ideology about what is best for children. We can hear it in one woman's defensive mockery of the questions parents ask her about the kind of care she provides: "Some of the things I'm asked, like how are you going to entertain her—come on. What do they want me to do? This isn't really a play school or nursery school. It's care but I do with them what I do with my own. I don't tap dance for the kids. I do play with them . . . but I'm not entertaining. Babies prefer to entertain themselves." Or we can hear it when another woman describes her understanding of "homelike" care and how it is distinguished from that offered in an institutional setting: "I have them watch me do things like baking. We walk around and talk about things outside. We talk to the cows. . . . I like them to have a good time, to be kids, to be themselves, not have to worry about every minute *planned*. If mothers want that they can send them to a preschool." And we can hear it in yet another provider's definition of good care: "Good care for me is a home atmosphere—not abc's, but playing and junk like that. We have kind of our schedules relating to kindergarten kids but other than that it is—homelike. I do some special things but more like if it happens it happens and if it doesn't it doesn't."

## Experiential Similarity to Mothering

Family day care providers not only choose homelike mothering as a *model* for child care, they also appear to *experience* caregiving much as mothers do. As they engage in the round of daily care they learn to love (or have affection for) nonresident children. They also find rewards and face problems similar to those identified by mothers.

### DEVELOPMENT OF ATTACHMENT

The literature on infant bonding would have us believe that what happens during the first moments or days of infancy provides the basis for a parent's subsequent nurturance. Those who emphasize this perspective might cast a skeptical eye on the notion of fierce attachments emerging when caregivers begin to nurture older children. Similarly, those who see a mother's love rooted in a biological link may not recognize the possibility of the kind of attachment I am describing here. Nor would those who see affection as being derived only from a long-term interest in—or "possession" of—a child.[20]

My stance differs from these. I believe that intense affection *can*, and indeed often *does*, emerge from the process of caregiving; conversely, I would suggest that caregiving is only meaningful (and pleasurable) in the context of concerned attachment.[21] The setting in which this kind of care takes place is, in some respects, especially well suited to the development of attachment.[22] Home-based caregiving does not interpose competing goals; the children often remain with the same individual for many years; care is not fragmented among a variety of different caregivers. And, as we have seen, most family day care providers neither have claim to—nor do they want to claim—a kind of professional status that makes particularistic attention and affection irrelevant. Moreover, I argue that the fact that this kind of caregiving has elements of a market relationship does not preclude the possibility of affection emerging.[23]

Seventy-seven percent of the questionnaire respondents agreed with the statement, "I get emotionally involved with the children in my care." The discussions in interviews reveal this same intense emotional engagement in the work and how it emerges from the activity of giving the full range of care over time to a child:

> [One child] came to me when he was six months old and I had him up until he was two. He was like my own because I'd have him from 7:00 in the morning till 6:30, 7:00 at night from Monday through Friday and some Saturdays. And it's like this kid's my own. This is the kid I was second momma to. It's like, "Momma I want cookie." I even trained that kid—I potty trained him. [The mother] did the nighttime bit but I did the daytime. The talking—everything. I watched this kid grow up.

Of course, not all providers become equally involved with the children in their care. Those with large groups find the process of engagement more difficult. And providers don't become equally attached to all the children in their groups. More easily than mothers, they admit to having favorites (although these are not necessarily the children the mothers think are the favorites). But all providers acknowledge that affection grows ("You learn to love the kids as you love your own") and that it is a significant reward of their daily activities. They also suggest that loss is a major problem.

## OTHER REWARDS AND SATISFACTIONS

Providers also speak about other rewards and satisfactions in language that is like that of mothers. From her interviews with fifty-eight middle-class and fifty-six working-class mothers, Mary Georgina Boulton identified the ways in which mothering gave women a sense of meaning, value, and purpose.[24]

First, she noted that, while a child's dependence might be a burden, mothers derive great satisfaction from being needed. Family day care providers also speak about being relied on and loved by the children in their care, and they present this as a positive feature of their work. Nancy Bingham said, "Cassie left the other day and told me she loved me. Things like that are the reward. What can you have more than a child that loves you?"

Second, Boulton noted the rewards a mother derives from the opportunity children give "to relive experiences from the past altered to be as she would have liked them to be." Many day-care providers also find fulfillment in rectifying the past. In fact, one respondent, when asked why she had opened a family day care home, stated simply, "I wanted to make life better for these kids than it was for me." Conversely, some find occasions for reciprocity. They can repay others for the care they received as children. Those women who were themselves reared by baby-sitters or foster parents proudly carry on a tradition of surrogate care.[25]

The women also take pride in the children and find rewards in "accomplishments" they can attribute directly to their care. Many have a story to tell about change in a specific child's behavior. And family day care providers spoke, as did Boulton's mothers, of the more passive pleasures derived from observing the children "doing all the cute things children do." Just as the women initially said that they were providing "homelike" care, as if that needed no further elaboration, some women did not indicate a specific gratification of caregiving but, when asked, simply said, "the same rewards a mother gets."

## PROBLEMS AND DISSATISFACTIONS

Family day care providers also discussed the same kinds of problems that Boulton and many others have identified.[26] The contemporary organization of maternal child care relies on a single individual with full responsibility for that care. Family day care duplicates this structural arrangement. Moreover, because a family day care provider generally takes care of more children than does the contemporary mother, the demands on her time and energy may well be greater while her possibility of going out or altering the arrangements are reduced.

Boulton's mothers indicated that this setting for child care resulted in isolation from rewarding company: Few people came to visit and the mothers found it hard to pack up their children to go out. Many family day care providers make these same complaints with a vengeance. (Others, however, note that the visits from parents in the morning and afternoons or scattered through the day are ample occasions for sociability. And some are deeply embedded in extended kin networks, which provide them with visits and phone calls.[27])

Finally, the middle-class respondents in Boulton's sample felt that as the children monopolized their attention, they lost a sense of individuality. And again we find a parallel with family day care providers who say that because they are constantly dealing with "kid stuff," they feel their own integrity and awareness of a larger world to be threatened.

## *Difference from Mothering*

Given this alignment with mothering as a model for care, it is not surprising that providers resist an outsider's attempt to get them to differentiate between how they feel about their own children and about the children of others. "Do you feel differently about your own children and the other children in your care?" I asked naively. The question got a uniform nonanswer: "I treat them all the same."

In part, of course, in emphasizing treatment, the family day care provider attempts to reassure the questionner that she does not let an intense bond with her *own* children stand in the way of fairness. However, I do not think this is the entire explanation. The evasion is also a form of public denial that her *feelings* are different.[28] Having dismissed professional caregiving, she embraces mothering. Having done so, she can not easily speak about the manner in which she deviates from this ideal.

A real contradiction is present. Mothering is something a family day care provider can not and does not want to achieve. Motherhood confers the privilege to mold and to keep; other people's children can not be molded and kept.[29] To think otherwise creates a situation where one can only be hurt. Motherhood denies a financial calculus and limits; for a day-care provider to refuse reimbursement entirely or fail to establish limits to the care one will give creates a situation where one will be exploited.[30] The family day care provider can not answer a question about feeling easily because there is no simple stance to take toward a model that is both an ideal and a threat. We can hear this confusion when providers use a "but" to describe their feelings: "I love these children *but* they're not my own"; "I enjoy caring for children *but* it is a job for me."

If we hold open the possibility that intense affection can emerge from daily caregiving, and if we believe the providers when they say that they want to be "like a mother," then we have to recognize that they are in a difficult position. As noted, they expect that they will become close to these children and they see the development of love as appropriate. But the relationship between a family day care provider and a child in her care is framed by the ambiguous relationship between the provider and the child's parents. Control and intimacy are two key issues. A mother balances trust and distrust, weighing her own interest in shaping her child against the need to "let go." She also balances her need to remain primary in the child's affection against the child's need to be cared for with a loving nurturance when away from home. She places the provider in a contradictory position when she simultaneously asks the provider to make decisions and feel strongly about her child *at the same time* as she attempts to manage the provider's relationship with her child. The "nurturing, enduring, and noncontingent relations governed by feelings of morality," which are the hallmark of (ideal) family life, can only partially emerge in the context of the "impersonal, competitive, contractual and temporary" relations of the market.[31] Mediating between these two sets of norms, the provider experiences her caregiving as "interrupted": She can neither assume the authority necessary for shaping a child nor fully allow the development of attachment. Both emotional and economic realities intervene.

## LIMITED AUTHORITY

Competent and successful caring for children relies on certain skills. While providers may denigrate their abilities, they can also recognize that they have acquired knowledge about children in general as well as intimate knowledge about the individual children who come to them. Moreover, because the family day care provider is dealing with many children at once, discipline and the imposition of routines are not just matters of individual style, but practical necessities. All children have to nap at the same time, eat the same food, and follow the same rules.

The women find satisfaction in exercising their skills, but they are often thwarted in their attempts to do so. Feminist analysis has uncovered the many ways in which a mother's confidence is undermined by the authority of male experts.[32] Family day care providers, perhaps, experience even more "interruptions." First, as noted above, parents give explicit instructions pertaining to the care of their own children. These instructions can undermine a provider's confidence; they also remind the provider that her authority is limited.

Second, the State of Vermont defines appropriate care for children through regulations. For regulated providers the intrusions take the form of guidelines about safety, numbers, nutrition, and the contested area of discipline. Resistance to regulation is sometimes grounded in the fact that it touches on the provider's privilege to offer care in the way she thinks is best in the privacy of her own home. But even unregistered providers feel these restraints. If they have already been observed by a state licenser, they may have been required to cut back on the number of children; if they have not yet been observed, they may be attempting to conceal themselves. Among all providers, increased public attention to child abuse can be grounds for less demonstration of affection between providers and children:[33] "Now it's really child abuse this and child abuse that. I'm afraid to get too close. I can still hug them and stuff. But still, in the back of my mind I don't want anyone accusing me. . . . You think about it, what do you classify as child abuse or sexual abuse or verbal abuse?"

Finally, providers are aware of a "public" that judges their actions. As Ruth Bolton said, her good name in the community was an important asset. Other providers as well know that their clientele relies on word-of-mouth recommendations. And they are aware that they are being watched by others in the community: "You can not control what people will say about how [an] injury occurred. [You are] in a business where the public is keeping an eye on you"; "You don't yell out the back door to the children because someone might hear you."

These intrusions sap the provider's authority. Although she may say that she does with others what she did with her own children, probing suggests that this "common sense" response is modulated by the consciousness that the child is not her own. One of the reasons providers so resent having sick children brought to them is because of this limitation: They feel they are placed in a particular bind when care demands the moment-to-moment exercise of an authority that is not theirs. Similarly, when providers speak about the burden of responsibility, there is an edge of anxiety about whether they can afford to allow the child to take the kind of risks a mother might: "I worry more about somebody else's child." Providers also say they try to put off questions about sex and religion, recognizing these as "private" matters best handled in the family: "I suggest they talk to their mother about that."

The most concrete manifestation of this difference shows up with respect to the issue of punishment.[34] Most providers believe that it is wrong—and even cruel—to spank someone else's child, even though many of them find it an appropriate disciplinary technique for their own children. In their discussions of this issue they interweave several themes: They are aware that their own limited attachment undermines their prerogative, that striking a child is a decision to be made by parents alone, that they would not want anyone to treat their children that way. One woman who did spank a child who was not her own justified it by incorporating the child into her family: "I think I've taken the initiative more and spanked Christopher. I feel more comfortable spanking my own—but he's like one of the family."

Providers do differ in the range of authority they find acceptable for themselves, and the longer children have been with them the more they seem to feel they can exercise a kind of parental authority. Moreover, their own needs to have acceptable working conditions can prompt them to actions that might clash with parents' wishes. Marjorie Black, for example, told how she initiated toilet training with Timothy (a mentally handicapped child)—balancing the parents' wishes to delay the process with her own need to have a four-year-old out of diapers. But even though she had the confidence to resist the parents in *this* situation, she said that she would never strike a child in her care. Although it is clearly difficult to establish precise boundaries, all providers acknowledge some issues that they see as the sole responsibility of the parents.

## LOSS

The most painful difference between mothering one's own child and mothering another's is the inevitability of loss. The relationship between loss and love is of a certain kind in mothering. We all know the possibility is there: Children get sick, injured, kidnapped. But mothers can not withhold affection because of this possibility. In loving children, as in loving anyone, we do not get the pleasures, the satisfactions of intensity, without allowing ourselves to be vulnerable to the pain. So we act *as if* the children are ours permanently; we engage in the fiction of the immortality of our own children. As Sara Ruddick writes,[35]

> Holding, preserving mothers have distinctive ways of seeing and being in the world that are worth considering. For example, faced with the fragility of the lives it seeks to preserve, maternal thinking recognizes humility and resilient cheerfulness as virtues of its practice. . . . Humility is a metaphysical attitude one takes toward a world beyond one's control. . . . Cheerfulness is a matter-of-fact willingness to continue, to give birth and to accept having given birth, to welcome life despite its conditions.

But for family day care providers, loss is a certainty; it can not be so easily overcome by humility and cheerfulness. These relationships are contingent: A parent can withdraw a child at any moment the parent decides that a different situation is preferable. Even when the situation is working well these relationships are temporary. They are bounded daily by the return of the mother and bounded ultimately by the child's maturity. Thus the limits of protection are narrowed. The day-care provider can ensure a loving and safe environment for specified hours;

she can not ensure that the child is being adequately clothed, fed, and nurtured during the hours that the child is with his or her own parents. Children go home at the end of the day, and the parents may or may not properly attend to the cough or diarrhea. Children leave for good after a couple of years, and the parents may or may not complete the job of teaching them to share or to have good manners.

In some ways the most painful losses are those that are initiated by a parent out of dissatisfaction. These losses threaten the provider's self-confidence as well as her relationship to a child. Providers speak about these losses with a special anguish:

> The mother decided she would get someone closer. That really hurt my feelings. I felt that I was not a good sitter. I even asked my husband, "Why is she taking him away from me?"

> One day she called me up and said she wasn't going to bring him back because she didn't think he was happy here. And that really bothered me and I asked, "Why don't you think he's happy here? What do you want me to do?" And she said, "It's nothing to do with you. I just don't think he is happy here. He doesn't want to go." . . . I was upset because I thought I did something wrong. I thought I had let his crying bother me too much . . . I started to wonder whether I should be taking care of other people's kids.

And even if the provider herself suggests a change for the child, the mother's hasty agreement can intensify her pain:[36]

> I lost two [children] about six months ago. The little girl was having trouble at home and we just couldn't pinpoint what it was at home. . . . And all of a sudden here one day she threw up . . . and she didn't make it to the bathroom. . . . "I'm coming," I said but I thought to myself, I'm not going to make it to her. . . . I had her since she was an infant . . . and I've gone over it time and time again. . . . And after that day she was really afraid to come. I kept her for six weeks and finally said to the mother, "She is so frightened and I hate to be the one to tell you this, why don't you try another baby-sitter." I was crushed. I miss them something wicked. . . . It was like I had let her down, because we were very close and she always enjoyed coming. It's not being able to figure it out is what troubled me.

But the more expected losses are anguish as well, and tears come to a provider's eyes when describing how loss interrupts relationships of love: "I lost one to kindergarten and some going closer to home. It's very hard. You feel like you're losing a part of you." When these losses are anticipated, a provider can do some of the work of grieving in advance. This might help them deal with the actual moment of parting; it can not alleviate the pain altogether.

The link between loss and affection is demonstrated in the frequency with which providers, when asked about their feelings about children, spontaneously speak about losing them: "I love these children. I feel terrible when I lose one." This constant awareness of loss makes becoming too attached to the children a risky proposition.

### FINANCIAL CONSTRAINTS

There is another reality as well. Family day care providers do this work, in part, because they need the money. If they become too attached to the children in their care, that is, if they identify too strongly with the model of mothering, they can neither ask for money at the end of the week nor impose restrictions on the hours of care they provide.

## *Detached Attachment*

In *The Managed Heart: The Commercialization of Human Feeling,* Arlie Russell Hochschild talks about the "feeling rules"—cultural expectations about what we should feel that we use to judge appropriate emotions in our relationships in both the public and private world.[37] In both realms Hochschild assumes that the feeling rule is clear: established by cultural norms in our social roles as mother, bride, or lover; established by company manuals in service work. But one problem for family day care providers is that there is no preordained feeling rule. They are supposed to be like mothers; they also have to be able to distinguish between what they feel and what real mothers feel so that they can handle the (externally imposed) limits to their authority, encompass loss, and impose their own boundaries around caregiving.

A second difference from Hochschild's analysis is also relevant. As we have seen, the context in which family day care providers work, and their ongoing involvement in the care of very young children, engender emotions that are structurally inappropriate. Family day care providers must fashion a feeling rule that enables them to draw a set of distinctions between the activity of caring for their own and the activity of caring for (kin and) nonkin as paid labor. They must also engage in the "emotional labor" of sustaining this distinction in how they feel. But because they are subject to the creation of strong, positive feelings, this emotional labor involves dismantling, or reducing the intensity of, these same feelings. They thus differ radically from an airline stewardess whose emotional labor entails the manufacture and pretense of warm sentiments in a context where neither feelings nor display come easily.

The final difference is that family day care providers do not work with an emotion superviser at hand: The task of emotional labor is self-directed. This freedom also entails a burden. They have to decide alone when they are being successful in their emotional labor—when they are feeling too much and when they are feeling too little. Being isolated, they lack access to the insights of others about how to handle their emotional dilemmas, or a work culture that might help relieve them of the intensity or set guidelines. For all of these reasons, I suggest that the human costs of family day care may well be different from the costs Hochschild identified.

The resolution to the dilemma of a commitment to mothering and the threat mothering poses is found in the creation of a feeling rule, a stance toward the children that I tentatively call "detached attachment." Although the providers do not explicitly acknowledge that what they offer is different from mothering, it clearly is. The feeling rule describes this difference that has to exist. As suggested already, it is characterized by a less claiming, less self-confident, and less intense affection for the children; it is marked also by the absence of identification with these children. (See Chapter 4.) It is not, however, the emotional detachment professional caregivers strive to achieve. Attachment persists. But the particular attachment they develop relies on the ongoing work of creating a space, a "distance" that saves them from an overwhelming emotional engagement: "I reserve something knowing that they're not mine"; "I hold back a little"; "I don't want to get too attached."

The capacity to create *and* sustain this detachment is one of the unrecognized skills acquired in the course of learning how to be a day-care provider. The more experienced providers said that they both were more willing to get involved emotionally *and* that they knew how to withdraw, how to find the right line. In many cases this capacity is acquired through the experience of not having sufficiently created distance in the past. A provider who talked about one child to whom she became "too" attached said she would not let it happen again: "I won't take one on from six months and watch it grow up like that again if I've got any feeling that they're going to be taken away from me. . . . I felt that I was doing a good job and I enjoyed [the child] just as much as [the parents] did, watching it grow up and being a part of its life. Maybe I did get too attached. I don't know."

Of course, there is some relief in the limits that providers create. As one woman said, "I have the pleasures of caring for them without the full responsibility." But this relief is contingent on a perception that the children are receiving competent care from their own parents. No such relief is possible when parents are seen as inadequate. And even when a child has parents assumed to be warm, loving, and capable, the provider's emotions are not easily turned off at the end of the day. In order to feel good about what she is doing, the day-care provider has to believe that she is offering something meaningful to the children. Because she denies that she has unique skills and abilities, and because she denigrates her own expertise, she can only achieve a sense of significance by establishing a bond.

The attempt to find the proper stance and the dilemmas entailed in doing so are illustrated by one provider's comments about having recently agreed to care for an infant:

> I don't think I want that emotional attachment—again. And the worrying and thinking about the baby like it's your own and then suddenly realizing when the baby's gone from your door you have no say in what happens to it. That's kind of hard to deal with because I invest a lot of emotional time with the kids to try to keep them happy and secure and everything. And then you wonder. They leave. . . . I think with the baby I'm trying to not get attached because I don't want to have to think about it or worry about it . . . but I know it's not going to work. . . . And I know after a matter of time it will be the same thing all over again. I'll be attached and thinking why's that mother doing that. And then thinking, you have nothing to say about it. It's not your kid. But in a way when you have them for so many hours it's hard to find that balance.

We can hear that providers have been successful in the emotional labor of creating and sustaining a distance when they talk about how they feel about their own children in contrast to the others for whom they care. Although they resist making these distinctions, when pushed they admit that caring for others involves a lowered affect and identification.

One of the first surprises of motherhood is the overwhelming love one feels for a new infant. To her dismay, a mother may soon come to realize that not only does she love this new being, but her very identity is wrapped up in it: The child becomes a reflection of the mother. If the child is praised, the mother feels gratified; if the child does not conform to social expectations, the mother believes she has failed. Day-care providers work to resist this identification with children who are not their own. Some say that they do feel that the children's behavior reflects on them. But most manage to keep themselves somewhat removed from this way of thinking. As a result, some situations are eased. Providers often speak about how well the other children behave for them.[38] Many find in the excellent behavior of the nonresident children evidence that they are "better" than the real mother; they delight in reporting how the child who was an angel all day threw a tantrum as soon as her mother walked in the door. They say that they can not understand these differences: "The kids are different when their parents come around. Eric has learned the best set of double standards I've ever seen. He does one thing here and is completely different at home. . . . He is a terror at home. I can't stand the kid when he's at home and with his parents. He's completely different . . . I don't know [why that is]." But some are aware of what must be the truth: that the children are expressing anger at having been left and that the children behave well for the providers because they are not engaged in the same kind of emotional relationship.[39]

The absent mother is critical to the development of this attitude. The mother is a prop the family day care provider can draw on to remind the *child* that his or her loyalties must rest elsewhere; in the process the provider deflects the child's attachment. Family day care providers feel strongly that to do otherwise would be wrong for the child, that the child has to be encouraged to "bond" with the mother. If the family day care provider fails to do this, she may find herself encouraging expectations she is unable to fill:

> I know Jodie really likes me. I know she does. I can tell. And I like Jodie. She's a nice little girl. But her mother has to be there for her. . . . I can't give what Jodie needs. I can give her the attention. I can care for her. I can make her feel good about herself. But I'm not her mother. You want to give the child what he [sic] needs without giving so much that you are interfering with the way he or she feels about his own parents.

Some providers talk very explicitly about how they "remind" the children that they are not their mothers, that the child's loyalty should remain elsewhere. One woman, who often took care of a child overnight, said that while the mother was away she would talk about "mommy" to the child and repeat constantly that "mommy is coming back."[40]

While the provider sees herself as protecting children (and parents), she is also clearly protecting herself. The provider needs this image of the mother as much, if not more than, the child, as a reminder of her own limited role. In the intervals of the mother's absence, her image is drawn on to deflect the *provider's* attachment. The failure to keep this image alive can have devastating emotional consequences, as one woman suggests:[41]

> With my nieces I'd have to stop and say to myself, "you're not their mother." For an example, the older one . . . had long hair and she wanted her hair cut. She wanted me to cut her hair. And I said, "Are you sure you want your hair cut?" And she said, "Oh, I'm sure I want it cut." And I said, "All right, after your bath tonight I'll cut your hair." And I did it and I never thought about it. And I put the kid to bed and I was upset all night. I said, I don't believe I cut her hair without asking her mother. . . . All night I just tossed and turned . . . I just agonized all night long about how I could do that *without even thinking of the mother.* Those girls were becoming more and more my own.

The manner in which providers talk about the emotional labor involved in bringing feelings in line with the feeling rule of detached attachment makes it clear that the process is a difficult and continuous one:

> *Question:* Can you talk about your feelings toward the children?
> *Answer:* I get very attached and yet I try to keep myself somewhat removed. The first year was hard because I got frustrated because I cared for them so much. I wished I could go home and tuck them in. You know, you see a little guy come in at 7:00 in the morning and you know he's not going to bed until 10:00, it just breaks your heart. Or to wake him [at the end of nap time] when he's the first one to go to sleep. That's the caring I feel for them. I do. I like to hold them if they cry. They need that. They don't get that if mom is working. . . .
> *Question:* You said you hold yourself back a little from loving the children, can you talk more about that?

*Answer:* I'm afraid to get too emotionally involved with them because it hurts if I see things happening in their private lives. I try not to look at them as my own kids because if I do. . . . It's hard to explain. I want to love them and treat them with lots of care. But I want to hold back a bit and not mother them too much because if I do the mothers resent that to some degree.

*Question:* So how do you hold back?

*Answer:* It is hard to describe. Maybe I don't hold them as much as when I had my own kids because there are six of them. I guess I don't hold back as much as I think I hold back. To me what happens here is just like when my three were at home. . . . But I can't put them in the car and take them into the grocery. It's as much a family setting as I can give but it's still not a family setting. . . . They have responsibilities just like my own girls do. And I'm doing with the kids what I did with mine. So maybe I'm not holding back as much as I think.

In each situation, with each child, the provider has to find the proper balance between attachment and distance. The distance is threatened constantly by the daily interaction with the children and the development of affection over time. It is threatened as well on occasions when parents abdicate responsibility. The distinction has to be recreated daily if the provider is not going to be consumed by concern or overstep her boundaries, and so that she can be prepared to lose the children.

The line between day care and mothering also has to be sustained so that the provider can impose her own limits on the care she will provide and request the financial reimbursement that is her due. Like other paid caregivers, providers do make calculations. They define work and nonwork hours; they can roughly assess cost and reward. When they do so, more often than not, they feel exploited. And, as I suggest below, when they do not feel that they are getting adequate rewards they may cease caring for certain children. But detached attachment is not the simple outcome of caregiving within the context of an exchange relationship. Certainly providers initially see a new child as an addition to their weekly income; certainly they refuse to care for difficult and disruptive children who make a mockery of their payment. But equally importantly, providers strive to achieve this stance of detached attachment *in order* to charge money. They have to limit their affection if they are to continue to be paid, to accommodate to payment as a condition (a fact) of the relationship between themselves and the children in their daily care. The issues covered in the preceding chapters—that these women begin this work out of a complex set of motivations, that caregiving of this sort is so diffuse that it defies calculation, that caregiving exists within a normative prohibition against this kind of calculation, and that the cultural taboo is extremely strong for women—all of these intensify the difficulties of mediating between an exchange and a social relationship vis-à-vis the children.

## Choice

While the context of family day care is similar to that of mothering, family day care providers, unlike mothers, can freely choose whether or not to care for a particular child. This is the flip side of the limitations imposed on them (of authority and impermanence) by a contractual relationship, the manner in which they can work the contract to their benefit. Since the notion of choice is so fundamentally opposed to the ideal of the good mother, the manner in which family day care providers handle this possibility lends further insight into the central issues discussed here.[42]

The provider's fragile emotional stance is threatened, from opposite directions, in two kinds of situations. First, their efforts to keep a distance are threatened when they are asked to care for a child who is neglected or abused by his or her own parents. The ambivalent relief of not feeling the full responsibility for the child's safety and development, of not having to care, is dependent on having someone else there to offer emotional and physical security. If that security is lacking, the provider's attempt to insert the mother into the gap is impossible. This situation shifts the burden of responsibility onto the day-care provider without giving her sufficient resources to accomplish it; the tension between feeling something should be done, and not wanting to make the emotional investment of doing it, can make these situations extremely painful.[43]

Just as providers differ in what they find as the appropriate degree of "detachment," so do they differ in how they respond to these situations. Many providers adamantly refuse to become involved in this kind of caregiving.[44] Sometimes they justify their decisions on the basis of the child's best interest. A child who needs more care than the provider can offer (given the demands of many children), is thrust out on the *same* grounds that the provider justifies the care she is offering. If she says she is offering greater one-on-one care than a center, she also delimits this by noting that she can not provide the one-on-one care that some abused and neglected children need. Sometimes this care involves physical maintenance that is missing at home and for which the provider does not have the time:

> One time I did have a state child . . . and it just pulled at my heart. . . . When the little girl came she just reeked and I bathed her. You know, I had fixed her up so cute. But I can't do that every day. I just don't have the time. And the next day she said to me, "Would you bathe me again?" I just cried over her but . . . I thought, I really can't do this. It's too hard alone.

They also justify their decisions by saying that it is not good for a child to be with others who have so much more and by noting that the time and effort that they have to put into one child can jeopardize the care they give to others. But they also reveal that the pain is too great, that these children call for an emotional investment they can not make. And although there is guilt involved in making these choices ("I could have done him some good"), fundamentally they feel they have no option but to rescue themselves from a situation that is too costly in emotional terms.

Alternatively, providers fantasize sometimes about adopting abused and neglected children; these fantasies provide them with the motivation to sustain a difficult relationship until it proves too troublesome:[45]

> I had a child I took care of for a couple of years. . . . At one point during the time I had the child I had tried to get the state to step in and really do something. It was a state-paid child in the first place so I knew that they were aware of the situation. But there was one point when she came in about ten in the morning and she had a mark on her bottom . . . and she went down for her nap and she woke up and she still had the mark and that really just blew my mind. Instant tears and the whole thing. She would stay for two or three days at a time sometimes because her mother was working and her schedule was nighttime and it was really crazy. So we had become very attached to the little girl at that point. I had to remove myself from the situation because I couldn't deal with it any more. . . . I was pregnant with Julie and I had asked the state to step in and they wouldn't. . . . I had tried to [adopt] her and I was told there was no way I

> could. . . . I felt if nobody is willing to do anything then neither am I because I can't endanger my family and my baby. . . . I was scared of being too attached to the child. We were really—I mean there would be days when . . . she would say, "Please, I don't want to go home" and she would start to cry and my kids would start to cry because they didn't want her to go home. It was causing too much problems.

One provider I interviewed after she had stopped doing this kind of work noted that it was such situations that precipitated her departure from child care. When asked why she stopped, she said, "Because it ceased to be neat." She then described two particular situations that had all the components providers want most to avoid:

> I had two boys whose mother was real nervous, a screamer. He was three and had been thrown out of seven centers. The mother said she had problems keeping him anywhere . . . and the mother sent bad food. She was strange. They were at my house nine hours and she would pick them up and throw them in the car. I also had two little girls whose mother was manic-depressive. The kids would be hungry and tired. They would cry and cry [and] the mother had no control over them in even making them put on a coat. When I had all four it was more than I could take emotionally. Basically I was so drained that by night I would be in tears. Because there's nothing you can do. They're not your kids and there's nothing you can do. You can't change their life-styles. I was worried about the boys being abused and the girls being neglected.

If abused and neglected children threaten "detachment," other kinds of situations threaten "attachment." Because family day care providers define their worth through emotional relationships, and because they draw on the satisfactions of these relationships as *part* of their compensation, they have to make the choice of not caring for children they can not learn to love. Dismissing "unlovable" children is also justified by the claim that this kind of situation is bad for the child. However, it is clear here as well that providers are protecting themselves:

> I had a little girl once. She was about three years old. And she was a totally obnoxious little kid. She was really smart

> but she was . . . I don't know what it was but we definitely had a problem. And I kept her about three days and then I told her mother that I had too many, that I couldn't handle another. She was just a little girl that I didn't feel comfortable with. . . . I wouldn't take care of a child I didn't like. It wouldn't be fair to the child or to me.

> I did sit for a child I didn't like. I had a boy who had a strange personality. We would have clashed if I kept him but the mother stopped working. He wasn't lovable and I couldn't hold him and hug him. The mother's older kids had problems—probably she was making the same mistake again. I might have told the mother it wasn't working out. I don't think there's anything wrong with people having personality clashes. The thing is with a kid you don't want to hurt their feelings. I wouldn't want my kid in a home where he wasn't at least liked, let alone loved, and I wouldn't want someone to give their kids a piece of candy and not mine.

Finally, difficult children (to the extent they can be distinguished from the abused and unlovable) enter the equation even more clearly. Neither attachment nor detachment is threatened as much as value, a calculation of effort versus rewards. The "social" perspective thus gives way entirely in some situations. Some providers say openly that they will not care for a child who makes a mockery of the exchange relationship:

> I did have to let two children go. One was a behavior problem—he dumped a gallon of milk on the carpet. He was younger but was too much with the other child. I just told the mother that I would repair the damages but that the child could not come any more. . . . The child was just so busy that it was too much work and too dangerous. It was not hard to get rid of him after he dumped the milk.

Providers also "get rid of" children when they have difficult relationships with parents or when parents refuse to pay the going rate. But, severing relationships because of a mother's failure to pay can also result in long-term guilt:

> I had two girls where the mother refused to give extra when I raised my fees. The mother said that her kids did not eat

that much food and didn't acknowledge that my time was worth something also. The kids ended up at the house of someone who screamed and yelled and made the baby a wreck. The mother ended up risking her two kids for 25 cents. That really upset me because the kids had been real sweet.

## Conclusion

The context in which family day care providers work aligns them with mothering. "Real" mothers find their work to be isolating, overwhelming, coerced and devalued; they also find enormous satisfactions and rewards in the activity of caring for their own children. Family day care providers experience both sides of the coin. But the model of mothering is particularly threatening to them: The ideal of deep emotional involvement and selfless giving draws them into too great an intensity and a denial of their own needs as workers. However, they can not withdraw completely: Too great a distance from children deprives them of emotional satisfaction. They attempt to resolve their dilemma through a stance of detached attachment. This fragile resolution is threatened daily.

Hochschild's discussion of the human costs of jobs requiring emotional labor focuses on the worker's estrangement from her own feelings. Providing family day care poses a different kind of threat. Mere display or pretense ("seeming to love the job") is a less central concern. And alienation from the self is less likely to be an issue because the women become genuinely attached to the children and can acknowledge openly the feelings generated in their daily activities. Rather, the challenge for these workers is to find a way to dampen acknowledged affections, to make their feelings appropriate to the structural conditions of their work. Thus while Hochschild sees burnout in service work having roots in a worker's too-wholehearted identification with the job, burnout among family day care providers may well have a different source.

# Chapter 4

# PROVIDERS AND THEIR FAMILIES

In the previous chapters I examined dilemmas providers face in their relationships with "outsiders." Here we turn to issues that emerge in relationships between providers and members of their own families, as they transform the home into the site of paid work. In each set of relationships—with husbands, children, and members of the extended family—providers have to negotiate with the expectation that they are there to fulfill a traditional unpaid domestic role.[1] They also have to protect their paid work against this same expectation.

Providers and their husbands often see family day care as an activity that can augment the household income without denying the family the benefits of a full-time wife and mother. Underlying this view is an assumption that paid and unpaid work can be merged relatively easily. As any reader of the contemporary literature on industrial home-work or telecommuting knows, however, these home-workers struggle to negotiate the simultaneous demands of employers and family members. Home-workers often find they can not meet production quotas unless they purchase supplemental care for their children and enlist the labor of family members; they work long hours for low pay and limited benefits.[2]

The literature on (nonwage) home-based work is less clear-cut about effects. As noted in the Introduction, analysts who focus on the dynamics of industrial home-work have often argued that because nonwage activities "at or from" the home emerge from a different relationship with the formal economy, they allow workers greater autonomy.[3] Alternatively, many analysts who easily combine the two types of paid work in the home argue that all of these activities can have advantages for women who want to remain at home.[4] Feminist historians argue differently about the effects of home-based work, even when they separate out cash-producing activities from unpaid domestic labor. They make two related points. The first is that these activities are not recognized as "real work," either by other family members or by the women themselves. The second is that these activities are entirely compatible with a traditional sexual division of labor.[5]

Karen Brodkin Sacks, for example, describes the involvement of women in a broad range of money-making activities such as "taking in piecework or boarders . . . , doing sewing, laundry or baking . . . , [or] running a small store or pushcart." And she argues that such informal activities have "played a key role in building working-class communities [that] heightened intracommunity dependence on the one hand and . . . gave it a margin of independence from outside (and likely hostile) interests on the other." She also notes that these "family and community links . . . provided a significant basis of support for sustained workplace resistance."[6] But she does not explore the possibility that these activities might *also* have provided women with the basis for challenging the very role with which they appear so congenial. Thus with Alice Kessler-Harris, she concludes,[7]

> Most jobs in the informal economy . . . were not only consistent with women's conventional roles at home, they reinforced them. Far from altering the balance of family relations, they perpetuated the notion that women could extend family income by being good wives and loyal family members. Moreover, they tied women into networks of kin and neighborhood activities that in turn tied the family into the social and economic life of the community, reinforcing the family's position within it and providing a larger context for women's hard work.

There is some truth to all of these perspectives, but at least as they may apply to the specific case of family day care, there remains a core of misperception as well. If family day care providers are not themselves wage employees, they are often locked into inflexible work patterns shaped by the needs of clients who are wage workers. If the work of family day care has some advantages over work outside the home, it has disadvantages as well. And, as we will see, if family day care is sometimes compatible with domestic responsibilities, it can also conflict with and disrupt these tasks. Providers and members of their families do not always initially think of family day care as a real job. But they often come to acknowledge that it makes a genuine contribution to family survival and imposes significant and legitimate demands on the provider's time and energy. Thus although the provision of family day care may reinforce traditional roles, it may also grant women the basis for resisting and challenging them; like other working women, family day care providers find in their employment both material and ideological grounds on which to make their own claims.

The first section of this chapter explores how the work of family day care is understood by both the provider and her husband and examines the broad contradictory tensions that result from transforming the home into the site of paid work. It then turns to the particular issues that emerge in relationships with spouses, children, and members of the provider's community.

## *Traditional Definition of Family Day Care: Care as Not Work*

Family day care providers enter the occupation from two different starting points. Some, like Rena Milks and Patsy Lincoln, add the responsibilities of family day care to their ongoing domestic activities; others, like Shelley Tompkins and Gerry Porter, substitute family day care for a prior involvement in paid employment outside the home. In both cases the work is necessary because the husband's wages fail to meet adequately the family's economic needs. And in both cases, because family day care is contrasted with the alternative of a wife's working outside the home, it is assumed she can fulfill obligations as defined by a traditional sexual division of labor.

### TRANSITION TO FAMILY DAY CARE

*Families in which the wife has not been employed outside the home.* In some families the provider and her husband reach an agreement early on in their married life that she will remain home, at the very least until the children are grown. This pattern may be chosen so that he can view himself as the breadwinner who supports his family solely through his own efforts: "He's all in favor of this. He's real traditional anyway. I think he likes it this way. He has a real strong sense of pride in providing for his family on his own and I guess maybe even though I'm bringing home money it's not like I'm a career woman out there. I don't think that would work with us." He may prefer, as well, that his family conform to the model with which he was familiar as a child; the fact that this model gives him knowledge of, and control over, his wife's movement is an added incentive: "I think all guys would like you to be home to know where you are. . . . That's the way his whole family is, that all the wives have always stayed home. His mother too. I guess that's why he's grown up with that view." A "traditional" family structure may also be justified in terms of a husband's particular routines. Many men are accustomed to coming home for a noon meal; a wife's work outside the home can disrupt these patterns. Patsy Lincoln said, "I would not like to work full-time [outside of the home]. I like being at home. My husband likes it. He wants me home for lunch. He would resist if I tried to work outside. His mother worked and he wants me around." Many men place children at the center of the decisions about family structure. One husband said, "We both felt strongly that we didn't want to [send the children to a sitter]. We think the mother should stay home so that she's there when they get home from school, and to see them off to school in the morning. That she's there."

As we have seen, the women have their own reasons for wanting to stay at home. Most share with their husbands the goal of maternal vigilance; some share as well the vision of a housewife as someone who does not work: "I'm a housewife and that's something that I wanted to do other than work. . . . I told him that I wasn't going to have anybody else baby-sit my kids on a permanent basis because they were my kids and I wanted them to learn from me what they should do and what they should not do." Some women find pleasures in the routines of domesticity. And many feel they have enough to do within the home and could not handle outside employment.

When women are viewed—by themselves and by their spouses—as already having a full (and demanding) set of domestic responsibilities, the involvement in family day care may be assumed to be the woman's choice of a way to use her free time. Family day care is thus defined as an activity grafted onto or emerging from a set of traditional responsibilities, rather than "as a clear cut alternative or a genuine extension of her working day."[8] The fact that women who were not previously employed outside the home often begin the occupation casually, as an occasional favor to friends or family members, or as a means to find playmates for a child, may also underlie the assumption that it is not true work. (Several women in this situation resisted my request for an interview on the grounds that they were *not* working and therefore had nothing to say about the occupation; one woman completely refused on these grounds.)

*Families in which the wife has been employed outside the home.* A second pattern is found among those women who have worked outside the home for some time after marriage or the birth of their children. In these cases, the decision to engage in family day care is often a more calculated one: The occupation is chosen as a *substitute* for paid employment outside the home. If these women begin less casually, however, they (and their husbands) believe they can thereby resolve the tensions incumbent on households in which both parents are employed. One man said,

> It was for everybody [that we made this change]. The tension now is nothing compared to the tension when we had to rush around and get ready to go to work. . . . The mornings were terrible. We were always rushed. We never got up on time. . . . Jessica would cry, Marilyn would be pissed off, and I would be pissed off and it's quarter to eight in the morning and that's no way to start your day every day. . . . It wasn't so much that Jessica was going to day care as it was everything that was involved with that. . . . What really started striking home to me was we'd go to the sitter—I shouldn't say sitter—the person doing day care and she would say, "Oh, could you be quiet, my child is still sleeping." It's like, I really don't want to hear that right now. . . . It certainly has improved.

Sometimes a husband may resist the idea, as Gerry Porter's did, on financial grounds; if the family is dependent on two incomes, he may be concerned about whether day care will bring in enough money: "I felt a little threatened financially at first." A traditional understanding that the expenses of child care come out of *her* wages, however, smooths the way to the realization that the overall household income might be increased if *she* stays home. (Although it is not always made explicit, it becomes clear that both providers and their spouses believe it is her work situation that causes the trouble.) For example, a woman who actually earned *more* than her husband when she worked outside the home spoke about the decision to do family day care in the following way:

> When we stopped and figured it out that I was going out to work and earning two hundred dollars a week and paying a hundred out in child care, fifty more out in taxes, and then you figure carfare, pantyhose, expensive clothes and not so expensive clothes, and a Coke a day, and then gas and the fact that we also put ourselves into the next tax bracket when I was going out to work, and it meant that we were paying Uncle Sam for me to go out to work.

Often the deciding factor, as with families that have always remained "traditional," is concern about the children. A husband said about the time when his wife was working outside the home, "I was torn because we were in financial straits. We really needed the money. But at the same time I didn't like the idea of my kids being at somebody else's house. So we came up with the idea of doing day care." Not surprisingly, husbands and wives in these situations might expect that additional gains will be forthcoming; in particular he might now assume that he is the "possessor" of a nonworking wife.[9]

Family day care may be defined then, not only as an activity compatible with the full-time job of being a housewife, but, among those who substitute family day care for wage work, as a welcome return to domesticity. Because family day care is keyed to the needs of young children, it is often viewed as a stage of life—until the youngest child goes to school, until the children have left the house. Among families in which the dominant ideal is that of a man supporting his wife, family day care may also be considered a temporary strategy to meet short-term financial needs—until the mortgage is paid off, until he finds a better job. The activity is thereby distinguished from a "real job" and her career concerns are shrugged aside:

> He's glad I stay home and raise the kids. I've been talking to him about after this baby's in kindergarten. I said, "What am I going to do for a job. All I ever did was be a secretary for a doctor or a secretary at [a local factory] and I hate sitting at a desk. It's just sitting inside all day. Boy I hate it. I hate it. What am I going to do. . . . Even now if I tried to go back—with all these kids coming out of school with all this computer knowledge and I have none—I'm going to have a hard time getting a job." And he said, "Well, we don't know how much we're going to be earning then. Maybe I'll make enough so you don't have to work."

Certain features of family day care further reinforce the perception that it is not real work. After all, the wife is, in fact, at home and involved in activities consistent with a traditional division of labor: caring for children, cooking, cleaning. With the decisions about how long to work negotiated personally with clients (within the norms of a social exchange), the constraints seem voluntary. The prevailing description of the activity as "baby-sitting" further undermines legitimacy. When women fail to report the incomes they earn, they do not even have official recognition they have worked. Husbands and wives alike can consequently easily "forget" that she is actually holding down a job.

## *Imposition of Family Day Care on the Household and Its Strains*

Paradoxically, family day care inevitably transforms the household and disrupts the traditional division of labor with which it is thought to be so congenial.

### TRANSFORMATION OF PRIVATE SPACE INTO PUBLIC SPACE

Family day care tends to take over the whole house. While other kinds of home-based work (including much home-work), might be confined to a single area, child care can not easily be contained. Some of the women say they would prefer an arrangement whereby they could keep day care separate from family life. Most do not have homes large enough to accomplish this goal, and many feel that to do so would defeat the ideal of homelike care.[10] Even if certain sections of the home are "off-limits" to day-care children, for the most part, and for much of the time, the household becomes a public space into which parents enter (often without knocking, as they would a store or a public building) and in which day-care children roam freely.[11]

Family day care providers are ambivalent about this transformation. Most providers accept it as necessary. For those women who have never experienced privacy—because they grew up in large, extended families—family day care feels like a comfortable continuation of an open household rather than a loss of domestic space. Some even welcome these intrusions as one of the casual benefits of work that is otherwise exercised in isolation.

Most women, however, also commented that this penetration of the public into the private domain left no aspect of their own lives free from scrutiny. They described getting up early in the morning and hurriedly cleaning to make their homes presentable for clients. And they felt guilty about imposing burdens on other family members—a husband who had to peek out of the door before making a dash to the bathroom, a child whose bedroom was rearranged daily for nap-time use.

Even when all "outsiders" have left and the mess is cleaned up, it is hard to transform the house back into private space. Each room shows the mark of children in the form of handprints on the wall of the corner used for "time out," or in the form of extra equipment:

> My room is invaded by a playpen, both my boys' bedrooms have playpens—they're just leaning against the wall on weekends. All their nice toys have to be put up high so nobody will break them.

> It's a lot of involvement. Not just with emotionally timing yourself for it but also with—you have to have the crib, you have to have the jumper chairs, you have to have the walkers—it's just a lot of hassle going into it. You have to learn to live around these things. It's not every family that wants to trip over a high chair for six years past the time when your own children got done using it. And right now we have two going.

Child care also takes a physical toll on the house. Although the images we receive from advertising suggest that only women are concerned with the details of domesticity, in reality men too have an investment in household appearances (if not in actual day-to-day household maintenance). In many families husbands put their own labor into the household both indirectly (by earning the money to purchase household furnishings) and directly (by building portions of the house, painting and wallpapering rooms, laying tiles or carpeting). These men are forthright in their expressions of resentment about the wear and tear accompanying home-based child care:

> It is a problem because the rooms where they spend 90 percent of their time are all brand new and we've talked about buying new furniture and I say no, not until she's done with the child care.

> I guess the difference is Betty's not materialistic and I am. . . . I want to have—she says a showpiece—and I say just a real nice home. . . . I just paid $1,100 for the couch and I don't want [the baby] drooling all [over it].

Both men and women find in the accumulation of material possessions a concrete reward for long hours put in at a job; in lives close to the margin, these possessions can not be replaced easily. As one provider said, "It's hard sometimes to see things that are broken or whatever but I think well, when they're gone, we'll repair them. It's just everything we have we have worked hard for." And it is paradoxical to have to wait until "they're gone" to have nice things when the added income from family day care places one in the financial position to achieve a more comfortable standard of living.

## DISRUPTED ROUTINES; OVERLAPPING TIME

Family day care overlaps with family routines in time as well as space. The women struggle to defend each sphere against the demands of the other.

Beginning the day is generally relatively easy. Because many working-class men leave for their jobs early, providers find they can handle their double burdens in the morning without much disruption. Of course, doing so comes at a cost: She may get up early to make sure the house is tidied and breakfast is on the table; she may stay up late the night before to pack lunches. Friction occurs more in the late afternoon and early evening. Providers feel strongly their domestic obligations at these times; they want to pay attention to their own children, to prepare dinner, or to give their husbands time in which to relax and unwind. They often feel very pulled.

Since the provider is working at home and has no bureaucratic protection against client demands, she has difficulty containing overlap. As noted in Chapter 2, parents assume that providers can cover for them if they are delayed at their jobs, and they frequently arrive late to pick up their children: "There's times when I really wish I had said five o'clock is the limit because I still have dinner to get for my family and sometimes it's really hard." Clients who are friends may unwittingly compound these pressures:

> At the end of the day—one of my moms used to do this too—it would be four o'clock and they'd come and get their kids and they'd want to stay and talk and tell you everything that happened and who they saw that weekend. And, you know, I want you to go home. I've got things [to do]. I want to cook supper. My kids need me now.

If day care impinges on family routines, the converse is also true. Providers resent it when their husbands interfere with their paid work: "Sometimes it's very hard if he's home. If he has to take a sick day he has nowhere to go. It's like you can't sleep in your bed, somebody has to take a nap there. It's hard for *me* too because this is my job and he's getting in the way. It is his home, but still it's hard." When her work becomes more visible, he may even try to control it in certain ways:

> The family's—how can I say it—they're lower income so the kids are kind of dirty at times and things like that. And James just—it bothers him having them around our kids all the time because he feels that he just doesn't want something to happen. For example, last weekend—[the mother] brought [the youngest child] in pants and I had to take them off and sew up both sides because they were torn. And I said, "I'm going to put Laura's pants on her," and he

> goes, "No, don't." And I said, "Why?" And he said, "Because if you do it this time, what's to say next time she's not going to send them in the same pants and you'll do it again." He doesn't really care for the kids that I have on weekends.

These daily struggles and tensions are exacerbated when, as is common, providers have a spouse who routinely stays home for all or part of the day. If a husband is accustomed to coming home for the noon meal, his wife has to prepare and serve his food as well as that of the day-care children. Some women report that their husbands find the presence of children at these times an annoyance: "He did [mind] at first . . . because when he came home for lunch he was so used to having it be just me that it was kind of infringing on his time to have other kids. I think he's resigning himself to the fact that for at least another year we'll have this going on." Thirty-seven percent of the questionnaire respondents said their husbands sometimes work at night. These women have the added burden of trying to keep children quiet so their husbands can sleep during the day. A man in this situation described how his schedule meshed poorly with that of his wife, "It bothers me because it's the end of Erica's day and it's the beginning of my day and those two times don't come together very well. . . . I have a hard time getting in synch with everybody else." Other work schedules also fit uneasily with family day care: When a man works four ten-hour days or is obligated to work through the weekend, children are present on his days off. One husband said, "With my job I never get my days off . . . except during the week . . . and a lot of times the kids are here. And like I said, this summer, if we go to the beach I don't want to bring two extra kids with us. . . . I don't want to share my time off. I have too much to do as it is."

The fact that this home-based work is caregiving intensifies some conflicts. Children can not simply be put aside until the needs of the home are met: "I can't feed my family when there is a kid here who hasn't had her dinner yet." In special circumstances providers feel they have to watch a child overnight or for an entire weekend:

> He doesn't mind except for the ones on the weekend. That bothers him because it is our time to be together and more or less spend time as a family. And like Sunday we used to go over to his mother's and then we'd go over and visit my mother. Now, with the kids [here], he either just goes up and visits [alone] or we have to wait until the kids leave.

## FAMILY MEMBERS AS UNPAID LABOR

The contact between family members and day-care children is not always so stressful. A man who does not enjoy having children around when he arrives home from work can easily make himself scarce: "Some days when he comes home they drive him completely nuts but he'll just go and do work somewhere else or something." If he is in a different mood, or if he genuinely likes children, he might stick around and play with them. One woman said, "He really likes the kids. If he gets home a little early and I want to start dinner then he will stay out with them and play." Her husband concurred: "I'll sit on the floor or on the couch and play with them . . . I'm attached to the ones that like me the best. . . . There's one little girl that is closer than the others."

But to a certain extent all providers—whether their husbands enjoy these interactions or not—have to monitor the behavior of their spouses. If the women grant their husbands the option of responding to the children or of avoiding them, they can not grant them the option of being unpleasant or mean. A family day care provider needs her husband's cooperation to make children feel safe, comfortable, and loved: "He's real good with the kids. They all run to him. And he'll spoil them rotten which I really like because *I don't want the kids to think he doesn't like them.*" (Emphasis added.)

She may need to impose affirmative responsibilities as well. Providers have lengthy and diffuse obligations to their clients. They work alone, without the structured breaks and time off of wage employees and without even the casual relief offered by coworkers. They have no space between home and work, and no time in which to take care of their own needs. They have to depend on family members from time to time:[12]

> When he's fixing fence he takes all of the kids with him. All of them. We say bring your boots tomorrow, we're fixing fence. And I can stay home and do whatever I want and he takes them all. And they just walk in the brook and he brings up juice and puts it in the brook for them. He shows them different places as nature walks and things like that.

In more egalitarian households providers claim this assistance as part of a fair exchange. One woman said, "I help him occasionally with things that he might come up with for work and if I have to go somewhere and it's nine o'clock and he doesn't have to be into work till ten o'clock, I don't think it's unreasonable of me to ask him to watch eight kids for an hour or so." Other providers simply say they have no choice but to make these demands.

This involvement has contradictory effects. On the one hand, the more the husbands become immersed in the daily activities of caregiving, the more they form independent attachments to the children. In the process they grow more accepting of the inevitable intrusions. One day-care provider described how her husband, who had originally told her she could do day care only if "he never saw the children," changed entirely: "Then all of a sudden—God, he's the one that brought the lady a watch—and he loves kids. He's just done a turnaround." One man said that when his wife talked about stopping he put pressure on her to continue, because "I just like having kids around." These pleasures clearly help alleviate the strains.[13]

On the other hand, relying on a husband can backfire in various ways. A man who feels that too much is being asked of him may demand that his wife give up day care altogether:

> I just don't enjoy it and I think if you're going to do something like this it should be under the ideal of conditions—if she could never leave them with me; if they weren't here when I come home from work. To me that sounds terrible but it's not that I don't want them around. . . . I just don't want the inconvenience of the situation. At first she was very upset [about my making her stop]. And I said, "Hey, it's going to get to the point where I'm going to refuse to take care of them. If you're so strong on this and you want to keep them I will never tell you that you have to give them up. That's your decision. But I will put limitations on what I'll do and I'm going to get to the point where I'm not going to allow myself to take care of them at all." . . . It's not that I really don't want her to do it. It's just that I don't want the inconvenience of having to take them to the beach or if she has to run upstreet I'm responsible for them. . . . I'm supposed to be painting my front fence. . . . It's an inconvenience.

A man may also define his involvement in ways that are compatible with, and thus reinforce, a traditional gendered division of labor. The husband who placed pressure on his wife to continue doing family day care because he enjoyed the children noted that his own involvement was always circumscribed:

> I wouldn't like it having [to care for] one that young . . . I don't like any part of changing them. I never did ours.

> That's funny because nowadays all modern husbands take care of the kids because the mother has to work and that's just the way the parents are. . . . It doesn't bother me as far as being here with them. I just don't like the real little ones. That's all because I wouldn't know what to do if something happened. I just don't feel at ease. But with any of the other ones I don't care.

Another husband placed similar restrictions on what he would do: "I don't change diapers because I can't stand to. I do my own kids because I am their father and that's what you do. Somebody else's kids—I'm sorry, this is not my job. . . . I have a weak stomach when it comes to diapers." These husbands reconfirm a division of labor in which women can be expected to engage in the dirty work of child care.

A man might also more broadly contrast his attitude toward children with that of his wife. If he says that he might take over or play with the children from time to time, he also says that he is not drawn to this activity as a woman is:

> I could never do day care. Like I said, my enjoyment with a bunch of kids would be to get a football or baseball or something like that and go out on the lawn and work them into a frenzy type of thing playing a game. But I'm just taking the dessert. I wouldn't want all the rest that goes with caring for a child all day long. . . . But *she* loves kids. She loves all kids, but especially little ones. She's the classic woman. If you brought a baby in she'd say let me hold the baby. I don't do that. I don't want to hold someone's baby.

He thus naturalizes her attitude and trivializes her endeavors.

Finally, it should be noted as well that providers place their husbands in extremely vulnerable positions. In a time of heightened awareness about the possibility of sexual abuse in all settings, including (and even especially) day care, a man's involvement in the care of young children may be regarded with suspicion.[14] The woman who said her husband took the children with him when he went to fix fences also said if *she* were looking for child care for her own children, she would seek a home in which there were no men around during the day. Two men spontaneously spoke about their concerns:

> One thing that has made me nervous with all this stuff that's going on about day care and I said to Erica, "I don't

> want to change any of these children, especially the little girls." Because I was afraid that something—I mean, I knew that I wasn't going to do anything. But what if something was said or something. . . . It's like this one instance I can think of. . . . The father is very protective of the child and will believe anything that she says. . . . That kind of made me afraid. We always had the feeling that he was looking for something to happen. . . . And I got nervous about that and I said, "I really would rather not change the diapers."

> I am horrified at the abuse kind of thing. . . . I've thought about it in the situation at home. It's like I kiss my daughter goodbye and she says, "Daddy kiss so and so goodbye." And no, I don't kiss so and so goodbye. I shake hands with her. I guess I'm paranoid about it because someone could walk in here right now, a boy or a girl, and point a finger at me and tell the policeman, "That's him," and my life from that day on is shot. And this happens to people. . . . I am so upset about this issue that I do keep my distance from the kids. Because there is a lot of press about it. . . . I'm not there enough really but yes, I am cautious. No I don't bend down and kiss each kid goodbye on my way to work or give them a pat on the rump. . . . I think guys are more susceptible of being accused of this.

By working at home, providers have placed themselves in a situation where the demands of each sphere not only overlap—both in space and time—but occasionally compete with the demands of the other. Family life can not be preserved intact against the intrusions of day care; nor can day care be insulated entirely from domestic concerns. And neither sphere offers a break from the other. Myra Marx Ferree argues that the involvement of working-class women in forms of paid work outside the home that might, to a middle-class observer, appear alienating and exploitative, can be explained by the fact that women find in such jobs relief from the demands of domesticity; conversely, working-class women find in their unpaid, domestic labor a similar alternative to wage work:[15]

> Just as the dominance and exploitation that occur within families are properly exposed by the contrasts that emerge when women participate in workplace relations, so the dominance and exploitation of paid jobs are properly critiqued by standards of relationship formed in families. . . .

> By trying to serve two masters, patriarchy and capitalism, women try to escape the total domination of either one.

Family day care providers face an entirely different situation. Neither sphere offers a direct contrast to the other: In both her paid and her unpaid work the family day care provider is involved in caregiving, bound (at least partially) to the norms of reciprocity, and subject to her husband's control. Like a woman employed outside the home, she is pulled in contradictory directions. Yet she is less able to give clear priority, even for short periods of time, to either sphere: "The thing that I have a hard time dealing with is this is my home but it's also my business. It's separating the two. I mean you can't."

The similarity of the tasks in her paid and unpaid work, and the sheer repetition of these tasks, dull the pleasures she finds in each: "Everything that used to be so much fun is now a chore. Our vacations consisted of going to my brother's and that's not a vacation. I mean it's wonderful to go down there and see everything and do everything. But you're still making the beds and getting dinner ready and watching the kids." She has no space and no time to call her own. The paid work confers no independent identity: "My son came home from school and said, 'Do you know mommy, the nurse in school is also a mother.' He was astounded that she could be two people." Not surprisingly, family day care providers believe that work outside the home is far easier: "When somebody says, 'Oh, how do you do it?' I say, 'It's a lot of hard work.' It's easy to go outside and work in the field. I worked there. I know. Boy, when I went to work at the hospital it was *wonderful*. I mean, I had my own desk, my own office. I had—I'm a social worker. When you're here, what do you say?" Those who have worked outside the home say of their current occupation, "It's probably the hardest job I've ever had."

## Renegotiating the Marriage Contract

As we have seen, although family day care is perceived as fitting easily into a gendered division of domestic labor, it also invariably disrupts the household and makes the fulfillment of domestic responsibilities difficult for the provider. If the family day care provider is not simply going to absorb this strain, she has to win, at a minimum, tolerance for the costs her work imposes on the family. A husband's acceptance of the demands of family day care is hinged on recognition that the demands are legitimate; it is also hinged on recognition of the material benefits derived from this work. The provider herself is (usually) committed to family day care for its intrinsic rewards (she is attached to the children; she finds pleasure in exercising a set of carefully honed skills) and for its "indirect" benefits (she enjoys access to an independent income; she needs the money she earns). She is often fighting for her own "survival."

## STRUGGLING FOR RECOGNITION

If the visibility of day care is a source of strain for providers, it can also be a potent weapon in her struggle to demonstrate that she is working—and working hard. Husbands who see their wives "on duty" from early in the morning until late in the afternoon develop an awareness of the job's persistent demands: "I'm sure he does [recognize that I have a job]. Especially the other day he stayed home—he took a personal day—and he realized I was busy." If casual observation doesn't drive the message home, a provider might actually leave the children with her husband for a brief period of time—not just because she needs his assistance, but to impress upon him how hard her work is and how much skill it requires.

The recognition that family day care is a job with legitimate demands is also clearly tied to the *material* benefits that derive from the work.[16] Almost all women *and* their husbands appreciate the money family day care brings in. They grow accustomed to the higher standard of living made possible by her earning power; they may also make investments that transform these earnings into an ongoing necessity.

On average, the women in this study contribute 37 percent of the total family income from their day-care earning.[17] The relative size of a woman's earnings is important. Among questionnaire respondents, agreement with the statement, "The people around me recognize that I have a real job," ranged from 34 percent among those earning less than a quarter of total family income to 67 percent among those earning more than two-fifths of total family income. The interviews confirm this statistical pattern. In those families where the wife's contribution is deemed essential, husbands openly acknowledge that their wives have no choice but to work at this time. They give verbal support to her endeavors: "I feel good about what she's doing. . . . It seems to be positive if you take the whole picture." They may also defend the work against the suggestion that it is trivial or unimportant. One husband said, "I get really mad when people say, 'Oh your wife baby-sits.' I say, 'No, she's not a baby-sitter, she works in day care.' . . . It's not like the kids are running around and she's sitting down watching a soap opera or chatting on the phone. She's there a hundred percent. I don't think people really realize."

In families where the wife makes a less significant contribution, husbands talk differently. They suggest that the family could survive without the money from family day care: "It lets her do a lot of things for the kids that maybe they normally would have to go without unless we counted pennies a lot more in other places." They may also be less willing to define what their wives are doing as real work.

And in families where the earnings from child care make little or no difference in the overall standard of living, a husband may be entirely dismissive:

> It makes no difference. She uses most of it for what she wants. A lot of time she sticks it into the budget. It seems like the more money you have the more you spend. . . . You just spend it. We don't have everything we want but we're not hurting. We're not needing. We're not deprived. [Her income] is definitely not needed. It's not something we need to survive or anything.

A family day care provider in this circumstance may even be admonished to cut back or to stop entirely. Even if she is allowed to continue, she may be well aware that she works at his sufferance. Rena Milks said,

> He's glad for the extra money to do, you know, it lets us do a little more things. Except right now with our situation financially—he's bought into the business he's been working for—so we really don't need the money. I think sometimes he's feeling that it's not worth it if I've had a really bad day and he comes home and has to hear about it. And in a way he wishes I weren't doing it because we don't have to financially.

(Paradoxically, because women who earn relatively little generally care for only a small number of children, the day care may intrude only minimally into family life. Even so, the work is resented more than it is in those families where day care becomes a more central burden on the household.)

Over time most providers say that they gain *some* legitimacy from their husbands. And they know that this acceptance is linked both to visibility and to their material contributions to the household's survival: "In the beginning I felt that he didn't realize what a hard job it was and what I was really doing and how much it contributed to the family income. But I don't feel that way now. He realizes what a hard job it is and what goes on all day and how loud it is in here and what it is making lunch for twelve children."

But providers indicate that this recognition has to be fought for repeatedly. The husbands in all of these families clearly have reasons for wanting to deny that their wives are working. Even if he doesn't make it explicit, a man may recognize that in defining child care as a real job, he has to give up the right to claim his wife's labor and support. One provider linked these issues in the way she answered the question of whether her husband recognized child care as a job:

> Sometimes yes and sometimes no depending on what mood he's in. There will be times when he'll come home and the dishes aren't done and the house is just a mess and he'll say why didn't you do this or why didn't you do that. And some days he realizes that I've had a hard day for some reason.

The absence of recognition may also be a strategy designed—by him, by her—to conceal from him the pain of not living up to social expectations. As the woman who noted that her husband had pride in supporting his family implied, she wanted to protect him from a real confrontation with the knowledge that his income did not stretch quite far enough. Some husbands themselves acknowledge the double pain of feeling they have failed to live up to their own images of a breadwinner and of seeing their wives struggle because of this failure:[18]

> It makes me mad . . . that I can't do what my father did or my uncles did. They could work and bring home enough money to pay the mortgage and all the bills. I couldn't begin to do that on my own now. It's hard because most males were brought up in that kind of situation. It's just . . . It would be nice if Dinah could not have to work until the kids were in school. That's a job in itself. . . . I live with [how hard she works]. . . . I sometimes don't listen [to her problems] as well as I should. I do understand what she's going through. But sometimes when she's having a hard time I'm scared because I don't know what to do.

Resistance may manifest itself in persistent denigration of her activities. One woman told me she found enormous comfort in her husband's respect for her work: "He'll brag to anyone and he'll say, 'She earns more money than I do and she works harder than anybody.'

His brother was starting to crap on me one day and he lit right into him and he said, 'Don't you ever laugh at what she does.'" Yet a moment later she said he frequently belittled her work's legitimacy by suggesting that she quit or take time off: "His answer for everything, if I'm having a bad day, is, well why don't you quit? Or why don't you take a year off?" A woman who made more money than her husband did said he repeatedly denied that her income was the earned result of hard work: "Well, sometimes he gets irritated because I make more than he does. He always tells me, '*I* have to work hard for *my* money.'"

Some men imply that the demands their wives experience are voluntary: They suggest that altruism, rather than the actual constraints of the job, underlies the persistent pressures. Some spouses may also preserve for themselves the "legitimate" job by refusing to allow their wives to claim the money they earn on income taxes: While this is justified as a strategy for saving money, nonreporting serves to make her income less important. Alternatively, husbands insist that their wives could not really be engaged in a serious occupation because they fail to explore its full money-making potential. Just as husbands frequently say that the extent to which their wives work hard is their own fault because they do not enforce limits, so do they often suggest that their wives could be making more money if they were more businesslike about it: "I feel that she could get more but she has feelings that this is what it's worth and she doesn't want to put pressure on other people." (Ironically, then, a man engages in a contradictory battle over the issue of legitimacy when he suggests that family day care *could* be transformed into "real" work. He may be doing so because he wishes that his wife would earn more money. He is also suggesting a mechanism whereby his wife could substantiate the very claims against which he is putting up resistance.)

Not surprisingly, men who know better sometimes "forget" that their wives are really working. One man said, "[When people ask] I say she runs a day care at home. That's what she does and that's what I tell them. I did make a goof on an insurance form once where it asked if she was employed. I wrote down 'no' and I heard about that." And men who at some times talk graphically about how hard family day care is and how much effort their wives put into their jobs, at other times assert with equal earnestness that they have protected their wives from having to work. Patsy Lincoln's husband, Mark, said,

> I never wanted her to work. When we first got married she worked before we had kids. And then she had Sonya and never worked outside the home since. I guess the thing that made me feel the strongest about that—I'll admit I'm old-

> fashioned—but I don't believe in women working period. But I'm not so thick-headed that I don't understand that nowadays they have to. And a lot of women want their own career and I'm fifty-fifty on that. I see their point and I don't see their point. You know what I mean. Because I'm old-fashioned that part. But I also see nowadays with the way things are and with the economic situation most of the time the mother and father have to work because of expenses. But I think it boils down to, I always told her she wasn't going to work or I really didn't want her to work. It wasn't that I ordered her not to work. It was just sort of a mutual agreement. I just didn't feel like having her work was good as long as we could afford not to because my mother had to work for years and I think it takes a lot out of the woman to work all those hours. To me they weren't put on earth to be the hard worker. It's hard enough work having to do the housework. If they have to do the housework as well as the work outside—except probably I know nowadays there's a lot of husbands that do the vacuuming and stuff and help out more and more because of the ERA's probably done that a lot. But I just felt it took a lot of years off my mother's life. I think she grew older, a lot older, than what normal people would if they didn't have to work out like that. That's why I didn't want my wife to have to go through it.

## CONTROL OVER MONEY

Research on the family has often assumed that men use their earning power to maintain control over the distribution of household monies. Some studies of working-class family life, for example, describe women who are ignorant of how much their husbands earn and are entirely dependent on the household allowance (with which they may struggle to make ends meet). Even when wives have some earning power of their own, it has been argued that women have little or no control in deciding how money is to be spent.[19] The evidence from this study contradicts this picture of total powerlessness: The women who make an economic contribution to the household have a voice in the family's financial decisions when they contribute their earnings into a common pool and, in a different way, when they keep their own earnings separate.

*Separate Accounting Families*. In about one-fifth of the households women keep their earnings separate from those of their husbands. This accounting system appears most often (although not invariably or exclusively) when the husband's income alone is deemed sufficient to cover household expenses. Women in these families control their own money:

> I keep it separate and what I do is I may pay off a bill I've made or if we'd like to have something that we wouldn't normally buy, I just put it aside. Like four years ago I saved up my money and had somebody build me a bookshelf and I've bought a kitchen appliance or just set it aside until such time as I wanted to do something with it. It was never anything I did out of necessity. More out of want—something I'd like to have or something I'd get for one of the kids. It's not something I'm in desperate need of. And a lot of times I'll take the kids to McDonalds for lunch so I'm using the money.

Maintaining this pattern demands vigilance. One woman who wanted her income to be separate lost her control over it when her husband began to use it in ways she disapproved of:

> I wanted that independence a little bit from my husband [but] before I knew it instead of going toward things that maybe were going to last for a while. . . . I noticed that we were buying my son a new bicycle every year. . . . It bothered me a little bit [because] I thought the money was going one way and it wasn't. . . . I let him get control of the money. . . . It happened that way. It just kind of slid that way. It's my money but it's gone before you knew it. . . . At Christmas it was crazy. He went out and bought these things and I couldn't understand it—all these extravagant things.

But even when they can sustain separate accounting, financial autonomy is not accompanied by legitimacy for one's work. Nor is it a base on which to claim relief from household responsibilities. In these families, family day care remains a "hobby"; it can not serve as the basis for renegotiation of the marriage contract.[20]

*Pooled Income Families.* In most of the households, the money that enters the family is pooled into a common pot.[21] Providers say both they and their husbands recognize that each contributes to the accumulation of household possessions: "It's a big joke. One of us will say, 'Well *I* bought that,' about something." And the women derive a feeling of importance from contributing their share and helping to make life easier:

> All of the income in our house is joined. It all goes into the same place. I place importance on it only in that it makes me feel like I'm contributing to the economics of the household. . . . I couldn't stay home and not work at all. We could probably make ends meet on Walt's salary. But it would be a very meager meeting.

In pooled-income families, the determination of who actually pays the bills seems to be neither a clear reflection of power (as it has been conceived in some studies) nor a burden imposed on the woman (as it has been characterized in others).[22] Usually the responsibility is delegated on the basis of expertise or facility:

> He had the checkbook for a couple of weeks. I let him run it and we were in the hole so quick we didn't know it and it just didn't work out so I take care of all the bills and everything. He gives [his check] to me, I write his name on the back, and after I cash it, I get some cash. He keeps taking it out of my pocketbook as he needs it. It burns a hole in his pocket so he just takes ten at a time.

> I usually just give all my checks to Martin at the end of the week and he pays the bills or whatever. I hate dealing with a checkbook. I just hate it—I don't really have that much to do with it. He decides what bills we should pay this week or next week or whatever.

Because many families run close to the margin, there is little room for independent decision making about how the income is spent: "It all goes in the checkbook and we pay the bills and Monday we have nothing left"; "It's all our money and it all goes into more or less one pot. You don't really have that much to worry about after spending anyway by the time you pay bills." Pooling incomes is a necessity:

> We've always thought about giving each other an allowance, saying so much is our money and we can do whatever we want. We've never got around to it. It seems like something always came up for the kids or unexpected doctor bills or tires for the car—always something. But I'd like to do that sometime.

But, where the combined incomes of the two allow discretionary spending, most providers say major decisions are made jointly: "We have common goals." Minor decisions can be made individually: "If I'm in Burlington at the craft fair and I see something I really like, I get it. And he does too." Because they have contributed income, the women are relieved of the burden of guilt when they do spend money:

> I feel like I have to feel like I'm contributing because I'm so used to it. And I just felt so incredibly guilty after a year had gone by and I hadn't worked. . . . I don't want to feel guilty that I'm buying something for [my son]. I need to contribute something.

Even so, providers and their husbands almost invariably think of the money as being separate, and they almost invariably define hers as extra *whether or not* it is an essential component of family survival. Providers and their spouses both say that his income is used for the unavoidable or necessary bills: the mortgage, the car payments, the utilities. In contrast, they say the money earned from family day care is used to pay for optional items—"small bills," groceries, and clothing. In describing how their incomes are used, providers often merge luxuries with obvious essentials such as food and taxes. When *his* money pays for these things, they are necessary; when *her* money does, they are extras: "What he makes there is mainly like insurance, taxes, and all that. What I make usually goes for food, clothing—whatever I find necessary to spend my baby-sitting money on or just to take the kids once a week to Middlebury and blow it." Another woman described it similarly: "Basically mine is used for extras or like taxes and stuff like that. Christmas presents or things that you could get away with if you didn't have."

The men characterize spending patterns the same way: "Of course, monetarily it's been very nice. . . . The money she earns is fun money basically to do the extras we want. We've done a lot of work on the house in the last year. I'm trying to build a garage. . . . So we've been able to get the extras. We could get along just fine without it but it's nice to have it."

There are, of course, rational explanations for some of these perceptions. First, her income is often less predictable than his and therefore can not be counted on in the same way. One provider said that her husband, in trying to balance the household budget, was continually frustrated by not knowing how much she would be earning the next week.[23] Since her money comes in weekly (and often in cash), she may see it go out in a less systematic way. The woman who said her family could make a "meager meeting" on her husband's salary, continued, "There would be no extras. And basically that's where my money goes. He gets paid every two weeks and I get paid every week so mine goes to groceries, bread and butter, the movies if you want to go. That sort of thing."

But it is also clear that these women are engaging in a fiction designed to preserve for men "a sense of manhood contingent on the shared belief that his paycheck is 'supporting the family.'"[24] As with the blue-collar families interviewed by Ellen Israel Rosen, this fiction has certain functions. Providers need a spouse's permission to engage in this kind of home-based work. This permission may be contingent on her not threatening his "manhood" even though they both know that her earnings relieve the strains of trying to survive on an inadequate paycheck. Providers also need assistance with both their paid and unpaid work. To the extent that she defines her earnings as a "help" to him, she may be in a better position to claim reciprocity. Finally, the women know that their own earnings alone (because they are small and because they come without benefits) are insufficient to maintain a household. By defining him as the breadwinner and herself as the housewife (who brings in "pin" money) she "reinforces his obligation to the family."

Predictably, women who actually make more money than their partners experience extreme tension in maintaining this fiction. We can hear this in Barbara Larson's discussion of how she and her husband deal with her greater earning power (some of which derives from care of the elderly). She feels he needs opportunities to increase his household contribution even though her burdens are thereby intensified; she also wants to protect him from knowing just how hard she works:

> In the ten years of our marriage, my income has been larger than his probably 70 percent of the time. And part of that is because of my college degree versus his not college degree. And part of it is because he was a student for a while. And I think at this point it's because I'm home and I'm earning money. He feels that he has to provide more. And he sees his success and his worth in the dollar amount that he can earn. And his self-esteem is very highly tied to that. That's why he's gone to the National Guard because he can earn more there for two weeks than he could in six to eight weeks at [his factory job]. . . . It's difficult for me not to have him here but it would be more difficult for him not to be bringing in the income. I think it has been [a source of

> tension] because there are times when I'd like to tell him it would be nice not to have to take care of kids.

Other women also struggled with the reality of earning more money than their husbands; this "admission" often was accompanied by tears, body language that suggested extreme discomfort, and a rapid attempt to change the subject.

## HOUSEWORK AND CHILD CARE

Recent studies of dual-earner families offer contradictory evidence about the division of household labor. Some researchers report that men do not take on a significant portion of housework and child care even when their wives are employed full-time. Others suggest that some men are doing more housework today than they did in the past. Some research attempts to specify the conditions under which men assume a larger share of domestic responsibilities.[25] Ferree, for example, argues that family negotiation about these issues "is more influenced by the relative equality of earnings between husband and wife than by their ideological support for women's equality."[26]

What happens to housework when women's paid work takes place inside the home? Is the ideological commitment to a traditional model of family life accompanied by a traditional division of labor? Are domestic responsibilities actually compatible with the work of family day care? Can the home-based worker translate her earning power into a claim for relief from household tasks?

Most providers and their husbands assume that when a woman stays home, she makes herself available to do housework. For example, John Bishop gave the following answer when asked if he did any of the housework when his wife worked as a secretary: "Some. Not as much as I should have, I'm sure. Somewhat. I'm sure I didn't do my share." Now that his wife has shifted to family day care, he said, "I just don't think about it. I think it has changed. She does get a chance to do some of those things during the day. . . . Probably I do a little less." Similarly, Paul Knutson, whose wife had never held a job outside the home, mused about what might happen if she did, "Even though she is working she is home during the day and she is able to do different things like get the evening meal started and different things like that whereas if she worked outside the home it would require a lot more planning, a lot more work on the rest of us to help out."

The women play into this. They too say they expect less of their husbands than they would if they held jobs outside the home: "Well, I think with me working at home and being able to catch up on things in the afternoon, most of it falls on me. . . . But I think if I worked outside the home where I couldn't do anything all day that would change. He would have to help me more and he wouldn't mind doing it."

If both spouses rationalize a gender-based division of housework as the inevitable result of her being home, they also justify it on other grounds. Some women believe in a division of "inside" and "outside" work: "We really have the kind of relationship where we have designated duties. I don't do anything outdoors. I never ever have. And he's the one that keeps the outside looking good so I basically do all the inside." Some protest they *prefer* to do the work because otherwise it might not be done adequately. Asked whether she received any help with the housework, one woman answered, "Very little, very little. And that's my fault. I take full blame for that. I used to feel that no one could do it like mom. It's crazy." Some are willing to accept inequities because they think he has the more demanding job: "He sure doesn't [help out around the home] but he works hard. He works at [a local factory] and he's busy all day long. When he comes home, he's tired." One woman said her husband helps "occasionally." "When he's here he tries. He hasn't done as much as he did when I was working outside the home but that's because of the long hours he puts in his job."

Ideology notwithstanding, the reality is that housework fits uneasily into the child-care day. A few providers said that they manage to go around their normal routines as they do when only their own children are home. But most accomplish little. Housework is done in the evening after an already-full workday: "By the time you get done at night you have your family to take care of—laundry or cleaning up and making snacks or thinking of lunch for the next day, or taking care of your children and what they need." Similarly: "As far as keeping my house, basically the only thing I can do during the day is laundry and dishes and prepare food. And occasionally I can vacuum. . . . But my basic housework day starts after 5:30."

There is no quantifiable data about the precise division of household labor, but the impression derived from discussions about this issue suggests a shift in orientation linked to a wife's contribution to the household income. As Ferree predicts, women who made a significant contribution to total family income frequently spoke as if they had the right to renegotiate responsibility for household tasks. Donna Burke, for example, who said she struggled with her husband over the definition of her job as work, also struggled to legitimize her claims for his participation in housework and child care:

> We're getting a little bit better. A little bit. But most of the time it's just, boy we don't have any clean laundry, the

> dishes need doing, or this that has to be done. And I say, "Well, I'm sorry. I work hard too and all you have to do is push the button on the washing machine." There's plenty he can do. . . . My mistake, when we first got married, I did everything. I didn't expect anything from him . . . because you know, I figured I wanted everything done a certain way anyways, and I always ended up doing it anyways. But I said, "No more." I finally learned. You can not be a superperson. There's no way you can do it. I said, "I'm sorry, but I'll have to have help." It took me a while to break down and be able to ask for help. I said, "I just can't do it all. If you want things done around here you are going to have to help." And he's getting better. It may be only that he takes the children and does something with them once in a while. But that's a big help. For a long time it was, "I'll do what I want to do and the kids are your responsibility." And I said, "Oh no." And he is a little bit better.

Another woman similarly drew on both the perceived difficulty of her job and her contribution to the family to force her husband's participation:

> He did [mind] in the beginning but I just kept saying, "This is a job for me and it's just as important as your job and you know everything can be done as long as everybody participates." It took him a while to understand how it was. You know, everybody thinks it's all fun and games to be home and take care of kids.

Women whose income contributions are less significant also get what they term "help"—their husbands wash up after dinner or do some of the vacuuming. But they also say they request assistance instead of claiming it, thus acquiescing to a gender-based understanding of domestic responsibility: "He will help—if I ask. He isn't one to volunteer." Or they said his "assistance" came only when *he* perceived her need. It therefore remained unpredictable and closed to negotiation. Vera Knutson, who said that she and her husband had "designated responsibilities," admitted that if this division of labor broke down, it did so only at his instigation: "On nights that I'm really tired he'll do all the dishes for me. . . . I'll cook the dinner and he'll say go sit down or something like that."

Even less "assistance" is forthcoming for family day care providers whose work is seen as optional. For example, Rena Milks, whose husband believed her child-care income was unnecessary, said the responsibility for housework remained exclusively hers: "Mostly I do it now because Rob doesn't. It was just kind of a decision because I'm home now." Meg Garber, whose husband resented having children present when he came home for lunch, also did all the housework because she wasn't "working": "Seven days out of the week I'm the one who does it. . . . If I were working he would help."

## LEISURE TIME AND ITS STRUGGLES

The combined responsibility for unpaid and paid work entails grueling and long days. Any leisure time (on a routine basis) is stolen from sleep: a few early morning minutes in which to exercise, read the paper, or simply sit quietly over a cup of coffee.

A fundamental inequality in power within the family is reflected in these stolen minutes measured against the extended (and protected) leisure time of men. The women describe how their husbands spend late afternoons and evenings reading the paper or watching television while they attend to housework and child care. Or they describe how their husbands, because they are always "on the move," avoid both the constraints and the responsibilities of the home: "He's never home anyway. He's one of those sports nuts. . . . He's never home"; "My husband is not one to stay home. He can not stand to stay inside. If he does stay home he's working in the garage or something."

If the women accept this inequality, by and large, resistance can be heard as well because they claim (sometimes deviously) additional fragments of time. For example, some take off as soon as their husbands arrive home: "After he gets home, I may just decide to go to do grocery shopping or anything just to get away for a little while. . . . It feels good just to get out for a little while by myself . . . I don't take the kids with me." Resistance can also be heard in the fact that the women make known some of their own needs, even when these needs directly conflict with those of their husbands. After a long day confined to the house, the women want some time away; after a long day away from the home, the men want to stay put. Patsy Lincoln, when asked whether there were any drawbacks to work at home, answered, "Oh definitely, because you're here twenty-four hours a day. And I get on these kicks sometimes on the weekends when I don't have these children I want to get out and do something different. And my husband's worked all week and he wants to stay home." Two husbands talked about this issue:

> It would be easier if she were working outside of the house because she could leave her job where she was. It just makes it hard because at the end of the day the kids go

> home but Claudia's still here and she likes to get away from here to get away from the job. And that makes it kind of hard because with my schedule we can't always just jump in the car and go somewhere. And Claudia would like to get away without the kids anyway and baby-sitters are very expensive so it makes it hard.

> Once I get home I'd rather stay put and Cathy would like to get out of here for a while.

In sum, the work of family day care providers takes place within a traditional definition of the sexual division of labor. Because providers have given at least nominal support to these notions and because they are seen as capable of fulfilling these expectations, an involvement in family day care does reinforce women's conventional roles, as Kessler-Harris and Sacks argue. At the same time, family day care providers draw on the visibility of their work and their contributions to household finances to challenge and resist these terms. And to some extent they appear successful as they claim power with respect to the distribution of the household's finances (within the material context of limited resources and the ideological context of the male as breadwinner). They may be less successful, however, in transforming the division of household work and gaining access to leisure time. Unlike paid work outside the home, their home-based work both appears to create the possibility for them to continue to do housework (because they are there) and limits their possibilities for leisure (because they are *still* there); it also adds the tensions of creating more housework and of putting their leisure needs in conflict with those of their husbands. Thus not only do these women, like other working women, have to fight against gender-based assumptions, they do so in a context explicitly designed to reinforce those very assumptions. If their failure is a measure of the persistence of patriarchal power, their resistance—fragmented and sputtering as it may be—challenges the perception of women as passive victims. It lends support to the notion that women struggle, albeit against overwhelming odds with which they often unwittingly collude, to achieve for themselves a self-defined and legitimated life.

## *Relationships with Their Own Children*

The decision to stay home, no matter how it may be combined with other interests, is justified by the needs of children. At a time when increasing numbers of women work outside the home and leave their children in the care of others, the ferocity of this commitment is somewhat surprising. Three factors can help explain why providers and their spouses are so insistent about this traditional model of child care.

First, a high proportion of the providers and their husbands experienced extensive family breakdown as children. Both women and men spoke about homes broken by divorce and death and being brought up by relatives (or, in a few cases, in orphanages) or by abusive and alcoholic parents. I can not say whether the frequency with which these problems occurred among the men and women in this study is greater than in the general population. But these individuals explicitly linked their dreams for their children with the goal of avoiding the pain that characterized their own lives. One provider talked about her life as the child of a single working woman: Although she had "fond" memories of the consistent care she had received from "sitters," she also had painful memories of never having enough time with her mother and of material deprivation. She was insistent that she wanted something different for her own child: "I don't want him to have to be brought up away from me. And I don't want him to wear second-hand clothes like I always did." One provider, who was raised by relatives, also used her experiences as a counter-model: "I remember how I felt as a child and I want to make it different for my children." One husband spoke about having been brought up in an orphanage and wanting to create for his children the stable family life that he never knew. And Mark Lincoln, who said he wanted to protect his wife from having to work outside the home, can remember his own sadness of thirty years ago: "I played all three sports and my parents were never there."[27]

Second, a precarious economic situation creates its own uncertainty. In her perceptive analysis of the lives of working-class families, Lillian Rubin argues that the distinction between middle-class and working-class family attitudes toward child rearing is not just a function of different resources with which to purchase child-care services, but is rooted in anxiety about the future:[28]

> Parents in professional middle-class families have a sense of their own success, of their ability to control their world, to provide for their children's future, whatever that might be. For them, the problem is not how to support the children through tomorrow, not *whether* they can go to college or professional school, but *which* of the prestigious alternatives available to them ought to be encouraged. For working-class parents, however, the future is seen as uncertain,

> problematic. For them, the question is most often *whether,* not *which*—and that "whether" more often asks *if* children will finish high school; *if* they will grow up without getting "into trouble"; *if,* even with maximum vigilance, they—the parents—can retain some control over their children's future. . . . Their own histories remind them about how easily children can get into trouble, how easily they stray from parental values and injunctions.

Both men and women in this study spoke about the significance of a parent's vigilance as a means to protect children from the "troubles" that afflicted them or their peers. A couple of the women quoted in the last chapter were explicit about how their own pasts shaped their current goals for their own and day-care children. Mark Lincoln hopes that in supporting *his* son's athletic activities, Jonathan can avoid the ever-increasing problems of adolescence: "I think there's so many added pressures on kids nowadays. Peer pressure is so great and the drug problem is so bad." Among some of these families a distrust of public institutions and the norms embedded there gives an additional justification for keeping their children "close to home and in the care of people who share parental values."[29]

Finally, an involvement in family day care feeds back on and reinforces this commitment. As I argued in Chapter 3, a provider finds confirmation of the importance of staying home with her *own* children in her observations of children who are separated from their parents all day, and in her assessment of what these parents are missing. Their husbands make similar observations. Mark Lincoln, forgetting that he worked hard when his own children were young, now "feels sorry for the Bousquet children" whose parents rarely see them; he also feels sorry for the father of these children who "has no chance [to work] days probably for another seven or eight years and by then with the exception of [the youngest child], the boys are going to be out of Little League or just about. And he would love to have the time to be here and be a coach. And he's not going to have that opportunity."

With the decision to embark on family day care so firmly entrenched in a notion of its benefits for children, both parents have difficulty discussing problems. When providers are asked how their own children have responded to family day care, they generally begin with a positive statement about its consequences. Only reluctantly do they acknowledge a gap between actual and anticipated effects. We can hear this in how Donna Burke gradually qualified her response to the question, "How do your children feel about your work?": "Oh, they love it. Well, it doesn't bother them too much. Occasionally they might get a little bit jealous." Providers not only have to acknowledge this gap, but they sometimes have to redefine "good" parenting. If they can not do so, they can not continue in the occupation. (See Chapter 7.)

## PRESCHOOL CHILDREN

The provider's ideal of good mothering for young children has been defined above. Providers believe in opportunities for free play, consistent discipline, and intense affection; they believe in "being there" for their children. They are partially able to enact this ideal. But the presence of other children can limit the extent to which a woman is available to her own children; the presence of other children also highlights in inadmissible ways the nature of the different and intense dynamic between a mother and her own child.

Many providers say that one or more of their children are threatened by the intrusion of other children into the private domain. Often the child mentioned as the one most hurt is one defined as being vulnerable for some *other* reason. Some women say that it is an oldest child who has had to learn to respond to a series of intruders including his or her own siblings:

> My four-year-old minds an awful lot. He has his days when he just loves it all but then he has his other days as well—like why do these kids come to this house all the time. But he's getting much better. But he does get a little touchy. [The younger child] is pretty good. Some days he needs a lot of hugs but he's usually no problem. But [the older] is—but [he] was the first child and then his brother came along and all these other kids came along and he was really threatened by that and he really likes to be "Mr. Center of Attention."

Others find that the youngest causes the most difficulty especially if she or he has to give up the status of "baby" in the family. And still others find it is a middle child who, lost in the shuffle anyway, has the most difficulty: "Tommy of all my kids feels the day care the most. But he also feels being in a family of four too. In one sense I feel bad about the fact that Tommy always has to share."

Providers also admit they have to put up with a range of distressing behavior patterns: One child may respond by becoming more whiney or clinging, another demands attention whenever the provider is caring for someone else. Children may respond with even more disruptive patterns: Some tattle on other children, hit or bite them, or throw temper tantrums.

Acknowledging these negative effects is extremely painful for a provider who has defined her role as being the "good" or even "perfect" mother, so she may be quick to minimize or deny them. She may suggest that the problems are the incidental results of a temporary situation: The new baby she is caring for is making it harder for her own child who now feels displaced; her son is missing a particular day-care friend who recently left. One woman, for example, said that her daughter was having a hard time because "the other ones are all younger and they don't talk as well so she doesn't have anyone to socialize with." She quickly added, "but she's getting a lot better."[30] The women also assert that the problems are easily balanced by the benefits. They say that their children learn how to share, that they have companions to play with on a daily basis, and that they become more independent.

But they can not always write off the negative aspects. If they say their children grow from sharing, they also say their children never have the option of *not* sharing:

> I found that my children have to share everything. They have to share their toys, they have to share their mother, they have to share their rooms—even their beds at times. I kind of feel . . . guilty about that at times. So that is my problem. That is me thinking that way. I mean my children get lost in the shuffle. That's what bothered me sometimes. You try to be fair to all of them. You don't give your child special priority.

And they acknowledge that, as a result, a child may even be less generous than she or he would be otherwise: "I think Emily is more giving than Jonah because he's always had to share his toys and whatever with everyone [whereas she had five years alone]. I think Emily's less selfish than Jonah is." Finally, they admit that although they are home, they have little time to spend with their own children. They can not entirely erase the pain they feel as they redefine good mothering in more limited terms than those motivating their involvement in the occupation: "I felt guilty because Peter was part of so many kids. I don't ever think I necessarily put him first. I remember feeling guilty that I was shortchanging Peter. He was just part of the gang." Similarly, "It feels like she's losing out from my doing day care. But I wanted to be home. It's a hard decision to make. I mean, if you have to work—I mean most people have to work. I wanted to be home but I wanted to be with my kids."

Providers have even more difficulty talking about a set of issues that touch on the distinctive nature of the relationship between a mother and her own child. As we saw in Chapter 3, most providers are unwilling to say they treat their own children any differently from the way they treat other people's children. In fact they take considerable pride in being fair—in giving equal treats, equal hugs, equal praise, and equal punishment—and they contrast themselves with other providers who do not act this way. But the presence of other children may highlight the fact that there *is* a different relationship; it may also exacerbate it.

Only reluctantly—and with probing—do providers admit that not only do they feel differently about their own children ("Of course, I would be lying if I said I didn't love mine more") but that they find themselves locked into different patterns of interaction. The first acknowledgment comes in the form of suggesting not only that other children act better for them than they do for their own parents, but that their *own* children are the most difficult to handle. Although some providers say that there are children who "have become comfortable enough they feel they can tease like mine do," or that they have "had children that have gotten familiar with me enough that if I yell or scream they're not intimidated," most providers agree that their own children test the limits more: "Other people's children are not as demanding. When you tell your children 'no' they always ask fifty times more. When I tell other people's children 'no' they don't ask again. . . . They are more obedient than your own"; "You know, your own kids don't seem to mind you as well as someone else's kids. . . . No child pushes me as much as my own."

When asked how they respond to these different behavior patterns, providers also acknowledge a different kind of treatment.[31] Some say they are harder on their own children, because their own know the rules and *should* be better:

> In a way I find myself being tougher on her because she knows what she's supposed to do and what she's not supposed to do. And with the [other] kids, they're just coming in for a while each day or something and you know, I figure it's hard for them to remember my rules and their parents' rules. But she knows what she can do and what she can't.

Some suggest they would find it difficult to "be as stern" with another person's child as with their own. And many say that because they can not—or will not—spank another person's child, they find themselves using different disciplinary techniques with their own:

> I don't spank the other ones and my daughter gets resentful because she knows that she can get spanked and the others

> can't. Like Ben has a tendency to run and jump on the couch and stuff, and if my daughter does it she just gets a swat and Ben gets put in the corner or something. Alison doesn't understand why she gets spanked for something and Ben doesn't.

Conversely, there are providers who say that they are easier on their own children. And still others say that they are inconsistent (sometimes easier, sometimes harder) and that this inconsistency constitutes an additional problem. Shelley Tompkins spoke at length about this issue:

> Sometimes I'm easier on Emma and sometimes I'm harder on her and I know it and I get mad at myself. When I'm easier I don't feel so bad until she starts getting bratty. And then I say, "Darn it, it's your own fault." All these toys here are my kids' toys and Emma has to share. . . . I don't handle [sharing of toys] the same way every time and that's a problem. Sometimes I'll let Emma have her own way around it and. . . . that's when I feel like I'm giving in to Emma. And then the times when I'm hard on her she might do something wrong and so will the other kids and she'll get in more trouble than they would. My attitude is sometimes, well you know better, you live with me. . . . So I hate myself for being that way.

But if providers can readily document these different interactions, they are reluctant to *explain* them. When asked to discuss why they thought that their own children were more difficult, providers invariably began by saying they didn't know. They then peeked at a possible truth: "I don't know. . . . your own children maybe they're a little more secure in you so they can test you more"; "I don't know why that is. They feel more secure maybe with their own parents? I don't know. They let their inner feelings out? They let their inner selves really show?"

Providers whose own children are no longer part of the day-care group allow themselves to understand these dynamics more fully. Like Patsy Lincoln they talk about having become more patient over time, about learning to relax and let children develop at their own pace; retrospectively they admit that they were harder on their own children because they cared so much about the outcomes of child rearing ("I expected my own to be perfect"). But a provider who still has preschool children can not easily acknowledge the extent to which identification with her own child locks her into a special kind of relationship, made visible by the difference in her feelings about other children, and exacerbated by her own different and occasionally inconsistent reactions. If the provider denies feeling differently about her own children, she has to find some other reason for her child's misbehavior; she may therefore have to contend with a sense of inadequacy about her own mothering. But if she acknowledges that her own child's misbehavior derives from her greater love for, and intense identification with, that child, and if she therefore acknowledges that different feelings result in somewhat different treatment (whether overt or covert) she loses in other ways: She can no longer claim that she is absolutely fair; she can no longer claim that she makes the children feel "like members of the family"; and she can no longer claim that she is "better" than the real mother—if she is simply better because she cares less, she isn't much better at all.

## SCHOOL-AGE CHILDREN

Many of these problems diminish when the provider's children are in school all day. At the same time, a new set of concerns emerges as the definition of good mothering changes. If young children "need" the daily and constant presence of a mother, older children "need" focused attention at specific times and for specific activities. When a woman cares for other children, she can not always be responsive.

Providers speak about the return from school as one time when their child's needs might be ignored or run into conflict with the needs of other children:

> We had a problem in the beginning when my kids got home and they wanted to tell me about their day and [the other children] wanted to tell me too because I was the first person they saw when they got off the bus. And it was like she's my mother, not yours, and it was real hard in that respect.

Two husbands also mention this issue:

> I wish my kids could explain some of their feelings because sometimes I think some of their days are just difficult. . . . It's like when Jimmy went to kindergarten last year and he'd come just at the time when Erica was serving lunch and he'd come in with all these neat things and Erica just did not have the time to sit down [with him]. I think that's one thing my children are missing out sometimes.

> I think it's tough on our boys when they come home from school and there's a house full and they don't get the attention they were used to before.

One husband even said he thought it might be better for his son to arrive at a day-care center where a provider would *have* to treat him with special consideration.

The inability to participate in school activities constitutes a problem for some women who realize the irony in the fact that although they are home *for* their own children, they can not do all that a good mother should. Cara Brown said, "That's been my biggest disappointment this year, not being able to go to my daughter's school when I wanted to. Yet here I was at home and I still couldn't leave."

Not only does day care distract a mother from responsiveness, it creates particular additional problems. A home geared to activities for small children can be a source of irritation to an older child. These children may also resent having their rooms used for naps and finding their toys broken. And they are more likely than younger children to articulate their resentment about the imposition of day care. A father said, "Maybe some of their toys have been moved or something like that. . . . They'll make it known that they're not happy about it."

Providers seek practical solutions to these problems: For example, an older child's room may be defined as "off-limits," or the provider may set aside a brief period in which she can pay attention exclusively to her own child. And, as with younger children, providers suggest that the advantages outweigh the disadvantages. These advantages also vary. Providers say it is good for their children to learn how to care for and interact with young ones. They say their children profit from being exposed to many kinds of people. As one husband put it, "I think it's good for the boys to see the different types of kids, different types of behavior. It gives our kids the chance to see the difference in what we say is right and wrong." And they tell the children directly that they might have to do without the "extras" if their mothers were not working.

## TEENAGE AND ADULT CHILDREN

Two new issues emerge with teenage and adult children. First, family day care providers have to decide how much to rely on their older children for assistance. Those who are reluctant—or unable—to renegotiate the sexual division of domestic labor may feel more comfortable imposing on their children. Many, when asked who did the housework, described each child's designated household responsibilities. Providers may also call on their older children for help in the tasks of family day care. Patsy Lincoln, whose husband said he would not watch a baby because he could not change diapers, found more capable relief in the form of her teenage daughter. Another woman, who cared for a larger-than-normal crew of children during the summer months, hired her three teenage sons as assistants. And the women believed these responsibilities encouraged independence and taught useful parenting skills.

When children have left the home and have children of their own, a new set of concerns arises. Should the provider care for her own grandchildren? If she does, should she charge money? No single pattern emerged from the interviews with the four women who included grandchildren in their day-care homes. Two women wanted family values to prevail, one thought she was a more reliable caregiver than her daughter (the child's mother), and one simply responded to a request. Only one of these women cared for the grandchild for free, two charged a reduced rate, and one charged the full amount. In all four cases the grandmothers felt that tensions with parents about control and intimacy were exacerbated in this kind of care, especially when their interactions were with a daughter-in-law. And two were saddened by their sense that by including grandchildren in a larger group of children, the "special" relationship was compromised.

Providers with young children face the most severe conflicts; they also have to do the most compromising. If they are "there" for their children, they can not always be fully available and responsive. Because the women in this position explain their occupational involvement primarily in terms of its benefits for their children, these conflicts and compromises can take an enormous emotional toll. When the provider continues in the occupation after her children are in school full-time, she may come to focus more on those benefits that are independent of her role as a mother to them. Nevertheless, with all children, as with her spouse, she has the constant problem of filling two roles simultaneously.

## *Relationships with Real and "Fictive" Kin*

As more women find employment in the labor force, family day care providers may appear to others (as they occasionally do to themselves and their husbands) as women who are simply "at home." As such, they become the repositories of the kinds of expectations for reciprocity that maintain community and kin networks.

These expectations are particularly intense for women who have remained in the communities in which they were raised and who are thus deeply embedded in networks of real and "fictive" kin.[32] Four of the providers I interviewed were all members of the same large family—two sisters, a sister-in-law, a niece. These women were bound to each other in complex ways: The two sisters shared, with other siblings, responsibility for the care of their elderly mother (on which days they looked after each other's children); each woman referred children to one of the others if they were fully enrolled themselves; and they relied on the same pool of relatives for backup assistance. Two other child-care providers I interviewed mentioned that they were caring for the children of women who had previously, as teenagers, baby-sat for their own children; in one of these cases, the tie extended back another "generation": Beth now cares for Joanne's children; when Joanne was a teenager she baby-sat for Beth's children; when Beth was a teenager, she baby-sat for Joanne. As we saw in Chapter 2, these kinds of bonds constitute one element of the social exchange between parents and providers. Yet providers do not always find their work allows them to meet these expectations: They have to protect their work against sociability; they also have to protect it against unpaid reciprocity.

Some providers find that, as with members of their nuclear family, the expectation for sociability from friends and kin conflicts directly with meeting the demands of their paid work. The women talk about having to "train" people not to call them during the day. But, while providers resist some of these expectations, they have competing needs in that these interactions can relieve the isolation of their work.

The expectations for care, as opposed to sociability, can be even more problematic. Some providers believe they can easily watch a relative's or neighbor's child from time to time on either a paid or an unpaid basis. (And some willingly care for such children on a regular, paid basis.) But almost all find these relationships troublesome: The expectation of reciprocity impinges on their efforts to create a businesslike approach to child care. One provider explained why she had decided to eliminate neighbors altogether from her clientele:

> My neighbor once called and said, "I want you to baby-sit for my child for the day." And then her friend called and said, "Would you baby-sit my child for the day?" And I said yes. And I planned to have the two extra. And then they called that morning and said, "We don't need your services." . . . I planned that day for them, I was ready for them, and then they called me at the last minute. And I said, uh-uh, I'm not going to be used that way. I made that policy I do not baby-sit for neighbors. It's the only way. I like my neighbors but I'd just as soon be able to say, I don't do that.

But disentanglement is not a fully appropriate or possible response because these same individuals can serve as a major resource for family day care providers who need backup support on both a regular basis and in emergencies, and because they can not always shed their community responsibilities. These complex webs can be detected when Bobbie Arnold explains why, although she said she "does not like caring for relatives," she was watching two nieces at the time of the interview. She felt trapped in this arrangement because of her own regular reliance for backup on the sister-in-law who usually looked after these nieces. She also felt trapped because she knew that if she refused this care, the burden would fall on her mother-in-law, toward whom she also feels some responsibility. "You live too close to relatives here," she said.

## Conclusion

Providers struggle to balance competing pressures in their relationships with clients—both parents and children. So too in their relationships with their own families, providers experience acute tensions from the effort to resolve contradictions. With their spouses they simultaneously accede to and resist patriarchal assumptions; in their relationships with children they attempt to fulfill but invariably redefine a core ideal of "good parenting"; and with members of their broader community, they are drawn into and strive to limit the hold of complex webs. Acknowledging the tensions that emerge in these relationships with family members is particularly difficult for providers: Not only does it entail a redefinition of purpose and self-identity, but it brings them face to face with unalterable constraints. As we will see in Chapter 7, only those who have left the occupation can openly admit to the experienced pain. Those still engaged in the field struggle with acceptance and denial.

# Chapter 5

# THE REGULATION CONTROVERSY

Family day care providers remain in the domestic domain; they do not thereby achieve privacy. This style of child care is increasingly drawing public—and often critical—attention. Observers may be quick to acknowledge that family day care providers can offer excellent substitute care; they also point to appallingly inadequate environments, and they note that parents are not always able to make appropriate judgments about (nor afford) adequate care.

To many, governmental regulation is one obvious and necessary solution to the problem family day care presents. Although they are not united about the best regulatory system, the precise content of regulatory standards, or whether standards should be established at the state or the federal level, most child-care advocates argue that effective monitoring can ensure at least minimal levels of safety for consumers.[1] They also note a number of additional possible benefits: increasing the stability and reliability of day-care providers, creating a role for licensers as sources of information for clients, providing a mechanism for corrective action in cases of neglect and abuse, and shifting responsibility from the individual to the broader society.[2] Many seek a requirement that family day care providers receive training. They focus on the enormous responsibility caregivers have in shaping the physical, emotional, and intellectual development of children who may spend more waking hours away from home than they do with their own parents. They suggest that intuition and informal experience may not be a sufficient base on which to build quality care. To support this position, they draw on the NDCHS finding that providers who were trained offered better-quality care (defined as a tendency to display more teaching, language/information activity, music/dramatic play, and comforting).[3] Regulation thus enters debates about family day care with the goal of protecting its consumers. In this way it differs from debates about the regulation of other kinds of home-based work, which focus on the protection of *workers*. Even when proponents of regulation recognize that the "rights" of consumers and providers may conflict, the bias is toward a concern for the most vulnerable party—children who can not speak for themselves.[4]

Although opponents of regulation draw on a different arsenel and operate from a different, and more conservative, political stance, they also generally ignore the needs of providers. Some argue on ideological grounds that it is inappropriate for the state to intervene in essentially private arrangements about child care; some are particularly opposed to the establishment of federal standards. (Some proponents of regulation distinguish between family day care involving nonrelatives and that involving relatives and acknowledge that regulation is inappropriate in the latter case.)[5] The glorification of "natural" motherhood is used to counter the argument that providers need training or that any kind of standards are necessary. As President Reagan said when addressing a group of business executives in 1981, "Mothers and grandmothers have been taking care of children for thousands of years without special college training. Why is it that certain states prohibit anyone without a degree in early childhood education from operating a day care facility?"[6] Many support their stand of opposition with more pragmatic arguments, suggesting that regulation will have a deleterious effect on the supply of providers, that regulation is unwieldy and ineffective, that it drives many providers "underground," that it will increase the cost of child care, and that it depletes scarce resources better allocated to salaries and direct services.[7] The lack of parent interest in and concern about regulation is used to bolster these arguments.[8] So too is the assertion that the proponents have exaggerated both the extent of the crisis and the efficacy of regulation as a solution.[9]

As this review of arguments suggests, the stakes are high. Some children in family day care may, in fact, be at risk. But this is not the only issue. We have argued that parents and providers are already engaged in difficult boundary disputes. The question of regulation frames the public-private question in a new way and introduces the state (as represented by its legislators and bureaucrats) as another interest group. Regulation thus provokes new questions: Can parents and providers be left alone to make decisions about, and allocate the responsibility for, child care? To what extent should the state be involved? How can the state's interest in protecting children be balanced with its interest in protecting family privacy? Will any attempt to resolve these issues inevitably serve the interests of one of the affected groups—children, parents, and providers—more than another?[10] And, if regulation is one dimension of the informal-formal economy continuum, what happens to family day care when it moves from one pole to another?

Curiously, providers are seldom heard from in these debates. We know little about the terms in which they define the issue of state regulation, why they choose to evade (or comply with) regulatory procedures, and whether or not actual differences between regulated and unregulated providers exist.[11] This chapter is an attempt to fill this gap. After presenting some information about the history of family day care regulation with specific attention to the situation in Vermont, I compare registered and unregistered providers. In so doing, I introduce a typology of providers; this kind of distinction was muted in the first half of this book where the emphasis was on the broader issues that transcended differences. The chapter then explores separately providers' reasons for evasion of or compliance with regulatory procedures. I argue that some traditionally offered explanations for resistance are abstracted from the daily life of family day care providers, and I suggest instead that this stance is a reflection of the major conflicts and constraints that are built into the occupation. Similarly, compliance can best be understood in the context of the availability of resources and the needs or interests with which some providers address these same occupational facts. In a final section I discuss provider experiences with state officials and with representatives of the other services offered in conjunction with the regulatory mechanism. I thus introduce a new set of relationships relevant to the family day care provider's daily life.

## A Brief History of Regulation

Until the 1970s most states either excluded family day care from regulation altogether or included it within a system of formal licensing that applied similar standards to family day care homes and child-care centers. In recent years many states have introduced a system of either voluntary or mandatory registration for the regulation of family day care homes. Registration usually entails self-certification among family day care providers rather than pre-approval inspection by a licensing agent; it is often associated with spot checks to ensure compliance. Registration has contradictory aspects: On the one hand, because its rules are generally less stringent than those applying to licensed facilities and because it does not require a visit by a licensing agent, it is perceived by some to be a form of deregulation; on the other hand, because of this "loosening of standards" it attracts larger numbers of providers and thus brings more homes within the regulatory net. By 1985 twenty-seven states required family day care providers to become licensed, another thirteen relied on registration, four states combined these two systems, and six states certified only those homes receiving public financing.[12] In spite of this new technique, the opponents of regulation can claim victory by default at this point: Although almost every state now has some system of licensing or registration on the books, most observers estimate that upward of 50 percent of all family day care remains unregulated in fact.[13]

Vermont's regulatory history parallels that of many other states. In 1982 Vermont instituted a two-tiered program of regulation, adding more lenient registration for family day care homes; center-based care and larger family day care homes remained subject to licensing regulations. Licensed day care had to meet State Fire Prevention and Building Codes and Environmental Health regulations; the licensee also had to participate in a minimum of six hours of training per year. In contrast, registered facilities did not have to meet as extensive building codes, and the caregivers were not subject to training requirements.[14] In order to become a registered provider, the applicant furnished the appropriate state agency with a signed registration statement indicating understanding of and compliance with the "Family Day Care Home Registration Standards of the Vermont Department of Social and Rehabilitation Services," and enclosed evidence of a heating-system inspection. She was also asked to distribute three letters of reference to individuals (unrelated to her) who could "attest to the registrant's physical and emotional capability of performing activities normally related to providing child care and to the registrant's ability to meet the Family Day Care Home Registration Standards"; these letters were to be sent "directly to the Division of Licensing and Regulation without prior review by the registrant."[15]

Registration was required of all providers who offered care to children from more than two different families. Registered providers could care for six children of preschool age full-time (no more than two of these children could be infants) and could care for an additional four school-age children on a part-time basis. The provider's own children were not included in these numbers. Women caring for any number of children from two or fewer families could remain unregistered. At the time of the study, regulation introduced few new resources into this system of child care although only registered providers had access to the federal Child Care Food Program (CCFP), could apply for state funds for capital improvements, and could have their names placed on lists made available through resource and referral centers. In some areas, registered providers were contacted by outreach workers and received a monthly newsletter; they were also notified of, and urged to attend, training opportunities. These "benefits" provide the context for understanding attitudes toward regulation and assessing its impact.

In Vermont, as elsewhere, registration has appeared to be attractive to providers who could not—or did not choose to—meet the conditions of licensing. By 1986 (the year in which this survey of registered providers was conducted), there were more than four hundred registered family day care homes. Easing of standards did not, however, mean complete regulatory success. A 1985 statewide study estimated that approximately 75 percent of preschool children received unregulated care from approximately twelve hundred different providers.[16] The proportion of those children in *legally* unregulated care was not assessed.

## *Differences Between Registered and Unregistered Providers*

Registered and unregistered providers differ in a few of their demographic attributes.[17] Although most providers in both groups are married, a higher proportion of registered providers are single (14 percent versus 6 percent). The number of children born to each woman is the same in both groups. Registered family day care providers, however, are older (mean age of 35.2 versus 32.9). As a result, fewer of the registered providers are caring on a full-time basis simultaneously for their own and other people's children (52 percent versus 77 percent). A higher proportion of registered providers have received some education beyond high school (54 percent versus 41 percent). Even so, a higher proportion of the unregistered providers come from families with total incomes above $25,000 (55 percent versus 41 percent).

There are also differences in the motivation for opening a family day care home between the two groups. Fewer registered providers say they chose this occupation in order to stay home with their own children (83 percent versus 91 percent) or because they could not afford alternative care for their children (23 percent versus 36 percent); more of them say that they could not find another job which was equally enjoyable (19 percent versus 10 percent). (A note of caution is necessary here: Although the differences between the two groups are statistically significant, the vast majority of the women in each group give the *same* responses to questions about motivation.) The registered providers also enter the occupation with more training than do the unregistered providers: 52 percent of the former group, in comparison with 28 percent of the latter, had received training for work with young children beyond that offered in the conferences or workshops made available to registered providers.

The structure of the work is different for the two groups of providers as well. Registered providers care for more children each week than do unregistered providers (an average of 7.7 versus an average of 4.6), they work with larger groups of children (a maximum of 8.2 versus a maximum of 6.1), and they work longer hours (an average of 48.7 per week versus 42.9). While they are no less likely than unregistered providers to take care of children overnight or during weekends, and are equally likely to accept children on a "drop-in" basis, they do protect their days off more rigorously. The fees they charge are similar to (if slightly lower than) those charged by unregistered providers. Even so, because they care for more children, for more hours, and bill more consistently (i.e., they are more likely to charge for sick days), they earn higher weekly incomes (mean of $196 versus mean of $118). They also earn, on average, a higher proportion of the family income (41 percent versus 28 percent).

Registered providers have been working in the occupation for more years than have unregistered providers (mean of 5.1 versus 4.1). They also anticipate staying longer: 41 percent of the registered providers say they think of family day care as a "permanent occupation" in comparison with 18 percent of the unregistered providers. Although the women in the two groups report equal satisfaction with the work of child care, registered providers report higher levels of stress: On a scale scored from 1 to 5 with a lower score indicating a higher degree of stress, the mean for registered providers was 2.2 in comparison with 2.4 for unregistered providers. The higher stress might result from the fact that registered providers not only take care of more children but also have more frequent problems with late payment, late pick-ups, and difficult and disliked children. In fact, if we control for the number of children in care, differences in stress levels disappear.

In the absence of longitudinal data, we can not say whether these differences precede or follow regulation. Nor can the bipolar distribution of providers distinguish among women at different stages of involvement in the regulatory system. Some of the registered providers had just completed this process; others had been registered for as long as four years; still others had been licensed before that. Some of the unregistered providers might have been considering registration as a possibility for the future; others were adamant about evasion.[18] Therefore, rather than attempt to speak about causality, I look at the differences in the context of the dilemmas discussed above.

## *Evasion of Regulation*

### TRADITIONAL EXPLANATIONS FOR RESISTANCE TO REGULATION

Several different explanations for evasion are tendered in the literature.[19] Two frequent explanations—that providers are ignorant of the requirement to register and that providers want to avoid the costs of doing so—are considered first.

Some argue that resistance to registration is the result of simple ignorance of the law.[20] This explanation can not account for the failure of the women in this study to register. Only 3 percent of the unregistered providers checked among alternative responses on a forced-choice questionnaire that they *had never heard of* registration or licensing; only 17 percent of this group checked the response indicating that they did not know about the procedures for becoming registered. Almost all of those interviewed had strong feelings about the issue.

Of course, even when aware of registration, providers do not necessarily have accurate information. In fact, many of those who assumed they were not required to register (half of those responding to the questionnaire) may well have been unaware of the content of the law. Fewer than half of all unregistered providers could say correctly how many children are permitted in a family day care home; the others were evenly divided between over- and under-estimators. In interviews women made such comments as, "You don't have to register unless you have seven children and I would never have that many"; or "None of my children are full-time. Only one of them comes more than three times a week. So I don't have to register." Ignorance about specific details of the regulation guidelines may thus be a matter of deliberate choice.

Other observers argue that a concern about anticipated costs produces evasion.[21] Registration places a cap on the number of children and therefore limits income. Because registration involves governmental notice, the possibility of evading taxes is reduced. And registration requires the purchase of such devices as smoke detectors, metal garbage cans, and fire extinguishers; it can also entail expensive home modifications. Anticipated costs alone, however, can not account for resistance to registration among this particular group of providers. First, as mentioned, those who are unregistered generally "choose" to have fewer children than do registered providers; only 13 percent of unregistered providers ever have more than six children present at any given time. Registration, then, rather than cutting off income for this group, might enable them to be more successful financially. The second issue—a desire to avoid paying income taxes—may have more validity. Many of the unregistered providers do not report the income they earn from family day care; the tax-free nature of those earnings is part of what makes family day care an attractive occupation. This is especially true of those women who are receiving other kinds of governmental support (e.g., AFDC) that would cease if they acknowledged their day-care incomes.[22] On the other hand, although providers readily admitted to concealing income, only one interviewed provider said that this was a reason for resisting registration, and some of the unregistered providers do report their incomes. Moreover, many of the *registered* providers are selective about income reporting as well. The last cost issue, that of the modifications entailed, also appears moot. Only 4 percent of the unregistered providers checked the response indicating that they could not afford the necessary purchases or modifications; in fact, many unregistered providers voluntarily comply with these requirements. Finally, at an absolute level, the unregistered providers have less pressing financial needs (average family income among unregistered providers is higher than among registered providers).

Other explanations for evasion, such as the assertion that providers regard licensing as a "complex government hassle and unnecessary intrusion," or that providers are fearful of the effects of regulation, are best understood as positions emerging from the provider's daily work as she negotiates her relationships with children, parents, and members of her own family.[23]

## EVASION AND THE DILEMMAS OF PROVIDERS

In each set of relationships providers face a series of dilemmas. Those who choose to remain unregistered perceive the impact of regulation on these ongoing concerns in largely negative terms.

*Relationships with Children.* A major dilemma for a family day care provider is how to define and defend her caregiving style. Almost all providers see themselves as offering homelike care and being like a mother to the children they tend on a daily basis; they generally rely on their own experiences (rather than formal training) as the basis for skill development. Regulation is perceived as a multifaceted threat to this style of care.

Some providers associate regulation with a greater emphasis on educational activities for the care of young children. They do not believe this alternative set of expectations is appropriate, and they view them as additional and unnecessary burdens to be imposed on a home setting.[24] Providers also want to preserve the right to make decisions about the care they offer. In 1984 a bill was passed in Vermont prohibiting the use of any kind of corporal punishment in public settings such as schools and day-care centers; among the most vociferous opponents of the bill were family day care providers who believed this legislation violated the rights of parents and providers to make decisions about discipline.[25] Two years later providers said a desire to preserve for themselves the right to implement this kind of discipline (when they had the backing of a parent) now stood behind their resistance to regulation: "I watched the debates in the papers about registration and licensing. If mommy says it's okay to smack the kids, then smack the kids, if you have permission." In fact, almost half (42 percent) of the unregistered providers agreed with the statement, "If a parent gives permission the day-care provider should be able to spank the child."

Providers associate regulation with more general restrictions as well. They defend the flexible nature of the care they offer; they suggest that governmental intrusion will inevitably curtail their ability to make accommodations:

> I had a lot of people call me for baby-sitting wanting to know if I was registered. They did not want their children in a registered day care because there's so much intervention. If I were registered and an inspector happened to come in on a certain day when I had one of the children that had the light temperature or a green runny nose, I would be closed down because you're not supposed to have those children around other children. And that's why day care has gotten the bad name. Because they can not be as accommodating with all the regulations as somebody who's not regulated can be. And it's too bad because the children suffer for it.

> I wanted to be flexible enough that if somebody called and said, "Could you just take my kid for the day?" I didn't want to have to sweat it out that [a licenser] or somebody is going to walk in the door that day and say, "Hey, you've got too many kids."

One provider drew on her experience with regulation for the care of the elderly to demonstrate how formal rules could interfere with responsiveness:

> I think it's appropriate but they take too much control away from you. I found that they didn't give you any leeway to be

> human. We're with our [elderly] people twenty-four hours a day and you're expected to behave the same way toward the people twenty-four hours a day in a businesslike manner and that's not why we're here. This is a business, yes, but we're dealing with people not commodities. And they're not the same way all the time and I know one day a month I'm a bitch.

Regulation is also linked with the possibility of scrutiny. Perhaps because these women rely so extensively on unmeasurable experiential preparation (and because they have limited education and training), they are unsure about whether they could "pass" a professional evaluation. This hesitation emerges as a total rejection of locating quality control in an outsider rather than in the provider's own assessment of her capabilities. Some unregistered providers believe, as do some registered ones, that regulation might be appropriate for *other* people who can not be trusted to exercise their own judgment. But they think that such individuals are not the rule: Only 28 percent of the unregistered providers agreed with the statement, "Because there are a lot of people who can not be trusted to care for children well, the government should supervise child care more carefully." And they differentiate between themselves and these exceptions: "It's a good idea because it helps to limit the number of kids a person is watching. I wouldn't take more kids anyway"; "I just don't see what the big deal is. I just feel if you can handle it then it's up to you. I don't know of any restrictions—I haven't looked into it. . . . I've done it for seven years now . . . I just figure if I don't take on any more than I can handle, I'm fine."

They also confront the issue of assessment head on, arguing that rules ignore the more subtle aspects of good care: "Quality comes from the make-up of the individual. Licensing provides externals—fire extinguishers, medicine up high. . . . As far as warmth, concern for a child's well-being, hugs, and understanding—that comes from inside a person, and no one can regulate one's thoughts."[26]

*Relationships with Parents.* As we saw in Chapter 2, relationships between providers and parents are enormously complex, alternating between two sets of contradictory norms as providers and parents define obligations and navigate the delicate issues of control and intimacy. In discussing why they refuse to register, providers reiterate their allegiance to the norms of a social exchange: "I not only baby-sat their kids, I was a mother to [the women]"; "I'm not registered because I do it mostly for my friends." They fear registration will substitute official certification for parental trust and that this substitution will inevitably erode whatever goodwill now prevails. One woman who had dropped her registration said she now felt less threatened by the possibility of a lawsuit. Although no one had ever threatened her in this way, she simply felt that as long as she was registered, "it could happen." The women also believe this substitution will diminish the significance of appreciation and trust as nonmaterial rewards:

> My girlfriend up the street said she knew me and if her kids had to be with somebody I was the first choice.

> The moms are intelligent enough to choose whether or not I am a good baby-sitter and they feel that I am. So I never felt the need to register. I feel that it should be the moms' decisions. I'm friends with everybody I baby-sit for and they know me and if they felt that I wasn't capable they wouldn't bring their children to me. And everybody I baby-sit comes first with their children. And I would hope that everybody would do that and realize—you can tell what a person is like by visiting or through word of mouth.

> I don't feel [registration] means much—the parents trust me.

As these comments demonstrate, the providers distinguish carefully between parental and official oversight. Most providers maintain an "open door" policy: "Parents come in and out and that's enough to protect the children." They are critical of parents who carelessly choose a family day care provider. But they see this kind of oversight as being sufficient: Eighty percent of the unregistered providers agreed with the statement, "Parents can judge for themselves whether or not another person will offer safe and good care for their child." In contrast, only 4 percent agreed with a statement suggesting that officials alone could ensure good care. They distinguish between a parent's intimate knowledge and official ignorance. And they defend parents' rights against arbitrary standards.

*Relationships with Families.* Even without regulation, almost all providers have difficulty mediating between familial and occupational concerns. Because registration can carry with it obligations to restructure the private domain, and to allow an outsider entry into it, providers believe it will inevitably undermine the right to resolve decisions in favor of the family. As I noted in Chapter 4, some family day care providers are under pressure to deny they are working at all; this is especially true when they are making only a small contribution to the family's standard of living. If they do not register with the state and if they do not report their incomes, they conceal the external signs of legitimacy that might threaten the implicit bargain they have made with their husbands. Most unregistered providers are caring for their own children. Having chosen to stay home in order to ensure the kind of care she believes is appropriate, a woman does not want to make adjustments in style or introduce distinctions between her own and other people's children.

The ideology of family privacy is *used* to defend these priorities. Although only a third of the unregistered providers said that opposition to government involvement was a reason for evasion, 52 percent agreed with a statement suggesting that child care in private homes should be immune from governmental oversight and 49 percent agreed with a statement suggesting that the government is already too involved in the life of its citizens. Unregistered providers can understand why parents might want the protection of regulation. Even so, they are committed to preserving their own privacy:

> I didn't want to have to hang a paper-towel rack in my bathroom because they're not allowed to use towels. I just don't want to rearrange my whole house. My house is clean and it's neat and it's childproof. . . . I didn't want the regulations. That's not really fair because if I had to send my child to child care I would probably want someone who's registered. . . . With all the child abuse that goes on, I think [registration] is appropriate. Yet that's touchy because it is still your house . . . you're talking about or your family and you don't want to change your whole life-style for it.

Two themes thus predominate as providers discuss resistance to regulation. First, they strive to find an orientation toward their work that resolves competing claims. They walk a fine line between understanding family day care as part of a woman's duty and viewing it as the expression of financial need, between establishing a social relationship with parents and accepting more contractual arrangements, and between seeing themselves as engaged in work that primarily responds to family needs and defining themselves as being involved in an independent entrepreneurial activity. They speak contemptuously of registered providers who they believe are simply in it for the money; they say registration has "a bad reputation" because it indicates a businesslike orientation toward the care of young children.

They are convinced that registration would inevitably transform their ongoing activities: "I wouldn't want that—it would be a business. I just feel like I'm mommy taking over for the daytime"; "Registration puts too much of a business slant on it—I didn't want it to be a business." Implicitly and explicitly they suggest that they are concerned about a possible redefinition of an activity they have balanced with and even subsumed within a traditional understanding of a woman's role.

An equally significant, and not entirely unrelated, problem for a family day care provider is how to maintain control—over her caregiving style and, more broadly, over her working conditions. Even without regulation, substantial limits to autonomy exist. Unregistered providers regard regulation as an additional constraint in an already overly constrained setting. They suspect that parents will become more exacting in their demands. They learn from friends, or they know from their own prior experiences (working as licensed providers or working in day-care centers), or they simply guess that registration can be a "hassle":

> Other people that I know who are registered or licensed have had major problems. One had a problem with an inspector outside of their home questioning the parents, another one had problems with them just walking in in the middle of the day, and another one had them walking in at 6:30 in the morning.

> I would probably close down rather than become registered because of the red tape and all the picky little things. The punishment thing is fine with me, but there are all kinds of little things [such as the requirement of] so much space [for each child]; there's just so much that it wouldn't be worth the aggravation. I'd rather close down than be licensed.

In short then, resistance to registration, or the motivation to evade regulatory efforts, appears rooted in several of the dilemmas facing family day care providers.[27] Their arguments may sometimes be wrapped in the ideological garb of opposition to governmental intrusion into the private domain. What is at stake, however, is the manner in which the provider has sought to make her work meaningful and satisfying within a specific set of ongoing constraints.

Unregistered providers have some limited success in defending these stakes by opting for the norms of the private domain rather than the norms of the market. These women represent a very early stage of occupational development (even if as individuals they have been involved in child care for many years). Given the material and ideological context in which *all* family day care providers offer care, and given the specific resources available to these particular women, they have reason to view privacy and informal negotiation as the best solution. But this stance carries its own dangers. They can not altogether circumvent state involvement. Their privacy may become so extreme as to be imprisoning: They can disentangle themselves neither from their domestic responsibilities nor from community expectations for reciprocity. They have only modest grounds on which to claim the reimbursement they want and need. And they forego those resources of the formal economy that can actually augment autonomy.

## *Understanding Compliance*

Registered providers have the same stakes at risk. They defend them in a different way.

*Relationships with Children.* There is almost no difference between registered and unregistered providers on the fundamental issue of caregiving style: 71 percent of the former and 83 percent of the latter group indicated strong agreement with the statement, "I think the role of the day-care provider is to be like a mother to the children in her care." Nor are there differences in the *ordering* of their caregiving priorities: Providers in both groups stress good nutrition and a homelike atmosphere; training in social skills and consistent discipline follow in importance; educational activities and a structured or planned day trail far behind. This suggests that registration neither alters the basic content of family day care nor selects out those providers with a set of more formal, educational concerns.

Other evidence confirms this conclusion. When asked (in my turnover survey; see Chapter 7) whether registration had an impact on the care of children, half of the registered providers responded affirmatively. Those who did so drew attention to the fact that registration provided useful guidelines. In interviews the providers made clear that the stylistic issues under consideration in these guidelines were those they already implemented (e.g., reliance on "time out" rather than corporal punishment, use of seat belts, limits on the total number of children). Registration is thus viewed as helping the provider sustain a stance she has previously decided on, particularly when pressures might otherwise cause her to violate her own beliefs or values: "I think it would be really easy to get overloaded and go over your limit if you're not registered"; "I think it's good that they say absolutely no [about corporal punishment] because for people to draw the lines sometimes is difficult"; "It's like with the amount of kids you have, they've got to set it somewhere. I feel like I'm being such a goody two shoes here. But I feel like they've got to draw the line somewhere because there's some people that would really get out of hand with that."

While they acknowledge that some unregistered providers might also be providing excellent care, they insist that without regulations abuses occur more frequently:

> I think everybody should be [registered]. I know there's some women out there that are really good that aren't registered. But there's a reason for the law. You can only handle so many kids. There's a lady down the road with twelve kids every day in a teeny tiny little house. And I don't think that's right for the kids. . . . But then there's a woman down the road who had an unregistered day care. . . . and from what I know about her she's real great. She has like four or five kids there and none of her own who are little. And I've heard wonderful things about her. And I feel real bad for those people [who get stopped] but the others—something should be done.

Nevertheless, there are some subtle shifts in caregiving style worth noting. There are differences between the registered and unregistered providers in the absolute weight women in each group place on the development of social skills and applying discipline consistently: The former think these issues are more important. However, the difference between the two groups is more pronounced (and only statistically significant) when a provider is caring for a small group of children, suggesting that registration is associated with more attention to a child's social development and with greater self-consciousness about discipline even when these changes are *not* determined by the demands of larger groups of children.

If registration is threatening to women concerned about evaluation, it is not surprising that those women who are more highly educated and more highly trained are less fearful. Education equips providers with the language skills necessary to defend their style; it might also enable them to meet licensers on an equal plane. Training—whether it is used or not—prepares them to articulate the value of specific features of the care they offer.

*Relationships with Parents.* All providers bitterly resent the abuses they believe they suffer at the hands of parents. Registered providers say they experience some of these problems more frequently. Because the regulatory process itself focuses attention on contractual issues, an awareness of these problems may be heightened through the act of registration alone; registration may also be sought by providers who are eager to avoid these kinds of conflicts when they decide to enlarge their clientele. Cara Brown, for example, said, "I decided if I was going to expand. . . . I would have to set some guidelines because I didn't want to have to take care of [sick children] all the time. . . . When I decided to really go out for it [and take more children] I sent for a couple of booklets I'd seen on operating a family day care. . . . I decided there were certain things I wanted to be covered on." Differences between registered and unregistered providers (with respect to the frequency of late pickups and late payment) disappear when we control for the number of children in the provider's daily care. A willingness to comply with registration may simply be a practical response to the problems associated with dealing with more clients.

The two problems that persist (when we control for numbers of children) impinge not only on contractual issues but on those of control and intimacy. Registered providers have more frequently had a child they found "difficult to care for" and have more frequently "disliked a child." (This latter problem only differentiates among providers who care for a small number of children.) A provider's attempt to deal with these situations might fundamentally threaten her relationship of implicit trust: She may even have to reject a parent's recommendation about discipline ("Parents always say, 'Well bop them if they need it.' I say, 'I'm not allowed' "), and she may have to refuse to care for a child altogether. She may thus *need* the intervention of a third party.

*Relationships with Families.* As long as a provider includes her own child in her family day care group, and as long as she cares for only a small number of additional children, she may claim (fragile as this claim may be) that her work is *for the family.* The claim is eroded when her own children no longer profit so directly from her staying home. She also has less reason to be opposed to intervention in issues of style since the care of her own children is no longer at stake. Earning a higher proportion of the overall family income gives her some power to redefine her involvement in the occupation vis à vis her husband (much as it gives her power with respect to other family issues). Registration may help legitimize this shift in priorities.[28] (Registration may also give her an occupational identity she can draw on to explain—to herself, to others—why, even though her children are now in school all day, she is *still* "at home.")

At the same time, this shift in orientation is not necessarily associated with acceptance of governmental intrusion into the private domain. If some providers use registration to help them create legitimacy, they also express ambivalence (similar to that expressed by unregistered providers) about whether the government should be involved in this kind of child care:

> I haven't found anything that's unfair. . . . but I have a problem with [regulation] in the first place—that you even have to be registered at all if you are taking care of more than two kids. . . . The state's always got their hands in everything. . . . The state just has to know who's doing what. . . . One of my big interests in doing day care was maybe that I could build up our income high enough that we could stop getting food stamps. . . . I guess what it really boils down to with us is that I'm just sick of the state having their hand in everything we do.

> In the overall view of things I don't know how I feel about it, whether it's a good thing [to have the government involved] in the long run or not. The big brother kind of thing. The government getting more involved kind of thing. Who knows what that will be like twenty years from now.

The two themes underlying resistance to regulation appear transformed among registered providers. Many of the differences between the two groups are relevant to the manner in which providers balance the social and market perspectives. Taken as a whole, the evidence does not suggest that the registered providers have completed this shift and that we should see them (as some of the unregistered providers would have us do) as cold-blooded calculators of reward and effort, driven by a business motivation rather than by affective, social, or familial orientations. This is not the case. Registered providers also speak contemptuously about women who are "in it just for the money," by which they mean *un*registered providers. They too find themselves giving free care and extending their work hours to accommodate children. They make these accommodations even when they have to violate the rules of registration. One woman, for example, who had already been caught by the inspectors for having more than the legally prescribed number of children in care, explains why this continues to happen on occasion: "I usually have just two infants. I hate to say no to anybody that I've taken care of before. . . . This last week and this week I've three children I haven't watched in about a year. The girl is two and I started taking care of her when she was six months old. . . . and the mother now has multiple sclerosis. And I won't say no to her."

But registered family day care providers have been in the occupation for a longer period of time, and they have learned to admit their own market interests ("After being in it for four years you have to look at it as a business"). They also have greater needs: Family income is lower among these women, and their work is more vital to that income. And they have indeed made family day care more of a "business"; they take care of more children, for more hours, in a more systematic way. Although only one half of the providers (in the turnover survey) said registration had benefits for *children*, four-fifths of them said registration had benefits for the *provider*. These included enrollment in CCFP, the availability of general information and resources, and access to clients:

> My sister was telling me about the benefits like the food program was available and the butter and the cheese programs. And then when I figured when you live out here, you can not get the price. . . . and I was really putting all my money into food and supplies. . . . I wasn't making a dime. Now I am on the food plan and boy does it help me. [Now] I'm not doing it for nothing.

All of the issues discussed above are indirectly relevant to autonomy: The registered providers seek more formal and contractual relationships as a mechanism for achieving self-determination. Registration abets this process in two additional ways.

First, regulation confers the protection of legality (70 percent said this was a reason for compliance). Providers do not want the hassles of being caught: "It is a law and this is my business. I didn't want to start this illegally and have somebody catch me and say, 'You're breaking the law,' and then have to go through registration and have it be nasty. They're very nasty when they catch people." Providers who have decided to enlarge their child-care group are often particularly concerned about getting this protection:

> I decided to become registered for the idea of going a little bit bigger and knowing that if I went bigger maybe somebody would report me as not claiming my income and things like that.

> I became registered because I wanted to take more children. If you want more than two families you have to be regis-

> tered so I did it. . . . I had always just had the two little kids and once in a while I'd have the extra kid around and I always felt guilty, as if somebody was going to be popping in at any minute. I figured if I was going to take that many kids . . . I didn't want to fool around with not being registered.

Second, regulation confers an occupational identity. Registered and unregistered family day care providers do not differ significantly in *most* of their attitudes. They do, however, differ in whether or not they mind being called baby-sitters: Whether the consciousness preceded or followed from registration, those who are registered resent it more. They feel they have the right to—and they want to claim—a status that distinguishes them from more casual caregivers and supports their claims to payment. A "reluctantly registered" provider showed that this shift sat uneasily on her shoulders: "I call myself a day-care provider. But I guess I am really just a baby-sitter."[29] In contrast, a voluntarily registered provider wanted this title:

> I say I run a day care. I don't baby-sit. I run a day care. We used to be baby-sitters and now we are a day-care provider or whatever. That [change] is important to me. I don't know. Sometimes I feel really funny having a college degree and staying home taking care of people's kids and on bad days or the wrong times of the month I might think why am I doing this. . . . I think that baby-sitters, and women who watch kids at home are pretty much down on the same level of the ladder as housewives and mothers have been considered in the last two generations. People haven't attached a lot of importance to that, and it's the same way with people who take care of kids. Sometimes I can see that in how some of these mothers react to me handing them my guidelines. . . . I think it's part of the way things have always been. But they probably are going to gain some respect for what day-care providers are doing because it is turning into more of an established type of business for a lot of people. But that's an outlook I think society has to change sooner or later . . . I think women are finding out that most baby-sitters are [having contracts] now—especially registered ones. . . . I think working parents are finding out this is the way it is.

In short, providers who want or need to transform this activity into a more profitable home-based business, and providers who are comfortable defining themselves in terms that modestly challenge the expectation that they care out of duty or altruism alone, focus on registration's benefits rather than its limits.[30] Registered providers already have some different resources with which to confront these dilemmas. At a later stage of occupational development, the additional benefits of the formal economy may compensate for the loss of privacy. Yet because the broader context for this form of home-based caregiving remains unchanged, registered providers do not thereby resolve persistent dilemmas. They wrestle with the same set of concerns as do their unregistered colleagues: Affection emerges in their relationships with children *and* parents; reliance on experience and ambivalence about commodification both undercut the market orientation; parents ignore contractual obligations, and they ask for (and receive) special consideration; and the providers' family members continue to make competing claims.

## *Experiences with State Officials and Outreach Workers*

The content of the relationships between providers and licensing agents and between providers and outreach workers deserves a close look.

### PATTERNS OF CONTACT WITH STATE OFFICIALS

*Unregistered Providers.* A provider can not, by evading regulation, ensure that the state will be irrelevant to her ongoing life: The existence of regulation (and the threat of observation) often affects her consciousness about what she does. It may also alter how she actually conducts her business. For those who have been noticed by a regulatory official, regulation assumes a more prominent and determining role.[31]

We know that most unregistered providers have heard of regulation. For those who think they are exempt from registration, this knowledge has only a minimal effect on daily activities. But those who believe they are not exempt may engage in efforts to conceal their activities; they may also live with some anxiety about being caught. Nancy Bingham, for example, said that she is "so busy that [she doesn't] have time to worry about the state finding out" about her. At the same time, she acknowledged that because she had heard about another family day care provider who was discovered when the state licensers followed her to her home, "we stay here." Anne-Marie Peck claimed she had no ideological conflict with registration but that she resisted it because she had too many children and giving one up "would kill me emotionally." On a day to day basis she found her anxiety about possible discovery to be one of the unpleasant realities of her job.

Some providers have already been caught. They have three practical alternatives: They can modify their care to remain within legal guidelines, they can leave the occupation altogether, or they can agree to come within the regulatory net.[32] Ruth Bolton represents the first of these options. One day while she was out for a walk with her day-care children, she was observed by a state licenser who followed her home. He demanded that she become registered or cease caring for children from more than two different families. She decided against registration partly for reasons having to do with cost: She did not want—and could not afford—to make the modifications on her house that would be necessary if she continued to have the children sleep upstairs. She also resented the threat to her autonomy: "As you get older you just don't want someone telling you what to do and to be on your back."

Marcia Palmer chose the second option. Marcia had the bad luck of opening her door one day to a state inspector who was asking for directions to another provider's house. Still involved in child care when interviewed, she was planning to retire from the occupation at the end of the month. She was bitter about what had happened, and she remained opposed to registration; Marcia's daughter, whom I interviewed after she had picked up several of her mother's clients, chose to offer family day care as an unregistered provider.

Providers who agree to comply with regulatory provisions after being caught, do so with varying stances. While some learn to accept and even appreciate regulation, others remains resistant:

> In a way I don't think it's fair the way some of the things are. If a person feels that they can take care of more than six children, why won't they let them? In the beginning when I first was taking care of kids it was mainly for a little extra income. And then they keep coming up with different laws and do's and don'ts and I'm sure that eventually I'll just get fed up with the whole thing and I'll just stop taking care of kids. Because every month there's something new that they're talking about doing and you get disgusted. I can understand a lot of the new things because of the child abuse that's going on. . . . It's just—it makes you mad. I want to take care of kids to bring in the income so I could stay home with my own kids and it's getting so you can't do as much as you want to.

*Regulated Providers.* As the last comment suggests, among regulated providers as well, state involvement can affect both their consciousness about what they should be doing and the ongoing reality of their work. However, because the registration procedures do not require an on-site inspection, and because the agency is understaffed, most providers never have any contact at all with a state official. They imagine what might happen if they were to be visited; they say the idea makes them "a little nervous." The procedures might thus have the effect of keeping providers "on their toes."[33] But most providers say this awareness does not affect what they do in any fundamental way: "I feel like I have to be so-so now and run it a little differently now, just in case I get checked up on or something. . . . But actually, I don't feel any difference. I could have a pigsty here and the kids would still be happy with me."

Some providers have been "checked up on" and not only casually, but as the result of a formal complaint.[34] Some have an easy time with these visits. One woman, for example, was caring for a child whose grandmother called the state and said that a child had been taken from the provider's home in an ambulance. Because the complaint was obviously false, the issue was easily resolved. But these visits can have a devastating impact. The providers' stories highlight the intrinsic conflicts between the state's obligation to respond to complaints and the rights and needs of the women offering this kind of child care.[35]

As a registered provider, Sherry Menard had been visited uneventfully several times by state licensers making routine checks. Her troubles began when she fired a high school student she had been employing to help her clean. The student lodged a complaint about mistreatment of children. As Sherry reports, two licensers showed up at her door unannounced and began to question her without telling her the content of the complaint. They also spoke independently to parents, telling them that they should look for different care since Sherry's services might be shut down. Several months passed without resolving the case; the uncertainty became so overwhelming that Sherry decided to stop providing child care. Like the unregistered providers forced into stopping or compliance, she remains angry and disappointed: "I have no other way to make a living and it's a very creative and good way for me to make a living. But I couldn't go on without knowing what was going to happen."[36]

We might note, however, that while providers would prefer to avoid observation, its absence also creates resentment. Providers mind that they reap little recognition for their efforts at compliance. Two-thirds of the registered providers who said they did not think that regulation was effective in improving child care indicated they felt this way because the rules were not enforced. Registered providers also mind that unregistered providers are allowed to evade the restrictions; they become the chief source of names of violators for state licensers.[37]

Even so, most providers mistrust the state. Only rarely—and often to preempt a complaint—do they call on licensers for help and support. (Only 9 percent of the registered providers in the turnover study said that they found the licenser a source of support for their work.) Priscilla Sabourin called the state when she was dealing with a mother who claimed that the previous provider had abused her child. Because Priscilla suspected that this claim had been fabricated, and because she was afraid that the same complaint might be made about her, she called her licenser for advice. Annie Flax called her licenser when a passerby berated her for allowing the children to wander too near the road; Annie was afraid the woman would follow through on her threat to report her negligence.

As all of these examples suggest, registration may be an important component of the context in which registered and unregistered providers work, and it confronts them with a new set of concerns. Among those unregistered providers who have had contact with state officials, a central issue becomes how to respond; among those who have not been observed, concealment may be paramount. Among registered providers the issue is how to take advantage of registration's resources without provoking its potential for disruptive intervention. But these issues are *salient* for only a few providers; for the majority, registration neither has a determining effect on the nature of their activities nor introduces a new set of significant ongoing relationships.

## PATTERNS OF CONTACT WITH OUTREACH WORKERS

Training and supervision of family day care providers is one of the chief benefits sought by those who favor regulation. As noted, at the time of this study, all training (except for that associated with enrollment in CCFP) was optional. It was offered to registered providers through the personnel of resource and referral and parent-child centers who made on-site visits, offered advice through telephone "warm lines" and newsletters, and arranged occasional workshops and conferences. The degree to which such resources were available varied within the state.

If resource and referral personnel insist they have something of value to offer family day care providers, family day care providers are equally insistent that their skills come largely from experience. (As we have seen, this insistence partially underlies resistance to regulation among some providers.) Yet many providers, whether or not they were registered, indicated on the questionnaire that they felt that training is important and that they personally would like to receive more training. An examination of the manner in which providers actually discuss training and make use of it when it is offered can help elucidate this seeming contradiction.

First, although two-thirds of the registered providers do indeed say that they want more training, only half of them ever participate in the available workshops and conferences; only one-fifth said on the turnover questionnaire that they found outreach workers an important source of support for their work. When asked why they don't participate in conferences, the providers give a variety of reasons. The absence of time and the presence of multiple demands loom large: "I'm too tired to go out in the evenings"; "There's no one to cover for me"; "I want to stay home with my family on weekends." They also say they do not believe they personally need the training. In fact, providers often suggest they believe training is important *for others.*

Many providers speak enthusiastically about workshops, conferences, and newsletters. Some talk about the ideas they get for activities and for planning a varied day. Most, however, are selective about the use they make of these resources, and they reject much of the information as being irrelevant, inappropriate, or out of touch with the reality of their lives. One provider, for example, casually dismissed the ideas suggested in a workshop on handling negotiations with parents: "As far as their advice and stuff—that will work with some people. . . . I just feel with a lot of these people that are giving out advice, it sounds great when they are talking about it but it can't be put into effect." Another provider was even more contemptuous:

> Dorothy Peterson is the woman that is kind of my go-between with the state and she suggested that I go [to a conference] and then I went to it. And I called and told her my opinion on it. I told her it was a waste of time. It didn't really deal with kids. It didn't help you with any situation. It was general stuff. It didn't have any specifics. . . . This was mostly just a waste of time.

On the other hand, both these women and many others spoke affirmatively about getting together with other providers. The woman who felt that the material offered could not be "put into effect" said the training did have other positive effects: "You know, what I think helps me out the most is going and listening to other people having the same concerns and stuff and just getting out." And the woman who felt her conference was a "waste of time" said she too valued a different kind of opportunity: "I like to go to the ones where you get a bunch of day-care providers together and they discuss what happened and what their situation is—things they have done you might learn from." Providers often speak about the support they receive from others "for the things you are already doing." Thus training might confirm, rather than challenge, their experientially based style of caregiving. At the same time, because they learn from others about the use of contracts and current rates, it strengthens some providers' hesitant movement toward a market orientation. And it gives support to a nascent occupational identity.[38]

The manner in which providers speak about their contact with the outreach workers who come to their homes confirms this interpretation of the importance of diffuse support rather than concrete information. A couple of the providers equated my visit to interview them with these other occasions: As one provider said, "Days like today when someone comes to visit . . . it makes it more worthwhile. The day-care trainer makes you feel like you are doing an important service and then you feel important."

## Conclusion

The evidence presented in this chapter suggests that regulation—as reality, as potential—has become a fact of life for most providers. Whether or not they comply with all of the requirements, registered providers are guided by a set of rules and are brought into contact with a network of state officials and outreach workers. No matter how adamantly unregistered providers oppose the concept of state involvement in the business of family day care, they too find regulation to be an element of the context in which they work.

The evidence suggests as well that evasion of regulation is rooted in the providers' perceptions of the implications of registration and, in particular, the manner in which regulation threatens to transform their ongoing relationships and limit the freedom with which they conduct their business. To the extent that some providers come to see regulation as a support, it appears that those who now stand outside of the regulatory net might move within its purview. But given the current regulatory bias minimizing provider concerns and the fact that regulation introduces few new resources into this system of child care, it is unlikely that regulation will soon attract all or even most providers.[39]

We can not evaluate here whether registered or unregistered providers offer better quality care to young children or whether training results in different kinds of interactions. Nevertheless, some assessment of the shifts associated with regulation is in order. In a study of lay midwives five years after a licensing system had been introduced, Rose Weitz and Deborah Sullivan found that the midwives had moved toward a more medical model of childbirth.[40] Although the midwives had initially offered their services in order to provide a distinct alternative to the hospital method of childbirth, in the years following licensure the midwives became increasingly sensitive to the potential for medical complications, more accepting of intervention, and more cautious in their selection of clients. They also moved away from a commitment to holistic care and introduced more hierarchical elements into their relationships with clients. Weitz and Sullivan attribute some of these changes directly to licensing: For example, the required training both heightened the midwives' awareness of pathology and created increased contact with medical personnel; the licensing process also forced more accountability on the midwives. The authors also suggest that these changes were not simply the result of licensure, but derived from social changes such as a growing social acceptance of midwifery (which meant their clients were more varied and might not share their ideological perspective), as well as from changes in their own lives such as a broader base of experience (which increased the likelihood of seeing problems), and from an enhanced desire to earn a living on their practice (which meant they had to reduce the time spent on each client).

Registration among family day care providers is associated with similar shifts. Ironically, these appear to have less to do with the content of child-care style than with relationships with parents and family members. Registered providers learn mechanisms for clarifying their relationships with clients (even if they are often unsuccessful in these attempts); they are more willing to impose their business activities on the household even when these activities do not directly serve the family's interest; and they come to think of themselves as having a distinct occupational status. Some of these changes can be directly attributed to regulation and its affiliated processes: Regulation does create opportunities for contact with a range of professionals, and it does offer services that assist the provider in transforming an informal activity into a more distinct occupation with tighter links to the formal economy. But, as was the case among the midwives, some of these changes have a more complex origin. As providers are brought into contact with others who share their occupational interests, they learn a sense of common identity. As more women enter the labor force, the demand for this service grows; what was once a set of casual arrangements achieves the public recognition and acknowledgment that the name "family day care" suggests.

All providers can now more easily enlarge their clientele and can advertise their services by calling on the new nomenclature. When providers choose, for whatever reason, to care for a larger number of children, a series of changes ensues. Not only are they more likely to be observed by state officials, but they are more likely to need the resources of registration. As they become more dependent on their child-care incomes, they want to maintain a steady stream of clients: Having their names placed on public lists is an advantage available only to providers who are registered. As they enlarge the pool from which they draw clients beyond the confines of kinship and friendship, opportunities for conflict (e.g., in child-rearing style) increase: An outside voice may become a significant resource. And as providers see more children they encounter pathologies outside the realm of everyday experience, for which they may come to need assistance from outreach workers.

While it might be tempting to line up these differences and assign a term such as "entrepreneur" or "small-business woman" to registered providers, the data preclude such an easy out. This study did not find that regulation resulted in *fundamental* shifts in orientation toward the content of family day care. Both registered and unregistered providers remain committed to providing homelike care, rely on the model of mothering, and root their skills in their own experience. Many providers use training to confirm and legitimize their own actions rather than as a mechanism for learning new child-care techniques; they find registration's guidelines acceptable in so far as they agree with their own decisions about style. They do not yet have access to all of the resources of the formal economy and they continue to adhere, albeit with somewhat diminished enthusiasm, to the norms of social exchange.

Of course, the differences between the effects of regulation on midwives and family day care providers may be attributed, in part, to the different kind of service each offers. Midwives do claim a distinctive knowledge base, and on this basis they allow hierarchy to creep into their relations with clients. But family day care providers are not yet claiming specialized expertise. Moreover, there are differences in the way licensing impinges on the two groups of women; for family day care providers licensure does not yet require extensive direct contact with professionals. The experiences of family day care providers also differ from those of other groups whose alternative services (e.g., shelters for battered women, hospices) have been regularized and formalized over time: Because family day care providers continue to be paid directly by consumers they are not subject to the demands of outside funding agencies; because family day care continues to be located in a private domain (though increasingly subject to public scrutiny), the providers remain free from both the protections and restraints of bureaucracy.[41] Resources are limited and cultural definitions lag. While registration might facilitate the movement toward a more regularized and impersonal business orientation, it alone is insufficient to enable providers to resolve in an entirely new manner the conflicting claims, interests, and concerns that mark this occupation. It does, however, take some of the possibilities for resolving these issues out of the hands of *both* parents and providers.

# *Chapter 6*

# A "DEVIANT" GROUP: PROFESSIONAL PROVIDERS

Professionalization represents another direction in which the activity of family day care could move. Ten of the seventy women interviewed for this study stand out from the majority of family day care providers because they say that they offer a "preschool program" in their homes.[1] In linking their activities to those of early-childhood educators, they explicitly align themselves with a more professional occupation.

Discussions of professionalization and the field of early-childhood education have two strands: a consideration of the possibility of ever achieving such a status and an assessment of the desirability of doing so. Those who hold out the goal of professionalization focus on specific actions participants might take to abet this process, such as requiring a CDA (Child Development Associate) credential for all child-care workers, assuming a common nomenclature, and educating the public about the occupation's important social functions. Drawing on the sociological literature describing the route other occupations have taken, William Ade, for example, summarizes a series of these necessary changes:[2]

> 1. Require a greater familiarity with the field's knowledge base. . . . 2. Identify and establish uniform criteria for admitting new members. . . . 3. Develop a more elaborate practitioner licensing process. . . . 4. Secure internal control of this licensing process. . . . 5. Demand a stronger position in the relationship with parents, school officers, and government.

Another group of observers believes that even with such actions the goal is unlikely to be achieved. To be successful, a profession must "steer away from a vocabulary that sounds too familiar to everyone."[3]

But, as Carole Joffe, for example, notes, "The problem for childcare workers is that the care of normal preschoolers is very familiar to everyone and especially to the parent-clients. Thus for a 'weak' profession, like early-childhood education, the main struggle with clients . . . is to be acknowledged as 'professional' in the first place—to make the leap from 'babysitter' to 'educator.'"[4] The overwhelmingly female composition of the profession may be another obstacle. Not only do women have low status in our society, but the prevailing cultural assumption is that women do this kind of work out of "love and duty."[5] In claiming expertise (and even the right to receive reimbursement for the care they give), early-childhood educators have to struggle to redefine "one of the main areas of social life of adult womanhood—the relationship with children and the responsibility of caring for them."[6]

Observers note barriers at the structural level as well. The escalating demand for child-care services, Joffe argues, may run counter to efforts to restrict entry into the field and thereby preclude the attainment of a distinctive "'license and mandate' . . . to deliver [these] services." Early-childhood education, she continues,[7]

> must compete for acceptance with neighboring professions, such as social work, and with a range of non-professional providers. . . . Although licensing requirements for childcare facilities exist in most states, they are often very casually enforced, and they usually deal only with the physical features of the facility, not with the qualifications of staff or the content of programs. Because childcare services are currently delivered under a hodgepodge of different arrangements, with minimal government regulation, it has been virtually impossible for any one group, such as early educators, to gain anything approaching 'exclusive control.'

Considerations of the desirability of professionalization take into account effects on both workers and clients. If some view the process as one that will bring autonomy, prestige, and economic rewards to workers, others are more skeptical. Some argue that professionalization might actually reduce the autonomy of practitioners when the process leads to a separation of conception and execution, as in a distinction between responsibility for the design and implementation of curriculum.[8] Others point to evidence suggesting that the marginal or semiprofessions have been most effective in gaining financial rewards when they view themselves as workers rather than professionals and allow unions to negotiate salaries.[9] From a somewhat different perspective, it can be argued that professionalization has proved especially problematic to women. The acquisition of a specialized knowledge base inevitably entails a denigration of the kinds of experiential knowledge women acquire through their informal work as caregivers. Even in the semiprofessions dominated by women, men often assume leadership, leaving women with the lower-paid (and sometimes more menial) positions.

With respect to clients (both children and parents) as well, observers find contradictory effects of professionalization. Proponents draw on the kind of evidence cited in Chapter 5 about the impact of training to buttress arguments for restricting occupational entry to those with formal credentials. But others argue that the acquisition of scientific knowledge can have problematic consequences. Kari Waerness describes this kind of learning:[10]

> In the context of science one understands from the position of an outsider, and learning means to develop the ability to formulate a body of principles based on what is common to a lot of phenomena and therefore independent of the peculiar and individual. . . . In science, one searches for predictability and control, the dominant criteria according to which scientific success is measured.

And she argues that this approach is inadequate for child rearing: "In the context of everyday life, it is foolish to seek 'certainty' in one's personal relations . . . because the relation between individuals is, by definition, something that cannot be subsumed under any kind of statistical generalization. Once that is done, the aspect of individuality vanishes." Moreover, the detachment of most professionals may be an especially inappropriate stance for those involved in the care of very young children. In fact, most professions have actually sought to shed caregiving tasks as part of the process of upward mobility.[11]

Professionalization also inevitably entails shifts in authority from clients to practitioners. Even more so than regulation, it may remove from parents control over the content and direction of child rearing. Many professionals, and in particular those whose activities receive state funding, find themselves involved in social control rather than social service.[12]

## *Characteristics of Professional Providers*

The stories of the ten women identified as professional providers can shed light on the question of what might happen if family day care providers acquired something beyond an occupational identity with entrepreneurial claims, and the problems entailed in their attempting to do so. These women differ from other family day care providers in a variety of ways.

On average, they were older (median age was thirty-eight) and more educated (eight of them had education past high school) than the other providers interviewed. They entered the occupation with more formal training and experience. Almost all of the professional providers had been in a classroom—as a teacher or as an aide—at some point in their lives. They are explicit about the relevance of this training and experience. When asked what they are good at, they highlight the acquisition of specific skills and concrete abilities that extend beyond patience and "maternal thinking."

They also experience the work differently. Only three of the women had their own children present during the child-care day. Although they generally had roughly the same size groups as the other women, these groups encompassed a narrower age range: None of the women cared for infants; only two watched older children after school. Eight of the women had a separate area of the house devoted exclusively to child care. Three hired assistants who came in at least once a week. Eight of the women included preschool activities as part of a longer day for the children in their care. As is the case for the majority of family day care providers, children arrived early in the morning and remained with them until mid- or late afternoon. The other two providers each offered limited sessions of preschool for children: One cared for children mornings only; the other held two separate sessions of her preschool. These two women are included in the analysis although they do not truly offer family day care because they were each in transition. The woman who offered separate sessions of preschool had formerly been a "traditional" family day care provider; her shift reveals insights about the difference between the two kinds of caregiving. The other woman was going to enlarge her preschool to include afternoon care in order to respond to the requests of parents for more time; her shift reveals the kind of pressures placed on women who attempt to limit caregiving within the home to a delimited, professional service.

The professional providers also claimed a different motivation for engaging in child care. Only a few of them mentioned a concern with being "at home." Most focused, instead, on the search for an occupational setting in which they could implement their own educational philosophy free from conflicting pressures. (Those women who do not have the certification necessary to obtain a teaching job in a school or day-care center viewed home-based care as a means to circumvent these requirements.) Carol Barnett, for example, had worked both in another woman's preschool and as a rehabilitation counselor. In each of those jobs she experienced personal conflicts with the official institutional mandate. Over time she formulated her own distinct goals: She wanted to offer care to a small group of children from low-income families; she wanted her school to be a "place where children *learned* while playing."

Thus if other family day care providers are impelled into caregiving by the particularistic requests of neighbors, family and friends, the professional providers view their mission in idealistic terms. They spoke about a general need for the kind of service they were offering and about their ability to meet this need. Some described themselves almost as "missionaries," with all its connotations of moral superiority: "I came to a rural area because I wanted to bring this kind of child care to a rural area. . . . I have ideas that I think would benefit the children and the community. Nothing is available here." Associated with this perspective is an identification of the deficits of those they are serving and an attempt to fill the gap with what they consider appropriate "cultural capital":[13] "I want [the children] to be exposed to nice—classical—music so that they have kind of an 'in,' an early comfort with sounds and experiences and activities that they might not have had without coming [to this preschool]. I want to help children to learn, to kind of make the world work for them."

## *Professional Care and Its Impact on Relationships*

A preschool program has a distinct meaning to the women under consideration. Most providers emphasize homelike care, with the elements of casual play, safety, nutrition, and discipline. If structure exists, it is based on the needs of children for adequate exercise, rest, and meals; occasional activities—coloring, nature walks, cooking—are introduced to flesh out the day. In contrast, professional providers derive structure from *programmatic* goals. These goals vary from woman to woman, depending on her particular skills and educational philosophy. Some are concerned with developing social skills: "A lot of kids had never been away from home before and were only children. I emphasized the social—learning to share and doing things by themselves, washing hands and going to the bathroom." Other are more concerned with advancing cognitive abilities: "I do kindergarten with the older ones and I provide a total preschool program"; "We went into colors and shapes, numbers and counting—all depending on the group. One group came more prepared so I did alphabet and adding with them." Still others focus on enhancing creativity: "I think I am particularly good at getting them to be interested in songs and music and dancing and creative expression." But all of them put program structure at the core of the day to differentiate what they do from what might happen in the home or in some other kind of child-care setting. As one provider said, "I believe in structure—that they know what's coming. I do not baby-sit. It is true I do child care but I believe in a total program. . . . I feel strongly about structure. . . . We have a theme each week and everything centers around the theme." The provider who formerly offered a more traditional kind of family day care, and cut back to a part-time preschool program, spoke about the difference: "I now do what I did during a whole day in day care. It's a lot more structured than what I was providing [before]."

For those who are working from a motivation to serve a group of children whom they believe might not otherwise have necessary skills, the differentiation between their care and that of mothers is made explicit and given a class base.[14]

## RELATIONSHIPS WITH CHILDREN

These women, then, are working with a different ideology about childhood and the role of education for young children; as several of these comments suggest, they are also drawing on a different model—that of a teacher rather than a mother—for the relationship between caregiver and recipient. As "teachers" they strive for greater detachment. Some encourage the children to use formal modes of address (e.g., Mrs. Smith or "Teacher"); similarly, they are less likely to refer to the children with the familial terms used by most providers.

Two aspects of the context in which they work abet this process. First, because they do not have to deal with their own children, issues of fairness and subjectivity do not arise. One provider thought about how her reactions differed when her own children were involved:

> When two children are having a dispute, when I'd see one of my own children having a dispute, there was a part of me tugging for my own kid. I was on his side. . . . We were still ultimately connected. . . . If children blow up here I don't have that kind of feeling. I'm objective. I'm aware sometimes where I'm being sensitive to both children. But I'm not on either side . . . and I can be more fair.

Another provider distinctly attributed structure to the fact that she had no children: "People who have their own children and are doing [day care] don't seem to have as much of a structured program as I do. It's more just come and play with my kids." Second, because they do not deal with very young children, they do not have to respond to needs that compete with teaching: "Right now I have a couple [of children] that are under two but when they grow up I prefer not so young. I really prefer the other. I prefer the teaching more than the care"; "I chose not to take small children because being a teacher I did not want to have very small ones."

In contrast to the women who seek rewards in attachment, the professional providers seek rewards in concrete achievements: "The work that I see hanging up there—it's production, it's something I can see. All of my children can write their names. Some of them couldn't even hold a crayon when they came here. I just love it. I guess it's all in the art of teaching . . . and that's why I like the preschool age." One woman said she wanted to give the children "a lot of creative experiences. They don't have to come out with a product. But by doing creative things they accomplish something." Seeing their role in less encompassing terms, these providers more readily recognize and adapt to limits to their authority: "I'm a person in their life. But mother means something different. Mother means an ultimate attachment. It's one of the few areas in tasks and things to do that there's a clear line where I don't belong. . . . I definitely do not feel like their mother. There's no struggle with that at all. . . . I had my children and that was plenty." Loss is also more easily accomplished. In fact, it is redefined as a new beginning for the child ("They go on to the next thing and I am glad for them") and for the provider: "When day-care children leave it bothers me. I wonder where they are. But I am a teacher and have children through the year. I get close. But as they leave others come in. I feel close to them but not so overly emotional that I can't handle that part. I look at the changes. It's time. I'm always excited to have a new group coming in."

If the professional providers are sometimes defensive about the distance they achieve, they believe they compensate with other aspects of their program:

> I guess I wonder about that, have I come on in too much of a distant way with them. [But] I think that even though I do come on as a teacher quite a bit—it's just my style—that they still like the security that I provide. They like the stimulation. What I'm lacking in the more casual, less structured, motherly-type provider, maybe I make it up in all sorts of fun things to do and bringing some beauty into their lives.

> I wouldn't say I am one of those day care providers that is overly mushy and wants them because they don't have

> their own. I don't have that. I want children of my own. But that's not the main reason that I am taking care of children. I like to sing with them and teach them. It's not like I can't live without them—I've heard other providers say that.

## RELATIONSHIPS WITH PARENTS

In Chapter 2, I suggested that the social perspective in relations between parents and providers is created—and sustained—by the provider's location in the domestic domain, the dynamics of attachment that develop between providers and parents, the uneasiness providers feel about claiming financial reimbursement for caregiving, and the fact that in the context of limited payment, nonmaterial rewards (including trust) become an essential component of the exchange. If registration bolsters the market perspective, it neither negates reciprocity as a basis for caregiving nor definitively creates legitimacy for the commodification of care. Professional providers work initially in a context of fewer social claims; they also strive to prevent their formation.

Three characteristics of the professional providers are relevant. First, they are not responding to particularistic requests for their services, and they are less likely to be enmeshed in their communities. Whereas 60 percent of the women who responded to the questionnaire were native Vermonters, only three of the professional providers were. Several were newcomers to the particular towns in which they were located; as such they did not have to negotiate claims of friendship and kinship. We could contrast, for example, Beth Forest, whose ties to one of her clients went back to the days when Beth baby-sat for her, with Karen Clark, who moved to her current home only because she viewed it as an appropriate site for her preschool—she knew none of the parents before they enrolled their children. Second, because many of the professional providers are older than the clients they serve, they are less likely to forge bonds around children's friendships or mutual interests. One of the professional providers commented explicitly on how her relationships with parents changed when she was free of these entanglements:

> I don't have problems with people pushing at the edges now because they are not really my friends. They meet me for the first time by bringing their child. It used to be the case when my own kids were the same age as the kids I was caring for—that was harder because they don't respect that you are doing a business, they don't pay on time and things like that. The way I work it now I get paid on time. It's much easier not to have a strong relationship with the parents.

Third, although to a great extent class congruity characterized the relationships between mothers and providers, in most cases of incongruity the mother had the higher social status. This pattern is reversed among professional providers. In some cases the provider's high social status underwrites the attitude of superiority described above. Implicitly, and sometimes explicitly, professional providers denigrate the parents with whom they work:[15]

> Very few of the children are from deprived backgrounds. They are not emotionally deprived. Most of the parents I've had have been well intentioned and take good care. But they are parents who don't have the same tastes in art and music I have. They have very few books, almost nothing on the walls, only a certain type of music. I think that children appreciate beauty when they are exposed to it. And they like it.

Professional providers also develop specific mechanisms to sustain distance from, and a professional stance with respect to, parents. By definition, they too offer their service in and from the domestic domain. But because many find room for a separate preschool space, they are less strongly associated with their family roles. They greet parents in the "classroom" rather than in the midst of cooking breakfast for their husbands or diapering a crying child. The identification of common interests between parents and providers is muted.

They also avoid opportunities for parents to make individual requests. Several of the providers said they initially met their clients in groups or by holding an "open house." They use these occasions as well as weekly newsletters to convey rules, which are applied universally. Cara Brown, a registered provider, described how difficult it was to enforce compliance with her contract: "One person said, when given the guidelines, 'I'm a very busy person and I don't know if I will have time to read it.' I charged her for times when she called without a twenty-four-hour notice. She got upset." In contrast, a professional provider commented, "I meet the parents in the spring before. I hold an open house and sit with the parents and talk about my regulations and my standards. I give out a form about what they have to expect for the year. I talk about payments. I get everything out in the open in the beginning." Similarly, although strict starting and closing times are not established solely to reduce contact, the collective arrival of parents tends to the same effect; it can also help resolve the problem of lateness. One provider said that at the end of each session she would have the children all dressed and ready to go ("The parents know that the children are waiting outside"). One provider, when a mother regularly came early and stayed to talk about her own problems, simply changed the opening hour.[16]

Some providers seek to enhance their professional stance by giving advice to and acting as a source of information for parents. One provider, worried that parents would not respect her because she had no children of her own, repeatedly offered evidence of her formal knowledge: "I give them photocopies of articles and they do respect me as someone who knows something about child care."

The fact that they believe they are not simply providing the same care that a mother gives underwrites their right to receive reimbursement. Whereas many of the other family day care providers prefaced remarks about wages with the proviso that they were not in it for the money, none of the professional providers did so. They too vary their rates. But they use objective criteria (e.g., whether or not a child is still in diapers) rather than a subjective assessment of the parent's capacity to pay.

## RELATIONSHIPS AT HOME

The professional providers impose stricter boundaries on their paid and unpaid work. Since many of them offer their child care in a space set aside specially for this purpose, that arrangement prevents it from spilling over into private space: "I like the concept of having children downstairs where they can not harm my space or themselves. I also have privacy upstairs for my own children." They also draw more distinct temporal boundaries. A significant minority of the family day care providers care for children overnight and on weekends and accept children on a casual or "drop-in" basis. Professional providers eschew these practices. They attribute their ability to do so to having defined themselves differently: "I'm not asked because I run it on a kind of professional basis. If I were doing *just* child care I would probably be asked more."

Boundary maintenance works in the other direction as well. The family and its demands are not allowed to intrude into occupational space and time. For the professional providers without young children, this separation is relatively easy: Their children return home at the end of the day when child care work is winding down. They also speak definitively about their right to impose this activity on the life of the household:

> I find my last two children are sick of what I'm doing. They'd like the house to be quieter. I have to tell them that this is my job—I say to them that this income helps us a lot and it is what mommy really likes to do. [It is] hardest on the one who is twenty-two and who is sensitive and a loner. But I have a right to do what I want to do.

Separation is more difficult for women with young children. Two of these women said they felt they were not being fair to their own children, and they dealt with their disappointment in the same way as the other providers—by redefining the meaning of motherhood: "I was disappointed in the beginning because I didn't have the quality time with my daughter I thought I would have. But it is more time than I could provide if I were working outside the home. So it is time and I'm not missing 'firsts.'" A third woman viewed her problems differently—and came up with a different solution. Because Carol's son had difficulty accepting his mother in the role of "teacher" and the transformation of his home into a "school," she sent him to another day-care provider during the instructional part of the day.

Professional providers strive to eliminate other domestic demands. They do not cook a noon meal for a spouse, and they limit housekeeping during the day to tasks directly associated with maintaining the preschool space. They are clear about their priorities: "I'm not cleaning my house and washing my windows. I can't carry on at home like daily living."

Whereas some providers see the use of family members for backup as part of an egalitarian exchange in a marriage or as part of the give and take of kinship relations, professional providers are less likely to rely on this kind of assistance. One woman who did use her husband in this way felt it was inappropriate:

> We try to keep our jobs somewhat separate. I try not to involve him into the day care unless I have to run down to the cellar and he can watch the children. I used to use the woman next door for respite and to go to the doctor and so on. She could cover nap time and things. But now she has a job. And since my husband works evenings and has more free time, I will use him to cover naps. He doesn't really like it but he knows that it is that or hire somebody for an hour so he does it. I really would rather not use him. But what else can I do?

And while most providers derive satisfaction from the intermingling of day care and family life, many professional providers would agree with one who said, "The key to my success has been keeping my business separate from my home life."

## RELATIONSHIPS WITH THE STATE

Professional providers favor regulation. The belief that their work is a distinct occupation and not just an extension of family life underlies this more ready acceptance: "I have no problem with the state telling what you can do—because it's not my home. This is my place of business. My husband is not allowed to come down in his nightrobe. This is my place of business. I have to keep things neat as part of the business." In fact, several of these women initially sought to be licensed in order to differentiate their activities from those of registered family day care providers; they failed often because of the more stringent requirements.

Active pursuit of regulation, however, does not ensure satisfaction with state policies. Professional providers are among the most serious critics of registration. They are disappointed that the process of regulation does not emphasize program development, and they view the regulatory effort as punitive rather than supportive of providers' efforts to give a high-quality service:

> I did have a John Jones as my licenser before and he was a weird one. I mean, I'm sorry the way licensing is, I really am. . . . because I feel that all they do is count numbers. There's so much more to day care than counting numbers. That is just such a trivia. He has come here two times and all he has ever done is count numbers. One time he came and he goes—really stupid—I was out here with a little one and he said, "When did you last change her pants?" I refused to answer that question. I absolutely refused to answer that question. I said, "I want to have a good relationship with you John but it's not going to be on that level, let me tell you right now." I said, "You know what I want from you in fact?" And I started to tell him. And he said, "How many children, let me count them." I hadn't seen him all summer and he said, "I've been in Minnesota at a symposium." And I said, "Oh, they taught you how to count to six?"

Most of the professional providers attend conferences and invite outreach workers to visit their homes. If, like other providers, they are critical of these activities, they do not subvert them. Their criticisms focus on the lack of sophistication, the lack of direction: "The trainer comes and she should be giving advice. Instead she just stands there and watches me and learns from me." They continue to participate, however, because they believe these activities are important to the process of professionalizing the occupation: "I would like to see it upgraded and I'm going to attend more."

## *New Dilemmas*

Professional providers appear to be fairly successful in their attempts to resolve three ongoing dilemmas: avoiding entanglements in intimate relationships with children; resisting many of the challenges to the market perspective; and maintaining boundaries between domestic obligations and paid work.

Even so, these women find it difficult to sustain a professional stance. Parents may accept distance; they do not always accept other attempts by the provider to redefine home-based child care. The providers who limited their child care services to less than a full working day found they repeatedly faced requests for additional time and that parents making such requests drew on assumed attachment ("She loves to be with you") and on assumed availability ("I didn't know you had anything else to do"). Many found that parents pressured for modifications of the program to meet an individual child's needs.

As we will see in Chapter 7, all providers are concerned about status, money, and isolation; professional providers speak about these issues in a distinctive way. Most family day care providers do not talk much about the objective status of their work; they view what they are doing as an extension of mothering. If they feel that mothering should have a higher status than it is currently accorded, they make few *independent* claims for family day care. Some providers do, of course, recognize that they are engaged in an occupation, and they resent the term baby-sitter. But for the most part even these women are seeking legitimacy for the transformation of family day care into a more formal exchange relationship (a business) rather than a professional occupation. (For example, the registered provider quoted in the previous chapter as being proud to call herself a day-care provider linked her status to that of mothers. She did not claim that she was doing something different.) In contrast, professional providers are conscious of status issues beyond those associated with payment:

> One thing I haven't liked—I feel I'm a professional—I do feel a lot of people who do it aren't—and people have made me feel as if "oh, you do that" just in the way that they treat me. It comes out that they think my job is not important. Or they say, you must get so sick of it being tied down. I resent that because this is my job. I try to say, don't you take your job seriously? I'm not home just minding my own children. This is my profession.

If both registered and unregistered providers have contempt for women who are "in it for the money," professional providers have contempt for women who provide child care without acquiring formal preparation: "I do know this is true, that there are a lot of uneducated people who feel they can do this work. I don't feel they are as qualified. But maybe that is what some people want. I'm not something for everybody. I do wish it were upgraded in some way. But who am I to say?" They blame parents for putting up with inadequate care and the state for allowing it to continue: "A lot of people who purchase child care want to have home influence and cut down on cost so they use families rather than strangers. . . . There should be public service announcements that tell parents how to purchase child care. . . . There should be general education about what children need in child care and then ways for people to be able to purchase that."

Professional providers also define the problem of isolation in specific terms and experience it in specific ways. They focus on their separation from colleagues; they regret the absence of a collective approach to child care: "I'm lonely in this job; I miss the team"; "I feel very isolated here. I am lonely and depressed. I miss the teachers' room." (In fact, two professional providers wept in frustration when speaking about this issue; in contrast, the more traditional family day care providers wept when speaking about children they had lost.) Visits by friends, neighbors, and clients do not fill this gap. Quite the contrary, they seek to avoid these interactions: "I can't really have visitors because it interferes in my program. Unless someone comes during nap time—but lots of times that is when I am getting ready for the next thing. I am a really structured person." But they miss the approval for, and confirmation of, the work they do. If most family day care providers find rewards in the parents' acknowledgment that they are doing a good job, the professional providers discredit this praise: "I think that the parents are happy with me. But I want them to be aware that I am working on skills with the children—that the water table is more than play." Having rejected parents, they seek reinforcement from those they consider professional peers:

> I can pick out the kids who go to kindergarten, who is going to be successful and who not. The teacher tells me that I am often right. I have a lot of contact with the school. . . . I do feel the kindergarten teacher respects me. She might tell me she is having trouble with a specific kid and ask me what to do. Sometimes the teacher will say she loves a particular group of children. Then, since most of them have come from me I feel real proud. They're mine.

Like isolation and status, money is an issue for all providers. Professional providers, however, focus not just on low earnings and late payments, but on not having enough money to sustain the program: They can not afford to repay the investments they have made in household renovations; they run short on those materials and supplies that are essential to their program; if the demand for their particular service is low, they have to admit children who are too young to take advantage of their special expertise. One woman feared that the inclusion of two-year-olds was transforming her service into "high class baby-sitting."

When interviewed, Sue North had been running a preschool in her home for just under a year. She prepared for my visit by jotting down a list of the ways in which her current job compared with her work as a kindergarten teacher. This list included many of the issues discussed above. Under "advantages" she started with being home with her own child. She then added the relief from bureaucratic hassles and conflicting institutional goals:

> I have a smaller number of children than I did when I was teaching so I can do more with them. I can make more of the snacks. I have no meetings. That was a big thing. . . . I was spending sometimes ten hours a week in meetings and that was time I could have spent working in my class. I don't have as much paper work—that's for sure. I guess you could say I'm in some ways my own administrator so whatever I choose to do as a theme or whatever I can do. This is going to sound maybe snobby but I can pick and choose my own clientele.

She balanced these with "disadvantages" which included not only the loss of "quality time" with her own child, but isolation from supportive colleagues, low status, high costs, and meager rewards:

> I have to buy my own materials. That comes out of the money that I make and I have no time to get the materials except for the weekends. I take home half of what I did when I was actually teaching. I pay my own health insurance because my husband isn't covered. . . . I have no paid sick days and vacations. I also have to provide extra insurance for the children. . . . It comes to about $125 a year. I get no professional support for problems. I'm used to having a speech pathologist or a nurse available. I do have some concerns with some of the children but I feel, even though I have worked with young children, that if I mentioned it in this situation I think that parents would take it as something that's none of my business. To many of them I'm just a "sitting service." Many of them still consider me a sitting service with a little extra things or something. But, I

> write lesson plans, and I buy my materials and I do all these things—and I'm looking at it as eventually down the road being recognized as a preschool. . . . I think one of the disadvantages, as I mentioned before, is that it's not recognized as a profession and it really is a profession I think. At least if I was going to send my child to somebody I would hope that they would look at it as something they were working at and not something they just had to do.

## Conclusion

Even if they lack professional status, child-care workers in institutional settings strive to achieve some differentiation between their activities and those of baby-sitters and mothers. They employ such mechanisms as task differentiation and hierarchy; at the very least they can draw on bureaucratic procedures for protection against particularistic claims.[17] For women who attempt this transformation in an informal setting the obstacles are greater: They can not present themselves as pure educators. Parents continue to view home-based caregivers as substitute mothers, and they make claims that assume altruism on the part of providers. They also seek ways to circumvent established rules and impose their own definition of good care. Financial pressures can preclude the creation of an ideal preschool group. The stringent standards of licensing forestall attaining that trapping of professionalism.

Professional providers *are* better able than their nonprofessional peers to sustain a market perspective and to achieve a limited autonomy. As some critics fear, however, they do so by rejecting nurturance and affiliation. Instead of identifying with their clients, they look outward to a community of professional colleagues; this alternative community gives them scant recognition. Thus they often find themselves more isolated and more self-conscious about their ambiguous status than do other family day care providers. And sometimes they wonder if they have made the right choice when everything they aspire to involves such struggle:

> I'm doing this because it's a calling in life, it's something I thought about a lot and decided to do. This is a career choice for me. But not many people think of it as a career. And I find it demeaning to work so hard, to have so much knowledge and so many skills and to get so little support. I did not want to *just* do child care. But I can't buy the materials I need to run a good program. Sometimes I can't even take care of my own survival.

# Chapter 7

# TURNOVER

Family day care is a short-term occupation. The median tenure of a family day care provider is three years. Within one year, 30 percent of registered providers have left the field; within two years more than 50 percent are gone.[1] While these figures might be lower than the turnover rates exhibited by center-based child-care workers, they are high enough to be a source of concern: to parents seeking to find reliable and consistent care for their children, to resource and referral agencies attempting to locate caregivers for parents, and to providers themselves searching for a satisfying home-based occupation.[2]

An extensive body of literature seeks to identify the reasons for turnover in a variety of occupations (including child care). Many offer useful insights into the process and the specific contribution of burnout, job satisfaction, and the availability of alternative occupations.[3] At the same time, these studies often tell us more about an outcome—turnover—than they do about the occupation in which this outcome occurs. In a critique of analyses of the experience of providing informal care for the frail elderly, Emily K. Abel argues,[4]

> Many . . . studies suffer from the shortcomings common to positivist social science. In order to establish connections between two variables it is necessary to abstract these variables from the context that gives them meaning. . . . In many studies . . . relational aspects of care are considered part of the background researchers seek (often unsuccessfully) to control. Thus even researchers who seek to tap the subjective responses of family members often fail to capture the emotional dynamics of caregiving.

This same criticism can be applied to studies of turnover in child care. They ignore personal relationships and the larger social context, which inevitably affect the meaning of such attitudes as "job satisfaction." "A related issue," Abel continues, "is that researchers often construct measures of complex phenomena that cannot easily be scaled." Thus, many studies of turnover seek to assess levels of stress. Such assessments inevitably fail to incorporate ambivalence, the extent to which stress in caregiving may coexist with—and, in fact, be unalterably intertwined with—satisfaction and joy.

In this chapter, I attempt to avoid these pitfalls by supplementing the quantitative data derived from a survey of seventy-five former day care providers with qualitative data derived from interviews with sixteen former providers *and* by focusing on contextual issues. As might be expected, I find the reasons for turnover linked to problems identified in earlier chapters of this book—as these problems are experienced in relationships with children, parents, members of their own family, and representatives of the state regulatory system. Many of these problems remained muted when providers were speaking from inside the occupation; some were even denied. But when they have time to reflect on the experience of family day care, providers reveal more fully the effort of balancing contradictory pressures and they acknowledge that sometimes the balancing act fails utterly. The analysis developed here ultimately serves as the basis for the policy recommendations in the final chapter.

## *Reasons for Leaving*

When providers were asked to cite the most important reason for *entering* family day care as an occupation, their answers were marked by a high degree of uniformity: 68 percent said that they wanted to stay home with their own children. There was far less uniformity in their answers to the question of the most important reason for *leaving* the occupation: No single response category accounted for more than a fifth of the respondents; many providers gave more than a single answer. In interviews as well the providers mentioned many different factors. Turnover is a complex process in which feelings about the occupation, ongoing occupational dilemmas, attitudes toward alternative employment possibilities, and material needs are merged.

Twenty percent of the providers who leave do so for reasons having nothing to do with the occupation itself. Older women retire, younger women give birth, women of all ages get sick, move, or are called on to respond to the needs of an elderly parent or a disabled husband. Even if we consider these as "extrinsic" reasons, we can also note that in many cases the organization of family day care permits the change if it doesn't impel it. Because the women doing this work may be perceived by others as "not working," they appear available to help assist a husband's business venture or to assume responsibility for the care of an ailing family member. Additionally, because the job carries no benefits (sick leave, disability pay), women who are temporarily disabled themselves have no alternative but to respond that they are not working. Many women drawn out of the occupation for these reasons regret leaving; some of them plan to resume their occupational role at a later time.

Of course, at one level, the explanation for leaving family day care among those without alternative constraints might be quite straightforward. Women begin because they want to stay home and care for their own children; when their own children are grown, they no longer have the impetus to do this kind of work.[5] And we do know that "stage of life" is a relevant factor for some providers—most providers do have their own children at home on either a full- or a part-time basis. But turnover rates do not vary dramatically with the age of the provider's youngest child (40 percent of those with a child of preschool age had left the occupation a year after the study in comparison with 60 percent of those with older children[6]) and very few (5 percent) providers actually gave as the most important reason for leaving that they had no more preschool children at home. (Many of the women with small children at home, if they stop doing family day care, either cease working for pay altogether or find an alternative home-based occupation.) Although the age of youngest child may be a contributing factor, it is rarely definitive. For example, Sally Wixted, when asked why she was leaving, gave this initial response: "My kids are all getting old enough to go to school and I just figured I would do it that long." Yet as she continued to discuss her feelings about the work of family day care, she acknowledged that she had not yet finished this stage of life (her youngest child had one more year before he started a half-day kindergarten program), that she continues to believe she must remain at home (she is substituting another home-based business for family day care), and that she is not certain she is leaving family day care permanently (she thinks it might be *easier* to do when her own children are no longer included in her child-care group). In fact, the more she talked, the more she suggested that a variety of factors had led her to reach the decision that, for now, she needed a change.

Moreover, among many women "stage of life" is negotiated. Although Judy Edwards had planned to provide child care in her home until her youngest daughter went to school, other factors intervened, and she had to weigh the needs of one child against her own needs and the needs of her other children:

> I had kind of thought that in another year or two I would stop anyways. . . . I kind of wanted to wait until my daughter was in kindergarten at least. The stress was high which was a big part of it. Also there was a transition happening with the families. I was at the point where I didn't want to take any new kids but was willing to commit to the kids I've had all along. . . . All the babies I had originally started with six years ago were all going into first grade this year so it seemed like the right time. Plus the insurance. . . . It just seemed that it wasn't worth it anymore working a twelve-hour day with added expenses and with having to take new kids—which is really the hardest, always getting new kids adjusted into the situation you've already established—and I just didn't have the energy for it. And my own children—now that the boys are going to be in school all day—it's too hard to go all day and when five o'clock comes I'm just not the kind of mother that I always hoped I would be at that time of the day. So I decided it was best for everybody.

In a somewhat different way, Sarah Stern revised her original estimate of how long she was going to remain in family day care, by reevaluating her child's maturity. This revision caused conflict with one set of clients:

> One person was very upset [about my stopping]. And her husband was very upset. Because they asked me when they started bringing their son here if I was going to be doing this until my son was going to be going into kindergarten and I said I planned to—and I did at that time. . . . But that wasn't what was in the cards. . . . I had stayed home with my son for four years. . . . For me that's the magic number. I always thought five was the magic number. I just realized when he turned four that he was ready.

A second plausible explanation—that women simply, after a time, do not like the activity of caring for young children—also fails to account for turnover. Some women do misjudge their own interests and the nature of family day care; they quickly learn that they are not cut out to do this work. But most providers, as is the case with center-based caregivers, find rich rewards in the daily interactions with small children and in the exercise of a set of experientially based skills.[7] They acknowledge the tedium, the repetitive nature of children's demands, the noise, the mess, and the squabbles. But if dealing with children is the most stressful aspect of their work, it is also the "best." When asked why they leave, they say, "It's not because of the kids."[8]

Many seek opportunities to work with children in a different setting. This search highlights the disingenuous nature of the response "it's not because of the kids"—a response that assumes (as does some of the feminist literature) that the experience of caregiving can be isolated from the context in which it occurs. Those who leave the field have found, ultimately, that the satisfactions they enjoy are spoiled by the difficulties of giving care in this setting.

If women give a variety of reasons for leaving, they also express shared concerns. The following discussion should sound familiar to the reader, since these providers reiterate problems identified while they were still in the occupation. The analysis is organized around contextual issues, starting with the immediate location of family day care in the domestic domain and moving outward to the broader social context for this work.

## PUBLIC CARE IN A PRIVATE SETTING

Situated in the private domain, family day care is experienced as an isolated and isolating activity; those who find "better" jobs often say that the opportunity for interaction with other adults is what makes these alternatives more desirable. Like mothers who care for their own children, and like other home-based workers, family day care providers have few such occasions: "I was tired of staying at home and not being around adults. I missed adults very much." In fact, as we saw in Chapter 3, their isolation might be more intense than that of other mothers.

As more women enter the wage labor force, there are fewer neighbors and friends who are also "at home" and available even to chat on the phone or to visit over a cup of coffee. Even if they are available, providers hesitate to call on these resources. Many already feel overburdened by the demands of community that fall on those few women still carrying on a "traditional" role; they are reluctant to increase the chances of requests for reciprocity or to engage in relationships which, because they cannot easily be confined, can disrupt their daily activities. If clients offer companionship—and for many providers clients not only become friends but constitute a major source of support—these ties too confound their attempts to clarify the boundaries between a social and a market perspective.

Providers find it difficult to forge links with others who do the same work. They occasionally make contacts through training opportunities or through their personal ties with women in the community.

They value these contacts for assistance, for help in designing policy, or for the opportunity simply to let off steam. But they rarely constitute a real support network. If professional providers bemoan the absence of colleagues who can sustain and legitimate their work, many of the other providers regret the absence of *any* kind of support.

Outreach workers have to cover too much territory to be of ongoing assistance; and they are seen by some as being affiliated with the regulatory mechanism. Providers consequently may be reluctant to ask for the help they need:

> I think a lot of home day care providers feel intimidated if they're having a really hard time and they have to pick up the phone and call somebody and say lookit, I'm really having a hard time, I need you to come over. Basically that's what Josie [the outreach worker] is there for. She's there to give you books and whatever. . . . And I think some kind of system has to be there because you really do feel like you're on your own at times and you're either going to take it out on your husbands—which a lot of women do—or some other provider. . . . I have three people who are home day care people that call me all the time, ranting and raving about some parent, or some kid or whatever. And you have to get it off your chest. I mean, I think it's dangerous. I think home day care is dangerous because you are by yourself and when you feel like going like this [she makes a shaking motion] there's less chance that you'll go like that than when you're working where some people are supporting you. And that scares me because of the children of course. . . . And I think that more has to be done. Like Josie kind of comes and she hangs out and she talks and she gives you books and she gives you toys but I don't think she really reads into what the situation is really like. . . . There's so many of us and I think she's only been here twice this year. . . . The whole program [is inadequate].

As this provider said, many women are thrust back on their own families for support. But this too can have its drawbacks. If husbands hear too much about the difficulty of doing family day care, they may tell their wives to abandon the activity altogether, particularly since they are reminded of their own failure to protect their wives from having to work.

Isolation also compounds the dilemmas of caregiving. Family day care providers are not just lonely, they *work* alone. If some find that every day brings new challenges and new excitement, others find they are stagnating. No one relieves them—even for brief periods of time—of the repetitive and constant demands of children. Ultimately some (36 percent) find that their health suffers: They report high blood pressure, headaches, back pains, and a greater susceptibility to illness.

The solution of "detached attachment" is difficult to sustain. The constant effort of maintaining distance can sap a provider's energy; over time she may find herself withdrawing. One provider explained at length how caregiving in a center-based context freed her from this struggle and thus enabled her to offer better care:

> I think that's part of what was making me burned out. I really felt that was where some of it was, from letting myself become too attached to the children. You have to keep a little bit of distance. Because, I think the fact that I had them here all the time they became . . . so much a part of my family that made it kind of crazy. . . . I haven't distanced myself from any of the children [at the center] but I don't have the hours with them. I think that makes a difference. . . . In a three-hour span you can't get as close. And you always know that there's somebody else that can take over there whereas [at home] there wasn't. I was their sole person for support, authority, love or whatever. I think [at the center] I always know there's somebody else who can step in and take over and do the same job that I'm doing and that makes a difference. You don't have to pull on yourself as much because you're not the be-all-and-end-all. . . . I think in ways it makes me feel freer to be able to communicate with [the children] and be with them . . . I don't have to feel I'm the only person who's going to get through to them.

Although family day care providers are isolated, they do not have the autonomy that sometimes accompanies solitary, entrepreneurial work. If "real mothers" have to produce children to the dictates of norms set by the broader society, and if they have limited opportunities for setting these norms, family day care providers have to respond to more direct and more numerous requirements. Parental oversight, state requirements, and, occasionally, the scrutiny of a husband all influence day-care style. Negotiating with these different parties causes stress.

Family day care providers do not even sustain true privacy by remaining at home. The public not only enters the domestic domain, it evaluates it. These evaluations extend beyond superficial issues such as cleanliness and spatial arrangements. A provider's husband and adolescent sons may be seen as potential threats to the safety of the children. Her children stand as representations of her caregiving capacity. Her background (whether or not she was brought up in a large family), her habits (smoking, drinking, cursing), her likes and dislikes, her passions and her rages are all assessed as parents seek care for their own children. There is no refuge from visibility; family day care providers are always public performers.

Domestic demands do not disappear as the woman takes on paid work in her home. The satisfaction of being "at home" constitutes one of the strongest appeals of the occupation; the stresses of being "at home" are also felt acutely, and they constitute a reason for leaving. Sometimes a husband insists, sometimes he merely withdraws support: "I put myself in a time frame, April vacation you're going to make this decision. My husband was pushing for me to give it up too. I was losing his support. He saw how overextended I was . . . and I was asking him for things . . . [like] leaving a list of things for him to do when he got home, maybe the dishes or something like that—because I had spent so much time on my job that the other things didn't get done." Sometimes women simply realize that the toll on their marriage is too great. But most often, they speak about the negative effects on their children: "When Tony started pushing eighteen months he got very jealous. It was incredibly stressful because every time I'd sit down with the [day-care] baby to give him a bottle, Tony would climb up on the kitchen table or do something like that. . . . He was very jealous and I felt he was missing a lot of 'mommy things.' When he was crying when I sat down with [the baby]—that broke my heart." And whether or not they actually say they leave for these reasons, providers allow themselves to speak openly, after the fact, about the strains they denied while still engaged in the occupation:[9] "I always wondered if I really benefited my kids by taking care of other people's kids at home because it was a lot more of my time and my patience was more worn out by the end of the day than it would have been if I had just had my own." They also say how much better family life is once they have stopped. Some focus on trivial or incidental family changes: For example, without four tricycles there is space in the garage to put the car away. Because they are not so tired of caring for children, they can allow their own children to have friends over to visit. In fact, they find renewed pleasures in these occasions: "I love having Billy come over [now]. . . . I feel like [his mother's] doing me a favor now when she lets him come. I can't believe I used to take money for that."

But sometimes the changes are more fundamental. They can

finally respond to pressing needs they had to ignore while engaged in family day care: "My youngest child is very active and aggressive and he takes a lot of my time. A lot of my time. By cutting down on the kids has given me more time with him. He goes to Early Essential Education (EEE) for his speech and I have to bring him there—and if I had more kids I couldn't do that and I couldn't work with him to help." They acknowledge greater family contentment: "They're all a lot happier. And my mother—she comes once a year at Christmas time—and she said that she felt that the children were less demanding on me for attention and that the household seemed a lot more stabilized. And I didn't ask her what she thought, but she just commented that she noticed that."

## THE BROADER SOCIAL CONTEXT

The need for child care is a consequence of women moving into the labor force. Social policy has lagged behind this change. Neither employers nor the government sufficiently fund child care; the structure of most waged labor is modeled on the norm of a male worker who could be assumed to have passed the responsibility for family life (including child care) onto his wife. But most women can not delegate these responsibilities; their wages are too low to enable them to pay adequately even for the support they need to continue working. The situation for single women is even worse. One consequence of these facts can be seen in the notoriously low wages of child-care workers of all kinds.[10]

But family day care providers are not just responding to the needs of others in offering their services; like those who enter the wage labor force, they too need to earn a second income to sustain their own families. Some women, because they have husbands who earn substantial salaries or because they do not have skills to sell on the open market, consider their earnings from day care to be reasonable: "I know a lot of people say the money's not good. But I couldn't have made that much doing anything else—and then to pay day care on top"; "There isn't a lot of competition for baby-sitting in [this town] . . . and I get three dollars an hour for two children from the same family. So I'm making six dollars an hour when I have all four girls. . . . That's good income."

Many, however, can not survive on what they earn from this endeavor. Family day care providers with total family incomes below $10,000 were three times as likely to have left the occupation after a year than were those with incomes above $20,000; the needs of some workers (both the women who provide care and the parents who purchase it) are thus subsidized by the wages of the spouses of family day care providers. Family day care may not be a desirable occupation, but it is restricted to those who have a supplemental source of income—and one that comes with benefits.[11]

If the limited resources for child care have broad economic roots, the impact is felt directly in relationships between parents and providers. Most parents have few options; they can not afford to pay generously for child care. If this is the source of their reluctance to acknowledge the provider's market demands, it is underscored by an emotional need to understand the transaction in the terms of a social exchange. Parents want to believe the provider is motivated by enjoyment and a womanly "duty to care." When parents resist commodification, the battle lines are drawn: "I was considering doing contracts and I talked to a few parents and they didn't like the idea too well. . . . And one mother said, 'Boy, you'd think this was a business.' Just like that. . . . I felt that it was like a business. I did enjoy working with the kids and that part was great. But it was a livelihood. I had to have income. And they didn't understand that." When providers weary of the battle, they leave the arena.

Other costs of an involvement in wage labor are pushed onto family day care providers as well. The providers tire of fielding the expectation that they will absorb the consequences of inflexible jobs for overextended parents. One of the women who still cares for a few children after school said that she left full-time child care in part for these reasons. She continues to have the same problems:

> The problem right now—like the little girl I have right now—her mother just assumes that I'm going to do transportation [to kindergarten] for the child. It's like, she's like my own so I will just automatically do this. And I told her that I could help her out when she needed help—but she just assumed I would do it. And more and more parents—they work from, say eight to five, and they're supposed to be here at five—and it might be six. . . . The people I have right now, I can't complain about. But the biggest problem is the parents—it's not the children, it's not discipline problems, it's not anything with the kids—it is the parents, just expecting more and more.

If other demands, whether implicit or explicit, are less tangible, they have the same roots. As more women work outside the home, caregivers of all kinds find their burdens increased. Schoolteachers complain about the emotional problems of children from broken or simply overwhelmed families. Family day care providers complain about the style of child rearing they feel accompanies a mother's employment and the obligation this creates for them to become the disciplinarian: "Sometimes it's hard, especially with one-parent families. I think there's a tendency to kind of overcompensate and let the child do anything because you feel guilty about not having the other parent, about going to work, about spending so much time away from this child. And so when the child is with the parent anything goes. And then they get to day care where that can't work." They may also feel called on to assume additional responsibilities: "I think things have changed since when I started. . . . With career-oriented parents that aren't spending time with their kids—and I found that more so in the last couple of years too—you have to give more. You're not just there to offer a fun day. I see kids being more insecure, needing more than, hey we're going to do this activity today—needing a lot more." Doing "more," however, confounds boundary problems. Susie Corbett told the following story as part of her explanation for why she could no longer handle the demands of family day care and was easing out of the occupation:

> One of the little girls I have in there, I talked to her parents about having her tested because I felt that she was behind in motor skills and everything and she didn't really have an imagination. And they did test her and she was behind and she was supposed to be worked with twice a week and the parents always cancelled at the last minute and she never really got worked with. So I ended up having [the EEE staff] come here to work with her which was a pain. I was a little upset at the parents because of it. But I felt that she shouldn't suffer because her parents couldn't fit that in their schedule. It was real hard because I didn't want to overstep my boundaries because it wasn't my child. But I could see her being frustrated with the other kids because she couldn't do simple little things and I offered it trying to make it no big deal if they came here. But it got to be that the instructor was calling me instead of them and I was helping with little things here. . . . I started out by saying [to the parents], do you notice that Samantha does this or that Samantha can't do this. And they didn't. . . . I'm sure that they had things to say about me when I wasn't around. But I always told them if you want me to mind my own business, if you think I am overstepping my bounds, just say so.

Although providers say they leave the occupation because of client resistance to market demands compounded by increased burdens (and this constitutes both a reason for leaving and a *worst* feature of the job), they acknowledge their own ambivalence about which norms should prevail. When asked what they would do differently if they were to reopen their homes to day-care children, or what advice they would give a woman starting this venture, providers speak adamantly about adherence to the market perspective: "I'd say get a contract. Spell out your rules"; "The one thing . . . is to sit down with the parents before you take on the child, to tell them the hours you are open and that you have a life afterwards too." At the same time, they confess that they were not able to do so for all the reasons mentioned earlier. They colluded in their own exploitation:

> I never had a written contract. I wanted the kids to be at home here and I wanted them to feel like they were going to an aunt's house or to grandma's house or something and it was a fun place to go and I felt if I had that business part of it there would be talk at home—there would be conflicts.

> I guess it was really my fault. I never was much of one to project myself or to put my foot down.

The failure to allocate resources reflects the social devaluation of child care, particularly when it takes place in a home. If we romanticize women's nurturance, and the virtues of a homelike setting, we are unwilling to accord it much respect. Regulation of day care may be justified by the state's interest in protecting children and overseeing an activity receiving financial support, but providers view it as relegating them to the position of children who can not be trusted; they also believe that it ignores the real content of day care, the skill required to run a good day-care home, and the effort entailed in responding to parents' needs: "People doing the regulations have never been in the situation. . . . They should take a harder look at it. . . . If the parents, children, and the providers are happy, that's the important thing. They don't take enough into consideration. They don't think about the emergencies, the snow days, etcetera, for reasons why a provider sometimes has too many kids." The money available to child-care providers—for training, for equipment—is unequally distributed. Family day care providers are pained by these manifestations of low status:

> To most people you're basically people who are at home, making money, because you want to stay home with your own children. Maybe that is a reason for some of us. But if it

> was just that that would be basically what we would be doing, just hanging out at home with our kids, trying to make a few extra dollars. I don't think people realize what the job entails and that it takes a special person to do the job and to do it right. . . . I think the home day cares are on the bottom of the list for most everything. . . . Anybody can become a registered day care which doesn't say a whole heck of a lot. . . . They always have the great trainings during the week [when home day care providers can't attend]—and then they do these little piddly ones for the home day care people. . . . Like they have day care–appreciation night each spring of every year and all the home day care people go and we get a flower and we have cookies and punch and it's just a little treat. And this year—I was about to stop [child care] and I said, "We hang around with kids all the time and eat cookies and drink punch and this is what you give us?" I said, "You should take us out to dinner. Or have champagne and caviar or something."

Parents participate in this social devaluation of caregiving. If they extol the virtues of the woman they have found to care for their child—and if they acknowledge that they couldn't do the work themselves—they attribute her skill to background factors ("she comes from a large family") or to her innate nurturance ("she just loves children"). Of course, this attitude can not be dissociated from the economic issues: One does not have to pay much for unskilled services. And parents have their own emotional reasons for wanting to deny the accomplishments of day-care providers.[12] No matter what the causes, providers grow weary of struggling with parents for evidence of appreciation. At the very least they want their rules respected. A woman who had ceased offering all-day care but continued to be available after school said:

> So there are times when I've been made aware that parents are apt to take you for granted. I think one of my biggest things now is that most of my kids are part-time. There's only one little boy that comes five afternoons a week. So I have to keep track of schedules and so on and I've tried to make it clear I'd like to have them call. . . . Well, they've been basically good. But every single one of them has forgotten to call me and you find out they've called the school but they forgot to call the baby-sitter. Well that makes me feel like I'm a number and not a name. And it makes me feel

> that—they've been out working and they've put their child in somebody else's care and I don't think they realize the sense of worrying about whether their kid's going to get back home from school or not. . . . So that's the parents—they take some of these things for granted. And I think it's because they've never been home to have to experience them. And they're all nice people. All nice people.

They also want their service valued and their skills acknowledged. They want to be treated as something more than "just a baby-sitter":

> I never felt that I was just a baby-sitter. I felt I was giving people a service and a good service . . . [but] I worked for mothers who found it very hard to say thank you because they had to give you money. And now all of a sudden I'm working for somebody who knows the word and I feel more appreciated. I think that's something that day care will never get. . . . You were providing a service and it was a good service—nobody ever said anything bad—but you never got feedback either. You never got that unless you asked for it. And I don't like to fish for it.

If day-care providers collude in their economic exploitation, so do they collude in their own devaluation. They disclaim their own skills ("I don't have any skills"); they naturalize their abilities ("Anyone who has been a mother can do this").

And they can not always articulate their needs. As we have seen, when parents offer to pay them more, they say money isn't everything; when parents show other signs of appreciation (bringing flowers or gifts), they discredit these gestures as well. In short, although the battle is fought with clients, clients alone can not supply the material rewards or the social prestige for a society that fails to value caregiving and the women who do this work.

## PUBLIC/PRIVATE BOUNDARIES AND MOTHERING

Chiara Saraceno, in her article, "Shifts in Public and Private Boundaries: Women as Mothers and Service Workers in Italian Daycare," discusses the manner in which broad social changes (including increasing numbers of women in the labor force and the growth of the service sector) and the state response to those changes (in the form of funding for day care) produced complicated and ambiguous relationships between clients and service workers. In the conclusion she writes:[13]

> The fact that this is also a women's story gives it another meaning as well. First, it shows how fragile and fluid are public/private boundaries in women's lives. Given the existing division of labor, it is left to women to make linkages between the two spheres, in their private or in their public capacities, as wives-mothers or as service workers. . . . The caring and service work remains attributed to women, who have to negotiate among themselves the share each has to take, according to her position in the family, and in the service structure. . . . Certainly in this process female gender roles are partially changed because the balance between public and private, and therefore the material conditions in which these roles are acted and defined, change. For example, the "mother role" can be extended to incorporate some kind of working experiences as well as a public role of relating to services and taking part in their management. And mothering itself can become a required dimension of service professions. But this does not mean that gender roles as such, and the sex/gender structure which supports them, are radically overthrown.

The American story is different from the Italian one on a number of grounds, not the least of which is the more limited direct state involvement in child-care services. And the situation of family day care providers is different from that of center-based workers. Nevertheless, many of the issues are the same because, whether in the United States or in Italy, and whether as center-based or home-based workers, broad social changes transform both the material conditions under which women's gender roles are enacted and the cultural meaning of those roles.

Family day care, even more than center-based care, illustrates the fragility and fluidity of public/private boundaries. Family day care providers are motivated by a desire to remain in the domestic domain, to serve a "traditional" role; they have to take on paid work because of changing economic realities. In the nineteenth century, "the permeable boundaries for women between unpaid and paid labor allowed nursing to pass back and forth when necessary";[14] the same is true of child care today. Family day care providers move, if not effortlessly, repeatedly, from unpaid care of their own children to a combination of unpaid care of their own and paid (and sometimes unpaid) care of other children while remaining in the domestic domain. Sometimes they move back to unpaid care of their own children (or other relatives); sometimes they move on to paid care of others in the public sphere. Many move back and forth between the public and private domains, in a remorseless and unrewarding search for a location in which to offer care without contradictions. And more so than in the past when women augmented the family income with home-based work (and thus merged paid and unpaid work in a single domain), their informal work activities involve them in the public sphere through state regulation.

As both unpaid caregivers to their own children and paid caregivers to children of working mothers, not only do they link and merge the two spheres, but they seek to establish "the share each has to take" in the new division of caregiving responsibilities. Boundary issues are often acute: Who is responsible for seeing that a child is adequately nurtured? How far can a day-care provider go without overstepping unstated limits or without increasing her own emotional costs?

Ironically, family day care providers who define themselves as "traditional mothers" facilitate a redefinition of mothering as a central activity of woman's gender role. They also bear some of the burdens of this process, including the contradiction of offering a service in which they don't really believe: "I think young children should be home with their parents. It was hard for me too to be providing that service when I don't think that's what's best for the kids." Another burden is the necessity of redefining their own mothering to make it congenial with the reality of the ongoing demands of their paid work. In caring for the children of working mothers—and their own at the same time—almost against their will, they allow mothering to be "extended to incorporate some kind of working experiences as well as a public role of relating to services and taking part in their management." The costs of this process—in the unmet needs of women *and* children—are negotiated as boundary issues, and (even more artificially) as issues of rules, resources, and respect, between two essentially powerless parties; they are also felt as real emotional burdens by women who sometimes feel compelled to pick up the slack even if they are not rewarded or even acknowledged for doing so.

At bottom they allow these transformations to rest on an unaltered definition of womanhood and thus in minimal changes in the sex/gender system. As long as working mothers can locate cheap, but competent, "replacements" they do not have to demand higher wages or greater job flexibility; they can continue to be exploited in the wage labor force, passing on (some of) the economic and emotional costs of their employment to another woman and her family. If some family day care providers can "get by" without charging high fees, the gap between a real wage and current earnings can be ignored; after all, women aren't in this "to make a killing," but to satisfy *other* needs, including the need to care. And because most family day care providers do indeed offer adequate care, women can still be assumed to acquire the essential skills through experience or gender socialization and therefore do not have to be given either material rewards or social prestige. The isolation of family day care providers and the lack of a real work culture preclude their having an effective base from which to make demands for these resources—even if they were ready to do so; their location in the private domain reinforces even as it undermines their dependence on their husbands and their subjection to patriarchy.

In short, family day care providers have to resolve the immediate conflicts of doing public caregiving in the private domain, find meaning and value in caregiving from a society that denies these rewards both to the activity and to the women who do it, and they have to negotiate the contradictions of shifting public/private boundaries. Daily they have to answer the question of what it means to be "like a mother" when they can not enjoy the privileges of mothering, and the very meaning of that activity is being redefined. By offering public child care, by engaging in paid work in the private sphere, they simultaneously challenge and reaffirm the "domestic code."

Individual attempts—and in the absence of an organization of day-care providers, individual action is the only possibility—at resolving these contradictions vary. If some women huddle more closely to the traditional experiential model of mothering and subscribe primarily to the terms of the social exchange, they deny themselves access to concrete resources (they receive no help through regulation and outreach workers), and they have no stance from which they can claim rewards. If some women opt for a more entrepreneurial identity, they are undercut by their own self-definition of being like a mother, and they continue to face parental resistance. The entirely different model—that of the professional child-care worker—creates its own dilemmas; in any case many women find this approach to child care inappropriate. Most women do not take a single stance, but vacillate among competing alternatives; they experience additional stress from this vacillation. The ultimate failure of individual solutions suggests a problem that has to be addressed on a broader scale.

## BURNOUT

While the causes of the difficulties family day care providers face have broad social roots, they are experienced as conflicts with other women. This is one of the tragedies of this situation—that mothers and child-care providers (each powerless in her own right), in spite of their common gender interests and their common interests in the well-being of the same children, resent each other for failing to meet needs they can not possibly meet.

Perhaps an even greater tragedy is that ultimately providers blame themselves. They experience as personal failure, as the enervating state of "burnout," their inability to withstand the strains of family day care. Burnout has been variously defined in the literature; most of these definitions isolate the components of emotional exhaustion, depersonalization, and (loss of) personal accomplishment.[15] Each of these factors emerged in the interviews conducted with women who had left the occupation.

Providers frequently described a sense of overwhelming weariness, of no longer being able to meet the demands of the day-care children—or even those of their own family members:

> It had just come to the point where I was really tired. And I loved the kids or I wouldn't be back in [center-based] day care. But it had come to the point where it was just too much. . . . It came to the point that I was really tired. I needed a change of pace.

> Everything became such a chore. Things that people had said to me over the years, like, "How can you manage so many children at one time? How can you stand all the noise and all the demands?" Well, over the years I couldn't understand what they were talking about. But then I just got really tired of the demands. And it was too much. And I wanted the kids to go away sort of. . . . I just knew I was tired and I didn't want to do it anymore. . . . I didn't want the demands of those children. I sort of didn't want the demands of my own children either. I just got really tired of children. I don't know how to say it more clearly than that. So I just had this overwhelming feeling that this was the end. I couldn't do it any more.

Depersonalization also showed up as a theme among some women who found themselves giving less good, and less intimate, care than they had previously. Of those who continued for some time after they had made the decision to stop providing family day care, 29 percent said they changed in that interval: 26 percent of these women said that they had become less patient; 21 percent, that they put in less energy.[16] One provider, for example, said that toward the end she found that she was allowing the children to play more on their own: "I wasn't myself. Although I guess I would play with the kids it probably wasn't as often that I got involved in actively playing with them. I think I probably relied a lot more on outside activities and inside activities that they could do and manage themselves." Another said she no longer offered new activities: "I was very enthusiastic and structured at the beginning but it became too much of a drain after a while. I stopped doing a lot of the stuff I had done—I ended up doing mostly maintenance care, providing the same environment day after day."

Providers also talked about a diminished sense of personal accomplishment. Many said they were no longer experiencing personal growth. They began to think longingly of alternative occupations in which they might learn something new. Others focused on the discouraging component of their work, on not being able to affect significantly the lives of children: "[I liked least] knowing that when the kids went home they'd be out on the streets, and seeing things they shouldn't. . . . I did it because I really wanted to, but it isn't something I'd want to do all the time. Because I hate knowing that the kids go back to that environment after all I try to do for them. One step forward and two steps back."

Finally, without specifying a specific component of burnout, providers simply noted the fact: "I really enjoyed it for the time that I did it—it worked well for me at the time. But it gets hard as you go along. You burn out."

## *Leaving the Occupation*

Movement out of the occupation resolves some of these problems for the individual: 45 percent of the providers said they were "very glad" to have stopped; an additional 23 percent were "somewhat glad." Of course, how providers feel about leaving varies with the reasons for doing so and on the work they subsequently find to do. Some of those who leave for strictly financial reasons, like those who are closed as a result of state intervention, are bitter about not being able to sustain a rewarding occupation. (Only 25 percent of these women said they were very glad to stop.) But others note that their new situations (whether they are working or not) relieve them of the stress of family day care; those who are working outside the home often speak affirmatively about opportunities for growth and self-esteem, and predictable (if not greater) financial rewards. And some are adamant about never having liked the job and being glad to be rid of it: "I'm glad I'm out of it and I'd never do it again."

Even so, almost all providers acknowledge loss. They miss the children:

> I still think about all of them. I miss them so much—everything—the fingerprints on the walls, messy rooms, wet toilet seats—I think that children are the greatest thing in the world and it was awful when I stopped. But I had to. It wasn't a job, it was a pleasure. I had one week off in twenty years and that was forced by my son. Most kids came at birth and stayed until they went to school. Some even came after school. It really was a great life.

They also miss the sense of identity, the self-definition of being a woman who cares. One woman, still in the transition stage—she had not yet found an alternative occupation—was having difficulty taking the children's pictures off the walls and was clinging to her larger investments (the stroller for three children, the water-sand table) "just in case." (Almost half of the providers said they would consider opening a family day care home again at some time.) But most providers recognize that if they are bewildered by the change, they are also ready to move on, and maybe even eager to do so:

> It was kind of bittersweet. I was feeling ready to move on and not be talking to children twenty-four hours a day and not having contact with any adults other than the parents. I was really excited about doing something new. But the last day, I was kind of teary.

> People have called me on the phone and asked me for day care since I stopped and I have said no. My license for the day-care registration ran out and I thought that would bother me that that wouldn't be open to me anymore. . . . And I thought it would bother me that that period of my life was over. But it didn't. I'm just sort of amazed because it's something that I've wanted to do for twenty years and all of a sudden I just have no desire. . . . It's just kind of a life change for me.

A third of the providers were not working at the time they answered the turnover questionnaire. Six of these were retired; eight were recovering from childbirth or illness. Several were waiting until their youngest children were in school (or until their children returned to school in the fall) to seek employment. A couple of women felt they needed time in which to relax and unwind:

> It's one thing about being stressed. I think it's hard to calm down again. You know what I mean. Little things bother

> me and I say, I can't believe this is bothering me. It wouldn't have bothered me three years ago. And I just want to be back to my old self again and be the kind of mother that I always thought I would be and that I was for a while.

Among those who were employed outside the home, the distribution of occupations was much as it had been before; among those for whom comparative data is available (that is information about occupations both before and after doing family day care), there is little evidence that providers experience radical career changes. This is not to say that day care is irrelevant to their occupational lives. If some find that the extended period out of the labor force hurts their chances of finding employment, more than half say they have acquired skills they can use on the job.[17] Because the child-care field is still fluid, and because many of these women live in communities where reputations are spread by word of mouth, a relatively high proportion (more than 10 percent) were able to parlay their skills into paid positions in day care centers:[18]

> Jessica Pack . . . has worked at the Tamarack Child Center for many years and they called her and she told them they would be nuts if they didn't hire me and they had better hire me right away before someone else did. So she single-handedly got me the job because they really respected her opinion. They also knew a lot of the people of the children I had watched and they knew that I had done day care. . . . I had connections with people there so they were able to check me out.

The experiences of these women (two among those I interviewed) highlight some of the crucial differences between home- and center-based care. Both of the women spoke of the many personal advantages of a caregiving setting that offered structured support and a sense of self-worth:

> I really do feel better about myself. It's nice. I feel differently. I don't even know where it's coming from other than the fact that I really do feel better. Maybe it's just getting out and getting to be with other people. . . . I still find myself using the wrong words at times but . . . it's nice being out and working and I still have the best of both worlds. I'm still with kids and that's what I want. . . . Actually, sitting here and talking with you today has made me realize that I feel better about myself. . . . I felt content and

> happy for a long time doing [family day care]. I don't think it was because I felt unhappy doing it that I gave it up. I just felt that I wanted to try something else. . . . I wanted to see what I could do. . . . And then in the end day care was where I belonged. I need to be able to nurture other people but I need that in return also.
>
> I had friends that really encouraged me to [look for a job in a day care center]. And I kept on saying, remember what I was saying last year about how I was really burned out. . . . And they said, but we think it will be different when you are at a center. And this is what you are good at. And they couldn't have been more right. I love what I am doing there so much—and I was so excited about working there I was able to go on a diet and lose twenty-five pounds. And I'm working with people, with other adults. There's a wonderful network at the Tamarack Child Center. I feel like I'm doing a different type job altogether.

Nevertheless, the not-infrequent movement of women from day care centers, back into home day care, and the exceedingly high turnover rates among institutional child-care workers, suggest that if this alternative setting resolves some of the contradictions of caregiving in this society, by no means does it resolve them all.

# CONCLUSION

I have tried to make this book the provider's story, told in her words, and from her point of view. In the process I have learned that there is more than one provider's story. Although all women in family day care face similar structural conditions, they do not all experience their work in the same way. Whether because they have access to different rewards, start with different personalities, or find themselves at different stages in their personal lives, they make different decisions about how to handle the dilemmas endemic to this occupation and, failing to resolve these dilemmas, they "burn out" at different times and for different reasons.

To understand fully the context in which family day care providers work, I have also had to go beyond these voices. The husbands of the women I interviewed had their own stories to tell; they were often poignant in their pain. If they sometimes supported their wives, they also represented a set of (gender-related) concerns that compounded the problems their wives faced in their attempts to merge paid and unpaid work, and to find recognition for doing so. The women who brought their children to the providers' homes had yet another set of needs. The same sex, a shared interest in the children, and even a genuine sense of attachment to and appreciation for a particular provider did not preclude disrespectful, and occasionally downright exploitative, behavior.

I also heard from state licensers, the personnel of resource and referral centers, outreach workers, center-based child-care workers and child-care advocates. Representatives of each group, while nominally supportive of family day care as a central component of the child-care picture, occasionally expressed attitudes or took stands denigrating this activity. Because state licensers placed the safety of children in a paramount position, they were critical of those who failed to register and often suspicious of those that did. Resource and referral services listed only those who register, even though those who care for children from fewer than two different families need not do so. Outreach workers often wanted to see substantial changes in the provider's style and the substitution of formal training for experientially based knowledge. Center-based child-care workers viewed home day care as undercutting them in their struggle for professional recognition. Child-care advocates, in highlighting the desperate need for resources often pointed to the worst abuses of current arrangements.[1]

Of course, sometimes these varying stands are the result of simple misunderstandings, stemming from a lack of effective communication among the different groups; at another level they result from different emphases and priorities. But they also represent real contradictions, and they are the outcome of real struggles over limited resources—in the size of the child-care pie and in the access to social goods both within and between families.

At some points, allowing all these different participants to speak for themselves has felt like an abdication of responsibility: I did not have to take a position myself or take a stand about the issues.[2] In this conclusion, in a partial way, I want to rectify this omission.

I will begin by stating three personal convictions about family day care.[3] The first is that family day care is likely to remain an important component of the child-care picture. There is both an available supply of the appropriate labor and a persistent demand for the service; this care is congruent with other political and economic priorities (even as these priorities change). Second, I think this is good. I acknowledge the concerns of critics, but I know that many of the women who do this work do it sensitively and well, and that when it is done in this manner, it meets the real needs of children and their parents. Finally, I am certain that family day care will change.

Some of these changes had already begun while I was conducting the research for and writing this book; they stem from many different sources, and they occur at many different levels. In the Vermont community in which I live, an arrangement known as the "Family Fund" was being developed by local child-care advocates, "to increase the supply, quality and affordability of child care" by offering resource and referral services, recruitment of new providers, training and support services for caregivers, flexible spending accounts for employees, redirection of tax savings into child-care assistance, seminars on selecting and paying for child care, and gradual development of a tuition assistance fund.[4] In the largest city in the state, citizens had voted on and defeated a proposal to subsidize through a "sin tax" the child-care expenses of working couples when those expenses exceeded 10 percent of the household's gross income.

Among the most important changes at the state level were: a revision in the regulations concerning licensing and registration, which introduced a training requirement of six hours for all registered providers; a change in the policy of licensers' making unscheduled visits and a clarification of the rights of providers regarding complaints; and a modification of reimbursement policies so that providers could charge parents for the difference between the state's reimbursement and their own customary fees. Between 1986 and 1989 the number of registered homes rose from approximately 400 to 1,375; the state budget for child care increased from $3.4 million in 1986 to $5.8 million in 1988, and the maximum income a family of four could earn to receive a state subsidy for child care rose from $18,912 in 1986 to $25,884 in 1989. The insurance community also responded, at least in Vermont, to the spread of home day care by changing policies so that this business could no longer be included as a rider on a homeowner's policy but had to be purchased separately: This increased average costs for a provider from between $120 and $150 a year to between $300 and $400 a year.

Nationwide, estimates of the number of employers (among those employing more than 100 workers) sponsoring child care in some fashion rose from 110 in 1978 to 600 in 1982 and to 3,300 in 1989.[5] At the federal level there were a variety of changes as well. A new IRS ruling made mandatory the reporting of the social security number of persons employed to provide child care. Another piece of legislation curtailed the practice of claiming both the dependent-care tax credit and the tax exclusion for dependent-care assistance provided by the parents' employers. And, although in 1987 twenty-eight states spent less in real dollars for child care funded through the Social Services Block Grant (formerly Title XX) than they did in 1981, as this book went to press major child-care legislation had been approved by both the House and the Senate.[6]

I might note that there are some contradictory tendencies in these changes. If, for example, the new IRS regulations are likely to increase the number of providers who have to report their incomes and therefore the number who might be compelled to register with the state, the changing insurance policies discourage providers from incorporating in this manner. Similarly, if some version of the proposed federal child-care legislation is funded and parents place pressure on providers to become registered so that they can be reimbursed for child-care expenses, the increased training requirements implemented at the state level may discourage providers from complying with regulation.

Taken as a whole, however, these changes represent more public awareness of the magnitude of the demand for child care and of the needs of at least lower-income families to receive help in purchasing this service. And some of the changes seem to recognize that family day care is a legitimate component of the child-care picture. But because the policy bias is toward meeting parents' needs, the needs of child-care workers are often ignored.

## *Family Day Care Systems*

In Vermont, as in the United States as a whole, family day care is largely haphazard, staffed by independent providers who have only minimal contact with the state and with the services provided by resource and referral centers. This is not the case in other countries. In Sweden, for example, family day care homes (municipal day nurseries) are an integral part of the services provided for preschool children. The private homes are inspected and approved by local authorities, and "day mothers" receive regular pay and social benefits such as holiday pay, health insurance, and pensions.[7]

Family day care systems exist in this country as well. In Minnesota, for example, the Greater Minneapolis Day Care Association, a private, nonprofit organization, helps parents find and afford child care, and funds child-care programs. It also serves family day care providers in a variety of ways, offering to its members a newsline, a toy-lending library, group health and dental insurance, training workshops, legal assistance, a van program, and access to a resource pool of equipment and supplies.[8]

These arrangements offer appropriate models for restructuring family day care. In the rest of this chapter, I discuss the benefits of family day care systems, which I believe would be best organized at a local level (with a governing board that includes parents and providers) and subsidized primarily by state and federal taxes.[9] This discussion focuses more on the needs to be served by these systems than on the precise structural arrangements that would ensure success.

The isolation of family day care providers is a major problem and one which, to a certain extent, is going to persist—by definition family day care providers work in a solitary setting. But the problems can be alleviated. For example, a system could offer a van service to transport the provider and her children to the library, a park, or an equipped municipal gym. It could keep open a "warm line" for providers to call for advice and support. It could also offer regular substitutes and respite care for emergencies. When asked what would make the work better for them, "someone to give me a break" was the item most often cited; those providers who are able, because they operate in a seller's market, to schedule for themselves a regular day off, speak of the vital importance of this practice. Visits from outreach workers could alleviate loneliness and act as a "safety net" for providers under stress; they might also offer both informal training opportunities (particularly around such issues as child development, nutrition, and educational activities) and occasions for the children to interact with another adult.[10]

These kinds of relief might help a provider sustain detached attachment. But occasional relief is not enough. Providers say they want training that responds to the reality of their situation, that meets their real needs. Implicitly they acknowledge they need help in understanding the processes of attachment and loss. Training could use the models available from hospice workers and therapists, models that acknowledge both the necessity for real emotional involvement and the importance of disengagement when the work is done. (At the same time, if training can help providers deal with the dilemma of detached attachment, all change need not come from this side. As "mothering" changes its definition to include loving care by someone who is not the mother, there must be shifts in the privileges that currently accrue only to the mother. Parents might have to acknowledge that, if they rely on another, they have to respect that person's interest in the child: These interests might include protected visitation and a voice in the decision about a change in the child's caregiving situation.[11])

Although the development of a supportive work culture might be difficult in the face of geographical isolation and a provider's overwhelming obligations (to clients as well as to her own family), simple structures could facilitate the benefits that accompany collegiality. One woman recommended a telephone tree or a "buddy system" so that providers reluctant to, or intimidated by the idea of, calling an outreach worker could have some way to "let off steam." Opportunities for providers to get together informally are now one of the latent functions of training opportunities; they could be made an explicit goal. Then too, if training responded to the real needs of providers (I have already mentioned the issue of detachment), it might be sought in its own right. The issues of negotiation with parents, and relationships within one's own family, might be popular—and appropriate—topics. And training might also reflect the fact that for many providers this work is short-term. Advice on how to find and apply for jobs, or information about career opportunities in school systems (sought by so many women), would ease problems associated with the transition out of the occupation.

Providers face financial pressures of two types. First, there are costs associated with the provision of family day care. A family day care system could relieve some of the providers' entrepreneurial difficulties by enabling them to purchase insurance (both that associated with running a business, and health, dental, and disability insurance) and obtain loans to assist them in making the improvements associated with regulation. It could also acquire supplies wholesale. Some equipment (both utilitarian objects like high chairs, as well as toys and books) could be shared on a rotating basis so that providers neither had to make their own investments, nor lodge bulky and expensive items permanently.

Second, providers clearly need help with income, and they need the typical benefits of wage employment such as paid sick days, paid vacations, pension plans, and contributions to F.I.C.A. An adequately funded system could pay *salaries* sufficient to support a family. These salaries could be structured around a base (providing care to two children, for example) with increments for each additional child, adjusted so as to support increased effort but discourage overloading. The pay scales could also incorporate different rates for different kinds of care to encourage providers to respond to pressing needs while rewarding them for doing so: for example, higher rates for children in protective services and for infants.

If salaries were paid to the provider from a central office, the parent-provider relationship would be relieved of one of the major sources of conflict. Even if parents were asked to contribute to the cost of this service, they would have less reason to charge a provider with the burden of proving that she was motivated by love as well as financial gain. A system could resolve other problems in these relationships as well. A clear formulation of each party's obligations would release providers from the responsibility of defending their decisions against particularistic claims.[12]

A family day care system might also offer a way to use the expertise of providers who have burned out or who need a break from direct care. Many women accumulate valuable knowledge over the course of their years as providers; at present much of this knowledge is lost when they leave the field. Two of the women who had not yet found employment but were certain that they were finished with family day care, spoke longingly about the possibility of working in administration or as a "resource" person. And these systems might have room for a variety of different kinds of providers, and a mechanism for matching clients' interests with providers' orientations.

Of course, a system will not solve all problems. At the very least, providers will continue to bear the strains of merging paid and unpaid work in a single location. They will also continue to have boundary disputes with parents. Moreover, a system of the kind envisioned here might not attract all providers; those most committed to the social perspective, and those who face obstacles (even if of their own making) to defining themselves as workers will continue to stand outside these arrangements. But the attractions might be great enough to overcome the hesitation of many women who now avoid regulation, and it will accomplish the same goals (ensuring safe and reliable care for children) without ignoring the needs of providers.[13]

As a society, we have a long way to go before we truly value caregiving and before we resolve the contradictions of contemporary social change. These recommendations are not a complete solution. But they do suggest ways in which some of the burden can be lifted from the shoulders of family day care providers so that they can more easily live up to the social expectations imposed on them.

## *Final Thoughts*

Much of the talk about *the family* and its virtues has been preempted by the political right in this country. Because they are struggling to sustain a traditional life-style, and the accompanying gender-based division of labor, many of the family day care providers might be viewed as being aligned with this political stance. Other of their deeply held convictions would tend to reinforce this impression. Many believe the government has become far too intrusive in our personal lives; they have contempt for those who rely on government "handouts." And many believe that women who work outside the home do so primarily for selfish reasons, such as their own careers or their craving for material possessions; in the process, the providers argue, children's needs are frequently sacrificed.

But this is not the whole picture. The work of family day care is also grounded in, and experienced as, a deep commitment to meeting the needs of children for stable and loving care. As providers enact their role, they recognize that such care does not depend on a biological or familial relationship with a child. They, too, on numerous occasions, benefit from the nurturance they offer; they find great rewards in watching and fostering growth. And they believe that good caregiving is grounded in the "mothering" experience and in intimate knowledge of the individual child. In each of these understandings—the commitment to children, the recognition of the rewards of "mothering," an appreciation of the experiential basis for caregiving—they stand on ground shared by (at least some) feminists, as well as (at least some members of) the political right. Moreover, in forging ties with children and with the parents of those children, in meeting the needs of members of their own families and (sometimes) of a broader network of real and "fictive" kin, family day care providers acknowledge the centrality of affective ties in their own lives. They act on the basis of an implicit (and sometimes explicit) understanding of community, of our fundamental interconnectedness and interdependence. In these commitments, too, they transcend political boundaries.

At the same time, unlike conservatives, who only look backward to an idealized past, to a vision of community in which women—and women alone—"naturally" chose to serve others (and thereby sacrifice their own needs), the political ideology of family day care providers is transmuted as a result of their daily activities. Perhaps because they bear some of the burdens of the current social transformation, they are compelled to acknowledge these changes. They know their own families can not get by without two incomes; they understand that the same is true for most of their clients. They know there is no going back. They also know that the wages women earn are barely sufficient to cover child-care costs, and they suggest both that these wages should be increased and that "something has to be done" to help ease the burdens on working couples. And they know that state intervention might be appropriate in some situations.

If they remain at home and enact traditional gender roles, they transform that home and those roles as they struggle for recognition and for a renegotiation of the sexual division of household labor. They ask their sons, as well as their daughters, to help with domestic tasks and to learn how to respond to the needs of younger children; some express considerable pride in how their children of both sexes acquire parenting skills through their participation in the activities of the family day care home. In caring for the children of others as well, they learn to respect individual differences and require behaviors that transcend gender roles. Whether it is because they have less of a personal investment in the children—or because of their own increased understanding of these matters—they find themselves responding openmindedly to a boy who plays with dolls or a girl who plays with trucks. In any case, at a practical level they have to make do—each member of the child-care group has to learn to get along with and play with others, to wear whatever clothes, and play with whatever toys, are at hand. Providers who say initially they believe in firm discipline, an authoritarian child-rearing style, often find that other methods work as well. Sometimes they have to find these other methods because of the rules surrounding their regulation; more often they themselves recognize that what is appropriate for one's own can not be applied to someone else's. As they find that discussion and "time out" can actually make child care easier, they sometimes wonder why they were so hard on their own—and if it was really good. Moreover, the work of family day care brings women into contact with a wide range of others, some of whom share their class position and social outlook, some of whom do not. They have to learn to find a new basis for understanding, to be open to views and attitudes that challenge their own.

From the base of their own experience, providers move toward a recognition of the need for autonomy in their own lives. Their understanding of this need is closer to a feminist vision of adult roles for women than it is that of the belief in individualism touted by the Right. As Susan Cohen and Mary Fainsod Katzenstein argue,[14]

> Individualism, for the Right, is encouraged by the family even as it must be, in another sense, sacrificed to the family. The Right maintains that the family is uniquely qualified to instill norms of independence and freedom in its young. Yet the exercise of this individualism is to happen outside, not within, the family. Within the family, community supersedes individuality. The choices men and women make inside the family are to be curtailed by the parameters of biology and tradition. Outside the family, however, individualism may flourish—but an individualism (feminist critics charge) that embraces only men.

But providers learn they can not sacrifice their own individualism/autonomy and still be effective social actors meeting their own and their families' needs at the same time as they meet the needs of the women and children who are their clients. Over time they have to develop—and learn to trust and value—their own caregiving style, even as it emerges from a complex mix of experience and formal training, practical necessity, and compromise. In the process of negotiation with parents, husbands, and state officials, they often find themselves developing new communication skills and acquiring the self-esteem to surmount their own socialization; they fight for and defend their own interests. Not surprisingly, some seek protection in privacy. In a patriarchal society women are rarely experienced in expressing their own needs for autonomous action, and they identify their interests with those of the domestic domain. Nor is it surprising that others express their goals in the terms of what I have called a market perspective or an entrepreneurial stance. In a capitalist society these are familiar ways to speak about self-interest. But the provider's quest goes well beyond any of these terms. They are seeking a measure of control over—and dignity for—the work they do. And in contrast to the more professional providers, most are unwilling (and unable) to abandon the broader pleasures of community in the process.

In their daily lives, then, at a narrow level, providers seek to balance a social and a market perspective, the norms of the public world and those of the private domain, affective and contractual relationships. At a deeper level, they are struggling to find a balance between autonomy and community. Because our society charges women with the burden of community, while granting men the privileges of autonomy; and because the necessary structural support for achieving this balance for members of *both* sexes is sorely lacking, family day care providers often "fail." But their stories are clear demonstrations of the truism that if caregivers are going to meet their own needs as well as those of care recipients, they must find that balance. Ensuring this basis for caregiving is, perhaps, one of the biggest challenges facing our society today.

# APPENDIX A

## *Methodology*

### *Setting*

The research on which this study is based was carried out exclusively in Vermont. Vermont has loomed large in the past twenty years as the place for those who were tired of the urban scene to escape to something more idyllic. These newcomers ("flatlanders," as they are called in Vermont) have certainly had an effect on the politics and the visible culture of the state. For the past six years a woman has been the governor—and even more surprising, she is a Democrat (and a Jew). Burlington's major theater hosts performances by Miriam Makeba, Randy Newman, and Joan Armatrading.

But in many ways Vermont remains much as it was before the influx, and the most significant changes (such as the demise of the family farm) have less to do with these newcomers than with broader political and economic events. Vermont remains white: It has a minority population of less than 1 percent; it is frequently labeled the whitest state in the nation.[1] Vermont continues to be a poor state: Although median family income rose from $8,928 in 1969 to $17,205 in 1979, the state lost ground relatively; in 1969 it was the nineteenth-poorest state; in 1979 it was the tenth poorest.[2] And Vermont is rural, hosting only one city large enough to count as a SMSA (Standard Metropolitan Statistical Area). In 1950 it was the forty-sixth most-rural state; in 1986 it ranked number forty-eight.[3]

For these reasons one might well wonder whether conclusions drawn from an analysis of family day care providers in Vermont could have anything but the anecdotal relevance of the deviant case. However, there are reasons for situating a study here that draw on this uniqueness; there are also reasons for suspecting that family day care in Vermont is not so unique at all.

First, the only large-scale study of family day care to date (National Day Care Home Study) looked exclusively at urban child care; my study provides an important counterweight, exploring family day care in an area in which it is more widely used.[4] Second, an analysis of the experience of white family day care providers and their relation-

*TABLE 2*
OVERVIEW OF CHARACTERISTICS OF
FAMILY DAY CARE PROVIDERS

| Provider Characteristics | Vermont | National Day Care Home Study | | |
|---|---|---|---|---|
| | | White | Black | Hispanic |
| Percent married | 86% | 84% | 52% | 80% |
| Median age | 32 | 34.7 | 46.6 | 44.8 |
| Median level of education | — | 12.2 | 11.4 | 9.6 |
| Percent with more than a high school education | 50% | — | — | — |
| Median family income | $20–25,000 | $13,500 | $6,750 | $9,000 |

SOURCE: Stephen J. Fosburg et al., *Family Day Care in the United States: Summary of Findings* (Washington, D.C.: Government Printing Office, 1981).

ships with white employing parents allows a focus on issues that arise from the nature of the work itself, without the complications of ethnic and racial factors.

At the same time, there are significant similarities between family day care in Vermont and family day care in other areas. For one thing, family day care providers in Vermont do not look that different from other (white) family day care providers in terms of their personal characteristics or working conditions (see Tables 2 and 3). Additionally, the dynamics of the work and the kinds of problems and tensions that the providers experience in Vermont are analogous to those that have been found in other large- and small-scale studies. And Vermont is representative of the newest regulatory development that substitutes registration for formal licensing procedures. Like other states, however, Vermont also has a large pool of unregulated family day care.

## *Data Collection*

I collected two very different kinds of data. Quantitative data derived from surveys of current and former family day care providers serve as the basis for generalizations about both the population of family day care providers in Vermont and reasons for leaving the occupation. In-depth interviews conducted with current and former family day care providers as well as a variety of other people in the day care provider's world serve as the basis for the analysis of the meaning of this work.

*TABLE 3*
WORKING CONDITIONS OF FAMILY DAY CARE PROVIDERS

| Working Conditions | Vermont | National Day Care Home Study | | |
|---|---|---|---|---|
| | | White | Black | Hispanic |
| Mean number of nonresident children per home | 4 | 3.8 | 3.8 | 2.7 |
| Mean number of nonresident related children per home | .5 | .3 | .5 | .8 |
| Percent of homes with one age group | 13% | — | 31% | — |
| Mean hourly fee per child* | $1.28 | $.70 | $.52 | $.51 |
| Mean weekly fee per child** | $52.50 | $26.36 | $22.65 | $17.80 |
| Mean weekly revenue from fees | $171.00 | $84.00 | $78.07 | $52.55 |

*NDCHS figure includes children who are cared for without charge.
**NDCHS figure does not include children who are cared for without charging. Vermont figure is based on weekly fees charged for full-time children.

## SURVEY DATA

*Current Family Day Care Providers.* In the summer of 1986 I mailed a questionnaire to the entire population of 463 family day care providers identified by Vermont as registered in that state. This mailing yielded 225 responses, or 49 percent of the total. The following summer I distributed questionnaires to 110 unregistered family day care providers. The location of unregistered family day care providers posed two problems. First, they do not appear on any published lists such as those available from the state for registered day care providers or those made available by resource and referral centers. Second, many unregistered providers attempt to maintain low visibility. If they are not reporting their incomes or if they are caring for more than the legal number of children, they seek to avoid recognition by state officials. The initial research strategy was to use advertisements that had appeared in two local newspapers. Unfortunately, a number of those who had advertised were no longer offering child care and some were registered providers. I also drove through various areas in the three counties under consideration and stopped in such places as general stores, parks, and post offices to ask about recommendations for names of family day care providers in the area. These two techniques provided an initial list of candidates for questionnaire distribution. Providers who agreed to participate were asked to recommend others they knew. The use of snowball sampling, then, constituted a third major strategy. (In the course of distributing questionnaires to unregistered providers, I picked up an additional 10 registered providers bringing the total for that group to 235.)

Both questionnaires covered a range of issues. The one directed at unregistered providers also asked a series of questions designed to assess attitudes toward state regulation, knowledge of these regulations, and the extent of voluntary compliance with them.

The question is sure to arise of how representative my questionnaire respondents are of both the national population of family day care providers and the broader population of family day care providers in Vermont. I look first at the registered providers. These providers look very much like the (white) registered providers in the National Day Care Home Study in both personal characteristics and working conditions, suggesting that I did not draw from a highly skewed population. (Because the state collects no data on the population of family day care providers, there is no way to assess how representative this sample is of the broader population of Vermont's providers.)

The distribution of responses for unregistered providers is skewed geographically since time and money limited the distribution of questionnaires to providers living on the western side of the state. Nevertheless, these data as well are analogous to those in the National Day Care Home Study of white unregulated providers.

*Former Day Care Providers.* During the summer of 1988 I conducted a telephone survey of sixty-three registered and twelve unregistered providers no longer involved in family day care.[5]

Questions in the telephone survey asked providers for information about their reasons for leaving family day care, current occupational activities, and experiences during the month prior to leaving the occupation. Some questions assessed attitudes towards child care in the same form as had been used on the first questionnaire; for the forty-two women who responded to both questionnaires, it was possible to do an analysis of change in attitudes over time. Two issues—sources of support and attitudes towards registration—that had not been included on the original questionnaire but emerged as significant areas of inquiry over the course of the study, were also included.

## INTERVIEW DATA

*Current Family Day Care Providers.* I also interviewed thirty-one registered providers (twenty-one of whom also completed questionnaires) and thirty-nine unregistered day care providers (fifteen of whom also completed questionnaires). Because I was particularly interested in allowing the description of family day care to emerge from the point of view of the providers themselves, the questions in the interview were open-ended. For example, the issues studied in the area of relationships between providers and children emerged from such questions as, "Could you tell me how you feel about the children in your care?" or "What do you want to be offering to the children in your care?" Areas of concern raised by women in the beginning of the study were pursued in subsequent interviews, and probing questions were designed to engender a fuller discussion of issues touched on superficially. This method precludes the possibility of using these data in a quantitative manner; not all interviews covered precisely the same material. However, with this method I feel confident that I am analyzing the experiences of family day care providers in a manner that reflects their reality rather than imposing an outsider's perspective. All names have been changed (as well as occasional details, such as a husband's occupation that might have identified a specific woman). I have tried to preserve the speech of the women and I have done only minor editing to conceal persons and places referred to by name and to avoid too many "you know's" or repetitions.

*Former Family Day Care Providers.* Between the summer of 1988 and the summer of 1989 I also conducted in-depth interviews with sixteen providers who had left the occupation or who were in the process of closing their family day care homes; eight of these women had been interviewed three years earlier while they were still engaged in family day care. Two of the women continued to offer after-school care to a small group of children who had previously been enrolled in their day care homes: One of the women was employed outside the home during school hours; the other was starting a different kind of home-based business.

*Other Interviews.* Several other groups were interviewed as well: nineteen mothers of children in family day care; seven spouses of family day care providers; eighteen center-based child care workers (as part of an earlier study);[6] and a variety of other persons whose occupational lives touch on family day care, such as state licensers, outreach workers, and resource and referral personnel.

## A Final Note

Although my own personal conviction is that child care can not remain just a woman's issue, with the exception of the husbands of family day care providers and state licensers I only interviewed women for this study. Most child-care providers are women. Also, the interviews with providers first and with mothers later suggested that most of the arrangements surrounding child care are made by women.[7] Providers spoke almost entirely about their interactions with mothers; they spoke little (but with more acceptance sometimes) about their interactions with fathers. Mothers said that they were responsible for child-care arrangements, and some even noted that the providers would not listen when their husbands gave information but would call them to check it out, or that if their husbands picked up the children, the provider would telephone in the evening with the daily rundown. The omission of men thus reflects a statistical reality rather than a normative prescription.*

*Recently over dinner in a local restaurant, I was discussing my research with a colleague who objected to my exclusive reliance on the voices of women. "Times are changing," she said, "men are involved in child-care decisions too." As we got up to leave, I went to say hello to a woman I had interviewed in her role as a mother using family day care. I asked her whether she had found a replacement for the provider she had been using, who had decided to seek employment outside of the home. She reported that she had just found a new woman who was willing to care for her child. As she told me this, her husband said, "I didn't know about that? What's going on?" My colleague, recognizing the mileage I was planning to get out of this incident, muttered, "You can't prove anything with just one case." I'm not so sure.

# APPENDIX B

## *Regulation of Family Day Care: Additional Information*

The following summarizes the Vermont standards for registered family day care homes in 1986.[1] This list is not complete. It does, however, indicate the major categories of standards and the most significant issues in these categories.

### STAFF

There shall be at least one caregiver with children at all times.

Caregiver shall be at least eighteen years of age and able to read and carry out the Family Day Care Home Registration Standards.

Caregiver shall not use or be under the effects of alcohol and/or drugs during the hours of care except medication prescribed by a physician. . . .

### PROGRAM

Care provided shall be reliable and consistent and shall include quiet and active play with indoor and outdoor activities. . . . Television viewing shall not be the major part of a child's daily activity.

The home shall provide care to not more than ten children present at any one time. Of these children present at any one time, not more than six shall be preschool children.

The home may not care for more than two children per caregiver, at any one time, who cannot quickly exit the home without assistance.

### DISCIPLINE

No person employed by or agent or a registered family day care home shall inflict or cause to be inflicted corporal punishment upon a child attending the home.

### CHILD ABUSE AND NEGLECT REPORTING

The registrant shall report to the department all instances of suspected child abuse or neglect. . . .

### ABUSE, NEGLECT, AND ILLEGAL ACTS

No person shall be employed as a staff member in, reside at, or operate a day-care facility, who has been convicted of a felony, or convicted of any offense involving abuse, neglect, or sexual activity with a child. . . .

RELATIONSHIPS BETWEEN PARENT AND REGISTRANT

Parents shall have free access to information about their child's daily activities and behavior, and free access to areas of the home used for child care while their children are in care.

RELATIONSHIPS BETWEEN REGISTRANT AND DEPARTMENT

Upon request, a registrant shall provide the department with a list of all the names and addresses of families served during the prior twelve months and the dates of service.

HEALTH AND SAFETY

A child who is ill or has a contagious condition may only be cared for in a family day care home when, in the opinion of the registrant and the parent(s) the child may be appropriately cared for, and there are not other children from other families present or when the degree of illness or contagious condition will not, in the opinion of the registrant, adversely affect the health of other children from other families in care.

The sewage-disposal system shall function properly. . . .

There shall be at least one properly functioning toilet and lavatory with hot and cold running water available for use by the children.

The home shall have an accessible first-aid kit. . . . Children in care shall be protected from hazardous conditions. . . .

Children shall be individually protected in car seats and/or seat belts. . . .

The home shall have an operating telephone with a list of emergency telephone numbers posted nearby. . . .

Portable heaters of the unvented kerosene type are prohibited in the home.

Children may be present and receive care on the first and second floor, provided there are two means of exit.

There shall be a properly installed and functioning approved smoke detector on each level the children occupy.

There shall be at least one easily accessible dry-chemical fire extinguisher. . . . This unit should be convenient to the kitchen area.

# NOTES

### *Introduction*

1. For *overviews* of the child-care problem see, for example, Children's Defense Fund, *A Children's Defense Budget* (Washington, D.C.: Children's Defense Fund, 1988); Martin O'Connell and David Bloom, *Juggling Jobs and Babies: America's Child Care Challenge* (Washington, D.C.: Population Reference Bureau, 1987); Claudia Wallis, "The Child Care Dilemma," *Time* 129 (June 22, 1987): 54–60. For *policy statements* see, for example, B. R. Bergmann, "A Workable Family Policy: Childcare, Income Support, Jobs," *Dissent* 35, no. 1 (1988): 88–93; Marian Wright Edelman, "Economic Issues Related to Child Care and Early Childhood Education," *Teachers College Record* 90, no. 3 (Spring 1989): 342–51; Sally Lubeck and Patricia Garrett, "Child Care 2000: Policy Options for the Future," *Social Policy* 18, no. 4 (1988): 31–37; National Association for the Education of Young Children, "Public Policy Report: Guidelines for Developing Legislation," *Young Children* 42, no. 3 (March 1987): 43–45; Robert J. Trotter, "Project Day-Care," *Psychology Today* 21 (December 1987): 32–38. For *surveys* of child-care use see U.S. Bureau of the Census, *Who's Minding the Kids? Child Care Arrangements: Winter 1984–85* (Washington, D.C.: Government Printing Office, 1987). For academic *evaluations* of the effects of day care on young children see Jay Belsky, "Two Waves of Day Care Research: Developmental Effects and Conditions of Quality," in Ricardo C. Ainslie (ed.), *The Child and the Day Care Setting: Qualitative Variations and Development* (New York: Praeger, 1984), 1–62; Jay Belsky, "A Reassessment of Infant Day Care," in Edward F. Zigler and Meryl Frank (eds.), *The Parental Leave Crisis: Toward a National Policy* (New Haven: Yale University Press, 1988), 100–19; Thomas J. Gamble and Edward F. Zigler, "Effects of Infant Day Care: Another Look at the Evidence," in Zigler and Frank, *Parental Leave Crisis*, 77–99; Alice Sterling Honig, "Research in Review: Compliance, Control and Discipline," *Young Children* 40, no. 2 (March 1985): 47–52; Deborah Phillips et al., "Child Care Quality and Children's Social Development," *Developmental Psychology* 23, no. 4 (July 1987): 537–43; Karl Zinsmeister, "Brave New World: How Day-Care Harms Children," *Policy Review* (Spring 1988): 40–48. For more popular articles addressing this issue see Earl C. Gottschalk, Jr., "Women at Work: Day Care Is Booming But Experts Are Split over Its Effect on Kids," *Wall Street Journal* (September 15, 1978): 1; Betty Holcomb, "Where's Mommy? The Great Debate over the Effects of Child Care," *New York* 20 (April 13, 1987): 72; Donna King and Carol E. MacKinnon, "Making Difficult Choices Easier: A Review of Research on Day Care and Children's Development," *Family Relations* 37 (October 1988): 392–98; Claudia Wallis, "Child Care: Effects on Children," *Time* 129 (June 22, 1987): 54–60; The *advice* to parents is discussed in Chapter 2, where a complete list of references can be found.

2. See Ad Hoc Day Care Coalition, *The Crisis in Infant and Toddler Child Care* (Washington, D.C.: Ad Hoc Day Care Coalition, 1985) and Fern Winston,

"Meeting the Day Care Crisis," *Political Affairs* 67 (March 1988): 5–9, for the use of crisis terminology. For an argument that the "crisis" has been exaggerated, see Ron Haskins, "What Day Care Crisis?" *Regulation: AEI Journal of Government and Society* 12, no. 2 (1988): 13.

3. This definition comes from Stephen J. Fosburg et al., *Family Day Care in the United States: Summary of Findings* (Washington, D.C.: Government Printing Office, 1981), 1.

4. Patricia Divine-Hawkins, *Final Report of the National Day Care Home Study*, 8 vols., U.S. Department of Health and Human Services (Washington, D.C.: Government Printing Office, 1981).

5. For a discussion of these limits, see Alfred J. Kahn and Sheila B. Kamerman, *Child Care: Facing the Hard Choices* (Dover, Mass.: Auburn House Publishing Co., 1987); Esther Wattenberg, "Family Day Care: Out of the Shadows and into the Spotlight," *Marriage and Family Review* 3, no. 3/4 (Fall/Winter 1980): 35–62. For the studies reviewed as well as other studies of family day care, see Benigno E. Aguirre, "Educational Activities and Needs of Family Day Care Providers in Texas," *Child Welfare* 66 (September–October 1987): 459–65; Mary Clurman, "Family Day Care: State of the Art," *Day Care and Early Education* 12 (Fall 1984); 22–23; Alice Collins and Eunice Watson, *Family Day Care* (Boston: Beacon Press, 1976); Brenda Krause Eheart and Robin Lynn Leavitt, "Training Day Care Home Providers: Implications for Policy and Research," *Early Childhood Research Quarterly* 1, no. 2 (June 1986): 119–32; A. C. Emlen et al., *Child Care by Kith* (Portland, Ore.: Oregon State University, 1971); A. C. Emlen, "Family Day Care for Children Under Three," paper presented at the International Symposium on the Ecology of Care and Education of Children Under Three, February 23–26, 1977, Max Planck Institute for Educational Research, Berlin; Elaine Enarson, "Toward a Theory of Waged Mothering: The Case of Family Day Care," unpublished paper, University of Nevada–Reno, 1987; Elaine Enarson, "Experts and Caregivers: Perspectives on Underground Childcare," in Emily K. Abel and Margaret K. Nelson (eds.), *Circles of Care* (Albany: SUNY Press, 1990), 233–45; Susan Groves, *Family Day Care: Economic and Work Related Factors Affecting the Persistence of Providers*, (Berkeley: Center for the Study, Education and Advancement of Women, University of California, 1984); Brian Jackson and Sonia Jackson, *Childminder: A Study in Action Research* (London: Routledge and Kegan Paul, 1979); Carol S. Klass, "Childrearing Interactions Within Developmental Home- or Center-Based Early Education," *Young Children* 42, no. 3 (1987): 9–13, 67–70; Jean Marzollo, "Child-Care Workers Speak Up," *Parents' Magazine* 62 (April 1987): 114–18; Alan R. Pence and Hillel Goelman, "Who Cares for the Child in Day Care? An Examination of Caregivers from Three Types of Care," *Early Childhood Research Quarterly* 2, no. 4 (December 1987): 315–34; Pat Petrie, "Day Care for Under 2's at Child Minders and in Day Nurseries," *Early Child Development and Care* 16, nos. 3–4 (1984): 205–15; June Solnit Sale, "Family Day Care: Potential Child Development Service," *American Journal of Public Health* 62, no. 5 (1972); June Solnit Sale, "Family Day Care: A Valuable Alternative," *Young Child* 28, no. 4 (1973): 668; June Solnit Sale, "Family Day Care: One Alternative in the Delivery of Developmental Services in Early Childhood," *American Journal of Ortho-*

*psychiatry* 43, no. 1 (1973): 37–45; Sandra M. Stith and Albert J. Davis, "Employed Mothers and Family Day Care Substitute Caregivers: A Comparative Analysis of Infant Care," *Child Development* 55, no. 4 (1984): 1340–48; P. V. Washburn and J. S. Washburn, "The Four Roles of the Family Day-Care Provider," *Child Welfare* 64, no. 5 (April 1985): 547–54; Esther Wattenberg, "Characteristics of Family Day Care Providers: Implications for Training," *Child Welfare* 56, no. 4 (April 1977): 211–29.

6. Garry Trudeau, *Calling Dr. Whoopee!* (New York: Henry Holt and Co., 1987); Nick Ravo, "Two Children Killed in Blaze at Brooklyn Day-Care Center," *New York Times* (November 25, 1986): B1, B4; Cathy Trost, "How Children's Safety Can Be Put in Jeopardy by Day-Care Personnel," *Wall Street Journal* (October 18, 1988): A1, A16; "Report Criticizes Two Relatives in Child's Fall in Texas Well," *New York Times* (January 13, 1988): A18.

7. R. L. Shortlidge et al., "Changes in Child Care Arrangements of Working Women," *Proceedings of the American Statistical Association* (1974): 209–18. See also the articles in the *Wall Street Journal* suggesting that too many restrictions on family day care providers might deplete the supply of this kind of care (Virginia Inman, "Stunted Growth: Day Care Laws Limit Private-Home Centers That Parents Like Best," *Wall Street Journal* [October 26, 1982]: 1; Cathy Trost, "Should a 'Mother Down the Block' Be Regulated as Day-Care Provider?," *Wall Street Journal* [October 18, 1988]: A16). For an example of portraits of women who have taken up this activity, see Lisa Wilson Strick, "A Homemade Solution to the Day Care Dilemma," *Woman's Day* (April 19, 1988): 26–30.

8. Kahn and Kamerman, *Child Care,* 8–10; see also U.S. Bureau of the Census, *Who's Minding the Kids?* No one knows how many children are in family day care homes nor how many family day care homes (and providers) exist. Three factors impede the arrival at firm estimates. First, most family day care is unregulated and therefore hidden from casual purview. Second, there are few comprehensive surveys of consumer use. Third, much of the care in another home is offered by relatives who may not be paid for their services (Kahn and Kamerman, *Child Care,* 213; Bureau of the Census, *Who's Minding the Kids?,* 11). Many studies exclude care by relatives when examining family day care. The Bureau of the Census report *Who's Minding the Kids?,* for example, makes a distinction among three kinds of care in another home: by grandparents, by other relatives, and by nonrelatives. While this distinction makes sense from the perspective of understanding parent choice, it does little to help us understand how many children are actually in family day care homes and how many providers there are. Kahn and Kamerman draw on four separate studies to arrive at their estimates. For another estimate, see Arleen Leibowitz, Linda J. Waite and Christina Witsberger, "Child Care for Preschoolers: Differences by Child's Age," *Demography* 25, no. 2 (May 1988): 205–20.

9. For studies of center-based child-care workers, see Carolyn Benson, *Who Cares for Kids: A Report on Child Care Providers* (Washington, D.C.: National Commission on Working Women, 1986); Glenn Collins, "For Child Care Workers, Poverty Level Wages," *The New York Times* (November 24, 1986): B18; Nora

Palmer Gould, "Caregivers in Day Care: Who Are They?" *Day Care* 10, no. 4 (Summer 1983): 17–21; Lana Hostetler, "Public Policy Report: The Nanny Trap: Child Care Work Today," *Young Children* 39, no. 2 (January 1984): 76–79; J. McClelland, "Job-Satisfaction of Child-Care Workers: A Review," *Child Care Quarterly* 15, no. 2 (1986): 82–89; Ludmilla Murphy, "Child Care Workers," *Occupational Outlook* 30 (Summer 1986): 29–32; John Myer, "An Exploratory Nationwide Survey of Child Care Workers," *Child Care Quarterly* 9, no. 1 (Spring 1980): 17–25; Willa Pettygrove and James Greenman, "The Adult World of Day Care," in James Greenman and Robert Fuqua (eds.), *Making Day Care Better* (New York: Teachers College Press, 1984), 84–105; Deborah Phillips and Marcy Whitebook, "Who Are Child Care Workers? The Search for Answers," *Young Children* 41 (May 1986): 14–20; Georgianna T. Roberts, "Status and Salaries of Our Profession," *Young Children* 8, no. 3 (March 1983): 18–19.

10. *Congressional Record*, Senate, 101st Congress, 1st Session, June 23, 1989: 7480.

11. The major child-care legislation under consideration exempts those who care for a single, related child from state and federal regulations. All the family day care providers discussed in this book were receiving payment for child care, and none cared for only one related child, although some had begun in this manner and some continued to offer unpaid care of relatives or care of relatives at a reduced rate.

12. Sara E. Rix (ed.), *The American Woman, 1988–89: A Status Report* (New York: W. W. Norton, 1988), 366; Vernon M. Briggs, Jr., "The Growth and Composition of the U.S. Labor Force," *Science* 238 (October 9, 1987): 178.

13. Briggs, *U.S. Labor Force*, 176–80; see also Howard V. Hayghe, "Rise in Mothers' Labor Force Activity Includes Those with Infants," *Monthly Labor Review* 109 (February 1986): 43–45; Howard V. Hayghe, "Employers and Child Care: What Roles Do They Play?" *Monthly Labor Review* 111 (September 1988): 34–44; Kahn and Kamerman, *Child Care*, 7; Elizabeth Waldman, "Labor Force Statistics from a Family Perspective," *Monthly Labor Review* 106 (December 1983): 16–20.

14. By 1995 two-thirds of all preschoolers will have mothers in the work force and need care on a part- or full-time basis. See also Susan Gordon, "America's Day-Care Crisis," *Entrepreneur* 17 (March 1989): 90–100; Hayghe, "Rise in Mothers' Labor Force Activity," 43; Hayghe, "Employers and Child Care"; Kahn and Kamerman, *Child Care*, 12; Barbara Kantrowitz, "Who Cares About Day Care? Millions of People but None of the Candidates," *Newsweek* 111 (March 28, 1988): 73.

15. For discussions of how feminists have looked at (and sometimes ignored) the issue of child care, see Judith D. Auerbach, "Locating Child Care in Sociology," paper presented at the Society for the Study of Social Problems, Annual Meeting, Chicago, August 14–16, 1987; Carole E. Joffe, "Why the United States Has No Child-Care Policy," in Irene Diamond (ed.), *Families, Politics and Public Policy: A Feminist Dialogue on Women and the State* (New York: Longman, 1983), 168–182; Sheila B. Kamerman, "Child Care Services: An Issue for Gender Equity and Women's Solidarity," *Child Welfare* 64, no. 3 (1985); Dorothy Miller, "Children's Policy and Women's Policy: Congruence or Con-

flict?" *Social Work* 32 (July/August 1987): 289–92; Barrie Thorne, "Re-Visioning Women and Social Change: Where Are the Children?" *Gender and Society* 1, no. 1 (1987): 85–109. For discussion suggesting that feminists have overlooked the needs of children in their proposals, see Valerie Suransky, *The Erosion of Childhood* (Chicago: University of Chicago Press, 1982).

16. Margaret Polatnick, "Why Men Don't Rear Children," in Joyce Trebilcot (ed.), *Mothering: Essays in Feminist Theory* (Totowa, N.J.: Rowman and Allanheld, 1983), 21–40; Andrew Hacker, *U/S: A Statistical Portrait of the American People* (New York: Viking Press, 1982); Derek Richardson, "Day Care: Men Need Not Apply," *Education Digest* 51 (January 1986): 58–59; Bryan E. Robinson, "An Update on the Status of Men in Early Child Care Work," *Child Welfare* 58, no. 7 (July–August 1979): 471–77; Bryan E. Robinson, "Vanishing Breed: Men in Child Care Programs," *Young Children* 43, no. 6 (September 1988): 54–58.

17. For comparisons of child-care policies in the United States and other countries, see Carolyn T. Adams and Kathryn T. Winston, *Mothers at Work: Public Policies in the United States, Sweden and China* (New York: Longman, 1980); Sheila B. Kamerman and Alfred J. Kahn, *Family Policy: Government and Families in Fourteen Countries* (New York: Columbia University Press, 1978); Sheila B. Kamerman and Alfred J. Kahn, *Child Care, Family Benefits and Working Parents: A Study of Comparative Policy* (New York: Columbia University Press, 1981); Sheila B. Kamerman, Alfred J. Kahn, and Paul Kingston, *Maternity Policies and Working Women* (New York: Columbia University Press, 1983); Mary Ruggie, *The State and Working Women: A Comparative Study of Britain and Sweden* (Princeton: Princeton University Press, 1984); Chiara Saraceno, "The Social Construction of Childhood: Child Care and Education Policies in Italy and the United States," *Social Problems* 3, no. 3 (February 1984): 351–63; Curtis J. Sitomer, "Day Care: A Global Perspective," *Christian Science Monitor* 73, no. 1 (May 1981): 14.

18. Reliance on resource and referral services for employees searching for child care is congruent with this objective; it is also supported by parents who state that this is a kind of help they need (G. A. Bogat and L. K. Gensheimer, "The Role of Information and Referral Services in the Selection of Child Care," *Children and Youth Services Review* 8, no. 3 [1986]: 243–56). For academic discussions of employer-sponsored child care, see Judith D. Auerbach, *In the Business of Child Care: Employer Initiatives and Working Women* (New York: Praeger, 1988); David E. Bloom and Todd P. Steen, "Why Child Care Is Good for Business," *American Demographics* 10 (August 1988): 22–27; Sandra L. Burud et al., *Employer Supported Child Care* (Dover, Mass.: Auburn House Publishing Co., 1984); Lisa R. Cole, "Child Care and Business," *Business and Economics Review* 35 (January–March 1989): 4–9; Hacker, *U/S: Statistical Portrait;* Sheila B. Kamerman, *Family Needs: The Corporate Response* (Pergamon Press, 1983); Renee Yablans Magid, "The Consequences of Employer Involvement in Child Care," *Teachers College Record* 90, no. 3 (Spring 1989): 434–43; Nancy Rubin, *The Mother Mirror* (New York: G. P. Putnam's Sons, 1984). See also U.S. Department of Labor, *Employers and Child Care: Benefiting Work and Family* (Washington, D.C.: Government Printing Office, 1989). Recently considerable attention has been

focused on this issue in the popular press. See, for example, Aaron Bernstein and Elizabeth Ehrlich, "Business Starts Tailoring Itself to Suit Working Women," *Business Week* (October 6, 1986): 50; Mark Bruno, "Day Care on the Job," *Newsweek* 106 (September 2, 1985): 59; Fern Schumer Chapman, "Executive Guilt: Who's Taking Care of the Children? And How Will Kids Raised by Nannies and in Day Care Centers Turn Out?" *Fortune* 115, no. 8 (February 16, 1987): 30; "Child Care: Get Your Boss to Help," *Changing Times* 40, no. 6 (October 1986): 8; Glenn Collins, "Day Care Finds Corporate Help," *The New York Times* (January 5, 1987): B5; Carol Dilks and Nancy L. Croft, "Child Care: Your Baby?" *Nation's Business* 74, no. 5 (December 1986): 16; Margaret Engel, "New Day Care Options: How Companies Are Meeting the Needs of Working Parents," *Glamour* 83 (May 1985): 136; Dana E. Friedman, "Child Care for Employees' Kids," *Harvard Business Review* 64 (March/April 1986): 28–38; Elizabeth K. LaFleur and Walter B. Newsom, "Opportunities for Child Care," *Personnel Administrator* 33 (June 1988): 146–54; Karen Rubin, "Whose Job Is Child Care?" *Ms.* 15 (March 1987): 32–39; Leonard Silverman, "Corporate Childcare: Playpens in the Boardroom or Productivity Investment?" *Vital Speeches of the Day* 51, no. 16 (June 1, 1985): 503.

19. For an argument that this might be changing, see Glenn Collins, "Wooing Workers in the 90's: New Role for Family Benefits," *The New York Times* (July 20, 1988): A1.

20. Administration representatives went on record as opposing governmental regulation of any sort at any level for child care. Although an interest in regulation of family day care homes grew, state standards vary widely (see Chapter 5); they have also been notoriously unsuccessful: Between 60 and 90 percent of all family day care remains unregulated. See Kahn and Kamerman, *Child Care*, 23; Margaret Malone, "Child Day Care: The Federal Role," Congressional Research Service (Education and Public Welfare Division, n.d.) on current government trends. On regulation specifically, see John R. Nelson, Jr., "The Federal Interagency Day Care Requirements," in Cheryl B. Hayes (ed.), *Making Policies for Children: A Study of the Federal Process* (Washington, D.C.: National Academy Press, 1982); D. Phillips and E. Zigler, "The Checkered History of Federal Child Care Regulation," *Review of Research in Education* 14 (1987): 3–41; Kahn and Kamerman, *Child Care*, 23.

21. Kahn and Kamerman, *Child Care*, 23. Until recently subsidies were limited largely to the Dependent Care Tax Credit. For discussions see Kahn and Kamerman, *Child Care*, 21; and Jane Bryant Quinn, "A Crisis in Child Care: Day-Care Help for Workingwomen Will Become the Most Essential Company Benefit of the 1990's," *Newsweek* 111 (February 15, 1988): 57. For an analysis of private-sector involvement in child care, see Angela C. Browne, "The Market Sphere: Private Responses to the Need for Day Care," *Child Welfare* 64, no. 4 (July–August 1985), 367–81; Katherine Ellis and Rosalind Petchesky, "Children of the Corporate Dream: An Analysis of Day Care as a Political Issue Under Capitalism," *Socialist Revolution* 2, no. 6 (November/December 1972): 9–28; Sharon L. Kagan and Theresa Glennon, "Child Care: In Defense of Choice," *Day Care* 9, no. 3 (Spring 1982): 54–57; Sarah Smith, "'La Petite Academy': Companies to Watch," *Fortune* 117 (May 9, 1988): 70.

22. In June 1989 the Senate passed an omnibus child-care bill, the Act for Better Child Care Services, a $10.3 billion five-year plan that would expand day care by providing direct grants to the states and help low-income working families by modestly increasing income tax credits. In March 1990, the House passed the Early Childhood Education and Development Act, a $27 billion five-year plan that would, like ABC, give states grants to help parents pay for and improve the quality of child care. The House bill also included money to expand Head Start and begin a new program of care in schools before and after classes for latchkey children. A major difference between the two bills remained in the area of how increased federal child-care assistance would be administered. The Senate bill relies primarily on direct grants to states for use at their discretion. The House measure relies more heavily on tax credits and block grants designated for child-care use. Immediately following the House vote, President Bush threatened to veto the legislation (Steven A. Holmes, "House, 265–145, Votes to Widen Day Care Programs in the Nation," *New York Times* [March 30, 1990]: A1). For debates on this legislation, see "Act for Better Child Care Services of 1989," *Congressional Digest* (February 1990): 33–67; "Child Care Legislation," *Congressional Digest* (November 1988): 258–87; Sandra Evans, "2.5 Billion Day Care Bill Proposed," *Washington Post* (November 20, 1987): 22; Erna Fishaut, "A Time to Dream," *Young Children* 43, no. 1 (November 1987): 20–22; Nancy Folbre and Heidi Hartmann, "A New Politics of Entitlement," *The Nation* (October 3, 1988): 263–66; George Gilder, "An Open Letter to Orrin Hatch," *National Review* (May 13, 1988): 32–34; Lawrence B. Lindsey, "Better Child Care, Cheaper," *Wall Street Journal* (July 5, 1988): 20; Mary McNamara, "At Last! A Major Push for Child Care," *Ms.* 16 (February 1988): 17–18; Laurence R. Seligman, "The Day Care Follies," *Fortune* 117 (February 15, 1988): 124; "Child Care for All," *Wall Street Journal* (June 7, 1988): 34; Robert Wright, "An Election Issue We Don't Need: Kids 'R' U.S.," *The New Republic* (August 22, 1988): 12–14.

23. See Joseph Davis and Phyllis Solomon, "Day-Care Needs Among the Upper Middle Classes," *Child Welfare* 59, no. 8 (September/October 1980); Leslie Tweeton, "The Day Care Problem," *Boston Magazine* 77 (May 1985): 180–81; Barbara Kantrowitz, "A Mother's Choice," *Newsweek* (March 31, 1986); "Child Care: The Bottom Line," *Children Today* 16, no. 4 (July–August 1987): 3; Robert W. Fuqua and Dorothy Labensohn, "Parents as Consumers of Child Care," *Family Relations* 35 (April 1986): 295–303. Ironically, a Reagan administration's child-care spokesperson insisted in mid-1986 that there was no evidence indicating a shortage of places because there is an unknown and indeterminate amount of informal care available that is as good or better than professional care (Kahn and Kamerman, *Child Care*, 103).

24. See David M. Blau and Philip K. Robins, "Child-Care Costs and Family Labor Supply," *Review of Economics and Statistics* 70, no. 3 (1988); Liliane Floge, "The Dynamics of Child-Care Use and Some Implications for Women's Employment," *Journal of Marriage and the Family* 47, no. 1 (February 1985): 143–54; Liliane Floge, "Changing Household Structure, Child-Care Availability, and Employment Among Mothers of Preschool Children," *Journal of Marriage and the Family* 51 (February 1989): 51–63; Marsha Hurst and Ruth E. Zambrana,

"Child Care and Working Mothers in Puerto Rican Families," *Annals of the American Academy: AAPSS* 461 (May 1982): 113–24; Gwen Morgan, "Who's Minding the Kids?" *Parents* (April 1987): 106–9; O'Connell and Bloom, "Juggling Jobs and Babies"; Harriet B. Presser and Wendy Baldwin, "Child Care as a Constraint on Employment: Prevalence, Correlates and the Bearing on the Work and Fertility Nexus" *American Journal of Sociology* 85, no. 5 (1980): 1202–13; Quinn, "Crisis in Child Care": 57; P. K. Robins, "Child-Care and Convenience: The Effects of Labor Market Entry Costs on Economic Self-Sufficiency Among Public-Housing Residents," *Social Science Quarterly* 69, no. 1 (1988): 122–36; Hal Straus, "The Day Care Dilemma," *American Health*, 7, no. 7 (September 1988): 61–66; Barbara Willer, "Quality or Affordability: Trade-offs for Early Childhood Programs," *Young Children* 42, no. 6 (September 1987): 41–3.

25. *Congressional Record*, June 23, 1989, 7483–84.

26. *Congressional Record*, June 23, 1989, 7483.

27. Davis and Solomon, "Day Care Needs"; Hurst and Zambrana, "Puerto Rican Families."

28. Kahn and Kamerman, *Child Care*, 211.

29. See, for example, Hacker, *U/S: Statistical Portrait*, on caregiving in formal organizations and Robyn Stone, Gail Lee Cafferata, and Judith Sangle, "Caregivers of the Frail Elderly: A National Profile" (Washington, D.C.: National Center for Health Services Research, 1986) on informal caregiving. For feminist discussions of caregiving, see Abel and Nelson, *Circles of Care;* Mary Georgina Boulton, *On Being a Mother: A Study of Women with Pre-School Children* (London: Tavistock Publications, 1983); Janet Finch and Dulcie Groves, *A Labour of Love: Women, Work and Caring* (London: Routledge and Kegan Paul, 1983); Berenice Fisher and Joan Tronto, "Toward a Feminist Theory of Caregiving," in Abel and Nelson, *Circles of Care*, 35–62; Hilary Graham, "Caring: A Labour of Love," in Finch and Groves, *Labour of Love*, 13–30; Hilary Land and Hilary Rose, "Compulsory Altruism for Some or an Altruistic Society for All?" in Philip Bean et al. (eds.), *In Defence of Welfare* (London: Tavistock, 1985), 74–96; Joan Tronto, "Beyond Gender Differences to a Theory of Care," *Signs* 12, no. 4 (Summer 1987): 644–63; Clare Ungerson, "Women and Caring: Skills, Tasks and Taboos," in Eva Gamarnikov et al. (eds.), *The Public and the Private* (London: Heinemann, 1983), 62–77; Kari Waerness, "On the Rationality of Caring," paper presented at the International Conference on the Transformation of the Welfare State: Dangers and Potentialities for Women, Bellagio, Italy, August 23–27, 1983; Kari Waerness, "Caring as Women's Work in the Welfare State," in Harriet Holter (ed.), *Patriarchy in a Welfare Society* (Oslo: Universitetsforlaget, 1984), 67–86.

30. A good review of this approach can be found in Alison M. Jaggar, *Feminist Politics and Human Nature* (Totowa, N.J.: Rowman and Allanheld, 1983).

31. Graham, "Caring: A Labour of Love," 27–28.

32. See, for example, Nancy Chodorow, *The Reproduction of Mothering* (Berkeley: University of California Press, 1971); Carol Gilligan, *In a Different Voice: Psychological Theory and Women's Development* (Cambridge, Mass.: Harvard University Press, 1982); and Jean Baker Miller, *Toward a New Psychology of Women* (Boston: Beacon Press, 1976).

33. Graham, "Caring: A Labour of Love," 17.

34. Emily K. Abel and Margaret K. Nelson, "Circles of Care: An Introductory Essay," in Abel and Nelson, *Circles of Care*, 4–34.

35. For discussions that focus more on contextual issues, see, for example, Cary Cherniss, *Staff Burnout: Job Stress in the Human Services* (Beverly Hills: Sage Publications, 1980); Cary Cherniss, *Professional Burnout in Human Service Organizations* (New York: Praeger, 1980); Timothy Diamond, "Nursing Homes as 'Trouble'" in Abel and Nelson, *Circles of Care*, 173–87; Sara Freedman, "To Love and to Work: The Ghettoization of Women's Labor in the Home and the School," unpublished paper, Cambridge, Mass., 1987; Karen Sacks, "Does It Pay to Care?," in Abel and Nelson, *Circles of Care*, 188–206; Ann Withorn, *Serving the People: Social Services and Social Change* (New York: Columbia University Press, 1984).

36. For useful discussions of this issue, see Rayna Rapp, "Family and Class in Contemporary America: Notes Toward an Understanding of Ideology," in Barrie Thorne and Marilyn Yalom (eds.), *Rethinking the Family: Some Feminist Questions* (New York: Longman, 1982), 168–87; Barrie Thorne, "Feminist Rethinking of the Family: An Overview," in Thorne and Yalom, *Rethinking the Family*, 1–24. Other observers have noted that the conceptualization of life as existing in entirely separate, and distinctive, private and public spheres has left us without a language with which to discuss work that transcends these distinctions. See, for example, the writing of Nona Y. Glazer, "Servants to Capital: Unpaid Domestic Labor and Paid Work," in Naomi Gerstel and Harriet Engel Gross (eds.), *Families and Work* (Philadelphia: Temple University Press, 1987), 236–56; Joan Smith, "The Way We Were: Women and Work," *Feminist Studies* 8, no. 2 (Summer 1982): 437–56; Margaret Stacey, "The Division of Labour Revisited or Overcoming the Two Adams," in P. Abrams et al. (eds.), *Practice and Progress: British Sociology 1950–1980* (London: Allen and Unwin, 1981), 172–91.

37. Thorne, "Feminist Rethinking of the Family," 18.

38. Susan M. Reverby, "The Duty or Right to Care: Nursing in Historical Perspective," in Abel and Nelson, *Circles of Care*, 132–49.

39. Arlie Russell Hochschild, *The Managed Heart: The Commercialization of Human Feeling* (Berkeley: University of California Press, 1983.)

40. For discussions of the resurgence and the effects of home-based work, see Sheila Allen and Carol Wolkowitz, "Homeworking and the Control of Women's Work," in *Feminist Review* (ed.), *Waged Work: A Reader* (London: Virago Press, 1986): 238–64; Sheila Allen and Carol Wolkowitz, *Homeworking: Myths and Realities* (Basingstoke, England: Macmillan, 1987); Lourdes Beneria and Martha Roldan, *Crossroads of Class and Gender: Industrial Homework, Subcontracting, and Household Dynamics in Mexico City* (Chicago: University of Chicago Press, 1987); Bettina Berch, "The Resurrection of Out-Work," *Monthly Review* 37, no. 6 (1985): 37–44; Kathleen Christensen, "Women and Home-Based Work," *Social Policy* 15 (Winter 1985): 54–57; Kathleen Christensen, *Women and Home-Based Work: The Unspoken Contract* (New York: Henry Holt and Co., 1987); Priscilla Connolly, "The Politics of the Informal Sector: A Critique," in Nanneke Redclift and Enzo Mingione (eds.), *Beyond Employment: Household Gender and Subsistence* (Oxford: Basil Blackwell, 1985), 14–54; Chris Gerry, "The

Working Class and Small Enterprises in the UK Recession," in Redclift and Mingione, *Beyond Employment*, 288–316; Laura McClure, "Homework's Horrors," *The Guardian* (November 5, 1986): 1; Magreth H. Olson and Sophia B. Primps, "Working at Home with Computers: Work and Nonwork Issues," *Journal of Social Issues* 40, no. 3 (1984): 97–112; "White Collar Homework: On the Upswing," *Personnel* 59, no. 5 (1984): 50–51; Alejandro Portes and John Walton, *Labour, Class and the International System* (New York: Academic Press, 1981); Joanne Pratt, "Hometelwork: A Study of Its Pioneers," *Technological Forecasting and Social Change* 25, no. 1 (1984): 1–14; Nanneke Redclift and Enzo Mingione, "Introduction," in Redclift and Mingione, *Beyond Employment*, 4; Martha Roldan, "Industrial Outworking, Struggles for the Reproduction of Working-Class Families and Gender Subordination," in Redclift and Mingione, *Beyond Employment*, 248–85; Maureen Sheehy, "Homework: Employment Option or Employment Risk," U.S. Department of Labor: National Commission on Working Women (Washington, D.C.: Government Printing Office, 1983); Ivan Szelenyi, "Structural Changes and Alternatives to Capitalist Development in the Contemporary Urban and Regional System," *International Journal of Urban and Regional Research* 5, no. 1 (1981): 1–4; Alvin Toffler, *The Third Wave* (New York: William Morrow, 1980); Tamara H. Wolfgram, "Working at Home: The Growth of Cottage Industry," *The Futurist* 18, no. 3 (June 1984): 31–34;

41. See, for example, Sheila Allen, *Production and Reproduction: The Lives of Women Homeworkers* (London: Routledge and Kegan Paul, 1983); for an exception see Jane Hoy and Mary Kennedy, "Women's Paid Labor in the Home: The British Experience," *Research in the Sociology of Work: Peripheral Workers*, vol. 2 (Greenwich, Conn.: JAI Press, 1983), 211–39.

42. See, for example, Eugene H. Becker, "Self-Employed Workers: An Update to 1983," *Monthly Labor Review* 107, no. 7 (1984): 14–18; France W. Horvath, "Work at Home: New Findings from the Current Population Survey," *Monthly Labor Review* 109, no. 11 (November 1986): 31–35.

43. Those who subdivide the informal economy further by whether the income is generated through legal or illegal means would introduce yet another criterion, which would distinguish among groups of providers. J. I. Gershuny and R. E. Pahl, "Work Outside Employment: Some Preliminary Speculations," *NUQ* (Winter 1979): 120–35; Stuart Henry, "Introduction," in Stuart Henry (ed.), *Informal Institutions: Alternative Networks in the Corporate State* (New York: St. Martin's Press, 1981), 1–23; Stuart Henry, "The Working Unemployed: Perspectives on the Informal Economy and Unemployment," *Sociological Review* 30, no. 3 (1982): 460–77.

44. Joan Smith, "Nonwage Labor and Subsistence," in Joan Smith et al. (eds.), *The Households and the World-Economy* (Beverly Hills, Calif.: Sage Publications, 1984), 72.

45. For evidence that women have always worked in the home, see Christine E. Bose, "Devaluing Women's Work: The Undercount of Women's Employment in 1900 and 1980," in Christine E. Bose, Roslyn Feldberg, and Natalie Sokoloff (eds.), *Hidden Aspects of Women's Work* (New York: Praeger, 1987): 95–116; Joan Smith, "The Way We Were."

46. The failure to make this distinction is also found among those who focus on home-work; see, for example, Allen and Wolkowitz, *Homeworking: Myths and Realities*, 27. The ambiguity can also be found in the writing of Alice Kessler-Harris and Karen Brodkin Sacks: "In addition, mothers and other non-wage earning adults in the family participated in what has come to be called an informal economy, where they provided significant amounts of cash for family needs and *stretched family income with their unwaged labor*" (emphasis added) (Alice Kessler-Harris and Karen Brodkin Sacks, "The Demise of Domesticity in America," in Lourdes Beneria and Catharine R. Simpson [eds.], *Women, Households and the Economy* [New Brunswick, N.J.: Rutgers University Press, 1987], 69.) For arguments against ignoring this distinction, see Joan Smith, "Nonwage Labor and Subsistence," and Allen and Wolkowitz, *Homeworking: Myths and Realities*, 17, 50.

47. Allen and Wolkowitz, *Homeworking: Myths and Realities*, 28.

48. Lenore Davidoff, "The Separation of Home and Work? Landladies and Lodgers in Nineteenth and Twentieth Century England," in Sandra Burman (ed.), *Fit Work for Women* (New York: St. Martin's Press, 1979), 64–97; Joan M. Jensen, "Cloth, Butter and Boarders: Women's Household Production for the Market," *Review of Radical Political Economics* 12, no. 2 (Summer 1980): 14–23.

49. Joan Smith, "Nonwage Labor and Subsistence," 77.

50. Two-thirds of these were registered providers; one-third were unregistered providers. These terms are explained in Chapter 5.

## *Chapter 1*

1. For an overview of these characteristics and the comparison with providers from the National Day Care Home Study, see Appendix A, Tables 2 and 3. For other studies of family day care providers, see also P. Lindsay and C. H. Lindsay, "Teachers in Preschools and Child-Care Centers: Overlooked and Undervalued," *Child and Youth Care Quarterly* 16, no. 2 (1987): 91–105; Alan R. Pence and Hillel Goelman, "Who Cares for the Child in Day Care? An Examination of Caregivers from Three Types of Care," *Early Childhood Research Quarterly* 2, no. 4 (December 1987): 315–34.

2. The proportion of female-headed households among provider families is almost the same as that among the population as a whole: 84.8 percent of Vermont families consist of married couples; 11.8 percent of all Vermont families are headed by females (U.S. Bureau of the Census, *1980 Census: Vermont* [Washington, D.C.: Government Printing Office, 1980], 43).

3. Some of the women I interviewed had cared for children before they had their own; most of them, like Sarah, did so in a client's home. When their first child was born, most of the women ceased caring for other people's children outside of their own homes. Several of the women who had been family day care providers before they had their own children said that they did not like the work at that time, but that after their own children were born they found it a more acceptable option.

4. Among married Vermont women age fifteen to forty-four, the number of children born per 1,000 women is 1.963 (U.S. Bureau of the Census, *1980 Census: Vermont*, 46). Sheila Allen, *Production and Reproduction: The Lives of*

*Women Homeworkers* (London: Routledge and Kegan Paul, 1983), suggests that the families of home-workers are somewhat larger than those in the broader population in which they are located; this finding is consistent with the data here since the older providers had more children. This suggests that many of the families with two children may still be "incomplete" and that those with only one child will add at least one more child to the family.

5. This is not to say that these children are irrelevant to their child-care decisions; many are still at home because they feel strongly that teenagers need a mother at home as much as younger children do.

6. A. C. Emlen, "Family Day Care for Children Under Three," paper presented at the International Symposium on the Ecology of Care and Education of Children Under Three, February 23–26, 1977, Max Planck Institute for Educational Research, Berlin.

7. Emmy Werner, *Child Care: Kith, Kin and Hired Hands* (Baltimore: University Park Press, 1984).

8. I did not ask about race on the questionnaire. Because Vermont is an extremely white state, I would not get enough nonwhite respondents to complete any kind of special analysis. Only one of the seventy women I interviewed was not white.

9. U.S. Bureau of the Census, *1980 Census: Vermont*.

10. For different assessments of the reasons why family day care providers enter the occupation, see Emlen, "Family Day Care"; Brian Jackson and Sonia Jackson, *Childminder: A Study in Action Research* (London: Routledge and Kegan Paul, 1979); Werner, *Child Care*.

11. U.S. Bureau of the Census, *1980 Census: Vermont*.

12. For a more detailed comparison of the occupations of family day care providers and the Vermont female labor force, see Margaret K. Nelson, "Providing Family Day Care: An Analysis of Home-Based Work," *Social Problems* 35, no. 1 (February 1988): 81.

13. As I will discuss in Chapter 6, some of these women consciously choose family day care as a site in which they can offer their services with much more autonomy and self-direction than they had working in institutional settings.

14. This may be especially true if we acknowledge the costs of going out to work (transportation, clothes, child care) and either the savings available to those family day care providers who do not report their incomes (as is the case for many of the unregulated providers) or the extensive deductions for operating a business in the home available to those who do report their incomes. On the other hand, child care also includes expenses (see below). Child-care workers, like other home-workers, frequently overlook these expenses when reporting their earnings (Jane Hoy and Mary Kennedy, "Women's Paid Labor in the Home: The British Experience," *Research in the Sociology of Work: Peripheral Workers*, vol. 2 [Greenwich, Conn.: JAI Press, 1983], 230).

15. In 1980, median annual earnings for Vermont's employed men ranged from $7,755 for those employed in farming, forestry, and fishing to $18,741 for those employed in managerial and professional specialty occupations. The occupations of the husbands of the family day care providers were distributed among the major occupational groups much like Vermont's male labor force as

a whole, with 24 percent in "managerial and professional specialty occupations," 22 percent in "technical, sales, and administrative support occupations," 9 percent in service occupations, 22 percent in "precision production, craft and repair occupations," 20 percent as "operators, fabricators, and laborers," and 4 percent in farming, forestry, and fishing.

16. The subject of how the proportion of income earned affects domestic relations will be considered in Chapter 4. I might note here that because these women are working in the informal economy (rather than as paid labor in the work force), the burden for maintaining these families and reproducing labor power is shifted from the sphere of wage labor to the family itself (Martha Roldan, "Industrial Outworking, Struggles for the Reproduction of Working-Class Families and Gender Subordination," in Nanneke Redclift and Enzo Mingione [eds.], *Beyond Employment: Household Gender and Subsistence* [Oxford: Basil Blackwell, 1985], 270). The second income sustains the family without placing pressure for higher wages on the husband's employer. Yet because this income does not carry benefits such as pensions or health insurance, the "primary earner" may be locked into a job that, although it does not pay enough to support the family, does offer resources without which the family's situation would be even more tenuous. At the same time, family day care providers—like women who stay home and raise their own children and care for the needs of their spouses—offer a service in a manner that relieves their clients' employers from the responsibility of making substantial contributions toward the cost of child care.

17. The fees that provide the basis for these incomes are discussed below. The statistics reported here were calculated in the following manner: I took the woman's reported weekly earnings and multiplied by fifty since most women report taking a vacation of two weeks or less; I then divided that statistic (for yearly income) by the total family income using the midpoint for the income category checked by the provider.

18. Allen and Wolkowitz, *Myths and Realities*, 63–70.

19. In many cases, women who can manage the expense and complications of child care with one child, find that the birth of a second precipitates them out of the wage labor force. One mother I interviewed was about to lose the family day care provider who was caring for her three children. Certain that she would be unable to locate anyone else with as reasonable rates (for the three), she felt she might have no choice but to open her own family day care home.

20. Allen and Wolkowitz, *Myths and Realities*, 73; Bettina Berch, "The Resurrection of Out-Work," *Monthly Review* 37, no. 6 (1985): 37–44; Kathleen Christensen, "Women and Home-Based Work," *Social Policy* 15 (Winter 1985): 54–7.

21. Three questionnaire respondents said that they opted for family day care as a career because of pressure from their spouse to remain at home. Roldan's 1985 study of industrial home-workers found that many women said their decision to work at home was influenced by their husbands.

22. Allen, *Production and Reproduction*, 85.

23. While these patterns of continuity describe some women, there is a deviant group that operates family day care homes in an explicit way as part of

a career. Again, the career is child care. But they are trained workers and seek family day care because it will provide them with optimum working conditions or will enable them to provide the kind of care they feel is appropriate. (For these women as well, the motivation might be combined with a desire to care for their own children.) (See Chapter 6.)

24. Kathleen Gerson makes a similar point in her discussion of the manner in which women make choices about motherhood and careers: "Women's adult choices are neither the predetermined outcome of early childhood socialization nor mere reflections of static, purely coercive social structures, although each of these factors plays a role. Women's decisions for or against motherhood and for or against committed employment develop out of a negotiated process whereby they confront and respond to constraints and opportunities, often unanticipated, encountered over the course of their lives. The process is dynamic, not stable and fixed. It depends on how women perceive and define their situations as well as on the objective circumstances that structure these perceptions. Because the structural arrangements that shape women's perceptions, motivations, and behavior are ambiguous and contradictory, decision making involves an active, at times difficult, effort to identify, choose between, and act on situational interests that are rarely obvious, consistent, or straightforwardly 'true.'" Kathleen Gerson, "How Women Choose Between Employment and Family: A Developmental Perspective," in Naomi Gerstel and Harriet Engel Gross (eds.), *Families and Work* (Philadelphia: Temple University Press, 1987), 283–84. See also Allen and Wolkowitz, *Myths and Realities*, 83–85; Lourdes Beneria and Martha Roldan, *Crossroads of Class and Gender: Industrial Homework, Subcontracting, and Household Dynamics in Mexico City* (Chicago: University of Chicago Press, 1987).

25. See Appendix A, Table 3 for a comparison of the working conditions of family day care providers in Vermont and those investigated by the National Day Care Home Study.

26. Alison I. Griffith and Dorothy E. Smith, "Coordinating the Uncoordinated: How Mothers Manage the School Day," Ontario Institute for Studies in Education, 1985; Dorothy E. Smith, "A Sociology for Women," in Julia Sherman and Evelyn Thornton Beck (eds.), *The Prism of Sex: Essays in the Sociology of Knowledge* (Madison: University of Wisconsin Press, 1979), 135–87.

27. Allen and Wolkowitz, *Myths and Realities*, also found that many homeworkers hold jobs in addition to their home-work.

28. Sheila Allen and Carol Wolkowitz, "Homeworking and the Control of Women's Work," in *Feminist Review* (ed.), *Waged Work: A Reader* (London: Virago Press, 1986); Laura McClure, "Homework's Horrors," *The Guardian* (November 5, 1986): 1; Roldan, "Industrial Outworking."

29. See Elaine Enarson, "Experts and Caregivers: Perspectives on Underground Childcare," in Emily K. Abel and Margaret K. Nelson (eds.), *Circles of Care* (Albany: SUNY Press, 1990), 233–45, for a discussion of the delivery of family day care in an area dependent on night work. Only 16 percent of the questionnaire respondents reported a work week of less than forty hours—some of these women provide a "preschool" program in their home with limited hours. (See Chapter 6.) Although these long hours are, as I suggest

above, the result of offering a service to employees in wage labor, I might note that many self-employed workers also work long hours. Eugene Becker, for example, reports an average of forty-nine hours a week for workers who are self-employed; see Eugene H. Becker, "Self-Employed Workers: An Update to 1983," *Monthly Labor Review* 107, no. 7 (1984): 14–18. Similarly, many women engaged in industrial home-work work long hours (Beneria and Roldan, *Crossroads of Class and Gender;* Kathleen Christensen, *Women and Home-Based Work: The Unspoken Contract* [New York: Henry Holt and Co., 1987]).

30. The group size reported here is similar to that reported in the National Day Care Home Study, which gave an average number of 3.8 nonresident children.

31. Group size varies with registration status; those who are not registered often keep group size down—in some cases in order to evade notice by the authorities. This issue is discussed further in Chapter 5.

32. They are often unsuccessful in sticking to these limits; sometimes they can not afford to exclude a client; more often they feel compelled out of obligation to respond to the need of a current client who wants now to bring her infant as well as her older child.

33. Helen Blank and Amy Wilkins, *Child Care: Whose Priority? A State Childcare Fact Book* (Washington, D.C.: Children's Defense Fund, 1985), 223; Amy Davenport et al., *The Economics of Child Care* (Montpelier, Vt.: Governor's Commission on the Status of Women's Childcare Task Force, 1985), 31.

34. For discussions of family day care as a location of care for special-needs children, see A. Chang and R. Teramoto, "Children with Special Needs in Private Day Care Centers," *Child and Youth Care Quarterly* 16, no. 1 (1987): 60–67; Dale B. Fink, "Child Care Dilemma, Family Day Care: An Option for Parents," *Exceptional Parent* 17, no. 2 (March, 1987); Sylvia Jones and Samuel Meisels, "Training Family Day Care Providers to Work with Special Needs Children," *Topics in Early Childhood Special Education* 7, no. 1 (Spring 1987): 1–12.

35. In 1980 the average annual pay for Vermont's full-time, year-round female employees was $9,089 or $177 a week; see U.S. Bureau of the Census, *1980 Census: Vermont*, 41.

36. Becker, "Self-Employed Workers," notes that self-employed workers earn on average 70 percent of what wage and salary workers earn; women who are self-employed in service work an average of $4,837 a year, or 53 percent of the $9,185 earned by wage and salary workers in similar occupations.

37. The National Day Care Home Study (Stephen J. Fosburg, et al., *Family Day Care in the United States: Summary of Findings* [Washington, D.C.: Government Printing Office, 1981]) found that providers often predicted accurately whether or not they would remain in the occupation. My analysis of this issue can be found in Chapter 7.

## *Chapter 2*

1. Andrew Hacker, *U/S: A Statistical Portrait of the American People* (New York: Viking Press, 1982); Ronald E. Kutscher and Valerie A. Personick, "De-

institutionalization and the Shift to Services," *Monthly Labor Review* 109, no. 6 (June 1986): 3–13; Janet Farrell Smith, "Parenting and Property," in Joyce Trebilcot (ed.), *Mothering: Essays in Feminist Theory* (Totowa, N.J.: Rowman and Allanheld, 1984), 199–212. Discussions of relationships between women in the service sector and women who use their services are divided into several types. For those that explore relationships between child-care workers and parents, see Alice M. Atkinson, "A Comparison of Mothers and Providers Preferences and Evaluations of Day-Care Center Services," *Child and Youth Care Quarterly* 16, no. 1 (Spring 1987): 35–47; Elaine Enarson, "Toward a Theory of Waged Mothering: The Case of Family Day Care." (Unpublished paper. University of Nevada–Reno, 1987.); Ellen Galinsky, "Parents and Teacher-Caregivers: Sources of Tension, Sources of Support," *Young Children* 43, no. 3 (March 1988): 4–13; Carole E. Joffe, *Friendly Intruders: Childcare Professionals and Family Life* (Berkeley: University of California Press, 1977); Susan Kontos and Wilma Wells, "Attitudes of Caregivers and the Day Care Experiences of Families," *Early Childhood Research Quarterly* 1, no. 1 (March 1986): 47–67; Chiara Saraceno, "Shifts in Public and Private Boundaries: Women as Mothers and Service Workers in Italian Daycare," *Feminist Studies* 10, no. 1 (1984): 7–30; Julia Wrigley, "Children's Caregivers and Ideologies of Parental Inadequacies: The Rise of Preschool Education," in Emily K. Abel and Margaret K. Nelson (eds.), *Circles of Care* (Albany: SUNY Press, 1990), 290–312.

2. Saraceno, "Shifts in Public and Private Boundaries," 7, 15.

3. Carol Stack, *All Our Kin* (New York: Harper and Row, 1974).

4. For discussions of domestic workers, see Jacklyn Cock, *Maids and Madams: A Study in the Politics of Exploitation* (Johannesburg: Ravan Press, 1980); Shelle Collen, " 'With Respect and Feelings': Voices of West Indian Child Care and Domestic Workers in New York City," in Johnnetta B. Cole (ed.), *All American Women: Lines That Divide, Ties That Bind* (New York: Free Press, 1986), 46–70; Lenore Davidoff, "The Separation of Home and Work? Landladies and Lodgers in Nineteenth and Twentieth Century England," in Sandra Burman (ed.), *Fit Work for Women* (New York: St. Martin's Press), 64–97; Bonnie Thornton Dill, " 'The Means to Put My Children Through': Child-rearing Goals and Strategies Among Black Female Domestic Servants," in LaFrances Rodgers-Rose (ed.), *The Black Woman* (Sage Publications, 1980), 107–23; Bonnie Thornton Dill, " 'Making Your Job Good Yourself': Domestic Service and the Construction of Personal Dignity," in Ann Bookman and Sandra Morgan (eds.), *Women and the Politics of Empowerment* (Philadelphia: Temple University Press, 1988), 33–52; Faye Dudden, *Serving Women: Household Service in Nineteenth-Century America* (Middletown, Conn.: Wesleyan University Press, 1983); Evelyn Nakano Glenn, *Issei, Nisei, War Bride: Three Generations of Japanese American Women in Domestic Service* (Philadelphia: Temple University Press, 1986); David Katzman, *Seven Days a Week: A History of Wage-Earning Women in the United States* (New York: Oxford University Press, 1978); Judith Rollins, *Between Women: Domestics and Their Employers* (Philadelphia: Temple University Press, 1985); Mary Romero, "Day Work in the Suburbs: The Work Experience of Chicana Private Housekeepers," in Anne Statham, Eleanor M. Miller, and Hans O. Mauksch (eds.), *The Worth of Women's Work: A Qualitative Synthesis* (Albany: SUNY Press, 1988), 77–92.

5. Charles Froland, "Formal and Informal Care: Discontinuities in a Continuum," *Social Service Review* 54 (December 1980): 572–87. See also Sara Lawrence Lightfoot, "Family-School Interactions: The Cultural Image of Mothers and Teachers," *Signs* 3, no. 2 (1977): 395–408; Sara Lawrence Lightfoot, *Worlds Apart: Relationships Between Families and Schools* (New York: Basic Books, 1978); Jean Ann Linney and Eric Vernberg, "Changing Patterns of Parental Employment and the Family-School Relationship," in Cheryl D. Hayes and Sheila B. Kamerman (eds.), *Children of Working Parents: Experiences and Outcomes* (Washington, D.C.: National Academy Press, 1983); E. Litwak, "Theoretical Bases for Practice," in R. Dobrof and E. Litwak (eds.), *Maintenance of Family Ties of Long-Term Care Patients: Theory and Guide to Practice* (Department of Health and Human Services. Washington, D.C.: Government Printing Office, 1981); Sandra Scarr, *Mother Care/Other Care* (New York: Basic Books, 1984).

6. Sheila B. Kamerman, "Women, Children, and Poverty: Public Policies and Female-Headed Families in Industrialized Countries," in Barbara C. Gelpi et al. (eds.), *Women and Poverty* (Chicago: University of Chicago Press, 1986), 269.

7. The domestic worker may not, however, be a member of a racial or ethnic minority. Most child-care workers in private households are white; many are young women engaging in this occupation for a short time (U.S. Department of Labor, Bureau of Labor Statistics, *Women in Domestic Work: Yesterday and Today* [Washington, D.C.: Government Printing Office, 1981]). Relationships between white employers and servants of racial and ethnic minority groups have been more thoroughly studied. See Cock, *Maids and Madams;* Colen, "Voices of West Indian Child Care"; Glenn, *Issei, Nisei, War Bride;* Dill, "Black Female Domestic Servants"; "'Making Your Job Good Yourself'"; Rollins, *Between Women;* Romero, "Day Work in the Suburbs." For discussions of class congruity between child-care workers and parents and the wages of child-care workers, see Carolyn Benson, *Who Cares for Kids: A Report on Child Care Providers* (Washington, D.C.: National Commission on Working Women, 1986); Florence Ruderman, *Childcare and Working Mothers: A Study of Arrangements Made for Daytime Care of Children* (New York: Child Welfare League of America, 1968); Julia Wrigley, "Children's Caregivers," in Abel and Nelson, *Circles of Care;* Caroline Zinsser, *Over a Barrel: Working Mothers Talk about Childcare* (New York: Center for Public Advocacy Research, 1987).

8. U.S. Bureau of the Census, *Who's Minding the Kids? Child Care Arrangements: Winter 1984–85* (Washington, D.C.: Government Printing Office, 1987). As the U.S. Bureau of the Census data show, there are also differences in the extent to which women with various social characteristics use *other* kinds of care.

9. A. C. Emlen, "Family Day Care for Children Under Three," paper presented at the International Symposium on the Ecology of Care and Education of Children Under Three, February 23–26, 1977, Max Planck Institute for Educational Research, Berlin; M. Golden et al., *The New York City Infant Day Care Study* (New York: Medical and Health Research Association of New York City, 1978).

10. M. R. Bradbard and R. C. Endsley, "What Do Licensers Say to Parents

Who Ask Their Help with Selecting Quality Day-Care?" *Child Care Quarterly* 8, no. 4 (1979): 307–12; D. R. Powell and J. W. Eisenstadt, "Parents' Searches for Child Care and the Design of Information Services," *Children and Youth Services Review* 4, no. 3 (1982): 239–53; Zinsser, *Over a Barrel*. A number of studies have shown that in spite of the growth of information and referral services, parents continue to rely on informal networks for the location of caregivers (G. A. Bogat and L. K. Gensheimer, "Discrepancies Between the Attitudes and Actions of Parents Choosing Day Care," *Child Care Quarterly* 15, no. 3 [1986]: 159–69; G. A. Bogat and L. K. Gensheimer, "The Role of Information and Referral Services in the Selection of Child Care," *Children and Youth Services Review* 8, no. 3 [1986]: 243–56).

11. Berenice Fisher and Joan Tronto, "Toward a Feminist Theory of Caregiving," in Abel and Nelson, *Circles of Care*, 35–62. See also Dill, "Black Female Domestic Servants," and "'Making Your Job Good Yourself.'"

12. Fisher and Tronto, "Toward a Feminist Theory"; *U.S. News and World Report*, "Getting the Best Child Care—Other than Mom (Interview with T. Berry Brazelton)," 99 (October 21, 1985): 70.

13. Half the mothers interviewed had the same level of education as the family day care provider and half had more education. What is entirely missing in this study is evidence of the interactions between providers and parents when *both* are drawn from ethnic and racial minorities as well as the white reliance on a minority provider. While this may limit the applicability of this study to areas in which family day care relies more heavily on an exploited underclass, it does ensure a focus on the dynamics of the relationships between providers and parents and the features of these relationships that grow out of the nature of the work itself rather than from underlying class, racial, and ethnic prejudices.

14. As demonstrated in Chapter 1, only 35 percent of the providers take care of children who receive state subsidies. Providers say they do not like to have to wait a full month until they are paid, that they feel the state reimbursements are too low, and that they mind the increased state involvement. Some of these complaints may be rationalizations for eliminating from their clientele a group of poorer women.

15. Luker explains similar differences (between pro-choice and pro-life advocates) as being rooted in different backgrounds (Kristin Luker, *Abortion and the Politics of Motherhood* [Berkeley: University of California Press, 1984]). Here, because I am looking at two groups of women with similar personal histories, these differences are difficult to explain in any way other than as the outcome of a complex set of factors (Kathleen Gerson, "How Women Choose Between Employment and Family: A Developmental Perspective," in Naomi Gerstel and Harriet Engel Gross [eds.], *Families and Work* [Philadelphia: Temple University Press, 1987], 270–88). For example, I interviewed two sisters, one a provider and the other a purchaser of family day care. A minority of the family day care providers are older women who grew up at a time when women did not work outside the home. These women are particularly critical of the younger women who use their services because they see them as putting an interest in personal growth and material goods before family

concerns. As I noted before, some of the providers are also clearly responding to their husband's wishes that they remain at home.

16. Selma Dendy makes a similar point in her essay about her experiences as a family day care provider: "Some of these children are in day care all day, five days a week; some are infants only a few weeks old when they begin care. Frankly, I couldn't have done that with my own children. . . . Sometimes I find myself passing judgment on these mothers: they are leaving babies who need them. Of course I am aware that it is because these women feel comfortable in going off to work each day. . . . Still, I sometimes wonder how they can do it" (Selma Dendy, "Mothering Others, Mothering My Own," in Ronnie Friedland and Carol Kort [eds.], *The Mother's Book* [Boston: Beacon Press, 1981], 77–78). For a discussion of a similar situation among abortion counselors, see Carole E. Joffe, *The Regulation of Sexuality* (Philadelphia: Temple University Press, 1986). The feeling that the service they are providing is, in some sense, "wrong" also contributes to burnout. (See Chapter 7.)

17. Among the most prominent books, see T. Berry Brazelton M.D., *Working and Caring* (Reading, Mass.: Addison-Wesley, 1985); Gloria Norris and Jo Ann Miller, *The Working Mother's Complete Handbook* (New York: New American Library, 1984); Sandra Scarr, *Mother Care/ Other Care* (New York: Basic Books, 1984); Bryna Siegel-Gorelick, *The Working Parent's Guide to Child Care* (Boston: Little, Brown, 1983). In the popular press, see, for example, "Day Care: Answers for Working Parents," *Changing Times* (August 1984): 30–34; Laural L. Dittmann, "Finding the Best Care for Your Infant or Toddler," *Young Children* 4, no. 3 (1986): 43–46; Janice Gibson, "Coping with Day Care," *Parents' Magazine* 60, no. 1 (August 1985): 110; Thelma Harms, "Finding Good Child Care: The Essential Questions to Ask When Seeking Quality Care for Your Child," *Parents' Magazine* 61, no. 2 (August 1986): 105; Bradley Hitchings, "Today's Choices in Child Care," *Business Week* (April 1, 1985): 104–5; Lilian G. Katz, "Care-Giver Relations," *Parents* 60 (January 1985): 114; Antonia van der Meer, "A Working Mother's Guide to Day Care," *Good Housekeeping* 203 (September 1986): 98–101; Jo Ann Miller and Gloria Norris, "Who's Minding Our Kids?" *Redbook* (March 1985): 4; Myryame Montrose, "What You Need to Know About Child-Care Alternatives; American Baby Basics, Part 7," *American Baby* 48 (July 1986): 55–63; Francene Sussner Rodgers and Michelle Seligson, "Mothers vs. Babysitters," *Parents* (August 1983): 62–8; Sandra Scarr, "A Child-Care Checklist: Choosing an Affordable, Safe and Happy Environment" *Ms.* 13 (January 1985): 95–98; Jacqueline Shannon, "Crisis in Child Care," *Health* 19 (October 1987): 29–33; Sally Shannon, "Searching for Good Child Care," *Washingtonian* 22 (October 1986): 182–99; Laurence F. Stains, "Day Care Nightmares," *Philadelphia* (September 1987); U.S. Department of Health and Human Services, Human Development Services, Administration for Children, Youth and Family, Day Care Division, *Parents' Checklist for Day Care* (Washington, D.C.: Government Printing Office, 1984); "Getting the Best Child Care—Other than Mom" (interview with T. Berry Brazelton), *U.S. News and World Report* 99 (October 21, 1985): 70. See also the list of books of advice in Carol E. MacKinnon and Donna King, "Day Care: A Review of Literature, Implications for Policy, and Critique of Resources," *Family Relations* 37, no. 2 (April 1988): 229–

36. Some of the articles are more sympathetic to the viewpoint of providers than are others.

18. *Changing Times* "Day Care: Answers for Working Parents"; Miller and Norris, "Who's Minding Our Kids?"; Stains, "Day Care Nightmares"; Jacqueline Shannon, "Crisis in Child Care," 31; Montrose, "What You Need to Know," 61.

19. *Time-Out: A Newsletter for Childcare Providers* (Childcare Resource and Referral, Burlington, Vt.), 1986–1988.

20. Vermont, Department of Social and Rehabilitation Services, *Journal for Family Day Care Homes* (Montpelier, Vt.: Division of Licensing and Registration, 1985).

21. There are manuals for, and articles giving advice to, women interested in establishing a family day care home. Some make it seem like an ideal solution for a woman who does not want to leave her own children. These sources generally urge licensing and establishing clear contracts. See, for example, Frances Alston, *Caring for Other People's Children: A Complete Guide to Family Day Care* (Baltimore: University Park Press, 1984); Alice Collins and Eunice Watson, *Family Day Care* (Boston: Beacon Press, 1976); Ludmilla Murphy, "Child Care Workers," *Occupational Outlook* 30 (Summer 1984): 29–32; Lisa Wilson Strick, "A Homemade Solution to the Day Care Dilemma," *Woman's Day* (April 19, 1988): 26–30; Leah Yarrow, "Starting a Home Day-Care Center," *Parents' Magazine* (August 1988): 64–8. Only a couple of the providers I interviewed mentioned that they had used this kind of resource, although many of the registered providers had spoken with an outreach worker or state licenser.

22. P. Ekeh, *Social Exchange Theory* (Cambridge: Harvard University Press, 1974); Claude Levi-Strauss, *The Elementary Structure of Kinship* (Boston: Beacon Press, 1969).

23. Stack, *All Our Kin*. The National Day Care Home Study confirms that providers charge less for relatives (Stephen J. Fosburg et al., *Family Day Care in the United States: Summary of Findings* [Washington, D.C.: Government Printing Office, 1981]). See also U.S. Bureau of the Census, *Who's Minding the Kids?*

24. Some studies have shown that when friendship develops, the child-care arrangements are more enduring. A. C. Emlen et al., *Child Care by Kith* (Portland: Oregon State University Press, 1971). Pence and Goelman suggest that friendship is more likely between a parent and a family day care provider than it is between a parent and a center-based caregiver (Alan R. Pence and Hillel Goelman, "Silent Partners: Parents of Children in Three Types of Day Care," *Early Childhood Research Quarterly* 2, no. 2 [1987]: 103–18).

25. Clair (Vickery) Brown, "Home Production for Use in a Market Economy," in Barrie Thorne and Marilyn Yalom (eds.), *Rethinking the Family: Some Feminist Questions* (New York: Longman, 1982), 151–67.

26. Susan Groves, *Family Day Care: Economic and Work Related Factors Affecting the Persistence of Providers*" (Berkeley: Center for the Study, Education and Advancement of Women, University of California, 1984). Providers also are hesitant to put a price on their service because they find intrinsic rewards from being able to stay home. In trying to assess (for me) whether the payment was

fair, one woman noted, "I guess it was okay . . . because I was lucky being home with my kids. I got to do a lot of things with my kids. . . . I can't judge it as fair pay."

27. Arlie Russell Hochschild, *The Managed Heart: The Commercialization of Human Feeling* (Berkeley: University of California Press, 1983).

28. Colen, "Voices of West Indian Child Care."

29. I might note here that if providers can believe that they are giving care freely they may feel less like servants performing the kind of personal service that the more powerful in this society can command from those who are less powerful. They thus feel less exploited (Kari Waerness, "On the Rationality of Caring," paper presented at the International Conference on the Transformation of the Welfare State: Dangers and Potentialities for Women, Bellagio, Italy, August 23–27, 1983).

30. I do not mean to imply that they can always shrug off these expectations. A friend who read an earlier draft of this chapter noted that her family day care provider asked both her and her husband for broad favors, ranging from helping on a remodeling project to picking up groceries.

31. Amy Davenport et al., *The Economics of Child Care* (Montpelier, Vt.: Governor's Commission on the Status of Women's Childcare Task Force, 1985). See also *State of Vermont: Supply, Demand and Need for Childcare* (Statewide System of Resource and Referral with the Childcare Resource and Referral Center of Chittenden County, 1988).

32. At one level, then, mothers are speaking as if they are employers. However, they do not like to think of themselves in this manner because they know they would then have to assume more responsibility (e.g., for fringe benefits). They also feel too dependent (see below) to see themselves in this role.

33. The fact that providers characterize themselves in the same way compounds the problem.

34. The other major reason for selecting family day care, that it can provide an intimate, homelike setting, is discussed below. Some women would have preferred a different kind of care altogether such as in-home care or a day-care center; both of these alternatives are more expensive and less available (especially for infant care) in this setting. These women have already made a compromise in settling on family day care. See Davenport et al., *Economics of Child Care; State of Vermont*.

35. Wrigley, "Children's Caregivers."

36. A couple of the parents I interviewed were upwardly mobile; they found that the sitter provided their child with an important opportunity to understand a way of life that was closer to that from which they themselves had come and with which the children would be in contact through visits with relatives.

37. Some studies have correlated satisfaction with care with parental control and input (Robert W. Fuqua and Dorothy Labensohn, "Parents as Consumers of Child Care," *Family Relations* 35 [April 1986]: 295–303).

38. The study compiled in 1988 by the Statewide System of Resource and Referral found that the percentage of (regulated) slots available for children

needing care ranged from a low of 15 percent in Bennington County to a high of 60 percent in Chittenden County (*State of Vermont*). See also Davenport et al., *Economics of Child Care,* for supply and demand three years earlier.

39. Colen, "Voices of West Indian Child Care"; Dill, "Black Female Domestic Servants" and "Making Your Job Good Yourself"; Glenn, *Isei, Nisei, War Bride;* Katzman, *Seven Days a Week;* Rollins, *Between Women;* Romero, "Day Work in the Suburbs."

40. M. Deutsch, "The Disadvantaged Child and the Learning Process," in H. Passow (ed.), *Education in Depressed Areas* (New York: Teachers College Press); Robert B. Innes and Sharon M. Innes, "A Qualitative Study of Caregivers' Attitudes about Child Care," *Early Child Development and Care* 15, nos. 2–3 (1984): 133–47; Douglas R. Powell, "The Interpersonal Relationship between Parents and Caregivers in Day Care Settings," *American Journal of Orthopsychiatry* 48, no. 4 (October 1978): 680–89; Edward F. Zigler and Pauline Turner, "Parents and Day Care Workers: A Failed Partnership?" in Edward Zigler and Edmund Gordon (eds.), *Day Care: Scientific and Social Policy Issues* (Boston: Auburn House Publishing Co., 1982), 174–82.

41. Parents use a variety of strategies for obtaining more information, including asking older children how well younger siblings are coping. They also "call" providers on incidents reported by their children. (For a discussion of the strategies used to obtain information by family members who have placed a relative in a nursing home, see Barbara Bowers, "Family Perceptions of Care in a Nursing Home," in Abel and Nelson, *Circles of Care,* 278–89.) Some evidence suggests that parents and providers in center-based care often evaluate the situation very differently and have different beliefs about child rearing. See Atkinson, "Comparison of Mothers and Providers Preferences"; Susan D. Holloway, Kathleen S. Gorman, and Bruce Fuller, "Child-rearing Beliefs within Diverse Social Structures: Mothers and Day-Care Providers in Mexico," *International Journal of Psychology* 23, no. 3 (1988): 303–17; Kontos and Wells, "Attitudes of Caregivers."

42. Change, however, is frequent among users of all kinds of child-care services (Liliane Floge, "The Dynamics of Child-Care Use and Some Implications for Women's Employment," *Journal of Marriage and the Family* 47, no. 1 [February 1985]: 143–54; Gwen Morgan, "Who's Minding the Kids?" *Parents* [April 1987]: 106–9).

43. Dill, "Making Your Job Good Yourself"; Innes and Innes, "Caregivers' Attitudes."

44. Collins and Watson, *Family Day Care.*

45. Innes and Innes, "Caregivers' Attitudes."

## *Chapter 3*

1. Some studies distinguish among provider "types" with respect to their orientation toward their work. See, for example, Esther Wattenberg, "Characteristics of Family Day Care Providers: Implications for Training," *Child Welfare* 56, no. 4 (April 1977): 211–29; P. V. Washburn and J. S. Washburn, "The Four Roles of the Family Day-Care Provider," *Child Welfare* 64, no. 5 (1985): 547–54. My interest, however, is less in differentiating among them in ways that might

be relevant to the kind of care provided than to focus on shared dilemmas. Thus I treat all of the providers together until Chapter 5 when I differentiate between registered and unregistered providers. For the other exception, see below.

2. Washburn and Washburn, "Four Roles," suggest that the top priority tasks for family day care providers, according to the providers themselves, "are those concerned with providing for the children's safety and understanding the children and their needs." Others have also studied the provider's distribution of efforts in a quantitative fashion (Stephen J. Fosburg et al., *Family Day Care in the United States: Summary of Findings* [Washington, D.C.: Government Printing Office, 1981]; Benigno E. Aguirre, "Educational Activities and Needs of Family Day Care Providers in Texas," *Child Welfare* 66, no. 5 [September–October 1987]: 459–65). My qualitative analysis reveals similar priorities.

3. See also Elaine Enarson, "Experts and Caregivers: Perspectives on Underground Childcare," in Emily K. Abel and Margaret K. Nelson (eds.), *Circles of Care* (Albany: SUNY Press, 1990), 233–45; Jean Marzollo, "Child-Care Workers Speak Up," *Parents' Magazine* 62 (April 1987): 114–18.

4. They also stress discipline in a narrower sense: 70 percent of the providers said they thought consistent discipline was "very important."

5. Margaret K. Nelson, "Waged Labors of Love," paper presented at the American Education Research Association Annual Meetings, Chicago, April 20–23, 1985.

6. Basil Bernstein, "Class and Pedagogies: Visible and Invisible," in Jerome Karabel and A. H. Halsey (eds.), *Power and Ideology in Education* (New York: Oxford University Press, 1977), 511–34.

7. Washburn and Washburn, "Four Roles," found this activity to be least important to family day care providers. The problem of housework is discussed further in Chapter 4.

8. Sara Freedman, "To Love and to Work: The Ghettoization of Women's Labor in the Home and the School," unpublished paper, Cambridge, Mass., 1987; Jeff Hearn, "Patriarchy, Professionalisation, and the Semi-Professions," in Clare Ungerson (ed.), *Women and Social Policy: A Reader* (London: Macmillan, 1985): 190–208; Carole E. Joffe, *Friendly Intruders: Childcare Professionals and Family Life* (Berkeley: University of California Press, 1977); Sara Lawrence Lightfoot, "Family-School Interactions: The Cultural Image of Mothers and Teachers," *Signs* 3, no. 2 (1977): 395–408; Sara Lawrence Lightfoot, *Worlds Apart: Relationships Between Families and Schools* (New York: Basic Books, 1978); Sandra Scarr, *Mother Care/ Other Care* (New York: Basic Books, 1984).

9. Lightfoot, *Worlds Apart*, 22.

10. Scarr, *Mother Care/Other Care.*

11. Chiara Saraceno, "Shifts in Public and Private Boundaries: Women as Mothers and Service Workers in Italian Daycare," *Feminist Studies* 10, no. 1 (1984): 20–21.

12. Rebecka Lundgren and Carol H. Browner, "Caring for the Institutionalized Mentally Retarded: Work Culture and Work-Based Social Support," in Abel and Nelson, *Circles of Care*, 150–72. Although some argue that family

day care providers are party to a work culture (Enarson, "Experts and Caregivers"), I suggest that they are sufficiently isolated on a daily basis that they independently learn how to resolve their ongoing dilemmas. Providers do say, however, that they speak with others doing similar work about routine issues, such as how much to charge, and to let off steam. Those who are registered also have access to a newsletter and visits from registration officials and trainers.

13. Kari Waerness, "Caring as Women's Work in the Welfare State," in Harriet Holter (ed.), *Patriarchy in a Welfare Society* (Oslo: Universitetsforlaget, 1984), 67–86.

14. Research on such issues as child abuse would have us believe that those abused as children have a strong tendency to become abusers themselves. Vincent J. Fontana, *Somewhere a Child Is Crying* (New York: Macmillan, 1973); Ruth A. Hitchcock, "Understanding Physical Abuse as a Life-Style," *Individual Psychology* 43, no. 1 (March 1987); 50–55; Blair Justice and Rita Justice, *The Abusing Family* (New York: Human Services Press, 1976). However, it is also possible for people to make a conscious decision not to repeat such abuse. More research should be dedicated to finding out how and why some people break the cycle.

15. See Sara Ruddick, "Maternal Thinking," in Joyce Trebilcot (ed.), *Mothering: Essays in Feminist Theory* (Totowa, N.J.: Rowman and Allanheld, 1983), 213–30. The contempt for training is not uniform. Some providers do want training but, as we will see in Chapter 5, they often subvert it.

16. See Esther Wattenberg, "Family Day Care: Out of the Shadows and into the Spotlight," *Marriage and Family Review* 3, no. 3/4 (Fall/Winter 1980): 35–62, for an interesting analysis of the kinds of skills family day care providers actually exercise in the course of their daily work.

17. Shellee Colen, "'With Respect and Feelings': Voices of West Indian Child Care and Domestic Workers in New York City," in Johnnetta B. Cole (ed.), *All American Women: Lines That Divide, Ties That Bind* (New York: The Free Press, 1986), 46–70.

18. Kristin Luker, *Abortion and the Politics of Motherhood* (Berkeley: University of California Press, 1984).

19. Myra Marx Ferree, for example, talks about housework as status production: "Family status production is work above and beyond that required for subsistence which serves to maintain and enhance the position of the family vis-à-vis other families in a hierarchy of social prestige." See Myra Marx Ferree, "Housework: Rethinking the Costs and the Benefits," in Irene Diamond (ed.), *Families, Politics and Public Policy* (New York: Longman, 1983), 154. Child-care activities are a major part of this process.

20. For discussions of bonding, see Ray Arney, "The Politics of Falling in Love with Your Child," *Feminist Studies* 6, no. 3 (1982): 54–70; Beverly Birns and Dale F. Hay, *The Different Faces of Motherhood* (New York: Plenum Press, 1988); Alice Balint, "Love for the Mother and Mother-Love," in Michael Balint (ed.), *Primary Love and Psychoanalytic Technique* (New York: Liveright Publishing Co., 1965), 91–108; Mary Georgina Boulton, *On Being a Mother: A Study of Women with Pre-School Children* (London: Tavistock, 1983); D. W. Winnicott, "The Theory of the Parent-Infant Relationship," *International Journal of Psycho-*

*Analysis* 41 (1960): 585–95. On the importance of the biological link, see Alice S. Rossi, "A Biosocial Perspective on Parenting," *Daedalus* 106, no. 2 (1977): 1–32. On parenting and possession, see Janet Farrell Smith, "Parenting and Property," in Joyce Trebilcot (ed.), *Mothering: Essays in Feminist Theory* (Totowa, N.J.: Rowman and Allanheld, 1984), 199–212.

21. This is not to say that those who have ceased caring about people may not continue to provide care; but even they might admit it is not "good care," and they find few rewards in the activity. Hilary Graham, "Caring: A Labour of Love," in Janet Finch and Dulcie Groves (eds.), *A Labour of Love: Women, Work and Caring* (London: Routledge and Kegan Paul, 1983), 13–30.

22. This setting also has considerable problems. Some of these were addressed in Chapter 1; others are addressed below.

23. The National Day Care Home Study found considerable continuity of care (Fosburg et al., *Family Day Care*). For discussions of attention and affection among caregivers, see Waerness, "Caring as Women's Work." Those who are reluctant to pay family members for giving care, who fear that payment will inevitably distort nurturing relations, are concerned that it will involve cold calculations, the weighing of (cash) rewards against effort. When care becomes an item of exchange, rather than the manifestation of reciprocity (or love), the argument goes, caregivers will limit their efforts and withhold them for higher pay. Certainly this sometimes happens. But the evidence from paid caregiving in other contexts suggests not only that people are drawn to the work for the opportunity to be of service but they derive enormous satisfaction from the establishment of intimate ties (Emily K. Abel and Margaret K. Nelson, "Circles of Care: An Introductory Essay," in Abel and Nelson, *Circles of Care*, 4–34; Lundgren and Browner, "Institutionalized Mentally Retarded," in Abel and Nelson, *Circles of Care*, 150–72). Even when caregivers find their efforts foolish by market standards, they do not necessarily hold back from responding to the needs of their clients (Waerness, "Caring as Women's Work"). The failure of paid caregivers to form attachments can often be attributed to the nature of the context in which they work: high turnover, many clients, fragmentation of caregiving activities, alternative responsibilities such as record keeping—all of these can impede the process of engagement (Timothy Diamond, "Social Policy and Everyday Life in Nursing Homes: A Critical Ethnography," in Anne Stratham, Eleanor M. Miller and Hans O. Mauksch [eds.], *The Worth of Women's Work: A Qualitative Synthesis* [Albany: SUNY Press, 1988], 39–56). The miracle is that in spite of these impediments, paid caregivers manage to remain concerned about clients. In fact, attachment to care recipients may be the best feature of an otherwise demeaning work situation (Bonnie Thornton Dill, "'Making Your Job Good Yourself': Domestic Service and the Construction of Personal Dignity," in Ann Bookman and Sandra Morgan [eds.], *Women and the Politics of Empowerment* [Philadelphia: Temple University Press, 1988]; Karen Brodkin Sacks, "Does It Pay to Care?," in Abel and Nelson, *Circles of Care*, 188–206).

24. Boulton, *On Being a Mother.*

25. Most of these women, however, do not want to duplicate this experience for their own children.

26. L. Comer, *Wedlocked Women* (Leeds: Feminist Books, 1974); Betty Frie-

dan, *The Feminine Mystique* (New York: W. W. Norton, 1963); H. Graham and L. McKee, *The First Months of Motherhood* (London: Health and Education Council, 1980); Sheila Kitzinger, *Women as Mothers* (New York: Random House, 1978); Carol Lopata, *Occupation Housewife* (New York: Oxford University Press, 1971); Ann Oakley, *Housewife* (New York: Viking Press, 1979); Adrienne Rich, *Of Woman Born: Motherhood as Experience and Institution* (New York: W. W. Norton, 1976). For an interesting discussion of the feminist critique of mothering, see Susan Cohen and Mary Fainsod Katzenstein, "The War over the Family Is Not over the Family," in Sanford M. Dornbusch and Myra H. Strober (eds.), *Feminism, Children, and the New Families* (New York: Guilford Press, 1988), 25–46.

27. Providers' ambivalence about these interactions—with parents and with kin—are discussed in the next chapter.

28. Alternatively, the nonanswer might be taken as an indication of the difficulty of separating treatment and feeling. Caregiving involves instrumental tasks and emotions. We care for someone because we care about them; when we care about someone we take care of their needs. But if it were just this difficulty, we might find that mothers could not separate the activities and the feelings. However, women can generally separate the two easily: I love my child but I hate changing diapers, getting up in the middle of the night, losing contact with the adult world, and so on.

29. I consciously avoid the use of the word "rights" to describe a mother's claims to her child even though this is a common terminology, used by observers as well as providers and clients (e.g., Carol Stack, *All Our Kin* [New York: Harper and Row, 1974]). The liberal notion of rights is structured on a view of individuals as autonomous entities; nurturance relies on a cooperative relationship between people. In a legal sense, of course, family day care providers do lack "rights" that mothers have: They can be prosecuted, for example, for simply spanking a child. And this limitation does affect the activity of providers. For this discussion, however, I prefer the notion of "privilege" since the provider's activities are constrained more by her inability to shape and keep a child than by the limitations in the area of rights *and* because I believe that being able to shape and keep a child is both a responsibility and a benefit. For other discussions see Janet Farrell Smith, "Parenting and Property," in Trebilcot, *Mothering;* Mary Lyndon Shanley, "Afterword: Feminism and Families in a Liberal Polity," in Irene Diamond (ed.), *Families, Politics and Policy* (New York: Longman, 1983), 357–61.

30. The fact that providers often engage in what can be called *self-exploitation* increases the significance of this possibility.

31. Barrie Thorne, "Feminist Rethinking of the Family: An Overview," in Barrie Thorne and Marilyn Yalom (eds.), *Rethinking the Family: Some Feminist Questions* (New York: Longman, 1982), 18.

32. Barbara Ehrenrich and Deidre English, *For Her Own Good: 150 Years of the Experts' Advice to Women* (New York: Doubleday, 1979); Alison M. Jaggar, *Feminist Politics and Human Nature* (Totowa, N.J.: Rowman and Allanheld, 1983).

33. Vermont, Department of Social and Rehabilitation Services, *Journal for*

*Family Day Care Homes* (Montpelier, Vt.: Division of Licensing and Registration, 1985). For interesting discussions of the issue of child abuse and how it can divide caregivers, see Susan Contratto, "Child Abuse and the Politics of Care," *Journal of Education* 168, no. 3 (1986): 70–79; Linda Gordon, "Child Abuse, Gender and the Myth of Family Independence: A Historical Critique," *Child Welfare* 64, no. 3 (May–June 1985): 213–24. For recent reports of sexual abuse in day-care settings, see David Finkelhor, and Linda Meyer Williams with Nanci Burns, *Nursery Crimes: Sexual Abuse in Day Care* (Newbury Park: Sage Publications, 1988).

34. I distinguish here between the broad kind of discipline, which is central to the provider's notion of what she is offering to children, and the specific methods of punishment for misbehavior that are employed. For public debates about the use of corporal punishment in day-care settings in Vermont, see *Burlington Free Press*, "Parents Still Have Control of Day-Care Discipline," Editorial (May 20, 1983): 12A; "Spanking in Day-Care Centers: Parents Should Make Decision," Opinions Page (February 15, 1984): 8A; "Snelling Puts Pen to Spanking Ban" (April 16, 1984): 6B; David Karvelas, "Day Care Spanking Opposed," *Burlington Free Press* (May 12, 1983): 1B.

35. Sara Ruddick, "Maternal Thinking," in Trebilcot, *Mothering*.

36. I might note that the mother tells this story somewhat differently. In the mother's version, *she* initiated the idea of moving the child to a new situation.

37. Arlie Russell Hochschild, *The Managed Heart: The Commercialization of Human Feeling* (Berkeley: University of California Press, 1983).

38. Sherri Griffin and Kathy R. Thornburg, "Perceptions of Infant/Toddler Temperament in Three Child Care Settings," *Early Child Development and Care* 18, nos. 3–4 (1985): 151–60.

39. Similarly, when they report, as many of them do, that their own children are the most difficult members of the group, the providers unconsciously reveal that the intense bond creates equally intense struggles. This issue is discussed in Chapter 4.

40. These reminders are not just to provide necessary reassurance to the child during a potentially traumatic separation; they serve the provider's interest in not allowing the child to become too attached.

41. By inserting the mother into the relationship—implicitly drawing a distinction between what she provides and what a mother offers—the day-care provider is also recreating a notion of mothering as something that exists only between a mother and her child. This kind of relationship she reserves for her *own* children. Thus mothering is not cheapened (which, paradoxically, it would be if it involved a monetary fee) by being confused with something different.

42. Because they can choose, they also differ from public caregivers who have to care for all those assigned to them. For interesting portrayals of choice in motherhood, see Shirley Glubka, "Out of the Stream: An Essay on Unconventional Motherhood," *Feminist Studies* 9 (Summer 1983): 223–35; Doris Lessing, *The Fifth Child* (New York: Alfred A. Knopf, 1988).

43. I am not including here those situations in which the provider feels the parent is marginally inadequate. As shown above, in such situations the

provider feels that she can compensate by "giving the child a little extra." She also finds rewards in being "better" than the real mother. She might also thereby derive some power in an otherwise powerless relationship.

44. Their discussions of these situations are often complicated by the fact that such children can be perceived as being—or actually are—more difficult to manage. I speak about difficult children below and concentrate here on the themes that prevail in discussions of abused and neglected children.

45. This is particularly likely to be the case when providers are locked into these relationships by strong ties of affection to the child or by ties of kinship to the parents.

## Chapter 4

1. This role has often been defined as the Domestic Code. For discussions see Karen Brodkin Sacks, "Generations of Working-Class Families," in Karen Brodkin Sacks and Dorothy Remy (eds.), *My Troubles Are Going to Have Trouble with Me: Everyday Trials and Triumphs of Women Workers* (New Brunswick, N.J.: Rutgers University Press, 1984), 15–38, and Alice Kessler-Harris and Karen Brodkin Sacks, "The Demise of Domesticity in America," in Lourdes Beneria and Catharine R. Simpson (eds.), *Women, Households and the Economy* (New Brunswick, N.J.: Rutgers University Press, 1987), 65–84.

2. Eileen Boris, "Homework and Women's Rights: The Case of the Vermont Knitters, 1980–1985," *Signs* 13, no. 1 (1987): 98–120; Kathleen Christensen, *Women and Home-Based Work: The Unspoken Contract* (New York: Henry Holt and Co., 1987); Lourdes Beneria and Martha Roldan, *Crossroads of Class and Gender: Industrial Homework, Subcontracting, and Household Dynamics in Mexico City* (Chicago: University of Chicago Press, 1987); Sheila Allen and Carol Wolkowitz, *Homeworking: Myths and Realities* (Basingstoke, England: Macmillan, 1987).

3. Allen and Wolkowitz, *Homeworking: Myths and Realities*, 7, 48.

4. See, for example, Magreth H. Olson and Sophia B. Primps, "Working at Home with Computers: Work and Nonwork Issues," *Journal of Social Issues* 40, no. 3 (1984): 97–112; "White Collar Homework: On the Upswing," *Personnel* 59, no. 5 (1984): 50–51; Maureen Sheehy, "Homework: Employment Option or Employment Risk," U.S. Department of Labor: National Commission on Working Women (Washington, D.C.: Government Printing Office, 1983).

5. Joan Smith, "The Way We Were: Women and Work," *Feminist Studies* 8, no. 2 (Summer 1982): 437–56; Kessler-Harris and Sacks, "Demise of Domesticity in America," in Beneria and Simpson, *Women, Households and the Economy*, 68.

6. Sacks, in Sacks and Remy, *Trials and Triumphs of Women Workers*, 28–30.

7. Kessler-Harris and Sacks, "Demise of Domesticity in America," 68–89.

8. Allen and Wolkowitz, *Homeworking: Myths and Realities*, 129.

9. In still other cases yet a different pattern prevails. As noted in Chapter 1, a substantial minority of the women interviewed were already engaged in other kinds of home-based work, such as caring for the elderly or being available for emergency foster-care placements. In these cases, as with the women who have predominantly remained in the home, family day care is

seen as an extra activity that is easily added to the other (income-producing) home-based work.

10. For an exception to this generalization, see the discussion of the "professional providers" in Chapter 6.

11. Alice M. Atkinson, "Provider's Evaluations of the Effect of Family Day Care on Own Family Relationships," *Family Relations* 37, no. 4 (1988), 403.

12. This need is different from the ways in which other kinds of home-work require the involvement of family members. If family members are brought in to supplement the labor of the home-worker so that she can meet production quotas or to enable her to earn enough to meet family needs, family day care providers use family members as an *alternative* source of labor. This kind of involvement does not, as in the case of home-based production, reduce the total hourly earnings. See Allen and Wolkowitz, *Homeworking: Myths and Realities*.

13. Some women gain additional satisfaction in seeing their husbands learn from them. The woman who said that she asked for assistance from her husband because she helped him with his work, also noted that this was a recent development: "I think I [used to feel] like gosh, maybe it's too much for him or he won't want that kind of responsibility. [But now] because we've had so many children come through over the years . . . I don't have to think now he won't know what to do. He also, maybe through observation of me, has alternatives. If a child is screaming he doesn't feel completely helpless. He feels able to try different things."

14. David Finkelhor and Linda Meyer Williams with Nanci Burns, *Nursery Crimes: Sexual Abuse in Day Care* (Newbury Park: Sage Publications, 1988).

15. Myra Marx Ferree, "Between Two Worlds: German Feminist Approaches to Working-Class Women and Their Work." *Signs* 10, no. 3 (1985): 534.

16. In a study of working-class women engaged in unionized jobs, Ellen Israel Rosen found that a third of the women were clear that their husbands did not like the fact that they were working outside the home, and another third said that their husbands were ambivalent. Rosen suggests that acceptance of a wife's employment varied in response to a man's earnings: "Women reported that husbands who were better earners (earning more than $15,000 a year) were less accepting of working wives than men who were poor earners (earning less than $10,000) a year" (Ellen Israel Rosen, *Bitter Choices: Blue-Collar Women In and Out of Work* [Chicago: University of Chicago Press, 1987], 102). The family day care providers interviewed in this study do not have to struggle for the "right" to work outside the home and therefore are in a different structural position than the women interviewed in Rosen's study. Nevertheless, responses from family day care providers (and their spouses) suggest that both acceptance of the demands of family day care, and recognition that their wives are working, are also keyed to the significance of a wife's contribution to the household.

17. This is lower than the average in the families interviewed by Rosen but higher than that in the families interviewed by Lillian Rubin (Lillian B. Rubin, *Worlds of Pain: Life in the Working-Class Family* (New York: Basic Books, 1976).

18. Curiously, this man himself was the product of a broken family and spent most of his life in a children's home. He clearly has a nostalgia for a life he never knew.

19. Mirra Komarovsky, *Blue Collar Marriage* (New York: Vintage Books, 1962); Lee Rainwater, Richard C. Coleman and Gerald Handel, *Workingman's Wife* (New York: Oceana Publications, 1959); Lillian Rubin, *Worlds of Pain;* Rosen, *Bitter Choices.*

20. This pattern is very different from the one noted by Rosanna Herz, who found that separate accounting systems indicated *more* power on the part of the wife. (Rosanna Herz, *More Equal than Others: Women and Men in Dual-Career Marriages* [Berkeley: University of California Press, 1986.]

21. A third pattern appears in some families where, by and large, the income is pooled but providers keep back a portion of their money for some special purpose such as a Christmas fund.

22. Lillian Rubin, *Worlds of Pain;* Rosen, *Bitter Choices.*

23. Moreover, providers themselves partially create this unpredictability by basing the energy with which they conform to the market perspective on the needs felt within the family.

24. Rosen, *Bitter Choices,* 104.

25. Sarah Fenstermaker Berk, *The Gender Factory: The Apportionment of Work in American Households* (New York: Plenum Press, 1985); Myra Marx Ferree, "She Works Hard for a Living," in Myra Marx Ferree and Beth Hess (eds.), *Analyzing Gender* (Newbury Park: Sage Publications, 1987), 322–47; Myra Marx Ferree, "The Struggles of Superwoman," in Christine Bose, Roslyn Feldberg, and Natalie Sokoloff (eds.), *Hidden Aspects of Women's Work* (New York: Praeger, 1987), 161–80; M. Meissner et al., "No Exit for Wives: Sexual Division of Labor and the Cumulation of Household Demands," *Canadian Review of Sociology and Anthropology* 12, no. 4 (1975): 424–39; W. Michaelson, *From Sun to Sun: Daily Obligations and Community Structure in the Lives of Employed Women and Their Families* (Totowa, N.J.: Rowman and Allanheld, 1985); G. Staines and J. Pleck, *The Impact of Work Schedules on the Family* (Ann Arbor, Mich.: ISR Press, 1983); Joan Vanek, "Time Spent in Housework," in N. Cott and E. Pleck (eds.), *A Heritage of Her Own* (New York: Simon and Schuster, 1979), 499–506.

26. Ferree, "She Works Hard," in Ferree and Hess, *Analyzing Gender,* 339.

27. Those families that provide foster care (several of the women), or have taken care of abused or neglected children, have yet a sharper reminder of the reality of family breakdown and its effects on children.

28. Lillian Rubin, *Worlds of Pain,* 85–86.

29. Ibid., 87.

30. Interestingly, although no provider acknowledged this, it is possible that offering family day care gives the provider a mechanism for discounting and remaining unconcerned about even serious behavioral problems. To the extent that the provider can claim that these problems are the result of the presence of day care, she has to acknowledge that day care has had a cost. On the other hand, she does not have to acknowledge that there are ways in which her own children have deep-seated developmental problems of their own.

31. Atkinson, "Provider's Evaluations," 402.

32. Carol Stack, *All Our Kin* (New York: Harper and Row, 1974).

## Chapter 5

1. Norris Class and Richard Orton, "Day Care Regulation: The Limits of Licensing," *Young Children* 35, no. 6 (1980): 12–17; John W. Lounsbury, "A Comparison of Interest Group Recommendations in Setting Day Care Licensing Standards," *Child Care Quarterly* 6, no. 4 (Winter 1977): 300; Donald J. Cohen and Edward F. Zigler, "Federal Day Care Standards: Rationale and Recommendations," *American Journal of Orthopsychiatry* 47, no. 3 (July 1977): 43–55; Edward F. Zigler and Kirby A. Heller, "Day Care Standards Approach Critical Juncture," *Day Care and Early Education* 7 (Spring 1980): 7–8; Gwen G. Morgan, "Regulation: One Approach to Quality Child Care," *Young Children* (September 1979): 22–27; Gwen G. Morgan, "Change Through Regulation," in James Greenman and Robert Fuqua (eds.), *Making Day Care Better* (New York: Teachers College Press, 1984), 163–84; Earline D. Kendall and Lewis H. Walker, "Day Care Licensing: The Eroding Regulations," *Child Care Quarterly* 13, no. 4 (Winter 1984): 278–90; Catherine J. Tobin, "Overhauling State Licensing Requirements: Making Quality Child Care a Reality," *Journal of Legislation* 12 (Summer 1985): 213–24; Kathryn T. Young and Edward F. Zigler, "Infant and Toddler Day Care: Regulations and Policy Implications," *American Journal of Orthopsychiatry* 56, no. 1 (January 1986): 43–55.

2. Elaine A. Anderson, "Family Day Care Provision: A Legislative Response," *Child Care Quarterly* 15, no. 1 (Spring 1986): 6–14; M. R. Bradbard and R. C. Endsley, "What Do Licensers Say to Parents Who Ask Their Help with Selecting Quality Day-Care?," *Child Care Quarterly* 8, no. 4 (1979): 307–12; Jake Terpstra, "Licensing of Children's Services," Children's Bureau, Washington, D.C. (November 1984); Karen Skold, "The Interests of Feminists and Children in Child Care," in Sanford M. Dornbusch and Myra H. Strober (eds.), *Feminism, Children, and the New Families* (New York: Guilford Press, 1988), 113–36.

3. Stephen J. Fosburg et al., *Family Day Care in the United States: Summary of Findings* (Washington, D.C.: Government Printing Office, 1981). See also Children's Defense Fund, *A Children's Defense Budget* (Washington, D.C. 1988); Terpstra, "Licensing of Children's Services."

4. Eileen Boris, "Regulating Industrial Homework: The Triumph of 'Sacred Motherhood,'" *Journal of American History* 71 (March 1985): 745–63; Eileen Boris, "Homework and Women's Rights: The Case of the Vermont Knitters, 1980–1985," *Signs* 13, no. 1 (1987): 98–120. It also differs from other debates about regulation in which issues such as prices and a free market are at stake (Morgan, "Change Through Regulation," 169; Terpstra, "Licensing of Children's Services").

5. For a summary of these debates as they applied to ABC, see "Child Care Legislation," *Congressional Digest* (November 1988), 258–87. The distinction between relative and nonrelative care was maintained in the Act for Better Child Care Services if only one child was involved.

6. President Reagan quoted in *Time* (October 19, 1981): 47.

7. Jaclyn Fierman, "Child Care: What Works—And Doesn't," *Fortune* (No-

vember 21, 1988): 165; Ron Haskins, "What Day Care Crisis?," *Regulation: AEI Journal of Government and Society* 12, no. 2 (1988): 13–21; Alfred J. Kahn and Sheila B. Kamerman, *Child Care: Facing the Hard Choices* (Dover, Mass.: Auburn House Publishing Co., 1987); Virginia L. Postrel, "Who's Behind the Child Care Crisis?," *Reason* (June 1989): 20–27; Susan Rose-Ackerman, "Unintended Consequences: Regulating the Quality of Subsidized Day Care," *Journal of Policy Analysis and Management* 3, no. 1 (1983): 14–30; see also Young and Zigler, "Infant and Toddler Day Care," 43–55.

8. See my discussion in Chapter 2; see also Cheryl S. Alexander and Ricka Keeney Markowitz, "Attitudes of Mothers of Preschoolers Toward Government Regulation of Day Care," *Public Health Reports* 97, no. 5 (1982): 572–78.

9. Haskins, "What Day Care Crisis?," 13–21.

10. It is perhaps because of these potential conflicts in needs and interests that there is no single feminist stance on this issue. If some feminists accept increasing state involvement as long as it is accompanied by state responsibility, and if some insist that the safety of children must, on occasion, supercede privacy rights, others argue that the interventions of a state with patriarchal priorities has often poorly served the interests of women. Then, too, women are involved in these issues from different (and sometimes oppositional) stances—as parents, as providers, as social workers, and as child-care advocates. Thus there can be no single solution acceptable for *all* women. For an interesting discussion of state involvement in the related issue of family violence, see Linda Gordon, "Family Violence, Feminism, and Social Control," *Feminist Studies* 12, no. 3 (Fall 1986): 453–78.

11. For example, Anderson's 1986 study of reasons why family day care providers do not agree to comply with licensing relies only on data from already-licensed providers who were asked why they thought some providers decided never to get licensed, as well as why they personally had chosen to do so. For a study that actually explores the attitudes of unregulated providers, see Elaine Enarson, "Experts and Caregivers: Perspectives on Underground Childcare," in Emily K. Abel and Margaret K. Nelson (eds.), *Circles of Care* (Albany: SUNY Press, 1990), 233–45.

12. Diane Adams, "Family Day Care Registration: Is It Deregulation or More Feasible State Public Policy?," *Young Children* 39, no. 4 (1984): 74–77; Kendall and Walker, "Day Care Licensing," 278–90; Morgan, "Change Through Regulation." For an overview of state licensing approaches, see Raymond C. Collins, "Child Care and the States: The Comparative Licensing Study," *Young Children* 38, no. 5 (1983): 3–11; see also Kateri K. Dames, "Registration for Child Care Homes," *Day Care and Early Education* (Fall 1983): 21–23. Studies demonstrate that when at least 20 percent of registered homes are visited, compliance is quite high (Gwen G. Morgan et al., "Gaps and Excesses in the Regulation of Child Day Care: Report of a Panel," *Reviews of Infectious Diseases* 8, no. 4 [July–August 1986]: 634–43). For evaluations of different regulatory standards, see Kahn and Kamerman, *Child Care;* Diane Adams, *National Survey of Family Day Care Regulations, Statistical Summary* (Eric Document Reproduction Service #220 207), 1982; Helen Blank and Amy Wilkins, *Child Care: Whose Priority? A State Childcare Fact Book* (Washington, D.C.: Children's Defense Fund, 1985); Dames, "Registration for Child Care Homes," 21–

23; U.S. Department of Health and Human Services, *Comparative Licensing Study; Vol. 5: Profiles of State Licensing Requirements, Family Day Care Homes* (Washington, D.C.: Government Printing Office, 1982); Morgan et al., "Gaps and Excesses," 634–43; June Solnit Sale, "Family Day Care: The Registration Controversy," *Day Care and Early Education* 8, no. 1 (Fall 1980): 10–14.

13. For an assessment of the effectiveness of regulatory efforts, see David A. Corsini, Steven Wisensale and Grace-Ann Caruso, "Family Day Care: System Issues and Regulatory Models," *Young Children* 43, no. 6 (September 1988): 17–23, and Morgan et al., "Gaps and Excesses," 634–43.

14. See Appendix B for a more thorough review of the regulatory requirements. In 1989, after the study was completed, these provisions were changed to include a training requirement of six hours for family day care providers (Vermont, Department of Social and Rehabilitation Services, "Family Day Care Regulations," [Waterbury, Vt., 1989]). This analysis was written before it was possible to assess the impact of these new standards on the number of regulated family day care homes in Vermont.

15. Vermont, Department of Social and Rehabilitation Services, "Family Day Care Regulations" (Waterbury, Vt., 1985).

16. Amy Davenport et al., *The Economics of Child Care* (Montpelier, Vt.: The Governor's Commission on the Status of Women's Childcare Task Force, 1985). A 1988 study of one county suggests that regulated slots are available for two-thirds of the preschool children needing child care; a variety of reasons, including the means of calculating need and available slots, suggest that this study overestimates the extent to which Vermont children are in regulated care (Burlington Child Care Council, *Final Report of the Burlington Child Care Council* [Burlington, Vt.: October 1, 1988]).

17. Neither of the two sets of data represents a random sample. Therefore, even though the reported differences between registered and unregistered providers are statistically significant, generalizations should be drawn with caution. Moreover, in spite of the fact that there were more registered than unregistered providers in the population in this study, the reader should remember that the actual proportion of providers in each of these two groups is, in fact, the reverse.

18. In fact, there is relatively little shifting back and forth between regulated and unregulated status. Of the sixty-three registered providers contacted as part of the turnover questionnaire, six had dropped their registration before they stopped providing care. One of the twelve unregistered providers who had stopped had become registered at some time during the previous year.

19. Anderson, "Family Day Care Provision," 6–14; Enarson, "Experts and Caregivers," in Abel and Nelson, *Circles of Care;* Fosburg et al., *Family Day Care;* Kahn and Kamerman, *Child Care.*

20. Adams, "Family Day Care Registration," 74–77.

21. Anderson, "Family Day Care Provision," 6–14.

22. At the same time, the extensive tax breaks available to home-based work mean that many providers pay no income taxes at all on their earnings.

23. Kahn and Kamerman, *Child Care,* 233; see also Sale, "Family Day Care," 10–14; and Adams, "Family Day Care Registration," 74–77.

24. Enarson, "Experts and Caregivers."

25. *Burlington Free Press*, "Spanking in Day-Care Centers: Parents Should Make Decision," Opinions Page (February 15, 1984): 8A; "Snelling Puts Pen to Spanking Ban," (April 16, 1984): 6B; see also David Karvelas, "Day Care Spanking Opposed," *Burlington Free Press* (May 12, 1983): 1B.

26. Enarson, "Experts and Caregivers."

27. Resistance is also multifaceted. Many of the providers gave more than one response to the question of why they chose to remain unregistered.

28. Single women face fewer of these conflicts altogether and so have less motivation for avoiding registration in the first place.

29. This term comes from Enarson ("Experts and Caregivers") to refer to providers who are registered as a result of being caught by a licenser.

30. For a somewhat different assessment of why providers agree to licensing, see Anderson, "Family Day Care Provision," 6–14.

31. During the first quarter of 1988, thirty-four family day care homes were reported to the state as operating illegally. Twenty-three of these reports were substantiated; twelve subsequently became registered and four reduced numbers. (Coley Baker, Director of Licensing, telephone conversation with author, May 5, 1989.)

32. Of course, providers can also continue to provide care and hope that they will not be caught; none of the providers I interviewed had done so.

33. Morgan et al., "Gaps and Excesses."

34. Clearly, the manner in which these cases are reported to me are one-sided. The cases I heard were all felt to be unsubstantiated by the provider. But the state does find evidence of real abuse and negligence—if infrequently. During the first quarter of 1988, there were twenty-seven reports of violations in registered family day care homes. They included four instances of corporal punishment (one substantiated), eleven cases of being over the legal numbers (two substantiated), four cases of "inappropriate care" (two substantiated), one case of child abuse (not substantiated), three cases of inappropriate discipline (not substantiated) and one case each of use of tobacco while handling babies, use of illegal drugs, lack of supervision and neglect (none of these were substantiated). (Author's conversation with Coley Baker.)

35. For a discussion of the conflicts in the licenser's role, see John W. Lounsbury and Diana Q. Hall, "Supervision and Consultation Conflicts in the Day-Care Licensing Role," *Social Service Review* 50 (September 1976): 515–23.

36. At the time I interviewed this provider, she had been contacted by others who had also had their registration revoked and suspended as a result of complaints against them. These providers had forced public attention on the issue of the legality of such actions. At the time of the interviews the licensers were doing spot checks and making unannounced visits; in fact part of the application process involved agreeing to allow this. At the time this book was actually written, these policies had changed. Licensers were no longer doing unannounced checks unless the complaint suggested an emergency. Even those visits designed to measure compliance were preceded by a letter. (Author's conversation with Coley Baker.)

37. Author's conversation with Coley Baker.

38. Unregistered providers use their less formal contacts in the same way. One unregistered provider, for example, told me that she had decided to charge for holidays after speaking with three other providers in her neighborhood.

39. The recent training requirement might also be counterproductive because it undermines the providers' insistence that the skills are experiential. To the extent that funding for family day care might increasingly be tied to regulation, the reverse might be true.

40. Rose Weitz and Deborah Sullivan, "Licensed Lay Midwifery and Medical Models of Childbirth," in Abel and Nelson, *Circles of Care*, 246–60.

41. The exception to this generalization is those children subsidized in whole or in part by the state.

## *Chapter 6*

1. I focus only on interviewed providers here because there was no room on the questionnaire for respondents to indicate this kind of an orientation toward their work. Of course, some of the respondents might also have defined themselves in similar terms if given the opportunity. I might also note that there were other interviewed family day care providers whose orientation toward their work approximated that of these ten women; categorization always involves an exaggeration of differences between groups.

2. William Ade, "Professionalization and Its Implications for the Field of Early Childhood Education," *Young Children* 37, no. 3 (March 1982): 25–33. See also Frank Ainsworth, "The Child Care Profession: Cause and Function," *Child Care Quarterly* 10, no. 2 (Summer 1981): 87–88; Jerome Beker, "Development of a Professional Identity for the Child Care Worker," *Child Welfare* 54, no. 6 (June 1975): 421–31; Bettye M. Caldwell, "A Comprehensive Model for Integrating Child Care and Early Childhood Education," *Teachers College Record* 90, no. 3 (Spring 1989): 404–14; Bettye M. Caldwell, "How Can We Educate the Americans About the Child Care Profession?" *Young Children* 38, no. 3 (March 1983): 11–17; Roy V. Ferguson and James P. Anglin, "The Child Care Profession: A Vision for the Future," *Child Care Quarterly* 14, no. 2 (Summer 1985): 85–101; Lana Hostetler and Edgar Klugman, "Early Childhood Job Titles: One Step Toward Professional Status," *Young Children* 37, no. 6 (September 1982): 13–19; Alan Keith-Lucas, "On Being Truly Professional," *Child Care Quarterly* 9, no. 4 (Winter 1980): 243–50; Carol J. Porter, "Professionalization and Day Care: Friend or Foe?" paper presented at the Conference on Child Care Education, University of Miami, Coral Gables, Fla., November 13, 1981; Douglas R. Powell, "The Role of Research in the Development of the Child Care Profession," *Child Care Quarterly* 11, no. 1 (Spring 1982): 4–11; Mary Ann Radomski, "Professionalization of Early Childhood Educators: How Far Have We Progressed?," *Young Children* 41 (July 1986): 20–23; Richard W. Small and Laura Dodge, "Roles, Skills and Job Tasks in Professional Child Care: A Review of the Literature," *Child and Youth Care Quarterly* 17, no. 1 (Spring 1988): 6–23; Karen VanderVen and Martha A. Mattingly, "Action Agenda for Child Care Education in the 80s: From Settings to Systems," *Child Care Quarterly* 10, no. 3 (Fall 1981): 278–88. For a very different approach, see Janna Dresden and

Barbara Kimes Myers, "Early Childhood Professionals: Toward Self-Definition," *Young Children* 44, no. 3 (January 1989): 62.

3. Harold Wilensky, "The Professionalization of Everyone?" *American Journal of Sociology* 70, no. 2 (September 1964): 149.

4. Carole E. Joffe, *Friendly Intruders: Childcare Professionals and Family Life* (Berkeley: University of California Press, 1977), 22.

5. Susan Reverby, "The Duty or Right to Care: Nursing and Womanhood in Historical Perspective," in Emily K. Abel and Margaret K. Nelson (eds.), *Circles of Care* (Albany: SUNY Press, 1990), 132–49; Barbara Melosh, *"The Physician's Hand": Work, Culture and Conflict in American Nursing* (Philadelphia: Temple University Press, 1982). For discussions of the impact of feminization on the process of professionalization, see also Joffe, *Friendly Intruders;* Hostetler and Klugman, "Early Childhood Job Titles," 13–19; Kathy Modigliani, "Twelve Reasons for the Low Wages in Child Care," *Young Children* 43 (March 1988): 14–15.

6. Chiara Saraceno, "Shifts in Public and Private Boundaries: Women as Mothers and Service Workers in Italian Daycare," *Feminist Studies* 10, no. 1 (1984): 20.

7. Joffe, *Friendly Intruders,* 21–22.

8. Jonathan G. Silin, "Authority as Knowledge: A Problem of Professionalization," *Young Children* 40 (March 1985): 41–46.

9. See the evidence in Heidi I. Hartmann and Diana M. Pearce, "High Skill and Low Pay: The Economics of Child Care Work," Executive Summary, Institute for Women's Policy Research, February 1989; see also Melosh, *"Physician's Hand."*

10. Kari Waerness, "On the Rationality of Caring," paper presented at the International Conference on the Transformation of the Welfare State: Dangers and Potentialities for Women, Bellagio, Italy, August 23–27, 1983.

11. Emily K. Abel and Margaret K. Nelson, "Circles of Care: An Introductory Essay," in Abel and Nelson, *Circles of Care,* 4–34.

12. Silin, "Authority as Knowledge," 41–46; Gerald Rupert Grace, *Teachers, Ideology and Control:* A Study in Urban Education (London: Routledge and Kegan Paul, 1978).

13. Pierre Bourdieu, "Cultural Reproduction and Social Reproduction," in Jerome Karabel and A. H. Halsey (eds.), *Power and Ideology in Education* (Oxford University Press, 1977), 473–86.

14. Their refusal to care for a dispersed age group or, among some, to take in after-school children, is designed to help protect this structure.

15. There is a great similarity between this approach and that of the "culture of poverty," which was the prevalent educational philosophy in the 1960s. See, for example, M. Deutsch, "The Disadvantaged Child and the Learning Process," in H. Passow (ed.), *Education in Depressed Areas* (New York: Teachers College Press, 1963).

16. If most of the professional providers rely on the technique of social distance to ensure client compliance with rules and regulations, one provider uses an altogether different approach. Judy Harris creates extremely close collaboration between herself and the parents to ensure that clients are aware

of her point of view and her needs. By doing so, Judy feels that she knows that she and the parent feel alike; she thus has more control. Whether this is an alternative model that could prevail among professional providers is impossible to tell in this small study.

17. For a good discussion of this process—and its problems—see Saraceno, "Shifts in Public and Private Boundaries," 7–30.

## *Chapter 7*

1. These figures were obtained by comparing lists of registered providers at different points in time.

2. For turnover among center-based caregivers, see *Child Care Information Exchange*, "Child Care in the News: The Good, the Bad, and the (Really) Ugly," no. 64 (December 1988), 7–10; Heidi H. Hartmann and Diana M. Pearce, "High Skills and Low Pay: The Economics of Child Care Work," *Executive Summary* (Institute for Women's Policy Research, February 1989); Mary Benson McMullen and Murray Krantz, "Burnout in Day Care Workers: The Effects of Learned Helplessness and Self-Esteem," *Child and Youth Care Quarterly* 17, no. 4 (Winter 1988): 275–80; Marcy Whitebook et al., "Who's Minding the Child Care Workers?: A Look at Staff Burnout," *Children Today* (January/February 1981): 2–6. For turnover in related occupations, see Barbara J. Fleischer, "Identification of Strategies to Reduce Turnover Among Child Care Workers," *Child Care Quarterly* 142, no. 2 (Summer 1985): 130–39; L. Hylton, *The Residential Treatment Center: Children's Programs and Costs* (New York: Child Welfare League of America, 1964); John Myer, "An Informal Survey of Child Care Workers," *Child Care Quarterly* 4, no. 2 (1975): 120; George Walker Rosenfeld, "Turnover Among Child Care Workers," *Child Care Quarterly,* no. 1 (Spring 1979), 67–69.

3. A range of overlapping explanations for turnover are cited in the literature. Burnout has been studied in a wide range of occupations. Cary Cherniss, *Professional Burnout in Human Service Organizations* (New York: Praeger, 1980); Herbert J. Freudenberger, *Burn-Out: The High Cost of High Achievement* (Garden City, N.Y.: Doubleday, 1980); John W. Jones (ed.), *The Burnout Syndrome: Current Research, Theory, Interventions* (Park Ridge, Ill.: London House Press, 1982); Christina Maslach, *Burnout: The Cost of Caring* (Englewood Cliffs, N.J.: Prentice-Hall, 1982); Whiton S. Paine, "The Burnout Syndrome in Context," in John W. Jones, *Burnout Syndrome*, 1–29; Whiton S. Paine, *Job Stress and Burnout: Research, Theory and Intervention Perspectives* (Beverly Hills: Sage Publications, 1982). Scholars suggest that in child care in particular the necessarily intense interaction between adult and child becomes more draining and less gratifying over time. Herbert J. Freudenberger, "Burn Out: Occupational Hazard of the Child Care Worker," *Child Care Quarterly* 6 (Summer 1977), 90–99; M. Mattingly, "Sources of Stress and Burn-Out in Professional Child Care Work," *Child Care Quarterly* 6 (Summer 1977): 127–37. A large number of studies have investigated the relationships between working conditions and job satisfaction, and between dissatisfaction and the decision to terminate employment. See, for example, F. Herzberg et al., *Job Attitudes: Review of Research and Opinion* (Pittsburgh: Psychological Service of Pittsburgh, 1957); A. I. Kraut, "Predicting Turnover of Employees from Measured Job Attitudes," *Organizational Behavior*

*and Human Performance* 13, no. 2 (1975): 23–43; E. A. Locke, "The Nature and Causes of Job Satisfaction," in M. Dunnette (ed.), *Handbook of Industrial and Organizational Psychology* (Chicago: Rand McNally, 1978), 1297–1349. Items that have been found to contribute to job satisfaction include salary, job content, job autonomy, responsibility, and role clarity (Fleischer, "Strategies to Reduce Turnover," 130–39; Rosenfeld, "Turnover Among Child Care Workers," 67–69). Five reviews of the literature report a consistently significant relationship between dissatisfaction with the job and the decision to leave employment. A. H. Brayfield and W. H. Crocket, "Employee Attitudes and Employee Performance," *Psychological Bulletin* 52 (1955): 396–424; Herzberg et al., *Job Attitudes;* Locke, "Job Satisfaction"; L. W. Porter and R. M. Steers, "Organizational Work and Personal Factors in Employee Turnover and Absenteeism," *Psychological Bulletin*, 80, no. 2 (1973): 151–76; V. Vroom, *Work and Motivation* (New York: Wiley, 1964). Scholars suggest a causal model relating burnout and job satisfaction: Stress and poor working conditions lead to job dissatisfaction; job dissatisfaction, in turn, leads to burnout and ultimately to turnover (David MacNeil, "The Relationship of Occupational Stress to Burnout," in John W. Jones, *Burnout Syndrome*, 68–88; Whitebook et al., "Staff Burnout"). Some scholars focus less on social-psychological and developmental variables than on the existence of opportunities that enable movement to another occupation. The interactions between the presence of alternative opportunities and the variables discussed above are presented in a model (W. H. Mobley, "Intermediate Linkage in the Relationship between Job Satisfaction and Employee Turnover," *Journal of Applied Psychology* 62, no. 2 [1977]: 237–40); job dissatisfaction leads to thoughts about quitting, which lead to a search for new alternatives, if those alternatives are perceived to exist; a comparison of alternatives with the present job then leads to intentions to quit or stay.

4. Emily K. Abel, "Informal Care for the Frail Elderly: A Critique of Recent Literature," unpublished paper, UCLA School of Public Health, n.d..

5. Other research, besides my own, finds that family day care is an occupation chosen by women who want to remain home while their own children are young (Elaine Enarson, "Toward A Theory of Waged Mothering: The Case of Family Day Care," unpublished paper, University of Nevada–Reno, 1987; Susan Groves, *Family Day Care: Economic and Work Related Factors Affecting the Persistence of Providers* [Berkeley: Center for the Study, Education and Advancement of Women, University of California, 1984]; Steven Fosburg et al., *Family Day Care in the United States: Summary of Findings* [Washington D.C.: Government Printing Office, 1981]; Alfred J. Kahn and Sheila B. Kamerman, *Child Care: Facing the Hard Choices* [Dover, Mass.: Auburn House Publishing Co., 1987]). As a corollary to this finding, it is suggested that turnover may have less to do with either burnout or dissatisfaction (or with some combination of the two) than with completion of a particular stage of life. Support for this hypothesis is provided by a study of child-care workers (Andrew L. Ross, "Mitigating Turnover of Child Care Staff in Group Care Facilities," *Child Welfare* 62, no. 1 [1983]: 63–67); see also W. E. Sobesky, "Youth as Child Care Workers: The Impact of the Stage of Life on Clinical Effectiveness," *Child Care*

*Quarterly* 5, no. 4 (1976): 262–73; Karen D. VanderVen, "Developmental Characteristics of Childcare Workers and Design of Training Programs," *Child Care Quarterly* 8, no. 2 (1976): 100–112.

6. By comparing consecutive lists of registered providers for March 1986 (the time of the original survey) and March 1987, and by adding departure from the occupation (if the provider's name was no longer on the list) as a variable to the original data, I was able to do some analysis of the factors related to turnover. Clearly this method was not precise: some providers might have been operating a day care home in a different district from the one in which their names appeared originally; some might have been operating under a different name as the result of marriage or divorce; and some might have been operating a day care home as an unregistered provider.

7. Whitebook et al., "Staff Burnout."

8. If caring for others is the best feature, caring for one's own is also a source of satisfaction. Some women, as we have seen, also reap satisfaction from the occasions on which they nurture other women as one component of their relationship with clients. More broadly, women are gratified by knowing that they are offering a needed and valued service, that they are fulfilling a female role of altruism and care.

9. On the turnover survey providers were significantly less likely to express agreement with the statement, "My children have adjusted easily to sharing me with others," than they had two years earlier when they responded to the original questionnaire.

10. In fact, many attribute center-based turnover rates directly to the low wages in the field. See Hartmann and Pearce, "High Skills and Low Pay"; Whitebook et al., "Staff Burnout."

11. The direct cost of providing day care in the home—particularly the cost of insurance—undercuts profits; state limitations on numbers of children (along with the prevailing "market rate" set by women's low wages in the labor force) ensure a cap. Women who take the full number of children allowed may be more likely than others to remain in the occupation; they also experience greater stress.

12. As Chiara Saraceno notes (talking about parents and center-based caregivers), mothers may have difficulty in accepting "the idea that other women are as good as or even better than they are themselves with their children, and as important in the children's experience." Chiara Saraceno, "Shifts in Public and Private Boundaries: Women as Mothers and Service Workers in Italian Daycare," *Feminist Studies* 10, no. 1 (1984): 3–30.

13. Saraceno, "Shifts in Public and Private Boundaries," 27.

14. Susan Reverby, "The Duty or the Right to Care? Nursing and Womanhood in Historical Perspective," in Emily K. Abel and Margaret K. Nelson, *Circles of Care* (Albany: SUNY Press, 1990), 132–49.

15. For discussions of the measurement of burnout, see Albert Einseidel and Heather Tully, "Methodological Considerations in Studying the Burnout Phenomenon," in Jones, *Burnout Syndrome;* Maslach, *Burnout*.

16. Significantly, providers who had left the occupation were less likely in the follow-up interview (in comparison with their responses to the initial

questionnaire) to say that they agreed with the statement "A day care provider should be like a mother to the children she cares for." Research indicates that when burnout is a causal factor in turnover, the period prior to departure is marked by lower productivity and a negative attitude toward work (Jones, *Burnout Syndrome*). For example, Rosenfeld ("Turnover Among Child Care Workers") found that residential treatment workers moved toward custodial care prior to leaving the occupation.

17. Numerous research reports have explored the issues surrounding reentry into the labor force among women who take time off for child rearing. D. Cox, "Panel Estimates of the Effects of Career Interruptions on the Earnings of Women," *Economic Inquiry* 22 (July 1984): 386–403; C. J. Erdwins and J. C. Mellinger, "Reentry Women After Graduation," *Journal of Genetic Psychology* 147 (December 1986): 437–46; W. E. Evans, "Career Interruptions Following Childbirth," *Journal of Labor Economics* 5 (April 1987): 255–77; E. Hoch et al., "Employment Decisions Made by Mothers of Infants," *Psychology of Women Quarterly* 9 (Spring 1985): 383–402; G. Stamp, "Some Observations on the Career Paths of Women," *Journal of Applied Behavioral Science* 22, no. 4 (1986); E. VanVelsor and A. M. O'Rand, "Family Life Cycle, Work Career Patterns, and Women's Wages at Midlife," *Journal of Marriage and the Family* 46 (May 1984), 565–73.

18. A couple of these women started their own centers outside the home.

*Conclusion*

1. See, for example, Children's Defense Fund, *A Children's Defense Budget: FY 1989* (Washington, D.C.: Children's Defense Fund, 1988).

2. Even so, sometimes I got in trouble with one group or another. At a policy conference, and in discussing my findings with child-care resource and referral personnel, my sympathetic portrayal of the reasons for providers' resistance to regulation provoked anger and outrage. At a conference of family day care providers, my critique of home-based employment irritated some women who asserted that it worked well for them. And when I stepped outside my role as an academic and helped to design a child-care policy for Middlebury College, which recommended that the college support employees' child-care costs *only* if they used licensed or registered care, I was browbeaten by staff members who claimed that the alternatives were better, cheaper, and more flexible.

3. I also start from a set of political convictions. The first is that, to solve the dilemmas highlighted in this book we need broad social change in the sex/gender system (and particularly in the way that system places the burden for child care almost exclusively in the hands of women), in the structure of wage labor, in the organization of profits derived from this labor, and in the role of the state in responding to the needs of its citizens. The second is that because many of these changes are unlikely to be realized in the forseeable future, we must work on incremental change while keeping in mind the broader goal.

4. *Open House,* Addison County Child/Care Training Program, P.O. Box 646, Middlebury, VT 05753.

5. Kirsten O. Lundberg, "What's New in Day Care? A Tool to Keep Women in the Workforce," *New York Times* (February 26, 1989): sec. 3, p. 13.

6. Children's Defense Fund, *Children's Defense Budget* (1988), p. 183.

7. Marrianne Karre et al., "Social Rights in Sweden Before School Starts," in Pamela Roby (ed.), *Child Care—Who Cares* (New York: Basic Books, 1973), 137–53; Mary Ruggie, *The State and Working Women: A Comparative Study of Britain and Sweden* (Princeton, N.J.: Princeton University Press, 1984).

8. Information from the Greater Minneapolis Day Care Association.

9. Parents might be asked to contribute also, particularly if their income is above the median income for the state. Employers might be taxed specially to help support child care.

10. One provider suggested the following idea: "One thing that I proposed [to the parent-child center] that was supposed to be put into the budget [for using state funds] and wasn't was hiring somebody to come around about once a week and just do projects or something with the kids. Like if you have a situation like Pat Markham who has babies and older children, and in the winter she just can't get the older kids out, you would know that that day that lady was coming to take your older kids out and build a snowman or whatever. Or if you were that kind of person who couldn't do a cooking project. And that person would come in and do that or direct stuff right there in the home. And not necessarily somebody that comes and sits there and talks to you, but somebody coming in and doing something with the kids. . . . If I knew that somebody was going to come once a week to play with the kids, even for an hour, I would look forward to it and I think the kids would look forward to it too."

11. Barbara Katz Rothman, *Recreating Motherhood* (New York: W. W. Norton, 1989), 259.

12. At a conference of family day care providers, those women who participated in a "system" were amazed to hear that other providers had hassles with parents about rules and regulations. Because they were backed up by written contracts, they felt secure in their defense of their own interests on these kinds of issues.

13. Because the kind of system described above will make family day care far more expensive than it is at present, it may lose its favored position. For a similar point (as well as some similar recommendations), see Alfred J. Kahn and Sheila B. Kamerman, *Child Care: Facing the Hard Choices* (Dover, Mass.: Auburn House Publishing Co., 1987).

14. Susan Cohen and Mary Fainsod Katzenstein, "The War over the Family Is Not over the Family," in Sanford M. Dornbusch and Myra H. Strober (eds.), *Feminism, Children, and the New Families* (New York: Guilford Press, 1988), 44.

## *Appendix A*

1. U.S. Bureau of the Census, *1980 Census: Vermont* (Washington, D.C.: Government Printing Office, 1980).

2. U.S. Bureau of the Census, *Statistical Abstracts of the United States* (Washington, D.C.: Government Printing Office, 1988).

3. *Statistical Abstracts*, 1988.

4. Stephen J. Fosburg et al., *Family Day Care in the United States: Summary of Findings* (Washington, D.C.: Government Printing Office, 1981).

5. In total 160 registered providers did not appear on the March 1988 lists of

registered family day care homes who had appeared on the list used in March 1986 as the basis for mailing the original survey; eighty-six (54 percent) of these providers had answered the original questionnaire; seventy-four (46 percent) had not. Of the eighty-six respondents to the original survey, forty (53 percent) participated in the study of turnover. For the registered providers who did not participate in the original survey, seven (9 percent) were still doing family day care; twenty-three (38 percent) of the remaining sixty-one participated in the study of turnover. In addition, fifty-five of the unregistered providers who had responded to the survey in the summer of 1987 were called: Twenty-four of these women were still doing family day care; twelve of the remaining thirty-one (39 percent) participated in the study of turnover.

6. Margaret K. Nelson, "Waged Labors of Love," paper presented at the American Education Research Association Annual Meeting, April 20–23, Chicago, 1985.

7. For a discussion of father's involvement in family day care, see Alice M. Atkinson, "A Comparison of Mother's and Provider's Preferences and Evaluations of Day Care Center Services," *Child and Youth Care Quarterly* 16, no. 1 (Spring 1987): 35–47.

*Appendix B*

1. Vermont, Department of Social and Rehabilitation Services, *Journal for Family Day Care Homes* (Montpelier, Vt.: Division of Licensing and Registration).

# BIBLIOGRAPHY


Abel, Emily K. n.d. "Informal Care for the Frail Elderly: A Critique of Recent Literature." (Unpublished paper, Los Angeles, Calif.: UCLA School of Public Health.)

Abel, Emily K., and Margaret K. Nelson. 1990. "Circles of Care: An Introductory Essay." In Emily K. Abel and Margaret K. Nelson (eds.), *Circles of Care*, 4–34. Albany: SUNY Press.

———. 1990. *Circles of Care.* Albany: SUNY Press.

Adams, Carolyn T., and Kathryn T. Winston. 1980. *Mothers at Work: Public Policies in the United States, Sweden and China.* New York: Longman.

Adams, Diane. 1984. "Family Day Care Registration: Is It Deregulation or More Feasible State Public Policy?" *Young Children* 39 (May): 74–77.

———. 1982. *National Survey of Family Day Care Regulations, Statistical Summary.* Eric Document Reproduction Service #220 207.

Ad Hoc Day Care Coalition. 1985. *The Crisis in Infant and Toddler Child Care.* Washington, D.C.: Ad Hoc Day Care Coalition.

Ade, William. 1982. "Professionalization and Its Implications for the Field of Early Childhood Education." *Young Children* 37, no. 3 (March): 25–32.

Aguirre, Benigno E. 1987. "Educational Activities and Needs of Family Day Care Providers in Texas." *Child Welfare* 66, no. 5 (September–October): 459–65.

Ainsworth, Frank. 1981. "The Child Care Profession: Cause and Function." *Child Care Quarterly* 10, no. 2 (Summer): 87–88.

Alexander, Cheryl S. and Ricka Keeney Markowitz. 1982. "Attitudes of Mothers of Preschoolers Toward Government Regulation of Day Care." *Public Health Reports* 97, no. 5: 572–78.

Allen, Sheila. 1983. *Production and Reproduction: The Lives of Women Homeworkers.* London: Routledge and Kegan Paul.

Allen, Sheila and Carol Wolkowitz. 1986. "Homeworking and the Control of Women's Work." In *Feminist Review* (ed.), *Waged Work: A Reader*, 238–64. London: Virago Press.

———. 1987. *Homeworking: Myths and Realities.* Basingstoke, England: Macmillan.

Alston, Frances. 1984. *Caring for Other People's Children: A Complete Guide to Family Day Care.* Baltimore: University Park Press.

Anderson, Elaine A. 1986. "Family Day Care Provision: A Legislative Response." *Child Care Quarterly* 15, no. 1 (Spring): 6–14.

Arney, Ray. 1982. "The Politics of Falling in Love with Your Child." *Feminist Studies* 6, no. 3: 54–70.

Atkinson, Alice M. 1987. "A Comparison of Mothers and Providers Preferences and Evaluations of Day-Care Center Services." *Child and Youth Care Quarterly* 16, no. 1 (Spring): 35–47.

———. 1988. "Provider's Evaluations of the Effect of Family Day Care on Own Family Relationships." *Family Relations* 37, no. 4: 399–404.

Auerbach, Judith D. 1987. "Locating Child Care in Sociology." Paper presented at the Society for the Study of Social Problems, Annual Meetings, August 14–16, Chicago.

———. 1988. *In the Business of Child Care: Employer Initiatives and Working Women*. New York: Praeger.

Balint, Alice. 1939. "Love for the Mother and Mother-Love." In Michael Balint (ed.), *Primary Love and Psychoanalytic Technique*, 91–108. New York: Liveright Publishing Co., 1965.

Becker, Eugene H. 1984. "Self-Employed Workers: An Update to 1983." *Monthly Labor Review* 107, no. 7: 14–18.

Beker, Jerome. 1975. "Development of a Professional Identity for the Child Care Worker." *Child Welfare* 54, no. 6 (June): 421–31.

Belsky, Jay. 1984. "Two Waves of Day Care Research: Developmental Effects and Conditions of Quality." In Ricardo C. Ainslie (ed.), *The Child and the Day Care Setting: Qualitative Variations and Development*, 1–62. New York: Praeger.

———. 1988. "A Reassessment of Infant Day Care." In Edward F. Zigler and Meryl Frank (eds.), *The Parental Leave Crisis: Toward a National Policy*, 100–19. New Haven: Yale University Press.

Beneria, Lourdes, and Martha Roldan. 1987. *Crossroads of Class and Gender: Industrial Homework, Subcontracting, and Household Dynamics in Mexico City.* Chicago: University of Chicago Press.

Benson, Carolyn. 1986. *Who Cares for Kids: A Report on Child Care Providers.* Washington, D.C.: National Commission on Working Women.

Berch, Bettina. 1985. "The Resurrection of Out-Work." *Monthly Review* 37, no. 6: 37–44.

Bergmann, B. R. 1988. "A Workable Family Policy: Childcare, Income Support, Jobs." *Dissent* 35, no. 1: 88–93.

Berk, Sarah Fenstermaker. 1985. *The Gender Factory: The Apportionment of Work in American Households.* New York: Plenum Press.

———. 1980. *Women and Household Labor.* Beverly Hills, Calif. Sage Publications.

Bernstein, Aaron, and Elizabeth Ehrlich. 1986. "Business Starts Tailoring Itself to Suit Working Women." *Business Week* (October 6): 50.

Bernstein, Basil. 1977. "Class and Pedagogies: Visible and Invisible." In Jerome Karabel and A. J. Halsey, *Power and Ideology in Education*, 511–34. New York: Oxford University Press.

Birns, Beverly, and Niza ben-New. 1988. "Psychoanalysis Constructs Motherhood." In Beverly Birns and Dale F. Hay (eds.), *The Different Faces of Motherhood*, 47–74. New York: Plenum Press.

Blank, Helen, and Amy Wilkins. 1985. *Child Care: Whose Priority? A State Childcare Fact Book.* Washington, D.C.: Children's Defense Fund.

Blau, David M., and Philip K. Robins. 1988. "Child-Care Costs and Family Labor Supply." *Review of Economics and Statistics* 70, no. 3: 374–81.

Bloom, David E., and Todd P. Steen. 1988. "Why Child Care Is Good for Business." *American Demographics* 10 (August): 22–27.

Bogat, G. A., and L. K. Gensheimer. 1986. "Discrepancies Between the Attitudes and Actions of Parents Choosing Day Care." *Child Care Quarterly* 15, no. 3: 159–69.

———. 1986. "The Role of Information and Referral Services in the Selection of Child Care." *Children and Youth Services Review* 8, no. 3: 243–56.

Boris, Eileen. 1987. "Homework and Women's Rights: The Case of the Vermont Knitters, 1980–1985." *Signs* 13, no. 1: 98–120.

———. 1985. "Regulating Industrial Homework: The Triumph of 'Sacred Motherhood.'" *Journal of American History* 71 (March): 745–63.

Bose, Christine E. 1987. "Devaluing Women's Work: The Undercount of Women's Employment in 1900 and 1980." In Christine E. Bose, Roslyn Feldberg, and Natalie Sokoloff (eds.), *Hidden Aspects of Women's Work*, 95–115. New York: Praeger.

Boulton, Mary Georgina. 1983. *On Being a Mother: A Study of Women with Pre-School Children*. London: Tavistock Publications.

Bourdieu, Pierre. 1977. "Cultural Reproduction and Social Reproduction." In Jerome Karabel and A. H. Halsey (eds.), *Power and Ideology in Education*, 473–86. Oxford University Press.

Bowers, Barbara. 1990. "Family Perceptions of Care in a Nursing Home." In Emily K. Abel and Margaret K. Nelson (eds.), *Circles of Care*, 278–89. Albany: SUNY Press.

Bradbard, M. R., and R. C. Endsley. 1979. "What Do Licensers Say to Parents Who Ask Their Help with Selecting Quality Day-Care?" *Child Care Quarterly* 8, no. 4: 307–12.

Bradley, Harriet. 1986. "Work, Home and the Restructuring of Jobs." In Kate Purcell et al. (eds.), *The Changing Experience of Employment*, 95–113. London: MacMillan Company.

Brayfield, A. H., and W. H. Crocket. 1955. "Employee Attitudes and Employee Performance." *Psychological Bulletin* 52: 396–424.

Brazelton, T. Berry, M.D. 1985. *Working and Caring*. Reading, Mass.: Addison-Wesley.

Bridgeland, William M., Philip R. Smith, and Edward A. Duane. 1985. "Child-Care Policy Arenas: A Comparison Between Sweden and the United States." *International Journal of Comparative Sociology* 26, nos. 1–2: 35–44.

Briggs, Vernon M., Jr. 1987. "The Growth and Composition of the U.S. Labor Force." *Science* 238 (October 9): 176–80.

Brown, Clair (Vickery). 1982. "Home Production for Use in a Market Economy." In Barrie Thorne and Marilyn Yalom (eds.), *Rethinking the Family: Some Feminist Questions*, 151–67. New York: Longman.

Browne, Angela C. 1985. "The Market Sphere: Private Responses to the Need for Day Care." *Child Welfare* 64, no. 4 (July–August): 367–81.

Bruno, Mark. 1985. "Day Care on the Job." *Newsweek* 106 (September 2): 59.

*Burlington Free Press*. 1983. "Parents Still Have Control of Day-Care Discipline." Editorial. (May 20): 12A.

———. 1984. "Spanking in Day-Care Centers: Parents Should Make Decision." Opinions Page. (February 15): 8A.

———. 1984. "Snelling Puts Pen to Spanking Ban." (April 16): 6B.

Burud, Sandra L., et al. 1984. *Employer Supported Child Care*. Dover, Mass.: Auburn House Publishing Co.

Caldwell, Bettye M. 1983. "How Can We Educate the Americans About the Child Care Profession?" *Young Children* 38, no. 3 (March): 11–17.

———. 1989. "A Comprehensive Model for Integrating Child Care and Early Childhood Education." *Teachers College Record* 90, no. 3 (Spring 1989): 404–14.

Chang, A., and R. Teramoto. 1987. "Children with Special Needs in Private Day Care Centers." *Child and Youth Care Quarterly* 16, no. 1: 60–67.

*Changing Times*. 1984. "Day Care: Answers for Working Parents." 38 no. 8 (August): 30–34.

———. 1986. "Child Care: Get Your Boss to Help." 40, no. 6 (October): 8.

Chapman, Fern Schumer. 1987. "Executive Guilt: Who's Taking Care of the Children? And How Will Kids Raised by Nannies and in Day Care Centers Turn Out?" *Fortune* 115, no. 8 (February 16): 30.

Cherniss, Cary. 1980. *Staff Burnout: Job Stress in the Human Services*. Beverly Hills: Sage Publications.

———. 1980. *Professional Burnout in Human Service Organizations*. New York: Praeger.

*Child Care Information Exchange*. 1988. "Child Care in the News: The Good, the Bad, and the (Really) Ugly." 64 (December): 7–10.

Child Care Licensing Position of the National Association for the Education of Young Children. 1984. *Young Children* 39 (January): 50–51.

*Children Today.* 1987. "Child Care: The Bottom Line." 16, no. 4 (July–August): 3–4.

Children's Defense Fund. 1986. *A Children's Defense Budget*. Washington, D.C.: Children's Defense Fund.

Children's Defense Fund. 1988. *A Children's Defense Budget*. Washington, D.C.: Children's Defense Fund.

Chodorow, Nancy. 1971. *The Reproduction of Mothering*. Berkeley: University of California Press.

Christensen, Kathleen. 1985. "Women and Home-Based Work." *Social Policy* 15 (Winter): 54–7.

———. 1987. *Women and Home-Based Work: The Unspoken Contract*. New York: Henry Holt and Co.

Class, Norris, and Richard Orton. 1980. "Day Care Regulation: The Limits of Licensing." *Young Children* 35, no. 6: 12–17.

Clurman, Mary. 1984. "Family Day Care: State of the Art." *Day Care and Early Education* 12 (Fall): 22–23.

Cock, Jacklyn. 1980. *Maids and Madams: A Study in the Politics of Exploitation*. Johannesburg: Ravan Press.

Cohen, Donald J., and Edward Zigler. 1977. "Federal Day Care Standards: Rationale and Recommendations," *American Journal of Orthopsychiatry* 47, no. 3 (July): 456–65.

Cohen, Susan, and Mary Fainsod Katzenstein. 1988. "The War over the Family Is Not over the Family." In Sanford M. Dornbusch and Myra H. Strober (eds.), *Feminism, Children, and the New Families*, 25–46. New York: Guilford Press.

Cole, Lisa R. 1989. "Child Care and Business." *Business and Economics Review* 35 (January–March): 4–9.

Colen, Shellee. 1986. "'With Respect and Feelings': Voices of West Indian

Child Care and Domestic Workers in New York City." In Johnnetta B. Cole (ed.), *All American Women: Lines That Divide, Ties That Bind*, 46–70. New York: Free Press.

Collins, Alice, and Eunice Watson. 1976. *Family Day Care*. Boston: Beacon Press.

Collins, Glenn. 1986. "For Child Care Workers, Poverty Level Wages." *The New York Times* (November 24): B18.

———. 1987. "Day Care Finds Corporate Help." *The New York Times* (January 5): B5.

———. 1988. "Wooing Workers in the 90's: New Role for Family Benefits." *The New York Times* (July 20): A1.

Collins, Raymond C. 1983. "Child Care and the States: The Comparative Licensing Study." *Young Children* 38, no. 5: 3–11.

Comer, L. 1974. *Wedlocked Women*. Leeds: Feminist Books.

*Congressional Digest*. 1988. "Child Care Legislation." (November): 258–87.

———. 1990. "Act for Better Child Care Services of 1989." (February): 33–63.

*Congressional Record*. 1989. U.S. Senate, 101st Cong., 1st sess., June 23.

Connolly, Priscilla. 1985. "The Politics of the Informal Sector: A Critique." In Nanneke Redclift and Enzo Mingione (eds.), *Beyond Employment: Household Gender and Subsistence*, 14–54. Oxford: Basil Blackwell.

Contratto, Susan. 1986. "Child Abuse and the Politics of Care." *Journal of Education* 168, no. 3: 70–79.

Corsini, David A., Steven Wisensale, and Grace-Ann Caruso. 1988. "Family Day Care: System Issues and Regulatory Models." *Young Children* 43, no. 6 (September): 17–23.

Cox, D. 1984. "Panel Estimates of the Effects of Career Interruptions on the Earnings of Women." *Economic Inquiry* 22 (July): 386–403.

Dames, Kateri K. 1983. "Registration for Child Care Homes." *Day Care and Early Education* 11 (Fall): 21–23.

Davenport, Amy, et al. 1985. *The Economics of Child Care*. Montpelier, Vt.: Governor's Commission on the Status of Women's Childcare Task Force.

Davidoff, Lenore. 1979. "The Separation of Home and Work? Landladies and Lodgers in Nineteenth and Twentieth Century England." In Sandra Burman (ed.), *Fit Work for Women*, 64–97. New York: St. Martin's Press.

Davis, Joseph, and Phyllis Solomon. 1980. "Day Care Needs Among the Upper Middle Classes." *Child Welfare* 59, no. 8 (September/October): 497–9.

Dendy, Selma. 1981. "Mothering Others, Mothering My Own." In Ronnie Friedland and Carol Kort (eds.), *The Mother's Book*, 72–82. Boston: Beacon Press.

Deutsch, M. 1963. "The Disadvantaged Child and the Learning Process." In H. Passow (ed.), *Education in Depressed Areas*. New York: Teachers College Press.

Diamond, Timothy. 1990. "Nursing Homes as 'Trouble.'" In Emily K. Abel and Margaret K. Nelson (eds.), *Circles of Care*, 173–87. Albany: SUNY Press.

———. 1988. "Social Policy and Everyday Life in Nursing Homes: A Critical Ethnography." In Anne Stratham, Eleanor M. Miller and Hans O. Mauksch (eds.), *The Worth of Women's Work: A Qualitative Synthesis*, 39–57. Albany: SUNY Press.

Dilks, Carol, and Nancy L. Croft. 1986. "Child Care: Your Baby?" *Nation's Business* 74, no. 5 (December): 16.

Dill, Bonnie Thornton. 1980. "'The Means to Put My Children Through': Child-rearing Goals and Strategies Among Black Female Domestic Servants." In LaFrances Rodgers-Rose (ed.), *The Black Woman*, 107–23. Beverly Hills: Sage Publications.

———. 1988. "'Making Your Job Good Yourself': Domestic Service and the Construction of Personal Dignity." In Ann Bookman and Sandra Morgan (eds.), *Women and the Politics of Empowerment*, 33–52. Philadelphia: Temple University Press.

Dittmann, Laural L. 1986. "Finding the Best Care for Your Infant or Toddler." *Young Children* 41, no. 3: 43–46.

Divine-Hawkins, Patricia. 1981. *Final Report of the National Day Care Home Study*, 8 vols. U.S. Department of Health and Human Services. Washington, D.C.: Government Printing Office.

Dresden, Janna, and Barbara Kimes Myers. 1989. "Early Childhood Professionals: Toward Self-Definition." *Young Children* 44, no. 3 (January): 62.

Dudden, Faye. 1983. *Serving Women: Household Service in Nineteenth-Century America*. Middletown, Conn.: Wesleyan University Press.

Edelman, Marian Wright. 1989. "Economic Issues Related to Child Care and Early Childhood Education." *Teachers College Record* 90, no. 3 (Spring): 342–51.

Eheart, Brenda Krause, and Robin Lynn Leavitt. 1986. "Training Day Care Home Providers: Implications for Policy and Research." *Early Childhood Research Quarterly* 1, no. 2 (June): 119–32.

Ehrenrich, Barbara, and Deidre English. 1979. *For Her Own Good: 150 Years of the Experts' Advice to Women*. New York: Doubleday.

Einseidel, Albert, and Heather Tully. 1982. "Methodological Considerations in Studying the Burnout Phenomenon." In John W. Jones (ed.), *The Burnout Syndrome: Current Research, Theory, Interventions*, 89–106. Park Ridge, Ill.: London House Press.

Ekeh, P. 1974. *Social Exchange Theory*. Cambridge: Harvard University Press.

Ellis, Katherine, and Rosalind Petchesky. 1972. "Children of the Corporate Dream: An Analysis of Day Care as a Political Issue Under Capitalism." *Socialist Revolution* 2 no. 6 (November/December): 9–28.

Emlen, A. C., et al. 1971. *Child Care by Kith*. Portland: Oregon State University Press.

———. 1977. "Family Day Care for Children Under Three." Paper presented at the International Symposium on the Ecology of Care and Education of Children Under Three, February 23–26, Max Planck Institute for Educational Research, Berlin.

Enarson, Elaine. 1987. "Toward a Theory of Waged Mothering: The Case of Family Day Care." Unpublished paper, University of Nevada–Reno.

———. 1990. "Experts and Caregivers: Perspectives on Underground Childcare." In Emily K. Abel and Margaret K. Nelson (eds.), *Circles of Care*, 233–45. Albany: SUNY Press.

Engel, Margaret. 1985. "New Day Care Options: How Companies Are Meeting the Needs of Working Parents." *Glamour* 83 (May): 136.

Erdwins, C. J., and J. C. Mellinger. 1986. "Reentry Women After Graduation." *Journal of Genetic Psychology* 147 (December): 437–46.

Evans, Sandra. 1987. "$2.5 Billion Day Care Bill Proposed." *Washington Post* (November 20): 22.

Evans, W. E. 1987. "Career Interruptions Following Childbirth." *Journal of Labor Economics* 5 (April): 255–77.

Ferguson, Roy V., and James P. Anglin. 1985. "The Child Care Profession: A Vision for the Future." *Child Care Quarterly* 14, no. 2 (Summer): 85–101.

Ferree, Myra Marx. 1985. "Between Two Worlds: German Feminist Approaches to Working-Class Women and Their Work." *Signs* 10, no. 3: 517–36.

———. 1987. "Family and Job for Working Class Women: Gender and Class Systems Seen from Below." In Naomi Gerstel and Harriet Engel Gross (eds.), *Families and Work*, 289–302. Philadelphia: Temple University Press.

———. 1987. "The Struggles of Superwoman." In Christine Bose, Roslyn Feldberg, and Natalie Sokoloff (eds.), *Hidden Aspects of Women's Work*, 161–80. New York: Praeger.

Fierman, Jaclyn. 1988. "Child Care: What Works—And Doesn't." *Fortune* (November 21): 165.

Finch, Janet, and Dulcie Groves. 1983. *A Labour of Love: Women, Work and Caring*. London: Routledge and Kegan Paul.

Fink, Dale B. 1987. "Child Care Dilemma, Family Day Care: An Option for Parents." *Exceptional Parent* 17, no. 2 (March): 18–21.

Finkelhor, David, and Linda Meyer Williams, with Nanci Burns. 1988. *Nursery Crimes: Sexual Abuse in Day Care*. Newbury Park: Sage Publications.

Fishaut, Erna. 1987. "A Time to Dream." *Young Children* 43, no. 1 (November): 20–22.

Fisher, Berenice. 1990. "Alice in the Human Services: A Feminist Analysis of Women's Work in the Caring Professions." In Emily K. Abel and Margaret K. Nelson (eds.), *Circles of Care*, 108–31. Albany: SUNY Press.

Fisher, Berenice, and Joan Tronto. 1990. "Toward a Feminist Theory of Caregiving." In Emily K. Abel and Margaret K. Nelson (eds.), *Circles of Care*, 35–62. Albany: SUNY Press.

Fleischer, Barbara J. 1985. "Identification of Strategies to Reduce Turnover Among Child Care Workers." *Child Care Quarterly* 142, no. 2 (Summer): 130–39.

Floge, Liliane. 1985. "The Dynamics of Child-Care Use and Some Implications for Women's Employment." *Journal of Marriage and the Family* 47, no. 1 (February): 143–54.

———. 1989. "Changing Household Structure, Child-Care Availability, and Employment Among Mothers of Pre-School Children." *Journal of Marriage and the Family* 51 (February): 51–63.

Folbre, Nancy, and Heidi Hartmann. 1988. "A New Politics of Entitlement." *The Nation* (October 3): 263–66.

Fontana, Vincent J. 1973. *Somewhere a Child Is Crying*. New York: Macmillan.

Fooner, Andrea. 1985. "Six Good Solutions for Child Care." *Working Women* 10, no. 4 (October): 173.

Fosburg, Stephen J., et al. 1981. *Family Day Care in the United States: Summary of Findings*. Washington, D.C.: Government Printing Office.

Freedman, Sara. 1987. "To Love and to Work: The Ghettoization of Women's Labor in the Home and the School." Unpublished paper, Cambridge, Mass.

Freudenberger, Herbert J. 1977. "Burn Out: Occupational Hazard of the Child Care Worker." *Child Care Quarterly* 6, no. 2 (Summer): 90–9.

———. 1980. *Burn-Out: The High Cost of High Achievement*. Garden City, N.Y.: Doubleday.

Friedan, Betty. 1963. *The Feminine Mystique*. New York: W. W. Norton.

Friedman, Dana E. 1986. "Child Care for Employees' Kids," *Harvard Business Review* 64 (March/April): 28–38.

Froland, Charles. 1980. "Formal and Informal Care: Discontinuities in a Continuum." *Social Service Review* 54 no. 4. (December): 572–87.

Fuqua, Robert W., and Dorothy Labensohn. 1986. "Parents as Consumers of Child Care." *Family Relations* 35 (April): 295–303.

Galinsky, Ellen. 1986. "What Really Constitutes Quality Care." *Child Care Information Exchange* 51 (September): 41–47.

———. 1988. "Parents and Teacher-Caregivers: Sources of Tension, Sources of Support." *Young Children* 43, no. 3 (March): 4–12.

Gamble, Thomas J., and Edward Zigler. 1988. "Effects of Infant Day Care: Another Look at the Evidence." In Edward F. Zigler and Meryl Frank (eds.), *The Parental Leave Crisis*, 77–99. New Haven: Yale University Press.

Gerry, Chris. 1985. "The Working Class and Small Enterprises in the UK Recession." In Nanneke Redclift and Enzo Mingione (eds.), *Beyond Employment: Household Gender and Subsistence*, 288–316. Oxford: Basil Blackwell.

Gershuny, J. I., and R. E. Pahl. 1979. "Work Outside Employment: Some Preliminary Speculations." *NUQ* (Winter): 120–35.

Gerson, Kathleen. 1987. "How Women Choose Between Employment and Family: A Developmental Perspective." In Naomi Gerstel and Harriet Engel Gross (eds.), *Families and Work*, 270–89. Philadelphia: Temple University Press.

Gibson, Janice. 1985. "Coping with Day Care." *Parents' Magazine* 60, no. 1 (August): 110.

Gilder, George. 1988. "An Open Letter to Orrin Hatch." *National Review* (May 13): 32–34.

Gilligan, Carol. 1982. *In a Different Voice: Psychological Theory and Women's Development*. Cambridge, Mass.: Harvard University Press.

Ginsburg, Gerri, Derek Richardson, and Marcy Whitebook. 1985. "Special Stresses of Infant Caregiving." *Day Care and Early Education* (Spring 1985): 22–24.

*Glamour*. 1985. "Editorial." *Glamour* 83 (April): 84.

Glazer, Nona Y. 1987. "Servants to Capital: Unpaid Domestic Labor and Paid Work." In Naomi Gerstel and Harriet Engel Gross (eds.), *Families and Work*, 236–56. Philadelphia: Temple University Press.

Glenn, Evelyn Nakano. 1986. *Issei, Nisei, War Bride: Three Generations of Japanese American Women in Domestic Service*. Philadelphia: Temple University Press.

Glubka, Shirley. 1983. "Out of the Stream: An Essay on Unconventional Motherhood." *Feminist Studies* 9 (Summer): 223–35.

Golden, M., et al. 1978. *The New York City Infant Day Care Study.* Medical and Health Research Association of New York City.

Gordon, Linda. 1985. "Child Abuse, Gender and the Myth of Family Independence: A Historical Critique." *Child Welfare* 64, no. 3 (May–June): 213–24.

———. 1986. "Family Violence, Feminism, and Social Control." *Feminist Studies* 12, no. 3 (Fall): 453–78.

Gordon, Susan. 1989. "America's Day-Care Crisis." *Entrepreneur* 17 (March): 90–100.

Gottschalk, Earl C., Jr. 1978. "Women at Work: Day Care Is Booming but Experts Are Split Over Its Effect on Kids." *Wall Street Journal* (September 15): 1.

Gould, Nora Palmer. 1983. "Caregivers in Day Care: Who Are They?" *Day Care* 10, no. 4 (Summer): 17–21.

Grace, Gerald Rupert. 1978. *Teachers, Ideology and Control: A Study in Urban Education.* London: Routledge and Kegan Paul.

Graham, Hilary. 1983. "Caring: A Labour of Love." In Janet Finch and Dulcie Groves (eds.), *A Labour of Love: Women, Work and Caring,* 13–30. London: Routledge and Kegan Paul.

Graham, H., and L. McKee. 1980. *The First Months of Motherhood.* London: Health and Education Council.

Griffin, Sherri, and Kathy R. Thornburg. 1985. "Perceptions of Infant/Toddler Temperament in Three Child Care Settings." *Early Child Development and Care* 18, nos. 3–4: 151–60.

Griffith, Alison I., and Dorothy E. Smith. 1985. "Coordinating the Uncoordinated: How Mothers Manage the School Day." Ontario Institute for Studies in Education.

Groves, Susan. 1984. *Family Day Care: Economic and Work Related Factors Affecting the Persistence of Providers.* Berkeley: Center for the Study, Education and Advancement of Women, University of California).

Hacker, Andrew. 1982. *U/S: A Statistical Portrait of the American People.* New York: Viking Press.

Harms, Thelma. 1986. "Finding Good Child Care: The Essential Questions to Ask When Seeking Quality Care for Your Child." *Parents' Magazine* 61, no. 2 (August): 105.

Hartmann, Heidi I. 1981. "The Family as the Locus of Gender, Class and Political Struggle: The Example of Housework," *Signs* 6, no. 3: 366–94.

Hartmann, Heidi I., and Diana M. Pearce. 1989. "High Skills and Low Pay: The Economics of Child Care Work." *Executive Summary* (Institute for Women's Policy Research, February).

Haskins, Ron. 1988. "What Day Care Crisis?" *Regulation: AEI Journal of Government and Society* 12, no. 2: 13–21.

Hayghe, Howard V. 1986. "Rise in Mothers' Labor Force Activity Includes Those with Infants." *Monthly Labor Review* 109 (February): 43–45.

———. 1988. "Employers and Child Care: What Roles Do They Play?" *Monthly Labor Review* 111 (September): 38–44.

Hearn, Jeff. 1985. "Patriarchy, Professionalisation, and the Semi-Professions." In Clare Ungerson (ed.), *Women and Social Policy: A Reader,* 109–208. London: Macmillan.

Henry, Stuart. 1981. "Introduction." In Stuart Henry (ed.), *Informal Institutions: Alternative Networks in the Corporate State*, 1–23. New York: St. Martin's Press.

———. 1982. "The Working Unemployed: Perspectives on the Informal Economy and Unemployment." *Sociological Review* 30, no. 3: 460–77.

Herrstrom, Staffan. 1986. *Swedish Family Policy*. Stockholm: Swedish Institute.

Herz, Rosanna. 1986. *More Equal than Others: Women and Men in Dual-Career Marriages*. Berkeley: University of California Press.

Herzberg, F., B. Mausner, R. O. Peterson, and D. F. Capwell. 1957. *Job Attitudes: Review of Research and Opinion*. Pittsburgh: Psychological Service of Pittsburgh.

Hickey, Mary, and Claudia Glenn Dowling. 1988. "Small World." *Life* (November): 150–58.

Hitchcock, Ruth A. 1987. "Understanding Physical Abuse as a Life-Style." *Individual Psychology* 43, no. 1 (March): 50–55.

Hitchings, Bradley. 1985. "Today's Choices in Child Care." *Business Week* (April 1): 104–5.

Hoch, E., et al. 1985. "Employment Decisions Made by Mothers of Infants." *Psychology of Women Quarterly* 9 (Spring): 383–402.

Hochschild, Arlie Russell. 1983. *The Managed Heart: The Commercialization of Human Feeling*. Berkeley: University of California Press.

Holcomb, Betty. 1987. "Where's Mommy? The Great Debate over the Effects of Child Care." *New York* 20, no. 13 (April): 72.

Holloway, Susan D., Kathleen S. Gorman, and Bruce Fuller. 1988. "Child-rearing Beliefs Within Diverse Social Structures: Mothers and Day-Care Providers in Mexico." *International Journal of Psychology* 23, no. 3: 303–17.

Holmes, Steven A. 1990. "House, 265–145, Votes to Widen Day Care Programs in the Nation." *New York Times* (March 30): A1.

Hom, P., R. Katerberg, and C. L. Hulin. 1978. "Comparative Examinations of Three Approaches to the Prediction of Turnover." *Journal of Applied Psychology* 64, no. 3: 280–90.

Honig, Alice Sterling. 1985. "Research in Review. Compliance, Control and Discipline." *Young Children* 40, no. 2 (March): 47–52.

Horvath, France W. 1986. "Work at Home: New Findings from the Current Population Survey." *Monthly Labor Review* 109, no. 11 (November): 31–35.

Hostetler, Lana. 1984. "Public Policy Report: The Nanny Trap: Child Care Work Today." *Young Children* 39, no. 2 (January): 76–79.

Hostetler, Lana, and Edgar Klugman. 1982. "Early Childhood Job Titles: One Step Toward Professional Status." *Young Children* 37, no. 6 (September): 13–19.

Hoy, Jane, and Mary Kennedy. 1983. "Women's Paid Labor in the Home: The British Experience." *Research in the Sociology of Work: Peripheral Workers* vol. 2, 211–39. Greenwich, Conn.: JAI Press.

Hughes, Robert, Jr. 1985. "The Informal Help-Giving of Home and Center Childcare Providers." *Family Relations* 34, no. 3 (July): 359–66.

Hurst, Marsha, and Ruth E. Zambrana. 1982. "Child Care and Working Mothers in Puerto Rican Families." *Annals of the American Academy: AAPSS* 461 (May): 113–24.

Hylton, L. 1964. *The Residential Treatment Center: Children's Programs and Costs.* New York: Child Welfare League of America.

Inman, Virginia. 1982. "Stunted Growth: Day Care Laws Limit Private-Home Centers that Parents Like Best." *Wall Street Journal* (October 26): 1.

Innes, Robert B., and Sharon M. Innes. 1984. "A Qualitative Study of Caregivers' Attitudes about Child Care." *Early Child Development and Care* 15, nos. 2–3: 133–47.

Jackson, Brian, and Sonia Jackson. 1979. *Childminder: A Study in Action Research.* London: Routledge and Kegan Paul.

Jaggar, Alison M. 1983. *Feminist Politics and Human Nature.* Totowa, N.J.: Rowman and Allanheld.

Jensen, Joan M. 1980. "Cloth, Butter and Boarders: Women's Household Production for the Market." *Review of Radical Political Economics* 12, no. 2 (Summer): 14–23.

Joffe, Carole E. 1977. *Friendly Intruders: Childcare Professionals and Family Life.* Berkeley: University of California Press.

———. 1983. "Why the United States Has No Child-Care Policy." In Irene Diamond (ed.), *Families, Politics and Public Policy: A Feminist Dialogue on Women and the State,* 168–82. New York: Longman.

———. 1986. *The Regulation of Sexuality.* Philadelphia: Temple University Press.

Jones, John W. 1982. *The Burnout Syndrome: Current Research, Theory, Interventions.* Park Ridge, Ill.: London House Press.

———. 1982. "Staff Burnout and Employee Counterproductivity." In John W. Jones (ed.), *The Burnout Syndrome: Current Research, Theory, Interventions,* 127–38. Park Ridge, Ill.: London House Press.

Jones, Sylvia, and Samuel Meisels. 1987. "Training Family Day Care Providers to Work with Special Needs Children." *Topics in Early Childhood Special Education* 7, no. 1 (Spring): 1–12.

Justice, Blair, and Rita Justice. 1976. *The Abusing Family.* New York: Human Services Press.

Kagan, Sharon Lynn. 1988. "Current Reforms in Early Childhood Education: Are We Addressing the Issues?" *Young Children* 43, no. 2 (January): 27–32.

Kagan, Sharon L., and Theresa Glennon. 1982. "Child Care: In Defense of Choice," *Day Care* 9, no. 3 (Spring): 54–57.

Kahn, Alfred J., and Sheila B. Kamerman. 1987. *Child Care: Facing the Hard Choices.* Dover, Mass.: Auburn House Publishing Co.

Kamerman, Sheila B. 1983. *Family Needs: The Corporate Response.* Fairview Park, N.Y.: Pergamon Press.

———. 1985. "Child Care Services: An Issue for Gender Equity and Women's Solidarity." *Child Welfare* 64, no. 3: 259–71.

———. 1986. "Women, Children and Poverty: Public Policies and Female-Headed Families in Industrialized Countries." In Barbara C. Gelpi et al. (eds.), *Women and Poverty,* 41–64. Chicago: University of Chicago Press.

Kamerman, Sheila B., and Alfred J. Kahn. 1978. *Family Policy: Government and Families in Fourteen Countries.* New York: Columbia University Press.

———. 1981. *Child Care, Family Benefits and Working Parents: A Study of Comparative Policy.* New York: Columbia University Press.

Kamerman, Sheila B., Alfred J. Kahn, and Paul Kingston. 1983. *Maternity Policies and Working Women.* New York: Columbia University Press.

Kantrowitz, Barbara. 1986. "Changes in the Workplace." *Newsweek* (March 31): 57.

———. 1986. "A Mother's Choice," *Newsweek* (March 31).

———. 1988. "Who Cares About Day Care? Millions of People but None of the Candidates." *Newsweek* 111 (March 28): 73.

Karre, Marianne, et al. 1973. "Social Rights in Sweden Before School Starts." In Pamela Roby (ed.), *Child Care—Who Cares?*, 137–53. New York: Basic Books.

Karvelas, David. 1983. "Day Care Spanking Opposed." *Burlington Free Press* (May 12): 1B.

Katz, Lilian G. 1980. "Mothering and Teaching—Some Significant Distinctions." In Lilian G. Katz (ed.), *Current Topics in Early Childhood Education,* vol. 3, 47–63. Norwood, N.J.: Ablex Publishing Co.

———. 1985. "Care-Giver Relations." *Parents* 60 (January): 114.

Katzman, David. 1978. *Seven Days a Week: A History of Wage-Earning Women in the United States.* New York: Oxford University Press.

Keith-Lucas, Alan. 1980. "On Being Truly Professional." *Child Care Quarterly* 9, no. 4 (Winter): 243–50.

Kelly, James. 1981. "Visions of Voluntarism: Calling for a Return to a Self-Help Society." *Time* (October 19): 47.

Kelly, M., Patricia Fernandez, and Anne M. Garcia. 1985. "The Making of an Underground Economy: Hispanic Women, Home Work and the Advanced Capitalist State." *Urban Anthropology* 14, nos. 1–3 (Spring, Summer, Fall): 59–90.

Kendall, Earline D., and Lewis H. Walker. 1984. "Day Care Licensing: The Eroding Regulations." *Child Care Quarterly* 13 no. 4 (Winter 1984): 278–90.

Kessler-Harris, Alice, and Karen Brodkin Sacks. 1987. "The Demise of Domesticity in America." In Lourdes Beneria and Catharine R. Simpson (eds.), *Women, Households and the Economy,* 65–84. New Brunswick, N.J.: Rutgers University Press.

Kimmick, Madeline H. 1985. *America's Children: Who Cares?* Washington, D.C.: The Urban Institute.

King, Donna, and Carol MacKinnon. 1988. "Making Difficult Choices Easier: A Review of Research on Day Care and Children's Development." *Family Relations* 37 (October): 392–98.

Kingsley, Ronald F., and Cheryl Cook-Hatala. 1988. "A Survey of Child Care Workers: Implications for Administrators Regarding Job Stress and Satisfaction." *Child and Youth Care Quarterly* 14, no. 4 (Winter): 281–87.

Kitzinger, Sheila. 1978. *Women as Mothers.* New York: Random House.

Kivikink, R., and B. Schell. 1987. "Demographic, Satisfaction, and Commitment Profiles of Day-Care Users, Nursery-School Users, and Babysitter Users in a Medium Sized Canadian City." *Child and Youth Care Quarterly* 16, no. 2: 116–30.

Klass, Carol S. 1987. "Childrearing Interactions Within Developmental Home- Or Center-Based Early Education." *Young Children* 42, no. 3: 9–13, 67–70.

Komarovsky, Mirra. 1962. *Blue Collar Marriage*. New York: Vintage Books.

Konrad, Walecia. 1985. "Corporate Day Care Attracts Top Male Employees, Too." *Working Woman* (November): 31.

Kontos, Susan, and Wilma Wells. 1986. "Attitudes of Caregivers and the Day Care Experiences of Families." *Early Childhood Research Quarterly* 1, no. 1 (March): 47–67.

Kraut, A. O. 1975. "Predicting Turnover of Employees from Measured Job Attitudes." *Organizational Behavior and Human Performance* 13, no. 2: 233–43.

Kutner, Laurence. 1988. "Searching for Day Care: How to Tell the Good from the Bad." *New York Times* (February 4): 17–18.

Kutscher, Ronald E., and Valerie A. Personick. 1986. "Deinstitutionalization and the Shift to Services." *Monthly Labor Review* 109, no. 6 (June): 3–13.

LaFleur, Elizabeth K., and Walter B. Newsom. 1988. "Opportunities for Child Care." *Personnel Administrator* 33 (June): 146–54.

Land, Hilary, and Hilary Rose. 1985. "Compulsory Altruism for Some or an Altruistic Society for All?" In Philip Bean et al. (eds.), *In Defence of Welfare*, 74–96. London: Tavistock.

Leibowitz, Arleen, Linda J. Waite, and Christina Witsberger. 1988. "Child Care for Preschoolers: Differences by Child's Age." *Demography* 25, no. 2 (May): 205–20.

Lessing, Doris. 1988. *The Fifth Child*. New York: Alfred A. Knopf.

Levine, Art. 1987. "Second Thoughts About Infant Day Care." *U.S. News and World Report* 102, no. 2 (May 4): 73.

Levi-Strauss, Claude. 1969. *The Elementary Structure of Kinship*. Boston: Beacon Press.

Lightfoot, Sara Lawrence. 1977. "Family-School Interactions: The Cultural Image of Mothers and Teachers." *Signs* 3, no. 2: 395–408.

———. 1978. *Worlds Apart: Relationships Between Families and Schools*. New York: Basic Books.

Lindsay, P., and C. H. Lindsay. 1987. "Teachers in Preschools and Child-Care Centers: Overlooked and Undervalued." *Child and Youth Care Quarterly* 16, no. 2: 91–105.

Lindsey, Lawrence B. 1988. "Better Child Care, Cheaper." *Wall Street Journal* (July 5): 20.

Linney, Jean Ann, and Eric Vernberg. 1983. "Changing Patterns of Parental Employment and the Family-School Relationship." In Cheryl D. Hayes and Sheila B. Kamerman (eds.), *Children of Working Parents: Experiences and Outcomes*. Washington, D.C.: National Academy Press.

Litwak, E. 1981. "Theoretical Bases for Practice." In R. Dobrof and E. Litwak (eds.), *Maintenance of Family Ties of Long-Term Care Patients: Theory and Guide to Practice*. Department of Health and Human Services. Washington, D.C.: Government Printing Office.

Locke, E. A. 1978. "The Nature and Causes of Job Satisfaction." In M. Dunnette (ed.), *Handbook of Industrial and Organizational Psychology*, 1297–1349. Chicago: Rand McNally.

Lopata, Carol. 1971. *Occupation Housewife*. New York: Oxford University Press.

Lounsbury, John W. 1977. "A Comparison of Interest Group Recommendations in Setting Day Care Licensing Standards." *Child Care Quarterly* 6, no. 4 (Winter): 300.

Lounsbury, John W. and Diana Q. Hall. 1976. "Supervision and Consultation Conflicts in the Day-Care Licensing Role," *Social Service Review* 50 (September): 515–23.

Lubeck, Sally, and Patricia Garrett. 1988. "Child Care 2000: Policy Options for the Future." *Social Policy* 18, no. 4: 31–37.

Luker, Kristin. 1984. *Abortion and the Politics of Motherhood*. Berkeley: University of California Press.

Lundberg, Kirsten O. 1989. "What's New in Day-Care? A Tool to Keep Women in the Workforce." *New York Times* (February 26): sec. 3, p. 13.

Lundgren, Rebecka, and Carole H. Browner. 1990. "Caring for the Institutionalized Mentally Retarded: Work Culture and Work-Based Social Support." In Emily K. Abel and Margaret K. Nelson (eds.), *Circles of Care*, 150–72. Albany: SUNY Press.

McClelland, J. 1986. "Job-Satisfaction of Child-Care Workers—A Review." *Child Care Quarterly* 15, no. 2: 82–89.

McClure, Laura. 1986. "Homework's Horrors." *The Guardian* (November 5): 1.

MacKinnon, Carol E., and Donna King. 1988. "Day Care: A Review of Literature, Implications for Policy, and Critique of Resources." *Family Relations* 37, no. 2 (April): 229–36.

McMullen, Mary Benson, and Murray Krantz. 1986. "Burnout in Day Care Workers: The Effects of Learned Helplessness and Self-Esteem." *Child and Youth Care Quarterly* 17, no. 4 (Winter): 275–80.

McNamara, Mary. 1988. "At Last! A Major Push for Child Care." *Ms.* 16 (February): 17–18.

MacNeil, David. 1982. "The Relationship of Occupational Stress to Burnout." In John W. Jones (ed.), *The Burnout Syndrome: Current Research, Theory, Interventions*, 68–88. Park Ridge, Ill.: London House Press.

Magid, Renee Yablans. 1989. "The Consequences of Employer Involvement in Child Care." *Teachers College Record* 90, no. 3 (Spring): 434–43.

Malone, Margaret. n.d. "Child Day Care: The Federal Role." Congressional Research Service, Education and Public Welfare Division, Washington, D.C.

Marshall, Nancy, et al. 1990. "Double Jeopardy: The Costs of Caring at Work and at Home." In Emily K. Abel and Margaret K. Nelson (eds.), *Circles of Care*, 266–77. Albany: SUNY Press.

Marzollo, Jean. 1987. "Child-Care Workers Speak Up." *Parents' Magazine* 62 (April): 114–18.

Maslach, Christina. 1982. *Burnout: The Cost of Caring*. Englewood Cliffs, N.J. Prentice-Hall.

Maslach, Christina, and A. Pines. 1977. "The Burnout Syndrome in the Day Care Setting." *Child Care Quarterly* 6, no. 2: 100–13.

Maslach, Christina, and S. E. Jackson. 1981. *The Maslach Burnout Inventory*. 2nd ed. Palo Alto, Calif.: Consulting Psychologists.

Mattingly, M. 1977. "Sources of Stress and Burn-out in Professional Child Care Work." *Child Care Quarterly* 6, no. 2 (Summer): 127–37.

Meer, Antonia van der. 1986. "A Working Mother's Guide to Day Care." *Good Housekeeping* 203 (September): 98–101.

Meissner, M., E. W. Humphrey, S. M. Meis, and W. J. Shen. 1975. "No Exit for Wives: Sexual Division of Labor and the Cumulation of Household Demands." *Canadian Review of Sociology and Anthropology* 12, no. 4: 424–39.

Melosh, Barbara. 1982. *"The Physician's Hand": Work, Culture and Conflict in American Nursing*. Philadelphia: Temple University Press.

Michaelsen, W. 1985. *From Sun to Sun: Daily Obligations and Community Structure in the Lives of Employed Women and their Families*. Totowa, N.J.: Rowman and Allanheld.

Miller, Dorothy. 1987. "Children's Policy and Women's Policy: Congruence or Conflict?" *Social Work* 32 (July/August): 289–92.

Miller, Jean Baker. 1976. *Toward a New Psychology of Women*. Boston: Beacon Press.

Miller, JoAnn, and Gloria Norris. 1985. "Who's Minding Our Kids?" *Redbook* 164, no. 4 (March): 4.

Mobley, W. H. 1977. "Intermediate Linkage in the Relationship Between Job Satisfaction and Employee Turnover." *Journal of Applied Psychology* 62, no. 2: 237–40.

Modigliani, Kathy. 1988. "Twelve Reasons for the Low Wages in Child Care." *Young Children* 43 (March): 14–15.

Montrose, Myryame. 1986. "What You Need to Know About Child-Care Alternatives: American Baby Basics, Part 7," *American Baby* 48 (July): 55–63.

Morgan, Gwen G. 1984. "Change Through Regulation." In James Greenman and Robert Fuqua (eds.), *Making Day Care Better*, 163–84. New York: Teachers College Press.

———. 1979. "Regulation: One Approach to Quality Child Care." *Young Children* 34, no. 6 (September): 22–27.

———. 1987. "Who's Minding the Kids?" *Parents* (April): 106–9.

Morgan, Gwen G., Carol S. Stevenson, Richard Fiene, and Keith O. Stephens. 1986. "Gaps and Excesses in the Regulation of Child Day Care: Report of a Panel." *Reviews of Infectious Diseases* 8, no. 4 (July–August): 634–43.

Murphy, Ludmilla. 1986. "Child Care Workers." *Occupational Outlook* 30 (Summer): 29–32.

Myer, John. 1975. "An Informal Survey of Child Care Workers." *Child Care Quarterly* 4, no. 2: 120.

———. 1980. "An Exploratory Nationwide Survey of Child Care Workers." *Child Care Quarterly* 9, no. 1 (Spring): 17–25.

National Association for the Education of Young Children. 1987. "Public Policy Report: Guidelines for Developing Legislation." *Young Children* 42, no. 3 (March): 43–45.

Nelson, John R., Jr. 1982. "The Federal Interagency Day Care Requirements." In Cheryl B. Hayes (ed.), *Making Policies for Children: A Study of the Federal Process*. Washington, D.C.: National Academy Press.

Nelson, Margaret K. 1985. "Waged Labors of Love." Paper presented at the American Education Research Association, Annual Meeting, Chicago, April 20–23.

———. 1988. "Providing Family Day Care: An Analysis of Home-Based Work." *Social Problems* 35, no. 1 (February): 78–94.

*New York Times*. 1988. "Report Criticizes Two Relatives in Child's Fall in Texas Well." (January 13): A18.

Norris, Gloria, and Jo Ann Miller. 1984. *The Working Mother's Complete Handbook*. New American Library.

Oakley, Ann. 1979. *Housewife*. New York: Viking Press.

O'Connell, Martin, and David Bloom. 1987. *Juggling Jobs and Babies: America's Child Care Challenge*. Washington, D.C.: Population Reference Bureau.

Olson, Magreth H., and Sophia B. Primps. 1984. "Working at Home with Computers: Work and Nonwork Issues." *Journal of Social Issues* 40, no. 3: 97–112.

*Open House*. 1989. Addison County Child Care Training Program. P.O. Box 646, Middlebury, VT 05753.

Paine, Whiton S. 1982. "The Burnout Syndrome in Context." In John W. Jones. (ed.), *The Burnout Syndrome: Current Research, Theory, Interventions*, 1–29. Park Ridge: Ill.: London House Press.

———. 1982. *Job Stress and Burnout: Research, Theory and Intervention Perspectives*. Beverly Hills: Sage Publications.

Pence, Alan R., and Hillel Goelman. 1987. "Silent Partners: Parents of Children in Three Types of Day Care." *Early Childhood Research Quarterly* 2, no. 2 (June): 103–18.

———. 1987. "Who Cares for the Child in Day Care? An Examination of Caregivers from Three Types of Care." *Early Childhood Research Quarterly* 2, no. 4 (December): 315–34.

*Personnel*. 1984. "White Collar Homework: On the Upswing." *Personnel* 59, no. 5: 50–51.

Peterson, Susan Rae. 1984. "Against 'Parenting'." In Joyce Trebilcot (ed.), *Mothering: Essays in Feminist Theory*, 62–9. Totowa, N.J.: Rowman and Allanheld.

Petrie, Pat. 1984. "Day Care for Under 2's at Child Minders and in Day Nurseries." *Early Child Development and Care* 16, nos. 3–4: 205–15.

Pettygrove, Willa, and James Greenman. 1984. "The Adult World of Day Care." In James Greenman and Robert Fuqua (eds.), *Making Day Care Better*, 84–105. New York: Teachers College Press.

Pettygrove, Willa, et al. 1984. "Beyond Babysitting: Changing the Image and Treatment of Child Caregivers." *Young Children* 39 (July): 14–21.

Phillips, Deborah A., and Michael Kiernan. 1988. "Child Care Legislation: Common Ground and Controversy." *Child Care Information Exchange* 62, no. 9: 23–26.

Phillips, Deborah A., and Marcy Whitebook. 1986. "Who Are Child Care Workers? The Search for Answers." *Young Children* 14 (May): 14–20.

Phillips, Deborah A., and Edward F. Zigler. 1987. "The Checkered History of Federal Child Care Regulation." *Review of Research in Education* 14: 3–41.

Phillips, Deborah, et al. 1987. "Child Care Quality and Children's Social Development." *Developmental Psychology* 23, no. 4 (July): 537–43.

Polatnick, Margaret. 1984. "Why Men Don't Rear Children." In Joyce Trebilcot (ed.), *Motherhood: Essays in Feminist Theory,* 21–40. Totowa, N.J.: Rowman and Allanheld.

Porter, Carol J. 1981. "Professionalization and Day Care: Friend or Foe?" (Paper presented at the Conference on Child Care Education, University of Miami, Coral Gables, Fla., November 13.)

Porter, L. W., and R. M. Steers. 1973. "Organizational, Work, and Personal Factors in Employee Turnover and Absenteeism." *Psychological Bulletin* 80, no. 2: 151–76.

Portes, Alejandro, and John Walton. 1981. *Labour, Class and the International System.* New York: Academic Press.

Postrel, Virginia L. 1989. "Who's Behind the Child Care Crisis?" *Reason* (June): 20–27.

Powell, Douglas R. 1978. "The Interpersonal Relationship Between Parents and Caregivers in Day Care Settings." *American Journal of Orthopsychiatry* 48, no. 4 (October): 680–89.

———. 1982. "The Role of Research in the Development of the Child Care Profession." *Child Care Quarterly* 11, no. 1 (Spring): 4–11.

——— and J. W. Eisenstadt. 1982. "Parents' Searches for Child Care and the Design of Information Services." *Children and Youth Services Review* 4, no. 3: 239–53.

Pratt, Joanne. 1984. "Hometelwork: A Study of Its Pioneers." *Technological Forecasting and Social Change* 25, no. 1: 1–14.

Presser, Harriet B., and Wendy Baldwin. 1980. "Child Care as a Constraint on Employment: Prevalence, Correlates and the Bearing on the Work and Fertility Nexus." *American Journal of Sociology* 85, no. 5: 1202–13.

Quinn, Jane Bryant. 1988. "A Crisis in Child Care; Day-Care Help for Workingwomen Will Become the Most Essential Company Benefit of the 1990's." *Newsweek* 111 (February 15): 57.

Radomski, Mary Ann. 1986. "Professionalization of Early Childhood Educators: How Far Have We Progressed?" *Young Children* 41 (July): 20–23.

Rainwater, Lee, Richard C. Coleman, and Gerald Handel. 1959. *Workingman's Wife.* New York: Oceana Publications.

Rapp, Rayna. 1982. "Family and Class in Contemporary America: Notes Toward an Understanding of Ideology." In Barrie Thorne and Marilyn Yalom (eds.), *Rethinking the Family: Some Feminist Questions,* 168–87. New York: Longman.

Ravo, Nick. 1986. "Two Children Killed in Blaze at Brooklyn Day-Care Center." *New York Times* (November 25): B1, B4.

Redclift, Nanneke, and Enzo Mingione. 1985. "Introduction," in Nanneke Redclift and Enzo Mingione (eds.), *Beyond Employment: Household Gender and Subsistence,* 1–12. Oxford: Basil Blackwell.

Reverby, Susan. 1990. "The Duty or Right to Care: Nursing in Historical Perspective." In Emily K. Abel and Margaret K. Nelson (eds.), *Circles of Care,* 132–49. Albany: SUNY Press.

Rich, Adrienne. 1976. *Of Woman Born: Motherhood as Experience and Institution.* New York: W. W. Norton.

Richardson, Derek. 1986. "Day Care: Men Need Not Apply." *Education Digest* 51 (January): 58–59.

Rix, Sara E. (ed.). 1988. *The American Woman, 1988–89: A Status Report*. New York: W. W. Norton.

Roberts, Georgianna T. 1983. "Status and Salaries of Our Profession." *Young Children* 8, no. 3 (March): 18–19.

Robins, P. K. 1988. "Child-Care and Convenience: The Effects of Labor Market Entry Costs on Economic Self-Sufficiency Among Public-Housing Residents." *Social Science Quarterly* 69, no. 1: 122–36.

Robinson, Bryan E. 1979. "An Update on the Status of Men in Early Child Care Work." *Child Welfare* 58, no. 7 (July–August): 471–77.

———. 1989. "Vanishing Breed: Men in Child Care Programs." *Young Children* 43, no. 6 (September): 54–58.

Rodgers, Francene Sussner, and Michelle Seligson. 1983. "Mothers vs. Babysitters." *Parents* (August): 62–68.

Roldan, Martha. 1985. "Industrial Outworking, Struggles for the Reproduction of Working-Class Families and Gender Subordination." In Nanneke Redclift and Enzo Mingione (eds.), *Beyond Employment: Household Gender and Subsistence*, 248–85. Oxford: Basil Blackwell.

Rollins, Judith. 1985. *Between Women: Domestics and Their Employers*. Philadelphia: Temple University Press.

Romero, Mary. 1988. "Day Work in the Suburbs: The Work Experience of Chicana Private Housekeepers." In Anne Statham, Eleanor M. Miller, and Hans O. Mauksch (eds.), *The Worth of Women's Work: A Qualitative Synthesis*, 77–92. Albany: SUNY Press.

Rose-Ackerman, Susan. 1983. "Unintended Consequences: Regulating the Quality of Subsidized Day Care." *Journal of Policy Analysis and Management* 3, no. 1: 14–30.

Rosen, Ellen Israel. 1987. *Bitter Choices: Blue-Collar Women in and out of Work*. Chicago: University of Chicago Press.

Rosenfeld, George Walker. 1979. "Turnover among Child Care Workers." *Child Care Quarterly* 8, no. 1 (Spring): 67–69.

Ross, Andrew L. 1983. "Mitigating Turnover of Child Care Staff in Group Care Facilities." *Child Welfare* 62, no. 1: 63–67.

Rossi, Alice S. 1977. "A Biosocial Perspective on Parenting." *Daedalus* 106, no. 2: 1–31.

Rothman, Barbara Katz. 1989. *Recreating Motherhood*. New York: W. W. Norton.

Rowan, Carl T., and David Mazie. 1985. "Day Care in America: A Special Report." *Reader's Digest* 126 (June): 103–8.

Rubin, Karen. 1987. "Whose Job Is Child Care?" *Ms.* 15 (March): 32–39.

Rubin, Lillian B. 1976. *Worlds of Pain: Life in the Working-Class Family*. New York: Basic Books.

Rubin, Nancy. 1984. *The Mother Mirror*. New York: G. P. Putnam's Sons.

Ruddick, Sara. 1983. "Maternal Thinking." In Joyce Trebilcot (ed.), *Mothering: Essays in Feminist Theory*, 213–30. Totowa, N.J.: Rowman and Allanheld.

Ruderman, Florence. 1968. *Childcare and Working Mothers: A Study of Arrangements Made for Daytime Care of Children*. New York: Child Welfare League of America.

Ruggie, Mary. 1984. *The State and Working Women: A Comparative Study of Britain and Sweden*. Princeton: Princeton University Press.

Sacks, Karen Brodkin. 1984. "Generations of Working-Class Families." In Karen Brodkin Sacks and Dorothy Remy (eds.), *My Troubles Are Going to Have Trouble with Me: Everyday Trials and Triumphs of Women Workers*, 15–38. New Brunswick, N.J.: Rutgers University Press.

Sacks, Karen. 1990. "Does It Pay to Care?" In Emily K. Abel and Margaret K. Nelson (eds.), *Circles of Care*, 188–206. Albany: SUNY Press.

Sale, June Solnit. 1972. "Family Day Care: Potential Child Development Service." *American Journal of Public Health* 62, no. 5: 668.

———. 1973. "Family Day Care: A Valuable Alternative." *Young Children* 28, no. 4.

———. 1973. "Family Day Care: One Alternative in the Delivery of Developmental Services in Early Childhood." *American Journal of Orthopsychiatry* 43, no. 1: 37–45.

———. 1975. "Watch Family Day Care Mothers Work Together to Improve Services." *Children Today* 36: 22–24.

———. 1980. "Family Day Care: The Registration Controversy." *Day Care and Early Education* 8, no. 1 (Fall): 1–14.

Saraceno, Chiara. 1984. "Shifts in Public and Private Boundaries: Women as Mothers and Service Workers in Italian Daycare." *Feminist Studies* 10, no. 1: 7–30.

———. 1984. "The Social Construction of Childhood: Child Care and Education Policies in Italy and the United States." *Social Problems* 3, no. 3 (February): 351–63.

Scarr, Sandra. 1984. *Mother Care/Other Care*. New York: Basic Books.

———. 1985. "A Child-Care Checklist: Choosing an Affordable, Safe and Happy Environment," *Ms.* 13 (January): 95–98.

Seligman, Daniel. 1988. "Debating Dinosaurs, Measuring Muscles, Playing to the Yuppies, And Other Matters." *Fortune* 117 (February 15): 123–4.

Seligman, Laurence R. 1988. "The Day Care Follies." *Fortune* 117 (February 15): 124.

Shanley, Mary Lyndon. 1983. "Afterword: Feminism and Families in a Liberal Polity." In Irene Diamond (ed.), *Families, Politics and Policy*, 357–61. New York: Longman.

Shannon, Jaqueline. 1987. "Crisis in Child Care." *Health* 19 (October): 29–33.

Shannon, Sally. 1986. "Searching for Good Child Care." *Washingtonian* 22 (October): 182–99.

Sheehy, Maureen. 1983. "Homework: Employment Option or Employment Risk." U.S. Department of Labor: National Commission on Working Women. Washington, D.C.: Government Printing Office.

Shortlidge, R. L., et al. 1974. "Changes in Child Care Arrangements of Working Women." *Proceedings of the American Statistical Association:* 209–18.

Siegel-Gorelick, Bryna. 1983. *The Working Parent's Guide to Child Care*. Boston: Little, Brown.

Silin, Jonathan G. 1985. "Authority as Knowledge: A Problem of Professionalization." *Young Children* 40 (March): 41–46.

Silverman, Leonard. 1985. "Corporate Childcare: Playpens in the Boardroom or Productivity Investment?" *Vital Speeches of the Day* 51, no. 16 (June 1): 503.

Sitomer, Curtis J. 1981. "Day Care: A Global Perspective," *Christian Science Monitor* 73, no. 1 (May): 14.
Skold, Karen. 1988. "The Interests of Feminists and Children in Child Care." In Sanford M. Dornbusch and Myra H. Strober (eds.), *Feminism, Children, and the New Families*, 113–36. New York: Guilford Press.
Small, Richard W., and Laura Dodge. 1988. "Roles, Skills and Job Tasks in Professional Child Care: A Review of the Literature." *Child and Youth Care Quarterly* 17, no. 1 (Spring): 6–23.
Smith, Dorothy. 1979. "A Sociology for Women." In Julia Sherman and Evelyn Thornton Beck (eds.), *The Prism of Sex: Essays in the Sociology of Knowledge*, 135–87. Madison: University of Wisconsin Press.
Smith, Janet Farrell. 1984. "Parenting and Property." In Joyce Trebilcot (ed.), *Mothering: Essays in Feminist Theory*, 199–212. Totowa, N.J.: Rowman and Allanheld.
Smith, Joan. 1982. "The Way We Were: Women and Work." *Feminist Studies* 8, no. 2 (Summer): 437–56.
———. 1984. "Nonwage Labor and Subsistence." In Joan Smith et al. (eds.), *The Households and the World-Economy*, 64–89. Beverly Hills: Sage Publications.
Smith, Sarah. 1988. "'La Petite Academy': Companies to Watch." *Fortune* 117 (May 9): 70.
Sobesky, N. E. 1976. "Youth as Child Care Workers—Impact of State of Life on Clinical Effectiveness." *Child Care Quarterly* 5, no. 4: 262–73.
Stacey, Margaret. 1981. "The Division of Labour Revisited or Overcoming the Two Adams." In P. Abrams et al. (eds.), *Practice and Progress: British Sociology 1950–1980*, 172–91. London: Allen and Unwin.
Stack, Carol. 1974. *All Our Kin*. New York: Harper and Row.
Stains, Laurence F. 1987. "Day Care Nightmares." *Philadelphia* (September): 29.
Stith, Sandra M., and Albert J. Davis. 1984. "Employed Mothers and Family Day Care Substitute Caregivers: A Comparative Analysis of Infant Care." *Child Development* 55, no. 4: 1340–48.
Stone, Robyn, Gail Lee Cafferata, and Judith Sangle. 1986. "Caregivers of the Frail Elderly: A National Profile." Washington, D.C.: National Center for Health Services Research.
Straus, Hal. 1988. "The Day Care Dilemma." *American Health* 7 no. 7 (September): 61–66.
Strick, Lisa Wilson. 1988. "A Homemade Solution to the Day Care Dilemma." *Woman's Day* (April 19): 26–30.
Suransky, Valerie. 1982. *The Erosion of Childhood*. Chicago: University of Chicago Press.
Szelenyi, Ivan. 1981. "Structural Changes and Alternatives to Capitalist Development in the Contemporary Urban and Regional System." *International Journal of Urban and Regional Research* 5, no. 1: 1–4.
Thorne, Barrie. 1982. "Feminist Rethinking of the Family: An Overview." In Barrie Thorne and Marilyn Yalom (eds.), *Rethinking the Family: Some Feminist Questions*, 1–24. New York: Longman.

———. 1987. "Re-Visioning Women and Social Change: Where Are the Children?" *Gender and Society* 1, no. 1 (March): 85–109.

*Time-Out: A Newsletter for Childcare Providers.* 1986–1988. Childcare Resource and Referral Center, Burlington, VT 05401.

Tobin, Catherine J. 1985. "Overhauling State Licensing Requirements: Making Quality Child Care a Reality." *Journal of Legislation* 12 (Summer): 213–24.

Toffler, Alvin. 1980. *The Third Wave.* New York: William Morrow.

Tronto, Joan. 1987. "Beyond Gender Differences to a Theory of Care." *Signs* 12, no. 4 (Summer): 644–63.

Trost, Cathy. 1988. "How Children's Safety Can Be Put in Jeopardy by Day-Care Personnel." *Wall Street Journal* (October 18): A1–A16.

———. 1988. "Should a 'Mother Down the Block' Be Regulated as Day-Care Provider?" *Wall Street Journal* (October 18): A16.

———. 1989. "Ohio Day-Care Standards Called Success—State's Experience May Bolster Case for U.S. Rules." *Wall Street Journal* (April 17): A5C.

Trotter, Robert J. 1987. "Project Day-Care." *Psychology Today* 21 (December): 32–38.

Trudeau, Gary. 1987. *Calling Dr. Whoopee!* New York: Henry Holt and Co.

Tweeton, Leslie. 1985. "The Day Care Problem." *Boston Magazine* 77 (May): 180–81.

Ungerson, Clare. 1983. "Women and Caring: Skills, Tasks and Taboos." In Eva Gamarnikov et al. (eds.), *The Public and the Private,* 62–77. London: Heinemann.

U.S. Congress. Senate. *Act for Better Child Care Services of 1987* (ABC). 100th Cong., 1st sess. 1987.

U.S. Bureau of the Census. 1980. *1980 Census: Vermont.* Washington, D.C.: Government Printing Office.

———. 1987. *Who's Minding the Kids? Child Care Arrangements: Winter 1984–85.* Washington, D.C.: Government Printing Office.

U.S. Department of Health and Human Services. 1982. *Comparative Licensing Study; Vol. 5: Profiles of State Licensing Requirements, Family Day Care Homes.* Washington, D.C.: Government Printing Office.

———. Human Development Services. Administration for Children, Youth and Family, Day Care Division. 1984. *Parents' Checklist for Day Care.* Washington, D.C.: Government Printing Office.

U.S. Department of Labor, Bureau of Labor Statistics. 1981. *Women in Domestic Work: Yesterday and Today.* Washington, D.C.: Government Printing Office.

*U.S. News and World Report.* 1985. "Getting the Best Child Care—Other than Mom (Interview with T. Berry Brazelton)." 99 (October 21): 70.

VanderVen, Karen. 1979. "Developmental Characteristics of Childcare Workers and Design of Training Programs." *Child Care Quarterly* 8, no. 2: 100–12.

——— and Martha A. Mattingly. 1981. "Action Agenda for Child Care Education in the 1980's: From Settings to Systems." *Child Care Quarterly* 10, no. 3: 278–88.

Vanek, Joan. 1983. "Household Work, Wage Work and Sexual Equality." In A. Skolnick and J. Skolnick (eds.), *Family in Transition,* 499–506. 4th ed. Boston: Little, Brown.

VanVelsor, E., and A. M. O'Rand. 1984. "Family Life Cycle, Work Career Patterns, and Women's Wages at Midlife." *Journal of Marriage and the Family* 46 (May): 565–73.

Vermont, Department of Social and Rehabilitation Services. 1985. *Journal for Family Day Care Homes.* Montpelier, Vt.: Division of Licensing and Registration.

———. 1989. *Journal for Family Day Care Homes.* Montpelier, Vt.: Division of Licensing and Registration.

Waerness, Kari. 1983. "On the Rationality of Caring." (Paper presented at the International Conference on the Transformation of the Welfare State: Dangers and Potentialities for Women; Bellagio, Italy, August 23–27.)

———. 1984. "Caring as Women's Work in the Welfare State." In Harriet Holter (ed.), *Patriarchy in a Welfare Society,* 67–86. Oslo: Universitetsforlaget.

Waldman, Elizabeth. 1983. "Labor Force Statistics from a Family Perspective." *Monthly Labor Review* (December): 16–20.

*Wall Street Journal.* 1988. "Child Care for All." (June 7): 34.

Wallis, Claudia. 1987. "The Child Care Dilemma," *Time* 129 (June 22): 54–60.

———. 1987. "Child Care: Effects on Children." *Time* 129 (June 22): 54–60.

Walsh, Jean. 1987. "Report: Work and Family. Is 'Homework' the Answer?" *Ms.* (July/August): 122.

Washburn, P. V., and J. S. Washburn. 1985. "The Four Roles of the Family Day-Care Provider." *Child Welfare* 64, no. 5: 547–54.

Watson, Russell. 1984. "What Price Day Care?" *Newsweek* 104 (September 10): 14–21.

Wattenberg, Esther. 1977. "Characteristics of Family Day Care Providers: Implications for Training." *Child Welfare* 56, no. 4 (April): 211–29.

———. 1980. "Family Day Care: Out of the Shadows and into the Spotlight," *Marriage and Family Review* 3, no. 3/4: 35–62.

Werner, Emmy. 1984. *Child Care: Kith, Kin and Hired Hands.* Baltimore: University of Maryland Press.

Whitebook, Marcy, et al. 1981. "Who's Minding the Child Care Workers? A Look at Staff Burnout." *Children Today.*

Wilkins, Amy, and Helen Blank. 1986. "Public Policy Report. Child Care: Strategies to Move the Issue Forward." *Young Children* 42 (November): 68–72.

Willer, Barbara. 1987. "Quality or Affordability: Trade-offs for Early Childhood Programs." *Young Children* 42, no. 6 (September): 41–43.

Williams, Lena. 1989. "Child Care at Job Site: Easing Fears." *New York Times* (March 16): C1, C10.

Winnicott, D. W. 1960. "The Theory of the Parent-Infant Relationship." *The International Journal of Psychoanalysis* 41: 585–95.

Winston, Fern. 1988. "Meeting the Day Care Crisis." *Political Affairs* 67 (March): 5–9.

Withorn, Ann. 1984. *Serving the People: Social Services and Social Change.* New York: Columbia University Press.

Wolfgram, Tamara H. 1984. "Working at Home: The Growth of Cottage Industry." *The Futurist* 18, no. 3 (June): 31–34.

Wright, Robert. 1988. "An Election Issue We Don't Need: Kids 'R' U.S.." *The New Republic* (August 22): 12–14.

Wrigley, Julia. 1990. "Children's Caregivers and Ideologies of Parental Inadequacies: The Rise of Preschool Education." In Emily K. Abel and Margaret K. Nelson (eds.), *Circles of Care*, 290–312. Albany: SUNY Press.

Yarrow, Leah. 1988. "Starting a Home Day-Care Center." *Parents' Magazine* (August): 64–68.

Young, Kathryn T., and Edward Zigler. 1986. "Infant and Toddler Day Care: Regulations and Policy Implications." *American Journal of Orthopsychiatry* 56, no. 1: 43–55.

Zigler, Edward F., and Meryl Frank. 1988. *The Parental Leave Crisis: Toward a National Policy.* New Haven: Yale University Press.

Zigler, Edward F., and Kirby A. Heller. 1980. "Day Care Standards Approach Critical Juncture." *Day Care and Early Education* 7 no. 3 (Spring): 6–8.

Zigler, Edward F., and Pauline Turner. 1982. "Parents and Day Care Workers: A Failed Partnership?" In Edward Zigler and Edmund Gordon (eds.), *Day Care: Scientific and Social Policy Issues*, 174–82. Boston: Auburn House Publishing Co.

Zinsmeister, Karl. 1988. "Brave New World: How Day-Care Harms Children." *Policy Review* (Spring): 40–48.

Zinsser, Caroline. 1986. *Day Care's Unfair Burden: How Low Wages Subsidize a Public Service.* New York: Center for Public Advocacy Research.

———. 1987. *Over a Barrel: Working Mothers Talk About Childcare.* New York: Center for Public Advocacy Research.

# INDEX